"Management of Digital Ecosystems":
Dedicated to the Memory of
Prof. William I. Grosky
8/4/1944–11/13/2020

"Management of Digital Ecosystems": Dedicated to the Memory of Prof. William I. Grosky 8/4/1944–11/13/2020

Editors

Mirjana Ivanović
Richard Chbeir
Yannis Manolopoulos

Basel • Beijing • Wuhan • Barcelona • Belgrade • Novi Sad • Cluj • Manchester

Editors

Mirjana Ivanović
University of Novi Sad
Novi Sad
Serbia

Richard Chbeir
Université de Pau et des Pays
de l'Adour (UPPA)
Anglet
France

Yannis Manolopoulos
Open University of Cyprus
Nicosia
Cyprus

Editorial Office
MDPI
St. Alban-Anlage 66
4052 Basel, Switzerland

This is a reprint of articles from the Special Issue published online in the open access journal *Digital* (ISSN 2673-6470) (available at: https://www.mdpi.com/journal/digital/special_issues/MEDES).

For citation purposes, cite each article independently as indicated on the article page online and as indicated below:

Lastname, A.A.; Lastname, B.B. Article Title. *Journal Name* **Year**, *Volume Number*, Page Range.

ISBN 978-3-7258-0645-4 (Hbk)
ISBN 978-3-7258-0646-1 (PDF)
doi.org/10.3390/books978-3-7258-0646-1

© 2024 by the authors. Articles in this book are Open Access and distributed under the Creative Commons Attribution (CC BY) license. The book as a whole is distributed by MDPI under the terms and conditions of the Creative Commons Attribution-NonCommercial-NoDerivs (CC BY-NC-ND) license.

Contents

About the Editors vii

Preface ix

Dimitrios A. Koutsomitropoulos and Ioanna C. Gogou
Object Detection Models and Optimizations: A Bird's-Eye View on Real-Time Medical Mask Detection
Reprinted from: *Digital* 2023, 3, 12, doi:10.3390/digital3030012 1

Thomas Krabokoukis
Technology Tools in Hospitality: Mapping the Landscape through Bibliometric Analysis and Presentation of a New Software Solution
Reprinted from: *Digital* 2023, 3, 6, doi:10.3390/digital3010006 18

Najla Fattouch, Imen Ben Lahmar, Mouna Rekik and Khouloud Boukadi
Decision-Making Approach for an IoRT-Aware Business Process Outsourcing
Reprinted from: *Digital* 2022, 2, 28, doi:10.3390/digital2040028 34

Ietezaz Ul Hassan, Raja Hashim Ali, Zain Ul Abideen, Talha Ali Khan and Rand Kouatly
Significance of Machine Learning for Detection of Malicious Websites on an Unbalanced Dataset
Reprinted from: *Digital* 2022, 2, 27, doi:10.3390/digital2040027 52

Utku Demirci and Pinar Karagoz
Explicit and Implicit Trust Modeling for Recommendation
Reprinted from: *Digital* 2022, 2, 24, doi:10.3390/digital2040024 71

Sotirios Batsakis, Marios Adamou, Ilias Tachmazidis, Sarah Jones, Sofya Titarenko, Grigoris Antoniou and Thanasis Kehagias
Data-Driven Decision Support for Adult Autism Diagnosis Using Machine Learning
Reprinted from: *Digital* 2022, 2, 14, doi:10.3390/digital2020014 90

Georgios Gkougkoudis, Dimitrios Pissanidis and Konstantinos Demertzis
Intelligence-Led Policing and the New Technologies Adopted by the Hellenic Police
Reprinted from: *Digital* 2022, 2, 9, doi:10.3390/digital2020009 110

Olanrewaju Sanda, Michalis Pavlidis and Nikolaos Polatidis
A Regulatory Readiness Assessment Framework for Blockchain Adoption in Healthcare
Reprinted from: *Digital* 2022, 2, 5, doi:10.3390/digital2010005 131

Sandesh Pantha, Sumina Shrestha and Janette Collier
Use of Internet Technology among Older Adults in Residential Aged Care Facilities: Protocol for a Systematic Review and Meta-Analysis
Reprinted from: *Digital* 2022, 2, 3, doi:10.3390/digital2010003 154

Michael Max Bühler, Igor Calzada, Isabel Cane, Thorsten Jelinek, Astha Kapoor, Morshed Mannan, et al.
Unlocking the Power of Digital Commons: Data Cooperatives as a Pathway for Data Sovereign, Innovative and Equitable Digital Communities
Reprinted from: *Digital* 2023, 3, 11, doi:10.3390/digital3030011 161

Vassilios Krassanakis and Loukas-Moysis Misthos
Mouse Tracking as a Method for Examining the Perception and Cognition of Digital Maps
Reprinted from: *Digital* 2023, 3, 9, doi:10.3390/digital3020009 187

Daiju Kato and Hiroshi Ishikawa
Quality Control Methods Using Quality Characteristics in Development and Operations
Reprinted from: *Digital* **2024**, *4*, 12, doi:10.3390/digital4010012 . . . . **197**

About the Editors

Mirjana Ivanović

Mirjana Ivanović is a Full Professor at the Faculty of Sciences, University of Novi Sad, Serbia. She is a member of the National Scientific Committee for Electronics, Telecommunication and Informatics within the Ministry of Education, Science and Technological Development of Serbia, and a member of the Board of Directors of the Institute for Artificial Intelligence Research and Development of Serbia. She was a member of the University Council for Informatics for more than 12 years. She has authored or co-authored 14 textbooks, several international monographs, and >450 research papers, most of which are published in international journals and conferences. Her research interests include agent technologies, intelligent techniques, applications of data mining, and machine learning in medical domains and technology-enhanced learning. She is a member of Program Committees of >300 international conferences, Program/General Chair of several international conferences, and leader of numerous international research projects. She has delivered numerous keynote speeches at international conferences and visited many academic institutions all over the world as visiting researcher (Australia, China, Germany, Korea, Portugal, and Slovenia). Currently, she is Editor-in-Chief of the *Computer Science and Information Systems* journal.

Richard Chbeir

Richard Chbeir is a Full Professor in Computer Science at the University of Pau and Pays de l'Adour in Anglet. He received his PhD in Computer Science from INSA de Lyon (2001), and his Habilitation in Leading Research degree from the University of Bourgogne (2010). He is the director of LIUPPA labs and head of OpenCEMS industrial Chair (https://opencems.sigappfr.org/). His research interests are in data engineering, data semantics, and digital ecosystems aiming to unlock the hidden potential of heterogeneous data sets. He has authored numerous publications in international journals (*IEEE Transactions on Sustainable Computing*, *IEEE Multimedia*, *Information Systems*, *Web Semantics*, *Computing*, *Information Science*, and *Big Data Research*) and conferences (EDBT, ER, CAiSE, SOFSEM, SISAP, DEXA, ICEIS, COMAD, ICWS, SITIS, KES, and OTM), and actively participates in chairing international conferences (ACM SAC, MEDES, WISE, ADBIS, ICCCI, ACIIDS, ICWE, and IDEAS), shaping the direction of computer science research. He is also Associate Editor of several journals (*WWW*, *Computer Journal*, *SNAM*, *ComSIS*, *IJAIT*, and *JWE*), as well as Editor of the Digital Ecosystems track of *SN Computer Science*. Finally, he is the Chair of the French Chapter ACM SIGAPP.

Yannis Manolopoulos

Yannis Manolopoulos is a Professor of the Open University of Cyprus and Professor Emeritus of the Aristotle University of Thessaloniki. He is also a Member of the Board of the University of Macedonia, and a Member of Academia Europaea. Currently, he is also a student of the Graduate Program on Creative Writing of the Hellenic Open University. His research focuses on data management. He has co-authored 6 monographs and 10 textbooks (in Greek), as well as >350 journal and conference papers. He has received >18,000 citations from >2800 distinct academic institutions from >100 countries (h-index = 61). He has also received five best paper awards from the SIGMOD, ECML/PKDD, MEDES (2), and ISSPIT conferences. Currently, he serves on the boards of the journals *Digital* (Editor-in-Chief), *The Computer Journal* (Deputy Editor), *SN Computer Science* (Track Editor), *Information Systems*, *World Wide Web*, *Expert Systems*, *Data Science*, and *Analytics*. He has organized conferences in Australia, Brazil, China, Cyprus, France, Greece, Latvia, Lebanon, North Macedonia, Romania, Russia, Serbia, Slovakia, Tunisia, Turkey, and the UAE. He has supervised 27 doctoral graduates who have had careers in Germany, Ireland, Italy, Netherlands, Spain, the UK, the USA, as well as Cyprus and Greece.

Preface

Our community remember him not only as an excellent scientist, but also as a very generous, funny, and curious person, passionately delivering lectures and seminars. When one needed to brainstorm any new technologies or ideas, he was the person to speak to. He used to state that one of the luxuries of academia is the ability to learn every day. This volume is dedicated to his memory.

One of the pioneers of computer science recently passed away: William I. Grosky (or Bill for friends). He received his B.S. degree in Mathematics from MIT in 1965, his M.S. degree in Applied Mathematics from Brown University in 1968, and his Ph.D. degree from Yale University in 1971. William I. Grosky served as a Professor and Chair of the Department of Computer and Information Science at the University of Michigan-Dearborn (UMD). Before joining UMD in 2001, he was the Professor and Chair of the Department of Computer Science at Wayne State University, as well as an Assistant Professor of Information and Computer Science at the Georgia Institute of Technology in Atlanta. His research interests included multimedia information systems, text and image mining, and the semantic web. He was a founding member of Intelligent Media LLC, a Michigan-based company, whose interests are in integrating new media into information technologies. He delivered many short courses in the area of database management for local industries and was invited to lecture on multimedia information systems worldwide. He served as the Editor-in-Chief of the IEEE Multimedia magazine, as well as a Member of Editorial Boards of many journals in the field; in addition, he served as a Member of several Program Committees of conferences focusing on database and multimedia systems. He published three books and more than 150 papers in international conferences and journals.

His peers, students and friends, and our community remember him not only as an excellent scientist, but also as a very generous, funny, and curious person, passionately delivering lectures and seminars. When one needed to brainstorm any new technologies or ideas, he was the person to speak to. His impressive knowledge in Computer Science always allowed for constructive and enriching conversations. He used to state that one of the luxuries of academia is the ability to learn every day.

We, therefore, felt the need and duty to collect a series of papers by his students, friends, and colleagues, compiled in this volume dedicated to Prof. William I. Grosky, for which we are interested in article topics addressing a broad scope, thereby paying tribute to his rich scientific curiosity.

In the world of the Internet of Things (IoT), the rapid growth and exponential use of digital components have led to the emergence of intelligent connected environments, composed of multiple independent entities such as individuals, organizations, services, software, and applications, sharing one or several missions, focusing on the interactions and inter-relationships among them. The application of information technologies has the potential to enable the understanding of how entities request resources and, ultimately, interact to create benefits and added values, impacting business practices and knowledge. These technologies can be improved through novel techniques, models, and methodologies for fields such as big data management, web technologies, networking, security, human–computer interactions, artificial intelligence, e-services, and self-organizing systems, supporting the establishment of digital ecosystems and the management of their resources.

Phenomena of collective intelligence in connected environments have emerged where (i) the diversity and plenitude of shared resources, and (ii) users act both as content consumers and content providers. How can we make the most out of these vast amounts of easily searchable resources, capable of inferring new information and knowledge? Recent research advances have stimulated the development of a series of innovative approaches, algorithms, and tools for concept/topic detection or extraction, respectively. In the course of this volume, high-quality research papers were sought in the following areas:

Digital Ecosystem Infrastructure;
Data and Knowledge Management;
Computational and Collective Intelligence;
Semantic Computing;
Software Ecosystems for Software Engineering;
Big Data;
Services;
Trust, Security, and Privacy;
Software Engineering;
Internet of Things and Intelligent Web;
Cyber Physical Systems;
Social and Collaborative Platforms;
Human–computer Interaction;
Open Source;
Complex Systems and Networks;
Applications.

In the sequel, we briefly introduce the papers that have been accepted for inclusion in this volume. In particular, this volume contains the following 11 papers.

The paper by Dimitrios Koutsomitropoulos and Ioanna Gogou (University of Patras, Greece) focuses on object detection models and optimizations. Convolutional Neural Networks (CNNs) are well studied and commonly used for the problem of object detection thanks to their increased accuracy. However, high accuracy alone says little about the effective performance of CNN-based models, especially when real-time detection tasks are involved. There has not been sufficient evaluation of the available methods in terms of their speed/accuracy trade-off. This work performs a review and hands-on evaluation of the most fundamental object detection models on the Common Objects in Context (COCO) dataset with respect to this trade-off, their memory footprint, and computational and storage costs. The authors review available datasets for medical mask detection and train YOLOv5 on the Properly Wearing Masked Faces Dataset (PWMFD). Next, they test and evaluate a set of specific optimization techniques, transfer learning, data augmentations, and attention mechanisms, and report on their effect for real-time mask detection. Finally, they propose an optimized model based on YOLOv5s using transfer learning for the detection of correctly and incorrectly worn medical masks that surpassed more than two times in speed (69 frames/second) the state-of-the-art model SE-YOLOv3 on the PWMFD while maintaining the same level of mean Average Precision (67%).

The paper by Thomas Krabokoukis (Nelios EPE, Greece) examines technology tools in hospitality through bibliometric analysis. This study offers a comprehensive examination of the literature related to technology and tools in the hospitality industry. A bibliometric analysis was performed on 709 Scopus-indexed publications from 2000 to January 2023, with a focus on identifying key players, institutions, research trends, and the co-occurrence of keywords. The results shed light on the scientific landscape of technology and tools in the hospitality sector, emphasizing the significance of big data and the customer experience in the sharing economy. The study also presents the architecture of new software that offers guests the ability to customize their hotel stay, classified as part of the first cluster in the co-occurrence of keywords analysis. This approach highlights the growing importance of big data and customer experience, and makes a valuable contribution to the field by offering a tool for hotel booking customization. Furthermore, the study underscores the importance of collaboration between academic institutions and private companies in providing a mutually beneficial platform that exceeds the expectations of both hotels and guests.

The paper by Najla Fattouch, Imen Ben Lahmar (University of Sfax, Tunisia), Mouna Rekik (University of Sousse, Tunisia), and Khouloud Boukadi (University of Sfax, Tunisia) proposes a decision-making approach for an IoRT-aware business process outsourcing. In the context of Industry 4.0, business processes (BPs) aware of Internet of Robotics Things (IoRT) represent an attractive paradigm to automate the classic BP by using IoRT. Nonetheless, the execution of these processes within the enterprises may be costly due to the consumed resources, recruitment cost, etc. To bridge these gaps, the business process outsourcing (BPO) strategy can be applied to outsource a process to external service suppliers. Despite the various advantages of BPO, it is not trivial to determine which part of the process should be outsourced and which environment would be selected to deploy it. This paper deals with the decision-making outsourcing of an IoRT-aware BP to the fog and/or cloud environments. The fog environment includes devices at the edge of the network which will ensure the latency requirements of some latency-sensitive applications. However, relying on cloud, the availability and computational requirements of applications can be met. Toward these objectives, the authors realized an in-depth analysis of the enterprise requirements, where they identified a set of relevant criteria that may impact the outsourcing decision. Then, they applied the method based on the removal effects of criteria (MEREC) to automatically generate the weights of the identified criteria. Using these weights, they performed the selection of the suitable execution environment by using the ELECTRE IS method. Finally, they sought help from an expert to estimate the precision, recall, and F1 score of their approach. The obtained promising results show that this approach is the most similar to the expert result.

The paper by Ietezaz Ul Hassan, Raja Hashim Ali, Zain Ul Abideen (Ghulam Ishaq Khan Institute of Engineering Sciences and Technology, Pakistan), Talha Ali Khan, and Rand Kouatly (University of Europe of Applied Sciences, Germany) examines the significance of machine learning for the detection of malicious websites. It is hard to trust any data entry on online websites as some websites may be malicious, and gather data for illegal or unintended use. To make users aware of the digital safety of websites, the authors have tried to identify and learn the pattern on a dataset consisting of features of malicious and benign websites. They treated the problem of differentiation between malicious and benign websites as a classification problem and applied several ML techniques, such as random forest, decision tree, logistic regression, and support vector machines. Several evaluation metrics such as accuracy, precision, recall, F1 score, and false positive rate were used to evaluate the performance of each classification technique. Since the dataset was imbalanced, the ML models developed a bias during training toward a specific class of websites. Multiple data balancing techniques, such as undersampling, oversampling, and SMOTE, were applied to balance the dataset and remove the bias. Their experiments showed that after data balancing, the random forest algorithm using the oversampling technique showed the best results in all evaluation metrics for the benign and malicious website feature dataset.

The paper by Utku Demirci and Pinar Karagoz (Middle East Technical University, Turkey) focuses on explicit and implicit trust modeling for recommendation. Recommendation has become an inseparable component of many software applications, such as e-commerce, social media, and gaming platforms. Particularly in collaborative filtering-based recommendation solutions, the preferences of other users are considered heavily. At this point, trust among the users comes into the scene as an important concept to improve the recommendation performance. Trust describes the nature and the strength of ties between individuals and hence provides useful information to improve the recommendation accuracy, particularly against data sparsity and cold start problems. The trust notion helps alleviate the effect of these problems by providing additional reliable relationships between the users. However, trust information, specifically explicit trust, is not straightforward to collect and is only scarcely available. Therefore, implicit trust models have been proposed to fill in the gap. In this work, two specific sub-problems are elaborated on: the relationship between explicit and implicit trust scores, and the construction of a ML model for explicit trust. For the first sub-problem, an implicit trust model is devised and the compatibility of implicit trust scores with explicit scores is analyzed. For the second sub-problem, two different explicit trust models are proposed: explicit trust modeling through users' rating behavior and explicit trust modeling as a link prediction problem. The performances of the prediction models are analyzed on a set of benchmark data sets. It is observed that explicit and implicit trust models have different natures, and are to be used in a complementary way for recommendation. Another important result is that the accuracy of the ML models for explicit trust is promising and depends on the availability of data.

The paper by Sotirios Batsakis (Technical University of Crete, Greece), Marios Adamou (South West Yorkshire Partnership NHS Foundation Trust, UK), Ilias Tachmazidis (University of Huddersfield, UK), Sarah Jones (South West Yorkshire Partnership NHS Foundation Trust, UK), Sofya Titarenko (University of Leeds, UK), Grigoris Antoniou (South West Yorkshire Partnership NHS Foundation Trust, UK), and Thanasis Kehagias (Aristotle University of Thessaloniki, Greece) focuses on data-driven decision support for adult autism diagnosis using machine learning. Adult referrals to specialist autism spectrum disorder diagnostic services have increased in recent years, placing strain on existing services and illustrating the need for the development of a reliable screening tool, to identify and prioritize patients most likely to receive an ASD diagnosis. In this work, a detailed overview of existing approaches is presented and a data-driven analysis using ML is applied on a dataset of adult autism cases consisting of 192 individuals. The results show initial promise, achieving a total positive rate (i.e., correctly classified instances to all instances ratio) of up to 88.5%, but also point to the limitations of currently available data, opening up avenues for further research. The main direction of this research is the development of a novel autism screening tool for adults (ASTA), also introduced in this work, and preliminary results indicate that the ASTA is suitable for use as a screening tool for adult populations in clinical settings.

The paper by Georgios Gkougkoudis (Hellenic Police, Greece), Dimitrios Pissanidis (Independent Studies of Science and Technology College, Greece), and Konstantinos Demertzis (Hellenic Open University, Patras) reviews intelligence-led policing and the new technologies adopted by the Hellenic Police. In the never-ending search by Law Enforcement Agencies (LEAs) for ways to reduce crime more effectively, the prevention of criminal activity is always considered the ideal solution. Since the 1990s, intelligence-led Policing (ILP) was implemented in some forms by many LEAs around the world for crime prevention. Along with ILP, LEAs nowadays more and more turn to various new surveillance technologies. As a result, there are numerous studies and reports introducing some compelling results from LEAs that have implemented ILP, offering robust data around how the future of policing could be. In this context, this paper explores the most recent research, identifying where ILP stands today in Greece and to what extent it could be a viable, practical approach to crime prevention. In addition, it is researched to what degree new technologies have been adopted by the European Union and the Hellenic Police in their "battle" against crime. In conclusion, most technologies are at the research stage, and studies are underway in many areas.

The paper by Olanrewaju Sanda, Michalis Pavlidis, and Nikolaos Polatidis (University of Brighton, UK) proposes a regulatory readiness assessment framework for blockchain adoption in healthcare. Blockchain is now utilized by a diverse spectrum of applications and is proclaimed as a technological innovation that transforms the way that data are stored. This technology has the potential to transform the healthcare sector, especially in view of the prevalent issues of patient's data-privacy and fragmented healthcare data. However, there is no evidence-based effort to develop a readiness assessment framework for blockchain that combines all the different social and economic factors and involves all stakeholders. Based on a systematic literature review, the proposed framework is applied to Portugal's healthcare sector and its applicability is outlined. The findings show the unique importance of regulators and the government in achieving a globally acceptable regulatory framework for the adoption of blockchain technology in healthcare and also in other sectors. The business entities and solution providers are ready to leverage the opportunities of blockchain, but the absence of a widely acceptable regulatory framework that protects stakeholders' interests is slowing down the adoption of blockchain. There are several misconceptions regarding blockchain laws and regulations, which have slowed stakeholder readiness. This paper will be useful as a guideline and knowledge base to reinforce blockchain adoption.

The paper by Sandesh Pantha, Sumina Shrestha, and Janette Collier (La Trobe University, Australia) examines the use of Internet technology among older adults in residential aged care facilities. Internet usage may help promote the physical and mental health of older adults living in residential aged care facilities (RACFs). There is little evidence of how these older citizens use Internet services. This systematic review aims to explore the trends and factors contributing to Internet use among aged care residents. A systematic search has been conducted on nine online databases: MEDLINE, EMBASE, PsycInfo, CINAHL, AgeLine, ProQuest, Web of Science, Scopus, and the Cochrane Library. Two reviewers have independently conducted title and abstract screening, full-text reading, critical appraisal, and data extraction. Any discrepancies have been resolved by consensus. The methodological risk of bias has been assessed using the Effective Public Health Practice Project measure and the Joanna Briggs Institute checklist. The authors report a narrative synthesis of the evidence. Information on factors contributing to Internet use and their strength of association is reported. A meta-analysis and meta-synthesis is undertaken. This review provides information on the factors predicting Internet use among older adults in RACFs. The evidence from this review will help to formulate further research objectives and, potentially, to design an intervention to trial Internet access for these groups.

The paper by Michael Max Bühler (Konstanz University of Applied Sciences, Germany) et al. explores the case of unlocking the power of digital commons. Network effects, economies of scale, and lock-in-effects increasingly lead to a concentration of digital resources and capabilities, hindering the free and equitable development of digital entrepreneurship, new skills, and jobs, especially in small communities as well as in small and medium-sized enterprises (SMEs). To ensure the affordability and accessibility of technologies, promote digital entrepreneurship and community well-being, and protect digital rights, the authors propose data cooperatives as a vehicle for secure, trusted, and sovereign data exchange. In post-pandemic times, community/SME-led cooperatives can play a vital role by ensuring that supply chains to support digital commons are uninterrupted, resilient, and decentralized. Digital commons and data sovereignty provide communities with affordable and easy access to information and the ability to collectively negotiate data-related decisions. Moreover, cooperative commons (i) provide access to the infrastructure that underpins the modern economy, (ii) preserve property rights, and (iii) ensure that privatization and monopolization do not further erode self-determination, especially in a world increasingly mediated by AI. Thus, governance plays a significant role in accelerating communities'/SMEs' digital transformation and addressing their challenges. Cooperatives thrive on digital governance and standards such as open trusted application programming interfaces (APIs) that increase the efficiency, technological capabilities, and capacities of participants and, most importantly, integrate, enable, and accelerate the digital transformation of SMEs in the overall process. This review article analyses an array of transformative use cases that underline the potential of cooperative data governance. These case studies exemplify how data and platform cooperatives, through their innovative value creation mechanisms, can elevate digital commons and value chains to a new dimension of collaboration, thereby addressing pressing societal issues. Guided by the research aim, the authors propose a policy framework that supports the practical implementation of digital federation platforms and data cooperatives. This policy blueprint intends to facilitate sustainable development in both the Global South and North, fostering equitable and inclusive data governance strategies.

The paper by Vassilios Krassanakis and Loukas-Moysis Misthos (University of West Attica, Greece) investigates mouse tracking as a method for examining the perception and cognition of digital maps. This article aims to present the authors' perspective regarding the challenges and opportunities of mouse-tracking methodology while performing experimental research, particularly related to the map-reading process. They briefly describe existing metrics, visualization techniques, and software tools utilized for the qualitative and quantitative analysis of experimental mouse-movement data towards the examination of both perceptual and cognitive issues. Moreover, they concisely report indicative examples of mouse-tracking studies in the field of cartography. The article concludes with summarizing mouse-tracking strengths/potential and limitations, compared to eye tracking. In a nutshell, mouse tracking is a straightforward method, particularly suitable for tracking real-life behaviors in interactive maps, providing the valuable opportunity for remote experimentation; even though it is not suitable for tracking the actual free-viewing behavior, it can be concurrently utilized with other state-of-the-art experimental methods.

The paper by Daiju Kato (Nihon Knowledge, Japan) and Hiroshi Ishikawa (Tokyo Metropolitan University, Japan) examines quality control methods in development and operations. Since the software quality model was defined as an international standard, many quality assurance teams have used this quality model for software development in a waterfall model for quality control. On the other hand, in the case of DevOps, efficient product development is achieved by building a pipeline in the CI/CD process, placing testing tasks in the pipeline, and promoting the automation of testing tasks. However, in many DevOps projects, classical quality metrics such as defect rate and test coverage rate are often used to monitor quality progress, and this approach is development-oriented, making it difficult to see the quality status. Therefore, by classifying the quality provided by testing in the CI/CD pipeline by quality characteristics, it is possible to visualize the quality progress required for the released system and to consider how to manage it with a quality model, as well as to define software quality targets with quality characteristics before the project starts and to use quality characteristics as KPIs. To use quality attributes as KPIs, it is necessary to manage the test results of each pipeline and compare them with the results of previous builds. This paper explains how to visualize the quality ensured by the CI/CD process, which is essential for DevOps, and the benefits of using quality characteristics as KPIs, and proposes a method to achieve rapid and high-quality product development.

This reprint brings together a number of papers from diverse contemporary research domains, and we expect that a wider audience will find at least one interesting paper to study. In addition, we hope that the papers will inspire readers to further deepen their research or try to perform innovative work in some of the research areas presented in these papers. Finally, we are thankful for the hard work and enthusiasm of the authors of the accepted papers and the reviewers without whom the publication of the current volume would not be possible.

Mirjana Ivanović, Richard Chbeir, and Yannis Manolopoulos
Editors

Article

Object Detection Models and Optimizations: A Bird's-Eye View on Real-Time Medical Mask Detection

Dimitrios A. Koutsomitropoulos * and Ioanna C. Gogou

Computer Engineering and Informatics Department, University of Patras, 26504 Patras, Greece; gogou@ceid.upatras.gr
* Correspondence: kotsomit@ceid.upatras.gr

Abstract: Convolutional Neural Networks (CNNs) are well-studied and commonly used for the problem of object detection thanks to their increased accuracy. However, high accuracy on its own says little about the effective performance of CNN-based models, especially when real-time detection tasks are involved. To the best of our knowledge, there has not been sufficient evaluation of the available methods in terms of their speed/accuracy trade-off. This work performs a review and hands-on evaluation of the most fundamental object detection models on the Common Objects in Context (COCO) dataset with respect to this trade-off, their memory footprint, and computational and storage costs. In addition, we review available datasets for medical mask detection and train YOLOv5 on the Properly Wearing Masked Faces Dataset (PWMFD). Next, we test and evaluate a set of specific optimization techniques, transfer learning, data augmentations, and attention mechanisms, and we report on their effect for real-time mask detection. Based on our findings, we propose an optimized model based on YOLOv5s using transfer learning for the detection of correctly and incorrectly worn medical masks that surpassed more than two times in speed (69 frames per second) the state-of-the-art model SE-YOLOv3 on the PWMFD while maintaining the same level of mean Average Precision (67%).

Keywords: real-time object detection; medical mask detection; video surveillance; YOLOv5; PWMFD; COVID-19

Citation: Koutsomitropoulos, D.A.; Gogou, I.C. Object Detection Models and Optimizations: A Bird's-Eye View on Real-Time Medical Mask Detection. *Digital* **2023**, *3*, 172–188. https://doi.org/10.3390/digital3030012

Academic Editors: Mirjana Ivanović, Richard Chbeir and Yannis Manolopoulos

Received: 26 May 2023
Revised: 17 June 2023
Accepted: 27 June 2023
Published: 1 July 2023

Copyright: © 2023 by the authors. Licensee MDPI, Basel, Switzerland. This article is an open access article distributed under the terms and conditions of the Creative Commons Attribution (CC BY) license (https:// creativecommons.org/licenses/by/ 4.0/).

1. Introduction

Computer vision has become an integral part of modern systems in transportation, manufacturing, and healthcare. In the last decade, the task of object detection as a deep learning problem has accumulated immense scientific interest. Convolutional Neural Networks (CNN) have shown excellent results in extracting the abstract features of image data, thanks to their similarities to the biological neural networks of the human brain [1]. Their promising capabilities have motivated scientists toward inventions of new state-of-the-art object detectors resulting in a continuous increase in accuracy. Nevertheless, their performance is ambiguous when detection speed is considered, which is usually sacrificed in favor of accuracy. Conducting accurate object detection in real time is a realistic requirement of modern systems, especially embedded ones with hardware limitations. However, the available methods have yet to be fully evaluated as published research [2–5] tends to overlook the trade-off between accuracy and speed, compares models on different machine learning frameworks, or excludes newer models, resulting in indefinite results.

This work focuses on giving a solution to this problem by reviewing and evaluating some of the most fundamental CNN-based object detection models: Faster R-CNN [6] and Mask R-CNN [7] of the family of Region-based Convolutional Neural Networks (R-CNN) [8], RetinaNet [9], Single-Shot MultiBox Detector (SSD) [10], and You Only Look Once (YOLO) [11] and its newer versions [12–15]. The objective is to evaluate and compare them in terms of GPU memory footprint, computational and storage costs, as well as their speed/accuracy trade-off. We seek to reach fair conclusions by executing the models through a common pipeline, using the same machine learning framework, dataset, and GPU. At the same time, we ensure that our experiments can be reproduced through our accompanying open-source code.

In addition, we review and compare available datasets for medical mask detection; among the models we evaluate, we choose YOLOv5 as a highly efficient one to train for real-time medical mask detection on a topical and novel dataset that has yet to be extensively tested, the Properly Wearing Masked Faces Dataset (PWMFD) [16]. In view of the protective measures put in place during the COVID-19 pandemic, the need for real-time detection of correctly and incorrectly worn medical masks in data streams has become evident. According to the World Health Organization (WHO), the use of medical masks combined with other health measures is recommended for the containment of the virus [17]. In this context, we propose an optimized real-time detector of correctly and incorrectly worn medical masks. Next, we review, test, and investigate various optimization techniques used before in medical mask detection and report on their effect, including transfer learning, data augmentations, and attention mechanisms. For instance, transfer learning from larger and more diverse object detection datasets is expected to improve model accuracy.

The main contributions of this work are the following:

- A review and evaluation of state-of-the-art object detectors and an analysis of their speed/accuracy trade-off, using the same framework, dataset, and GPU. No other similar study has been published that includes YOLOv5 [15], whose performance has yet to be extensively tested.
- The accuracy and speed of YOLOv5s are evaluated for the first time on the newly developed Properly Wearing Masked Faces Dataset (PWMFD) [16]. Furthermore, the effects of transfer learning, data augmentations, and attention mechanisms are assessed for medical mask detection.
- A real-time medical mask detection model based on YOLOv5 is proposed that surpassed more than 2 times in speed (69 fps) the state-of-the-art model SEYOLOv3 [16] on the PWMFD while maintaining the same level of the mean Average Precision (mAP) at 67%. This increase in speed gives room for using the model on embedded devices with lower hardware capabilities, while still achieving real-time detection.

A preliminary version of this paper has appeared in [18]. In comparison, this article shows the following:

1. It presents new evaluation results of object detection models in terms of their accuracy and speed vs. computational performance (GFLOPS).
2. It includes new results demonstrating the (detrimental) effect of augmenting the model with Transformer Encoder (TE) Attention blocks.
3. It involves a more thorough description of the detection models reviewed and evaluated.
4. It includes a new section on the characteristics, availability, and usage of datasets suitable for medical mask detection.

All results are reproducible through our open-source code on GitHub (https://github.com/joangog/object-detection accessed on 1 June 2023) as well as the measurements' data. The weight file of our medical mask detector is also available on GitHub (https://github.com/joangog/object-detection-assets accessed on 1 June 2023) and on Hugging Face (https://huggingface.co/joangog/pwmfd-yolov5 accessed on 1 June 2023).

The rest of this paper is organized as follows: Section 2 reviews the current state of the art for object and mask detection and describes models from an architectural point of view. Section 3 is devoted to the comparative, hands-on evaluation of several object detection models, employing a uniform evaluation testbed and metrics and discussing observed tradeoffs. Section 4 presents a qualitative review of datasets that can be leveraged for implementing effective mask detection pipelines. The results of testing various optimizations for this task on well-performing models are shown in Section 5 along with our final proposed model. Finally, Section 6 summarizes the lessons learned and the outlook of our work.

2. Related Work

2.1. Object Detection Models

The development of AlexNet [19] in 2012 paved the way toward the CNN-based object detection models we know today. Introduced in 2014, R-CNN [8] was the first one to adopt the idea of region proposals for object detection, produced through a selective search algorithm. In 2015, its successor, Fast R-CNN [20], increased detection speed by computing a feature map for the whole image rather than for each proposal. It was improved further with Faster R-CNN [6] by replacing selective search with a more efficient fully convolutional region proposal network. In 2017, Mask R-CNN [7] was an extension of Faster R-CNN for image segmentation. In 2015, the first one-shot model was published, named YOLO [11]. Two iterations followed, YOLOv2 [12] and YOLOv3 [13], improving its performance with the addition of anchors, batch normalization, the Darknet-53 backbone, and three detection heads. In 2020, its development resumed with YOLOv4 [14]. It included the enhanced CSPDarknet53 backbone, a Spatial Pyramid Pooling (SPP) [21] layer, and a Path Aggregation Network (PANet) [22]. Shortly after, YOLOv5 [15] was launched with only small alterations. Its role as the fifth version of YOLO was a controversial subject as no official publication has been released to this day. Nevertheless, it shows promising results through consistent updates, which are worth investigating. As of January 2023, YOLOv8 was released. Early results appearing in Github (https://github.com/ultralytics/ultralytics accessed on 1 June 2023) show a consistent improvement to previous versions, both in terms of accuracy and speed; however, no scientific paper has been published reporting and/or comparing the results. Finally, SSD [10] proposed in 2016 and RetinaNet [9] in 2017 are two other notable one-shot models. The latter became known for introducing focal loss to combat foreground–background imbalance.

2.2. Models Description

The architecture of the models to be evaluated is described below, in terms of their backbone, number of parameters, and input size. The PyTorch Torchvision package provides SSD in two variants. The first is a lightweight version of SSD, the SSDlite320, with the backbone of the MobileNetV3-Large [23], which is optimized for mobile devices with a very small number of parameters, and an input image size of 320×320. The second variant, the SSD300, has as its backbone the larger VGG16 network with 16 layers of neurons (13 conv and 3 fc leaving out the 5 pooling layers) and an input size of 300×300. The SSD300 has 35.6 million parameters, while the SSDlite320 has about a tenth of them, i.e., 3.4 million.

Implementing RetinaNet in Torchvision uses the backbone ResNet-50 consisting of 50 layers and 34 million parameters. For Faster R-CNN, two variants with different backbones are provided, one with MobileNetV3-Large and the second with ResNet-50. For the MobileNet variant, there are two versions with different input sizes, one with 800×800 and the other with 320×320. Also included is Faster R-CNN's version for the segmentation problem, the R-CNN Mask with Resnet-50 backbone, which produces simultaneously segmentation masks as well as bounding boxes. Mask R-CNN has a few more parameters than Faster R-CNN due to its additional functionality.

In the PyTorch implementation of G. Jocher's YOLOv3, the backbone of Darknet53 is used, as in the original implementation in the Darknet framework. Two further variants are provided, YOLOv3-tiny and YOLOv3-spp. YOLOv3-tiny is a smaller version of YOLOv3, which replaces some conv layers of the backbone with pooling layers and removes one of the three heads of YOLOv3, the one for small objects, to reduce computational costs. It consists of only 8.8 million parameters compared to YOLOv3 which has 61.9 million. YOLOv3-spp is virtually the same as YOLOv3, but one of the conv layers has been replaced by an SPP layer which helps the network to perceive the characteristics of the image at various levels of resolution, which only slightly increases the number of parameters to 63 million.

For YOLOv4, the PyTorch implementation by T. Xiaomo is used, which employs the improved backbone of CSPDarknet53, as in the original YOLOv4 implementation of the

Darknet framework, and in total consists of 64.4 million parameters. Finally, G. Jocher's YOLOv5 is distributed in five variants, n, s, m, l, and x, depending on the size of the network, of which we will consider n, s, m, and l. The number of its parameters ranges from 1.9 million up to 47 million depending on the variant. YOLOv5 uses a backbone based on CSPDarknet53 with some modifications in the implementation of the CSP Bottleneck. All the above implementations of YOLO can accept any input size. However, in order to ensure the validity of the results, we define the input size as the size of the data with which the pretrained models we use were trained. This size is 640 × 640 for YOLOv3 and v5, and 608 × 608 for YOLOv4.

2.3. Speed/Accuracy Trade-Off of Object Detection Models

In recent years, several reviews of modern object detection models have been published. In 2019, a survey [2] was conducted on the improvements in object detection in the last 20 years. Nonetheless, the survey merely reported on the performance of the models in question in the related bibliography. No experiment was performed to measure their accuracy and speed. In contrast, another review in the same year [3] included an experimental evaluation of more than 26 models on the Visual Object Classes (VOC) [24] and Common Objects in Context (COCO) [25] datasets. Although both accuracy and speed were measured, the trade-off between the two parameters was not analyzed. Moreover, the tested models were implemented in different machine learning frameworks and programming languages, thus obscuring the detection speed.

Two studies published in 2017 [4] and 2018 [5] assessed the speed/accuracy trade-off of object detection models using the same framework. In [4], the Tensorflow implementations of Faster R-CNN [6], SSD [10], and Region-based Fully Convolutional Network (R-FCN) [26] were evaluated on COCO [25] based on their speed/accuracy trade-off while testing different backbones, image resolutions, and number of region proposals. In [5], a similar analysis was conducted using the same models with the addition of Mask R-CNN [7] and SSDlite [27]. The aspect of memory consumption and detection speed on different devices was investigated as well. Nevertheless, both studies did not take into account newer models, such as YOLOv5 [15] and RetinaNet [9].

2.4. Medical Mask Detection

Initially, interest in medical mask detection was limited. After the outbreak of COVID-19, numerous medical mask detection models were proposed to limit infection.

In 2020, the Super-Resolution and Classification Network [28] was designed and trained using transfer learning. In 2021, RetinaFaceMask [29] was introduced, a one-shot model based on RetinaNet, using transfer learning from a human face dataset to the Masked Faces for Face Mask Detection Dataset (MAFA-FMD) made by the authors. In the same year, a hybrid medical mask recognition model [30] combining ResNet-50 [31] with a Support Vector Machine (SVM) was proposed, after being trained on both real-world and synthetic data using transfer learning. Later, in [32], the authors replaced the SVM with YOLOv2 [12]. A medical mask detector published in [33] was based on Inception-v3 [34] and trained on a synthetic mask dataset using transfer learning from a general object dataset and several data augmentations.

Despite achieving near-perfect accuracy, the above models were not evaluated on their detection speed. In view of this, a real-time mask detection model was designed, SE-YOLOv3 [16] and trained on the novel Properly Wearing Masked Face Detection (PWMFD) dataset created by the authors. It introduced a Squeeze-and-Excitation (SE) attention mechanism [35] to YOLOv3, achieving a 66% mAP and 28 fps. However, its performance was evaluated using a high-end GPU, rendering it unsuitable for lightweight devices. Moving to YOLOv4, the hybrid mask detection model tiny-YOLOv4-SPP was proposed [36]. It significantly reduced the training time while increasing the accuracy compared to the original tiny-YOLOv4, but the aspect of real-time detection was not considered.

3. Materials and Methods

3.1. Evaluation Methodology of Object Detection Models

We evaluate the object detection models shown in Table 1 in terms of memory consumption, computational and storage costs, as well as their speed/accuracy trade-off. The models include Faster R-CNN with two different backbones and image sizes, Mask R-CNN, RetinaNet, SSD and its memory-efficient version SSDlite, YOLOv3 with its SPP and tiny variants, YOLOv4, and YOLOv5, including its large, medium, small, and nano variants. For all models, we utilize the same framework, dataset, and GPU.

Table 1. Models evaluated on the COCO2017 dataset.

Model	Backbone	Image Size [a]
Faster R-CNN [6]	MobileNetV3-Large [23]	800
Faster R-CNN	MobileNetV3-Large	320
Faster R-CNN	ResNet-50 [31]	800
Mask R-CNN [7]	ResNet-50	800
RetinaNet [9]	ResNet-50	800
SSD [10]	VGG16 [37]	300
SSDlite [25]	MobileNetV3-Large	320
YOLOv3 [13]	Darknet53 [13]	640
YOLOv3-spp [13]	Darknet53	640
YOLOv3-tiny [13]	Darknet53	640
YOLOv4 [14]	CSPDarknet53 [14]	608
YOLOv5l [15]	Modified CSPDarknet [15]	640
YOLOv5m [15]	Modified CSPDarknet	640
YOLOv5s [15]	Modified CSPDarknet	640
YOLOv5n [15]	Modified CSPDarknet	640

[a] Given a value of N, the image size in pixels is N × N.

1. Framework: All models are implemented in PyTorch and are offered in the Torchvision package. The only exceptions are YOLOv3, YOLOv4, and YOLOv5, which are implemented in GitHub repositories (https://github.com/ultralytics/yolov3 accessed on 1 June 2023; https://github.com/Tianxiaomo/pytorch-YOLOv4 accessed on 1 June 2023; https://github.com/ultralytics/yolov5 accessed on 1 June 2023).
2. Dataset: The evaluation is performed on the val subset of the COCO2017 [25] dataset. COCO appears to be among the de facto standards for measuring accuracy and speed in modern object detection models as it strikes a balance between manageable size and adequate image scene density. It contains 118,000 examples for training and 5000 for validation belonging to 80 classes of everyday objects. In addition, COCO training has been extensively used in the past as a basis for transfer learning on the specific problem of medical mask detection. No training phase is performed as all models are already pretrained on the train subset. The data are loaded with a batch size of 1 to imitate the stream-like insertion when detecting in real time.
3. Environment: The code for the experiment is organized in two Jupyter notebooks (coco17 inference.pynb, analysis.pynb) and is executed through the Google Colab platform. We chose the option of a local runtime, which uses the GPU of our system (Nvidia Geforce GTX 960, 4 GB). Every model goes through the same inference pipeline.
4. Metrics: To estimate the memory usage of each model, we calculate the maximum GPU memory allocated to our GPU device by CUDA for the program. To quantify computational costs, Giga Floating Point Operations (GFLOPs) are counted using the

ptflops (https://github.com/sovrasov/flops-counter.pytorch accessed on 1 June 2023) Python package. The storage cost is derived from the size of the weight file of each respective model. We measure detection speed in frames (images) per second (fps). For accuracy, we use the mean Average Precision (mAP) of all classes. According to the COCO evaluation standard (https://cocodataset.org/#detection-eval accessed on 1 June 2023), Average Precision (AP) is calculated using 101-point interpolation on the area under the P-R (Precision–Recall) curve, as follows:

$$AP_{101} = \frac{1}{101} \sum_{R=\{0, 0.01, \ldots, 0.99, 1\}} P_{interp}(R) \qquad (1)$$

where

$$P_{interp}(R) = \max_{\tilde{R}: \tilde{R} \geq R} P(\tilde{R}) \qquad (2)$$

3.2. Memory Footprint

In Figure 1a, the higher the number of parameters and image size, the more GPU memory the model consumes. Interestingly, YOLOv4 has a 925 MB memory footprint that is 3 times more than models with roughly the same parameter count and image size, such as YOLOv3 (301 MB). In contrast, YOLOv3 utilizes approximately three-fourths of the memory consumed by YOLOv5l, despite having more parameters and the same image size. SSDlite, having the fewest parameters and smallest image size, uses merely 33 MB.

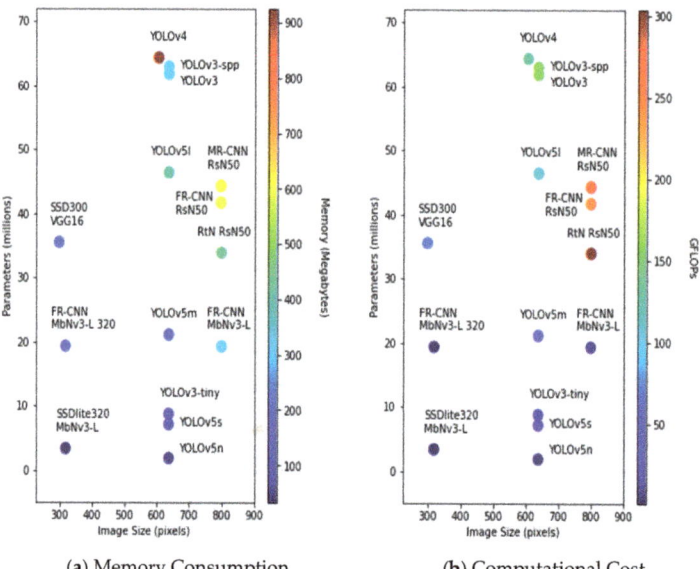

Figure 1. Memory footprint in Megabytes (**a**) and computational cost in GFLOPs (**b**) in relation to parameter count and image size of object detection models evaluated on the COCO2017 [25] dataset.

3.3. Computational Performance and Storage Costs

Firstly, the number of GFLOPs of a model is closely related to its number of parameters and image size. For instance, in Figure 1b, between the two implementations of Faster R-CNN with MobileNet-v3 and ResNet-50, the second executes 27 times more GFLOPs than the first while having just over twice the same number of parameters. In general, models that use the MobileNet-v3 backbone, i.e., SSDlite and Faster R-CNN, prove to be the least expensive in GFLOPs. Subsequently, comparing the two versions of Faster R-CNN with different image sizes, the one with size 800 costs almost 6 times more GFLOPs than the one with 320. The sole exception to the rule is RetinaNet and YOLOv3 which, despite having the same image size and fewer parameters than Faster R-CNN ResNet50 and YOLOv4, respectively, execute more GFLOPs than their counterpart.

According to Figure 2, storage cost increases linearly with the number of parameters in a model. Nevertheless, YOLOv3 and YOLOv5 cost significantly less storage space than models with an equivalent number of parameters.

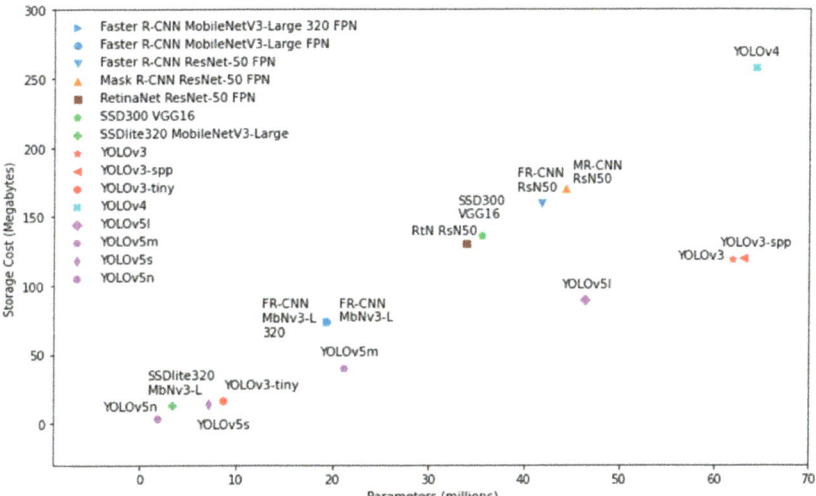

Figure 2. Relationship between storage cost in Megabytes and parameter count of object detection models evaluated on the COCO2017 [25] dataset.

3.4. Accuracy and Speed

For a fair comparison of the models' accuracy, it is necessary to evaluate this metric in terms of speed. There is no point in ranking the models based on their accuracy, if we do not understand the larger context in which a model manages to provide its degree of accuracy. This means that if a model achieves high accuracy but at the same time sacrifices a significant part of its speed for this purpose, then it becomes unsuitable for the problem of real-time detection. Accordingly, the same is true for the reverse.

Therefore, in Figure 3, we illustrate the trade-off between the speed (fps) and accuracy (mAP) of all models. An immediate observation is a decrease in speed as the accuracy of a model increases. On a general note, a favorable model would be one that achieves both high accuracy and speed. Thus, it would be found in the top right corner of Figure 3. All variations of YOLOv5 provide the best balance between accuracy and speed, whereas RetinaNet, SSD, SSDlite, and YOLOv3-tiny rank last.

3.5. Accuracy and Speed vs. Computational Performance

In Figure 4, we demonstrate the relationship between mAP and GFLOPs for each model. We notice that the higher the count of GFLOPs, the higher the accuracy, forming a hyperbolic curve of "$y = -\alpha/x + \beta$" between the two measures. Ideally, we strive to find a model that achieves the highest possible mAP for the lowest possible GFLOPs. According to this, the best performance is attained by the models of the YOLOv5 family, especially the medium and large variants, with Faster R-CNN MobileNetV3-Large rivaling the smaller variants. The worst mAP/GFLOPs balance is observed for YOLOv3-tiny, which shows the lowest mAP in comparison to other models of a similar level of GFLOPs, and RetinaNet, which executes far more GLOPs than other models of the same order of mAP.

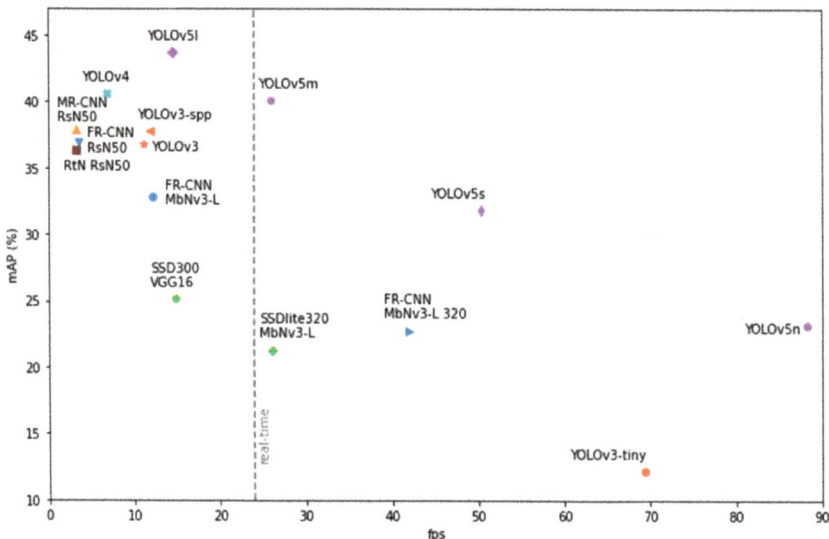

Figure 3. Speed (fps)/accuracy (mAP) trade-off of object detection models evaluated on the COCO2017 [25] dataset.

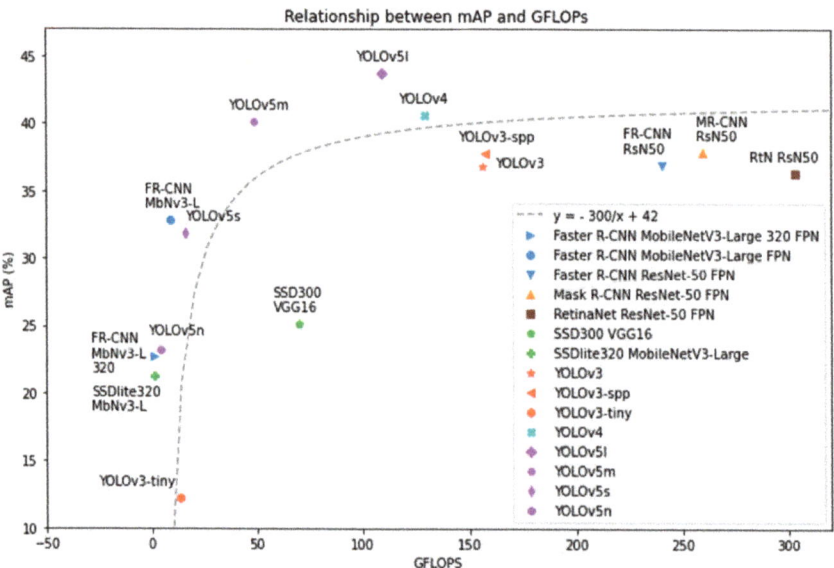

Figure 4. Relationship between mAP and GFLOPs for various object detection models.

Figure 5 illustrates the relationship between inference speed in fps and GFLOPs. We observe that it is approximated by a hyperbolic curve of the form "y = α/x". In other words, as the GFLOPs of a model increase, the fps decrease. Nevertheless, achieving the highest fps possible with the least amount of GFLOPs is favorable. Thus, we conclude that the most efficient model in terms of speed is YOLOv5n, with YOLOv3-tiny ranking second. The implementation of RetinaNet is the least efficient with the largest number of GFLOPs and the least fps.

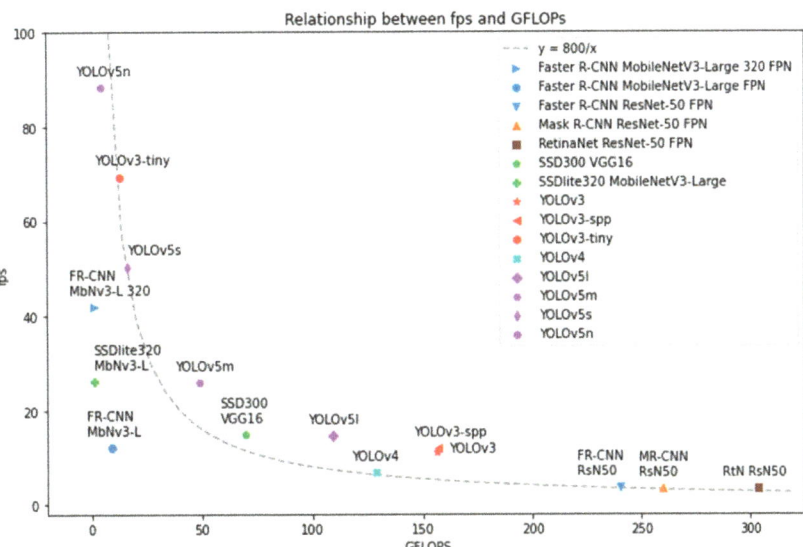

Figure 5. Relationship between fps and GFLOPs for various object detection models.

4. Datasets for Medical Mask Detection

For the problem of medical mask detection, we performed an extensive survey of the available datasets. The choice of a complex and diverse set is crucial for the development of a robust model. Although a model may exhibit maximum accuracy in a simplistic set, this does not necessarily hold in real conditions. The first datasets of medical masks have been appearing since 2017. However, since the outbreak of the COVID-19 pandemic, they have multiplied rapidly in number and some of them have already been used in medical mask detection systems. These datasets are analyzed below.

4.1. MAFA and MAFA-FMD

The Masked Faces (MAFA) dataset [38] was developed in 2017 by S. Ge et al. as the first dataset of faces with masks. It includes 30,811 non-synthetic images and a total of 35,806 masked faces divided across the number of images. On average, the faces of the set have a size of 143×143 pixels. A distinct characteristic of the dataset lies in the fact that the annotations of faces, in addition to the bounding box that encloses the face, include information about the orientation of the face, the degree of mask overlap, and the type of mask. In terms of orientation, faces are classified as left, left-front, front, right-front, and right, with the majority (71%) belonging to the front. In terms of degree of overlap, they are divided into weak, medium, and strong, depending on the number of areas they cover on the face, with the majority belonging to medium (81%). Finally, regarding the type of mask, the faces are grouped into simple, complex, body, and hybrid. In essence, "mask" is considered not only a medical mask but also a garment or part of the body, such as a hand.

In 2019, following the outbreak of COVID-19, the Masked Faces for Face Mask Detection Dataset (MAFA-FMD) [29] was formed as an improvement on MAFA. In particular, the labels of the original set were modified with the aim of specializing it in medical conditions, and the labels of persons who had not already been tagged were added. MAFA-FMD contains 56,024 identifications of persons who, unlike MAFA, also include faces without a mask at all. Faces are organized into three groups depending on whether a strictly medical mask has been placed correctly, wrongly, or not at all. Body parts or clothing used to cover the face are not considered valid masks and faces are classified as maskless. At the same time, the dataset was augmented with labels for low-resolution face samples i.e., smaller than 32×32 pixels. One disadvantage of MAFA-FMD is the imbalance of class samples, most notably the misplaced mask class with only 1388 samples compared to the other two classes with 28,233 and 26,463 samples, respectively.

4.2. RMFD and SMRFD

In 2020, a large dataset of medical masks was issued by Z. Wang et al., the Real-World Masked Face Recognition Dataset (RMFRD) [39]. RMFRD contains 95,000 images of 525 different public faces in frontal view, of which 5000 contain a face with a medical mask and 90,000 without. Alongside this set, the Simulated Masked Face Recognition Dataset (SMFRD) [39] was published. It was used to exploit already existing large-scale face datasets. For its construction, the creators placed medical masks on each face of such sets, in an automatic way, after developing the appropriate software. In total, it contains 500,000 images of 10,000 different people with one face in each image. The advantage of synthetic sets is that they enable the usage of large-scale datasets of common problems in our own, especially in cases where the problem is new and sufficient data do not yet exist. However, the introduction of synthetic information requires the researcher to take some initiatives based on their own perception about what data the problem needs. Thus, there is a danger that the model will form biases during training. For example, in the SMFRD set, synthetic masks added to faces are drawn from only one image of a medical mask. Therefore, if the model is faced with the detection of masks of various colors, shapes, and textures, it is very likely that it will not be able to generalize sufficiently. In conclusion, the use of synthetic sets must be accompanied by the use of image sets from real life to maximize the ability of the model to generalize. Both RMFRD and SMFRD categorize faces into only two classes, those who wear a mask and those who do not. However, the labels of the two sets do not include bounding boxes, so the sets are not suitable for detecting masks, only for recognition.

4.3. MaskedFace-Net

In 2020, MaskedFace-Net [40] was developed by A. Cabani et al., and it is the largest synthetic dataset of masks differentiating correctly and incorrectly placed medical masks. The facial images were drawn from the Flickr-Faces-HQ (FFHQ) set comprising faces of high diversity in terms of age, ethnicity, and environmental conditions. Then, a medical mask image was automatically added to them with varying degrees of overlap using a machine learning model to identify the parts of the face to which the mask attaches. MaskedFace-Net contains a total of 137,016 images and is a synthesis of two subsets developed by the creators, the Correctly Masked Face Dataset (CMFD) and the Incorrectly Masked Face Dataset (IMFD), with 67,193 and 69,823 images, respectively. In the IMFD set, faces are grouped into three subsets which are differentiated according to whether the mask does not cover the nose (80%), whether it does not cover the chin (10%), and whether it does not cover the nose and mouth (10%). Unlike the large-scale SMFRD dataset, MaskedFace-Net can be used for both recognition and detection and provides detailed analysis of faces with misplaced masks. Of course, like SMFRD, as a synthetic dataset, it is proposed to be used in conjunction with a non-synthetic set.

4.4. PWMFD

The Properly Wearing Masked Face Detection Dataset (PWMFD) [16] is a dataset of faces with medical masks developed by X. Jiang et al. in 2021. It includes 9205 non-synthetic images of faces from multiple sources. Specifically, 3615 were collected from the internet, 2951 from the WIDER FACE dataset, 2581 from MAFA, and 58 from RMFRD. There are three classes used to classify faces: faces with correct mask placement, with wrong mask placement, and without a mask. In the maskless class, not only persons who did not wear a mask were placed but also persons with body parts or objects covering a part of them. Thus, the set is an important tool to ensure the proper use of medical masks, even in cases of attempts to deceive the system. Of the 9205 images, a total of 18,532 faces are highlighted: 7695 in the correct placement class, 366 in the wrong placement class, and 10,471 in the maskless class. We observe a balance between correct and maskless classes, but the number of samples in the wrong mask class is relatively incomplete.

For implementing a medical mask detection and recognition system, we select PWMFD among the datasets reviewed. Initially, due to the nature of the problem, it is necessary for the dataset chosen to include markings for both the class and the coordinates of each face. Therefore, sets exclusively specialized in either detection or recognition, such as RMFRD and SMFRD, are not readily suitable. In addition, it is important that the dataset contains realistic and diverse images so that the model can generalize with a high degree of accuracy after training. Synthetic sets have limitations in this respect, such as SMFRD and MaskedFace-Net sets, which use a single mask format from a particular image to compose the set. To avoid prolonged training times, we need a balance between the dataset size and the percentage of realistic vs. synthetic images it contains rather than an arbitrary expansion with synthetic images. At the same time, PWMFD is also an average solution in terms of sample count per image, averaging two faces per image. A large count gives the model the opportunity to train in scenes with dense crowds of people, something that responds to realistic situations. After all, the PWMFD set is a synthesis of subsets of MAFA and RMFRD, enriched with additional data. Finally, as already mentioned, PWMFD allows the detection of misplaced masks as well, a significant advantage in real medical applications.

5. Results of Optimizations for Medical Mask Detection

5.1. Configuration

Dataset: To achieve desirable results, a realistic and diverse dataset for both localization and recognition of medical masks is required, one that is large enough to ensure high accuracy but does not exceed our hardware limitations. Therefore, we selected the newly created PWMFD [16] dataset, using its train and validation subsets to train and evaluate our model, respectively. It includes 9205 real-life images with 18,532 annotations of faces belonging to three classes: "with mask", "incorrect mask", and "without mask."

Environment: The code for the experiment was executed through Google Colab and was organized in three Jupyter notebooks (mask training.pynb, mask inference.pynb, analysis.pynb). Training was performed using the GPU provided by Colab (Nvidia Tesla K80, 12 GB) due to its memory facilitating a larger batch size, whereas the evaluation was performed using our local GPU (Nvidia Geforce GTX 960, 4 GB) because of its higher detection speed.

Training and Evaluation: During training, a batch size of 32 was used. Training lasted for 50 epochs, as more resulted in overfitting. The learning rate was updated according to the OneCycleLR [41] policy, with values in the range of [0.001, 0.01]. As an optimizer, Stochastic Gradient Descent was employed with a value of 0.937 for momentum and 0.0005 for weight decay. Cross-Entropy was used for classification loss and Complete Intersection over Union (CIoU) for localization loss. After training, the final weights were selected from the epoch with the highest mAP. During evaluation, inference was performed with a batch size of one to mimic the sequential input of data in real time. The COCO mAP and fps were measured as metrics.

5.2. Implementing Optimizations for Medical Mask Detection

According to our study in Section 3, YOLOv5 [15], and particularly its medium, small, and nano variants, provided the best balance between accuracy, speed, memory consumption, and computational and storage costs for real-time object detection. Its architecture is depicted in Figure 6. To implement our medical mask detector, we chose to train its small variant, YOLOv5s, on PWMFD [16] with an image size of 320, achieving 33% mAP and 69 fps. To elevate its performance, we experimented with various optimizations during training.

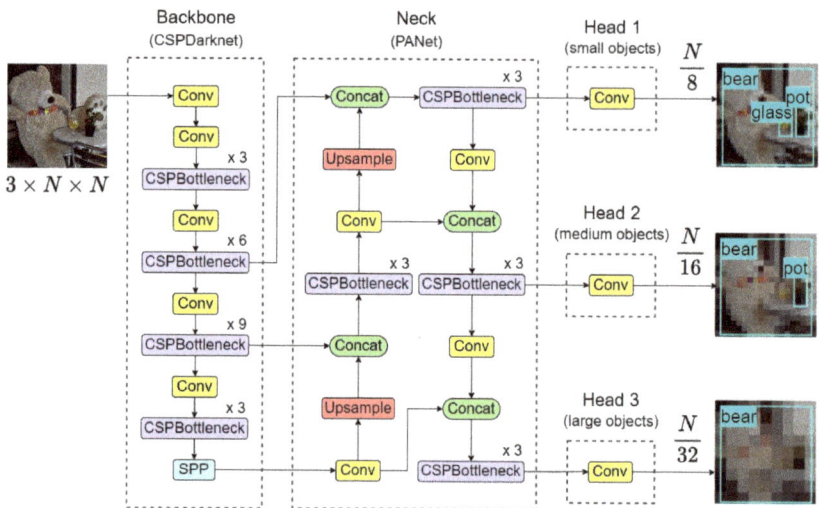

Figure 6. Architecture of YOLOv5 [15] consisting of a CSPDarknet [14] type of backbone, an SPP [21] layer, a PANet [22] as the neck, and three heads for the detection of objects of different sizes.

5.3. Transfer Learning

Inspired by the success of transfer learning in previous medical mask detectors [28–30,32,33], we applied weights pretrained on COCO [25] to PWMFD [16]. This technique is known for significantly decreasing training time and the need for a large dataset [42], both crucial in our case. We tested various training schemes for YOLOv5s on PWMFD, without transfer learning using random initial weights (row 1 in Table 2) and with transfer learning using the COCO weights (rows 2–4 in Table 2), while experimenting with freezing the weights of different layers before training. The highest mAP (38%) was achieved by freezing the pretrained backbone, that is, training only the head on PWMFD.

Table 2. Performance of YOLOV5s [15] on PWMFD [16] with various transfer learning (TL) and layer freezing schemes.

	mAP	mAP@50	mAP@75
No TL	0.33	0.59	0.33
TL + No Freeze	0.35	0.60	0.39
TL + Freeze Backbone	**0.38**	**0.63**	**0.43**
TL + Freeze All [a]	0.03	0.10	0.01

[a] Except output layer.

5.4. Data Augmentations

To prevent overfitting, we utilized the following basic data augmentations: translation, scaling, flipping, and Hue–Saturation–Value (HSV) transformations. Furthermore, we assessed the effect of two novel transformations, mosaic and mixup [43]. The first combined multiple images forming a mosaic, while the second stacked two images on top of one another with a degree of transparency. The potential benefits of mosaic and mixup for YOLO were explored in [14,16] for mask detection. We trained YOLOv5s with three different data augmentation combinations as shown in Table 3. Mosaic nearly doubled the accuracy (mAP 67%), but the addition of mixup was not beneficial.

Table 3. Performance of YOLOV5S [15] on PWMFD [16] with various data augmentation combinations.

	mAP	mAP@50	mAP@75
Basic Transformations [a]	0.38	0.63	0.43
Basic Trans. + Mosaic	**0.67**	**0.92**	**0.81**
Basic Trans. + Mosaic + Mixup	0.65	0.91	0.78

[a] Translation, scaling, flipping, and Hue-Saturation-Value.

5.5. Attention Mechanism with Squeeze-and-Excitation (SE) Block

In [16], by introducing two SE blocks to the backbone of YOLOv3 as an attention mechanism along with mixup and focal loss, the accuracy of YOLOv3 on PWMFD raised by 8.6%. The SE mechanism applies input-dependent weights to the channels of the feature map to create a better representation of the image. Focal loss is an improvement on Cross-Entropy loss that assists the model in focusing on hard misclassified examples during training. We applied the same strategy to YOLOv5. Our ablation study in Table 4 shows that these optimizations did not affect speed, but they impacted accuracy negatively. Therefore, they were not used in our final mask detector. Nevertheless, Figure 7 illustrates higher accuracy for small and medium-sized objects when using SE with mixup.

Table 4. Performance of YOLOV5S [15] on PWMFD [16] with selected optimizations from SE-YOLOV3 (Squeeze-and-Excitation attention mechanism, mixup, and focal loss).

	mAP	mAP@50	mAP@75	fps
No SE	**0.67**	0.92	**0.81**	69
SE	0.61	**0.93**	0.74	68
SE + Mixup	0.58	0.90	0.68	69
SE + Focal Loss	0.38	0.63	0.45	**71**
SE + Mixup + Focal Loss	0.37	0.62	0.43	70

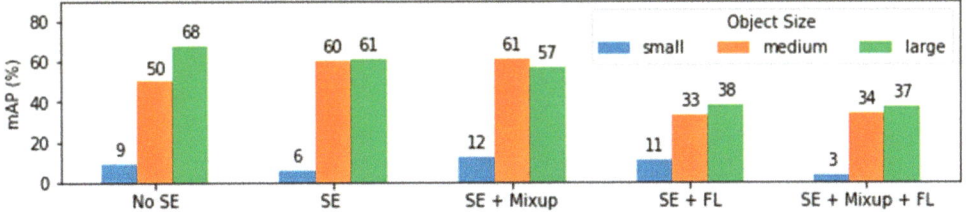

Figure 7. Accuracy of YOLOv5s [15] on PWMFD [16] for 3 object sizes (small: area < 32^2, medium: 32^2 < area < 96^2, large: area > 96^2 in COCO evaluation metrics) with selected optimizations from SE-YOLOv3 [16].

5.6. Attention Mechanism with Transformer Encoder (TE) Block

In the TPH-YOLOv5 model [44], the basic architecture of YOLOv5 was enhanced by adding a Transformer Encoder block as an attention mechanism at the end of the backbone and the beginning of each head. The purpose of the backbone addition is to enhance feature maps with information about the general context in which they appear, i.e., their relationship to neighboring objects. The purpose of the head addition is to improve feature maps on each output size scale. In addition, by using TE blocks, TPH-YOLOv5 improved the accuracy of locating small, densely placed objects. Based on the architecture of TPH-YOLOv5, we evaluated the insertion of TE blocks into YOLOv5s at the end of the backbone and at the beginning of each head. The structure of the TE block was the one implemented within the C3TR block in the official code repository of YOLOv5. The new C3TR blocks replaced the C3 blocks of YOLOv5 located at the end of the backbone and at the beginning of each head. A C3TR block, like the C3, consists of a CSPNet, except that in the former a TE block is nested and in the latter a bottleneck block.

Table 5 shows the influence of using TE blocks on the backbone, heads, and the architecture as a whole. We note that using TE blocks in each case did not improve accuracy. In fact, due to the addition of the new units, the speed dropped. Adding three TE blocks to the heads reduced the speed much more (−13 fps) than adding to the backbone (−1 fps). The drop in accuracy was not as dramatic (−5%) but still greater than the drop after adding to the backbone (−1%). The use of TE blocks across the architecture had the greatest decrease in accuracy (−7%) and speed (−14 fps). For a loose IoU boundary, we observed that using TE blocks did not affect accuracy as negatively as with a tighter limit, meaning that the generated bounding boxes with TE blocks are less "tight" around each object. We also noticed that using TE blocks solely on the backbone or heads improved the detection of medium objects but negatively affected accuracy on large and especially small objects. We conclude that for our problem, the use of the attention mechanisms we examined helped the model for medium objects in terms of accuracy, but not overall, and therefore we did not use them in the final model.

Table 5. Performance of YOLOV5S [15] on PWMFD [16] with and w/o TE blocks.

	mAP	mAP@50	mAP@75	fps
No TE Block	**0.67**	**0.92**	**0.81**	**69**
TE Block (Backbone)	0.66	0.90	0.78	68
TE Block (Heads)	0.62	**0.92**	0.76	56
TE Block (Backbone + Heads)	0.60	0.88	0.75	55

5.7. Final Optimized Model

Our final mask detector was based on YOLOv5s with transfer learning from COCO to PWMFD while freezing the backbone and uses mosaic and other basic data augmentations. According to Table 6, it is twice as accurate as the baseline YOLOv5s while being equal in speed. At the same time, when compared using PWMFD, it was as accurate and more than two times faster on our own lower-end GTX 960 GPU than the state-of-the-art SE-YOLOv3 on a GTX 2070. This significant increase in speed gives room for its use in embedded devices with lower hardware capabilities while still achieving real-time detection. Detection examples are illustrated in Figure 8.

Table 6. Performance of our optimized YOLOv5s compared to baseline YOLOv5 [15] and SE-YOLOv3 [16].

	mAP	mAP@50	mAP@75	fps
SE-YOLOv3 [a] [16]	0.66	**0.96**	0.79	28
YOLOv5s [15]	0.33	0.59	0.33	**69**
YOLOv5s + TL + Freeze BB + Mosaic	**0.67**	0.92	**0.81**	**69**

[a] With image size 320 and a GTX 2070 GPU.

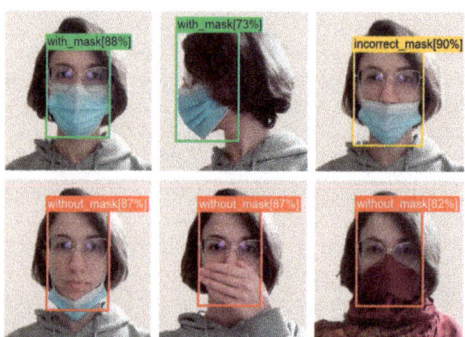

Figure 8. Detection examples using our optimized YOLOv5s model.

6. Discussion

Evaluating object detection models fairly is a task that requires multiple parameters to be addressed besides accuracy. Our goal is to provide an informative analysis of fundamental object detectors that also includes speed, accuracy, memory consumption, and computational and storage costs. YOLOv5 currently appears to provide the best balance between these parameters for real-time object detection. For the specific task of medical mask detection, our review and survey of currently available models and datasets can be useful for further designing end-to-end systems for public health administration and protection.

We also perform an evaluation of an inspiring set of potential optimizations for the task at hand. Using our findings, we propose an optimized YOLOv5s-based model for real-time mask detection to protect public health amidst the COVID-19 pandemic. Our optimizations led to increased accuracy (mAP 67%) that rivaled that of the state-of-the-art SE-YOLOv3 on PWMFD while being more than two times faster (69 fps). At the same time, applying the SE attention mechanism of SEYOLOv3 to YOLOv5s along with mixup improved the accuracy for small and medium-sized objects but not large ones.

In the future, we would like to research optimizations to combat the side effects on large objects, thus improving total accuracy. Moreover, our model does not utilize an important characteristic of data streams, the relationship between consecutive frames. This could be achieved by exploring object detection models that implement this using Recurrent Neural Networks. In addition, further optimized models such as YOLOv8 as well as Transformer-based models (ViTs) have yet to be fully evaluated specifically for the problem per se. Some of the optimizations we have tested and reported on have now been incorporated into v8, including mixup, for which we already concluded that it does not offer overall gains.

After the end of the pandemic, we are hopeful that with the help of our model the healthcare sector can be better prepared for a similar crisis. Our proposed optimizations may also be useful for other related problems, such as face detection.

Author Contributions: Conceptualization, D.A.K.; methodology, D.A.K. and I.C.G.; validation, I.C.G.; investigation, D.A.K. and I.C.G.; writing—original draft preparation, D.A.K. and I.C.G.; writing—review and editing, D.A.K. and I.C.G.; visualization, I.C.G.; supervision, D.A.K. All authors have read and agreed to the published version of the manuscript.

Funding: This research received no external funding.

Data Availability Statement: The data presented in this study are openly available at https://github.com/joangog/object-detection-assets.

Conflicts of Interest: The authors declare no conflict of interest.

References

1. Lecun, Y.; Bengio, Y. Convolutional networks for images, speech and time series. In *The Handbook of Brain Theory and Neural Networks*; The MIT Press: Cambridge, MA, USA, 1995.
2. Zou, Z.; Shi, Z.; Guo, Y.; Ye, J. Object detection in 20 years: A survey. *arXiv* **2019**, arXiv:1905.05055. [CrossRef]
3. Zhao, Z.; Zheng, P.; Xu, S.; Wu, X. Object detection with deep learning: A review. *IEEE Trans. Neural Netw. Learn. Syst.* **2019**, *30*, 3212–3232. [CrossRef] [PubMed]
4. Huang, J.; Rathod, V.; Sun, C.; Zhu, M.; Korattikara, A.; Fathi, A.; Fischer, I.; Wojna, Z.; Song, Y.; Guadarrama, S.; et al. Speed/accuracy trade-offs for modern convolutional object detectors. In Proceedings of the IEEE Conference on Computer Vision and Pattern Recognition, Honolulu, Hawaii, 21–26 July 2017; pp. 3296–3297.
5. Srivastava, A.; Nguyen, D.; Aggarwal, S.; Luckow, A.; Duffy, E.; Kennedy, K.; Ziolkowski, M.; Apon, A. Performance and memory trade-offs of deep learning object detection in fast streaming high-definition images. In Proceedings of the 2018 IEEE International Conference on Big Data (Big Data), Seattle, WA, USA, 10–13 December 2018; pp. 3915–3924.
6. Ren, S.; He, K.; Girshick, R.B.; Sun, J. Faster R-CNN: Towards real-time object detection with region proposal networks. In *Advances in Neural Information Processing Systems 28 (NIPS 2015)*; Neural Information Processing Systems Foundation, Inc.: Montreal, QC, Canada, 2015; Volume 28.
7. He, K.; Gkioxari, G.; Dollar, P.; Girshick, R.B. Mask R-CNN. In Proceedings of the 2017 IEEE International Conference on Computer Vision (ICCV), Venice, Italy, 22–29 October 2017; pp. 2961–2969.

8. Girshick, R.B.; Donahue, J.; Darrell, T.; Malik, J. Rich feature hierarchies for accurate object detection and semantic segmentation. In Proceedings of the IEEE Conference on Computer Vision and Pattern Recognition 2014, Columbus, OH, USA, 23–28 June 2014; pp. 580–587.
9. Lin, T.; Goyal, P.; Girshick, R.B.; He, K.; Dollar, P. Focal loss for ́ dense object detection. In Proceedings of the IEEE International Conference on Computer Vision 2017, Venice, Italy, 22–29 October 2017.
10. Liu, W.; Anguelov, D.; Erhan, D.; Szegedy, C.; Reed, S.; Fu, C.Y.; Berg, A.C. SSD: Single Shot Multibox Detector. In *ECCV 2016: Computer Vision–ECCV 2016*; Springer: Cham, Switzerland, 2016; pp. 21–37.
11. Redmon, J.; Divvala, K.; Girshick, R.B.; Farhadi, A. You only look once: Unified, real-time object detection. In Proceedings of the IEEE Conference on Computer Vision and Pattern Recognition 2016, Las Vegas, NV, USA, 27–30 June 2016; pp. 779–788.
12. Redmon, J.; Farhadi, A. YOLO9000: Better, faster, stronger. In Proceedings of the IEEE Conference on Computer Vision and Pattern Recognition 2017, Honolulu, Hawaii, 21–26 July 2017; pp. 7263–7271.
13. Redmon, J.; Farhadi, A. YOLOv3: An incremental improvement. *arXiv* **2018**, arXiv:1804.02767.
14. Bochkovskiy, A.; Wang, C.; Liao, H.M. YOLOv4: Optimal speed and accuracy of object detection. *arXiv* **2020**, arXiv:2004.10934.
15. Jocher, G.; Stoken, A.; Chaurasia, A.; Borovec, J.; Kwon, Y.; Michael, K.; Changyu, L.; Fang, J.; Skalski, P.; Hogan, A.; et al. ultralytics/yolov5: v6.0-YOLOv5n 'Nano' Models, Roboflow Integration, TensorFlow Export, OpenCV DNN Support. 2021. Available online: https://github.com/ultralytics/yolov5 (accessed on 1 June 2023).
16. Jiang, X.; Gao, T.; Zhu, Z.; Zhao, Y. Real-time face mask detection method based on YOLOv3. *Electronics* **2021**, *10*, 837. [CrossRef]
17. World Health Organization. *Advice on the Use of Masks in the Context of COVID-19: Interim Guidance*; World Health Organization: Geneva, Switzerland, 2020.
18. Gogou, I.C.; Koutsomitropoulos, D.A. A Review and Implementation of Object Detection Models and Optimizations for Real-time Medical Mask Detection during the COVID-19 Pandemic. In Proceedings of the 2022 International Conference on INnovations in Intelligent SysTems and Applications (INISTA), Biarritz, France, 8–12 August 2022; pp. 1–6.
19. Krizhevsky, A.; Sutskever, I.; Hinton, G.E. ImageNet classification with deep convolutional neural networks. In *Advances in Neural Information Processing Systems 25 (NIPS 2012)*; Curran Associates, Inc.: New York, USA, 2013; pp. 1097–1105.
20. Girshick, R.B. Fast R-CNN. In Proceedings of the IEEE International Conference on Computer Vision, Santiago, Chile, 7–13 December 2015; pp. 1440–1448.
21. He, K.; Zhang, X.; Ren, S.; Sun, J. Spatial pyramid pooling in deep convolutional networks for visual recognition. *IEEE Trans. Pattern Anal. Mach. Intell.* **2015**, *37*, 1904–1916. [CrossRef] [PubMed]
22. Liu, S.; Qi, L.; Qin, H.; Shi, J.; Jia, J. Path aggregation network for instance segmentation. In Proceedings of the IEEE Conference on Computer Vision and Pattern Recognition 2018, Salt Lake City, UT, USA, 18–22 June 2018; pp. 8759–8768.
23. Howard, A.; Sandler, M.; Chu, G.; Chen, L.C.; Chen, B.; Tan, M.; Wang, W.; Zhu, Y.; Pang, R.; Vasudevan, V.; et al. Searching for mobilenetv3. In Proceedings of the IEEE/CVF International Conference on Computer Vision 2019, Long Beach, CA, USA, 16–20 June 2019.
24. Everingham, M.; Gool, L.V.; Williams, C.K.I.; Winn, J.M.; Zisserman, A. The Pascal Visual Object Classes (VOC) challenge. *Int. J. Comput. Vis.* **2010**, *88*, 303–338. [CrossRef]
25. Lin, T.-Y.; Maire, M.; Belongie, S.; Hays, J.; Perona, P.; Ramanan, D.; Dollár, P. Microsoft COCO: Common Objects in Context. In *ECCV 2014: Computer Vision–ECCV 2014*; Springer: Cham, Switzerland, 2014; pp. 740–755.
26. Dai, J.; Li, Y.; He, K.; Sun, J. R-FCN: Object detection via regionbased fully convolutional networks. In *Advances in Neural Information Processing Systems 29 (NIPS 2016)*; Curran Associates, Inc.: New York, NY, USA, 2016.
27. Sandler, M.; Howard, A.; Zhu, M.; Zhmoginov, A.; Chen, L. MobileNetV2: Inverted residuals and linear bottlenecks. In Proceedings of the IEEE Conference on Computer Vision and Pattern Recognition 2018, Salt Lake City, UT, USA, 18–22 June 2018.
28. Qin, B.; Li, D. Identifying facemask-wearing condition using image super-resolution with classification network to prevent COVID-19. *Sensors* **2020**, *20*, 5236. [CrossRef] [PubMed]
29. Fan, X.; Jiang, M. RetinaFaceMask: A single stage face mask detector for assisting control of the COVID-19 pandemic. In Proceedings of the 2021 IEEE International Conference on Systems, Man, and Cybernetics (SMC), Melbourne, Australia, 17–20 October 2021; pp. 832–837.
30. Loey, M.; Manogaran, G.; Taha, M.H.N.; Khalifa, N.E.M. A hybrid deep transfer learning model with machine learning methods for face mask detection in the era of the COVID-19 pandemic. *Measurement* **2021**, *167*, 108288. [CrossRef] [PubMed]
31. He, K.; Zhang, X.; Ren, S.; Sun, J. Deep residual learning for image recognition. In Proceedings of the IEEE Conference on Computer Vision and Pattern Recognition 2016, Las Vegas, NV, USA, 27–30 June 2016; pp. 770–778.
32. Loey, M.; Manogaran, G.; Taha, M.H.N.; Khalifa, N.E.M. Fighting against COVID-19: A novel deep learning model based on YOLO-v2 with ResNet-50 for medical face mask detection. *Sustain. Cities Soc.* **2021**, *65*, 102600. [CrossRef] [PubMed]
33. Chowdary, G.J.; Punn, N.S.; Sonbhadra, S.K.; Agarwal, S. Face mask detection using transfer learning of InceptionV3. In *BDA 2020: Big Data Analytics*; Springer: Cham, Switzerland, 2020; pp. 81–90.
34. Szegedy, C.; Vanhoucke, V.; Ioffe, S.; Shlens, J.; Wojna, Z. Rethinking the inception architecture for computer vision. In Proceedings of the IEEE Conference on Computer Vision and Pattern Recognition 2016, Las Vegas, NV, USA, 27–30 June 2016.
35. Hu, J.; Shen, L.; Sun, G. Squeeze-and-excitation networks. In Proceedings of the IEEE Conference on Computer Vision and Pattern Recognition 2018, Salt Lake City, UT, USA, 18–22 June 2018.

36. Kumar, A.; Kalia, A.; Sharma, A.; Kaushal, M. A hybrid tiny YOLO v4-SPP module based improved face mask detection vision system. *J. Ambient Intell. Human. Comput.* **2023**, *14*, 6783–6796. [CrossRef] [PubMed]
37. Simonyan, K.; Zisserman, A. Very deep convolutional networks for large-scale image recognition. *arXiv* **2014**, arXiv:1409.1556.
38. Ge, S.; Li, J.; Ye, Q.; Luo, Z. Detecting masked faces in the wild with LLE-CNNs. In Proceedings of the IEEE Conference on Computer Vision and Pattern Recognition (CVPR) 2017, Honolulu, HI, USA, 21–26 July 2017; pp. 2682–2690.
39. Wang, Z.; Huang, B.; Wang, G.; Yi, P.; Jiang, K. Masked face recognition dataset and application. *IEEE Trans. Biom. Behav. Identity Sci.* **2023**, *5*, 298–304. [CrossRef]
40. Cabani, A.; Hammoudi, K.; Benhabiles, H.; Melkemi, M. MaskedFace-Net–A dataset of correctly/incorrectly masked face images in the context of COVID-19. *Smart Health* **2021**, *19*, 100144. [CrossRef] [PubMed]
41. Smith, L.N.; Topin, N. Super-convergence: Very fast training of neural networks using large learning rates. In Proceedings of the Artificial Intelligence and Machine Learning for Multi-Domain Operations Applications, Baltimore, MD, USA, 14–18 April 2019; pp. 369–386.
42. Tan, C.; Sun, F.; Kong, T.; Zhang, W.; Yang, C.; Liu, C. A survey on deep transfer learning. In *ICANN 2018: Artificial Neural Networks and Machine Learning–ICANN 2018*; Springer: Cham, Switzerland, 2018; pp. 270–279.
43. Zhang, H.; Cisse, M.; Dauphin, Y.N.; Lopez-Paz, D. mixup: Beyond empirical risk minimization. *arXiv* **2017**, arXiv:1710.09412.
44. Zhu, X.; Lyu, S.; Wang, X.; Zhao, Q. TPH-YOLOv5: Improved YOLOv5 Based on Transformer Prediction Head for Object Detection on Drone-Captured Scenarios. In Proceedings of the IEEE/CVF International Conference on Computer Vision (ICCV) Workshops, Montreal, QC, Canada, 10–17 October 2021; pp. 2778–2788.

Disclaimer/Publisher's Note: The statements, opinions and data contained in all publications are solely those of the individual author(s) and contributor(s) and not of MDPI and/or the editor(s). MDPI and/or the editor(s) disclaim responsibility for any injury to people or property resulting from any ideas, methods, instructions or products referred to in the content.

Article

Technology Tools in Hospitality: Mapping the Landscape through Bibliometric Analysis and Presentation of a New Software Solution

Thomas Krabokoukis

Nelios EPE, 10560 Athens, Greece; tkrabokoukis@nelios.com

Abstract: This study offers a comprehensive examination of the literature surrounding technology and tools in the hospitality industry. A bibliometric analysis was performed on 709 Scopus-indexed publications from 2000 to January 2023, with a focus on identifying key players, institutions, research trends, and the co-occurrence of keywords. The results shed light on the scientific landscape of technology and tools in the hospitality sector, emphasizing the significance of big data and the customer experience in the sharing economy. The study also presents the architecture of new software that offers guests the ability to customize their hotel stay, classified as part of the first cluster in the co-occurrence of keywords analysis. This approach highlights the growing importance of big data and customer experience and makes a valuable contribution to the field by offering a tool for hotel booking customization. Furthermore, the study underscores the importance of collaboration between academic institutions and private companies in providing a mutually beneficial platform that exceeds the expectations of both hotels and guests.

Keywords: hospitality technology; bibliometric analysis; customer experience; VOSviewer; Gephi; research trends

Citation: Krabokoukis, T. Technology Tools in Hospitality: Mapping the Landscape through Bibliometric Analysis and Presentation of a New Software Solution. *Digital* **2023**, *3*, 81–96. https://doi.org/10.3390/digital3010006

Academic Editors: Mirjana Ivanović, Richard Chbeir and Yannis Manolopoulos

Received: 8 February 2023
Revised: 22 February 2023
Accepted: 1 March 2023
Published: 3 March 2023

Copyright: © 2023 by the author. Licensee MDPI, Basel, Switzerland. This article is an open access article distributed under the terms and conditions of the Creative Commons Attribution (CC BY) license (https://creativecommons.org/licenses/by/4.0/).

1. Introduction

The tourism industry is a complex and multifaceted field of study, with a wide range of dimensions that have been developed over the years. Scholars have explored various topics such as metaverse [1], big data and innovation [2], technology and ICT [3,4], competitiveness [5], spatial inequalities [7], seasonality [6], and crisis management [8,9] to gain a deeper understanding of the factors that shape the tourism industry and its impact on society. In recent years, the integration of technology and tools into the hospitality industry has emerged as a rapidly growing area of research [10]. The implementation of digital solutions such as mobile apps and smart systems has been driven by the need to enhance the guest experience and improve operational efficiency in hotels and other accommodation providers [11]. As a result, a growing body of literature has emerged on the use of technology and tools in the hospitality sector, although this literature is diverse and dispersed, making it challenging to identify key actors, institutions, and trends in the field.

To address this challenge, this study employs bibliometric analysis to map the structure and dynamics of research on technology and tools in the hospitality sector. Bibliometric analysis is a widely used research method in various fields, including the hospitality industry, for understanding the scientific landscape and key actors, institutions, and research trends within a specific field of study [12]. This powerful tool enables the creation of a comprehensive overview of the scientific literature and helps to identify the most relevant papers, authors, institutions, and trends within a specific field of research [13].

In this study, the literature on technology and tools in the hospitality sector will be analyzed through a bibliometric lens. The study will focus on the temporal distribution of relevant publications, citation metrics, and co-authorship patterns. By utilizing various metrics such as citation counts and co-citation analysis, this study aims to identify the most prevalent and highly cited publications, as well as the leading organizations and countries participating in the co-authoring network. Additionally, this study will seek to identify the most important keywords and highlight the relationships between them using tools such as VOSviewer and Gephi.

In addition to the bibliometric analysis, this study presents a proposed software solution for the hospitality industry. The proposed software focuses on customizing hotel reservations and aims to improve the overall customer experience. The software architecture is designed to account for the bibliometric analysis findings and integrates advanced technologies to provide customized and personalized experiences for guests. This software solution offers a new and innovative approach to improving the guest experience, providing a starting point for further research and development in this area.

The hospitality industry is constantly seeking new and innovative ways to improve the customer experience. This study addresses this need by combining bibliometric analysis and the development of a proposed software solution. The bibliometric analysis identifies the main authors and organizations in the field, providing a foundation for future research and development. The main objectives of this study are, therefore, to identify the key authors and organizations in the field for potential synergies and to propose a software solution that meets the identified needs of the hospitality industry.

The structure of the paper is as follows: the Section 2 outlines the bibliometric techniques employed in the study, the Section 3 displays the outcomes of the analysis, the Section 4 covers the proposed software solution, and the Section 5 summarizes the key findings and their implications.

2. Materials and Methods

The methodology of this study is based on bibliometric analysis, a widely recognized and established research method [14–16] that utilizes quantitative measures to analyze and evaluate the scientific literature in a specific field of study. The purpose is to map and understand the structure and dynamics of research on technology and tools in the hospitality sector. Bibliometric analysis is mainly helpful in identifying key actors, institutions, and research trends within a given field and can provide valuable insights into research gaps and opportunities, as well as the impact of research activities [13,17]. It is crucial to be aware of the limitations of the bibliometric analysis and to interpret the results with caution [17,18].

In this study, data were collected from the Scopus database, one of the largest and most reputable sources of abstracts and citations of research literature, and exported to VOSviewer and Gephi software. VOSviewer and Gephi are popular in bibliometric analyses thanks to their user-friendliness, ability to handle large datasets, and production of high-quality visualizations. VOSviewer is a powerful and user-friendly software tool that is specifically designed for visualizing and analyzing bibliometric networks. It allows for the exploration of the underlying structure of a research field and the identification of key themes, authors, and journals. Gephi is another widely used software tool for visualizing and analyzing complex networks. It is particularly useful for exploring the topology of the network and for identifying the most important nodes and communities. While R language, bibliometrix, or SCImat are also commonly used for bibliometric analysis, this study used these tools as they offer a more intuitive and efficient way to analyze the data, allowing for a more comprehensive and accurate understanding of the bibliometric landscape.

VOSviewer uses the co-citation analysis method, which is a method of bibliometric analysis that uses the co-citation of papers to identify the relationships between manuscripts in a specific field of research [15–18], and Gephi is a tool used for network visualization and analysis [19]. The data for this study were extracted for the period spanning from 2010 to mid-January 2023, as detailed in Table 1, which outlines the specific terms and constraints used to gather the database of 709 references. Scopus includes over 22,000 academic journals and other scholarly sources from more than 5000 international publishers and over

70 million records. Additionally, the enhanced version of Scopus allows for the use of a data visualization dashboard, which was employed in this study.

Table 1. Data retrieval constraints and parameters for the Scopus database.

Data	Constraints and Parameters
Database	Scopus
Search field	Title, abstract, keywords
Keywords	"Hospitality technology tools" OR "hotel experience tools" OR "guest experience" OR "digital hotel tools"
Open access	All
Years	2000–2023
Author name	Exclude undefined names
Subject area	All
Publication stage	All
Document type	All
Source title	All
Affiliation	All
Funding sponsor	All
Country	All
Source type	All
Language	All
Search string	(TITLE-ABS-KEY (hospitality AND technology AND tools)) OR (TITLE-ABS-KEY (digital AND hotel AND tools)) OR (TITLE-ABS-KEY (hotel AND experience AND tools)) OR (TITLE-ABS-KEY ("guest experience")) AND PUBYEAR > 1999 AND PUBYEAR < 2024 AND (EXCLUDE (PREFNAMEAUID, "Undefined"))
Data extracted	12 January 2023
Number of publications	709

The time frame of 2010 to mid-January 2023 was selected for the bibliometric analysis in order to capture long-term trends in research and facilitate comparisons across time periods. This duration provides a more comprehensive overview of the field, allowing for the identification of key developments over a significant period. The choice of 2023 as the end point of the data collection ensures that the analysis is current and reflects the most recent developments in the field. This is particularly important in bibliometric studies, as it allows for a more accurate assessment of the current state of the field and offers valuable insights to guide future research.

The data were analyzed in two steps: first, to identify the most highly cited papers in the field of technology and tools in the hospitality sector, and second, to create a bibliometric map of the field of technology and tools in the hospitality sector, which was used to identify critical actors, institutions, and research trends.

2.1. Citation Analysis

Citation analysis is a widely employed technique in bibliometric research that involves quantifying the number of times a specific paper or author has been cited within other publications [12,20]. This method allows researchers to evaluate the impact and influence of a particular paper or author within a specific field of study. Through the examination of citation patterns, researchers can identify the most highly cited papers and authors within a field, as well as the main research trends and key actors [12,21,22]. Additionally, citation analysis can be utilized to assess the performance of academic institutions and journals, as well as to identify potential research gaps and opportunities within a field [19].

2.2. Co-Authorship Analysis

Co-authorship analysis is a method used in bibliometric research to identify patterns of collaboration among authors in a specific field of study. This method is particularly useful in identifying key actors, institutions, and research trends within a given field and identifying research gaps and opportunities. Co-authorship analysis can be performed at different levels of analysis, including the individual author, the institution, and the country [14,20]. In this study, co-authorship analysis was performed at the country level to identify patterns of collaboration among authors from different countries in the field of technology and tools in the hospitality sector. The country unit of analysis is particularly useful in identifying international collaborations and in understanding the global distribution of research activities in a given field [12,17,20]. The results of the co-authorship analysis at the country level were used to identify the most active countries and institutions in the field of technology and tools in the hospitality sector, as well as to understand the dynamics of international collaborations in this field.

2.3. Co-Occurrence of Keywords Analysis

Co-occurrence of keywords analysis is another method of bibliometric analysis used to identify the relationships between keywords in a specific field of research, the main themes and subtopics within a research topic, and the key actors and institutions working in that field. As a result, it is useful in identifying emerging trends and research gaps within the topic [21]. However, it is important to note that the co-occurrence of keywords analysis should be used in conjunction with other research methods, such as citation analysis, in order to provide a comprehensive understanding of the research topic. Additionally, one must be aware of the limitations of the co-occurrence of keywords analysis, such as the potential for bias in the selection of keywords, and interpret the results with caution [12,17]. This study involves analyzing the co-occurrence of keywords in a set of publications to identify the most frequently co-occurring keywords and the patterns of association between them [12,17].

3. Results

Table 2 provides a breakdown of the different types of documents included in the dataset used in this study. The majority of the sources were articles and conference papers, accounting for a total of 62.76% and 20.45% of the dataset, respectively. These two types of documents are considered to be the most prevalent forms of scholarly communication in the field of technology and tools in the hospitality sector. The presence of a high proportion of articles and conference papers in the dataset suggests that this study has captured a broad and representative sample of the literature in this area. Additionally, it indicates that the study has captured the most recent and up-to-date research.

Table 2. Distribution of document types in the retrieved sample.

Document Type	Total Publications	Percentage (%)
Article	445	62.76
Conference paper	145	20.45
Book chapter	70	9.87
Review	24	3.39
Book	11	1.55
Note	10	1.41
Letter	2	0.28
Editorial	2	0.28
Total	709	100

The next most prevalent type of document in the dataset is book chapters, which make up 9.87% of the sources. This suggests that the study has also captured research that is disseminated in monographic works. The remaining types of documents, including reviews, books, notes, letters, and editorials, make up a relatively small percentage of the dataset, indicating that they are less prevalent forms of scholarly communication in the field of technology and tools in the hospitality sector. Furthermore, the overwhelming majority of studies, approximately 96%, were written in English, while the remaining studies were authored in various other languages, including Spanish, Portuguese, Russian, French, German, Italian, and Japanese.

3.1. Results of the Citation Analysis

Figure 1 illustrates the temporal distribution of related publications and their corresponding total citations over the years of examination. The left axis represents the number of publications, depicted through bars, which exhibits an upward trend in recent years. The right axis, representing the number of citations through a line graph, also reflects a similar pattern. It is noteworthy that a slight decline in the number of citations is observed post-2020, which may indicate a higher rate of publications within this timeframe. Despite this, there is significant interest in the concepts examined within the tourism industry, as evidenced by the increasing trend in both publications and citations over the years of examination.

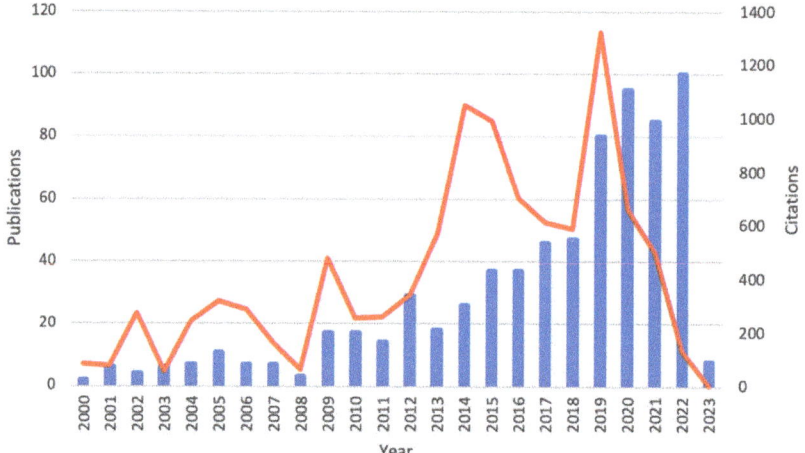

Figure 1. Temporal distribution of the literature: a comparison of total publication (bars) and citation counts by year for the period 2000–2023 (lines).

Table 3 presents the citation metrics of the 709 publications analyzed in this study. The total number of citations for these publications is 10,051, spanning over 12 years. This results in an average of 837.6 citations per year, or 59.1 citations per paper. The data show that the average number of citations per author is 63.0 and the average number of authors per paper is 4.4.

Table 3. Citations metrics.

Metrics	Data
Publications	709
Number of citations	10,051
Years	12
Citations per year	837.6
Citations per paper	59.1
Citations per author	63.0
Authors per paper	4.4

Table 4 presents the general citation structure of the publications analyzed in this study, providing an overview of the distribution of citations among the publications of the dataset. As shown, 28.07% of the articles received no citations and 65.87% received less than 52 citations. Moreover, 3.39% of the articles received between 52 and 103 citations, 1.27% received between 104 and 154 citations, 0.71% received between 155 and 205 citations, 0.42% received between 206 and 256 citations, and 0.28% received more than 256 citations.

Table 4. Distribution of citations.

Number of Citations	Number of Publications	% Accumulated Articles
0	199	28.07
<52	467	65.87
<103	24	3.39
<154	9	1.27
<205	5	0.71
<256	3	0.42
<512	2	0.28
Total	709	100

Table 5 illustrates the top 10 most cited papers in our database. The papers are ranked based on the number of citations received, with the paper written by Xiang et al. (2015) receiving the highest number of citations at 510. These cover a wide range of topics related to the hospitality industry, including big data and text analytics in relation to hotel guest experience and satisfaction, customer engagement with tourism brands, technological disruptions in services, and consumer satisfaction in green hotels. The authors of the papers come from diverse backgrounds and institutions, including universities and research centers. Overall, the table highlights the importance of understanding the consumer experience and the role of technology and sustainability in the hospitality industry.

Table 5. Top 10 most cited publications.

No.	Authors	Title	Citations
1	[23]	What can big data and text analytics tell us about hotel guest experience and satisfaction?	510
2	[24]	Customer Engagement With Tourism Brands: Scale Development and Validation	332
3	[25]	Technological disruptions in services: lessons from tourism and hospitality	226
4	[26]	Are your satisfied customers loyal?	210
5	[27]	Understanding the consumer experience: An exploratory study of luxury hotels	205
6	[28]	Differentiating hospitality operations via experiences: Why selling services is not enough	202
7	[29]	The accommodation experiences cape: a comparative assessment of hotels and Airbnb	201
8	[30]	Improving consumer satisfaction in green hotels: The roles of perceived warmth, perceived competence, and CSR motive	185
9	[31]	Exploring user acceptance of 3D virtual worlds in travel and tourism marketing	169
10	[32]	Adoption of voluntary environmental tools for sustainable tourism: Analysing the experience of Spanish hotels	162

3.2. Results of the Co-Authorship Analysis

Of the 1286 organizations, only 4 meet the threshold of a minimum number of three documents, as shown in Table 6. The table presents the top organizations in the co-authorship of organizations analysis. The first column shows the organization's name, the second column shows the number of documents (publications) produced by the organization, and the third column shows the number of citations received by these documents. Cardiff Metropolitan University, with 3 documents and 43 citations, is the top organization. The second organization is Rosen College of Hospitality Management, University of Florida, with 9 documents and 197 citations. The third organization is the School of Hotel and Tourism Management, The Hong Kong Polytechnic University, with 4 documents and 160 citations. The fourth organization is Universidade Europeia, Lisbon, with 4 documents and 47 citations. These organizations have made significant contributions to the topic of hospitality and tourism management, as evidenced by their high number of publications and citations.

Table 6. Top organizations in the co-authorship of organizations analysis.

No.	Organization	Documents	Citations
1	Cardiff Metropolitan University, United Kingdom	3	43
2	Rosen College of Hospitality Management, University of Florida, United States of America	9	197
3	School of Hotel and Tourism Management, The Hong Kong Polytechnic University, Hong Kong	4	160
4	Universidade Europeia, Lisbon, Portugal	4	47

Of the 93 countries, 21 meet the threshold of a minimum number of 10 documents, as shown in Table 7 and Figure 2. The table shows the number of documents and citations for each country and the total link strength between them. The total link strength is a measure of the collaboration between countries, where a higher link strength means more collaboration. The United States of America is at the top of the list, with 177 documents and 4872 citations. The United Kingdom follows with 62 documents and 1077 citations. China is in third place, with 47 documents and 458 citations, and other countries on the list include Australia, India, Malaysia, United Arab Emirates, Hong Kong, New Zealand, Canada, Italy, South Korea, France, Greece, Spain, Thailand, Turkey, Taiwan, Portugal, Russian Federation, and Germany. The data suggest that the authors in these countries have a strong collaboration with each other in terms of co-authorship and citations.

Table 7. Top countries by co-authorship productivity in organizational analysis.

No.	Country	Documents	Citations	Total Link Strength
1	United States of America	177	4872	55
2	United Kingdom	62	1077	40
3	China	47	458	31
4	Australia	36	827	20
5	India	59	544	15
6	Malaysia	27	167	11
7	United Arabia Emirates	10	117	11
8	Hong Kong	17	566	9
9	New Zealand	11	99	9
10	Canada	12	283	8
11	Italy	22	265	8
12	South Korea	13	201	8
13	France	12	229	8
14	Greece	20	89	5
15	Spain	39	635	5
16	Thailand	13	60	5
17	Turkey	15	309	4
18	Taiwan	14	207	43
19	Portugal	31	239	2
20	Russian Federation	22	175	2
21	Germany	10	73	1

The co-authorship of countries analysis provides a deeper understanding of the patterns and trends in the co-authorship of countries in the network. The analysis yielded six clusters, each representing a grouping of countries based on their patterns of collaboration in the network. This analysis provides a deeper understanding of the patterns and trends in the co-authorship of countries in the network. The first cluster (red) encompasses France, Greece, India, South Korea, and Spain, indicating a high degree of collaboration among these countries. The second cluster (green) includes Italy, Portugal, Turkey, the United Arab

Emirates, and the United Kingdom. The third cluster (blue) encompasses China, Germany, Hong Kong, and the United States of America. The fourth cluster (yellow) includes Australia, New Zealand, and the Russian Federation. The fifth cluster (purple) encompasses Canada and Taiwan and the sixth cluster (light blue) includes Malaysia and Thailand, with both clusters indicating a lower degree of collaboration among these countries.

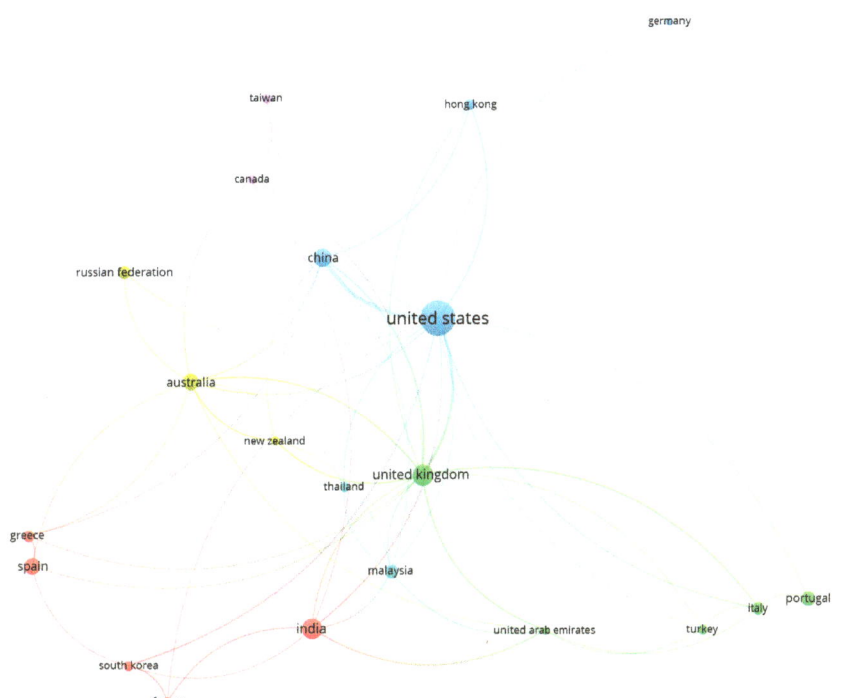

Figure 2. Visualization of the co-authorship of countries analysis.

The analysis of the co-authorship network using Gephi software revealed some interesting insights. The total number of nodes (authors) in the database was 1810 and the total number of edges (citations) was 1922. Utilizing Gephi's network visualization capabilities, an understanding of the overall structure of the network was achieved, patterns in the connections between authors were identified, and distinct groups within the network were highlighted, known as modularity classes. These classes represent groups of authors that are more densely connected than other nodes in the network, providing insight into potential research interests or collaboration patterns among the authors.

The analysis revealed a high degree of community structure in the network, as indicated by the modularity index of 0.895 [19]. This suggests that the authors in the network tend to be more connected to other nodes within the same group or cluster than to those outside of it, potentially indicating similar research interests or collaboration on similar projects. The modularity classes were used to identify the group of authors that are most tightly connected, with the highest class (purple color) having a 25.75% representation, as shown in Figure 3. The elements in this class are the authors and the number of elements, in this case, 465, represents the number of authors that have been grouped.

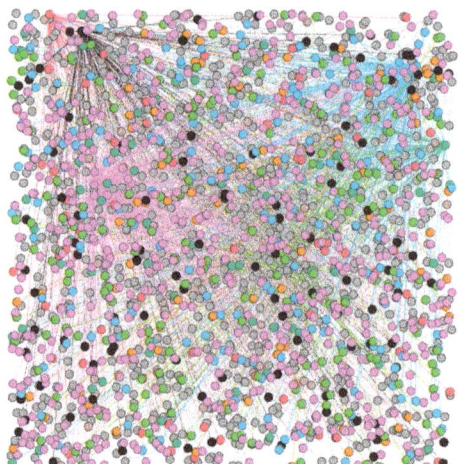

Figure 3. Visualization of the co-authorship of modularity analysis in Gephi.

3.3. Results of the Co-Occurrence Analysis

An analysis of the co-occurrence of keywords in the authors' papers was conducted using VOSviewer software. Of the 2069 total author keywords, a threshold of seven appearances was set to identify the most prevalent keywords. This analysis produced six clusters, with the highest co-occurring keywords being tourism (46), hospitality (46), guest experience (33), and hotels (29). Table 8 presents a summary of the top 15 keywords, including their number of occurrences and total link strength, while Figure 4 illustrates the network mapping of the co-occurrence of keywords analysis. The clusters were then labeled and analyzed to gain insights into the prevalent themes and patterns in the authors' research.

Table 8. Top keywords in the co-authorship of organizations analysis.

No.	Keyword	Occurrences	Total Link Strength
1	Hospitality	46	55
2	Guest experience	33	25
3	Hotels	29	22
4	Customer satisfaction	24	26
5	COVID-19	22	20
6	Social media	21	23
7	Hotel industry	21	18
8	Airbnb	20	16
9	Technology	19	30
10	Hospitality industry	19	15
11	Hotel	17	23
12	Service quality	16	16
13	Customer experience	15	15
14	Satisfaction	15	10
15	Sharing economy	13	13

Cluster 1 (red), titled "Big Data and Customer Experience in the Sharing Economy", contains keywords related to the use of big data and the customer experience in the context of the sharing economy, specifically in the context of companies such as Airbnb and TripAdvisor. The keywords "Airbnb", "big data", "customer experience", "customer satisfaction", "guest experience", "machine learning", "online reviews", "sentiment analysis", "sharing economy", and "TripAdvisor" all relate to the use of data and customer experience in the sharing economy. This cluster highlights the growing importance of utilizing big data and advanced technologies such as machine learning in understanding and improving customer experiences in the sharing economy.

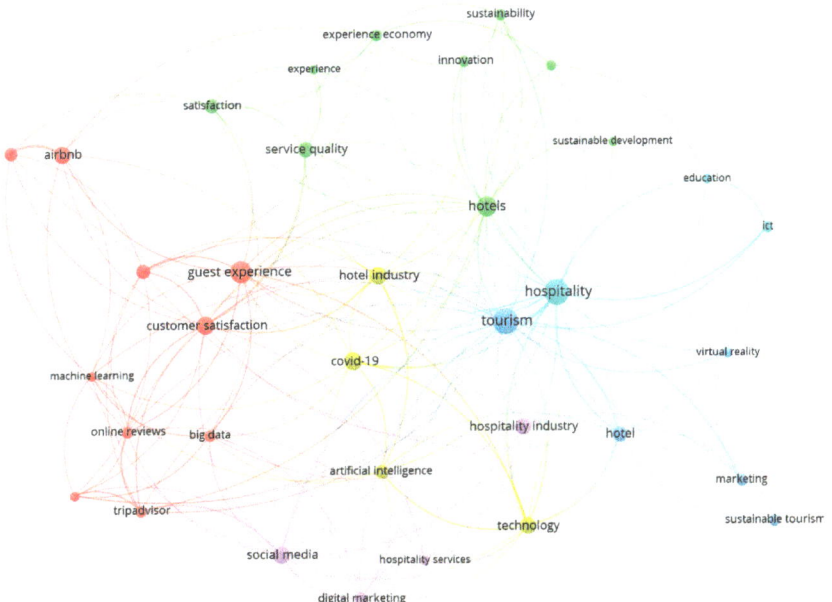

Figure 4. Visualization of the co-occurrence of keywords analysis.

Cluster 2 (green), titled "Innovations in Hospitality Management and Sustainability", contains keywords related to the topics of hospitality management, innovation, and sustainability. The keywords "experience", "experience economy", "hospitality management", "hotels", "innovation", "satisfaction", "service quality", "sustainability", and "sustainable development" all relate to the growing importance of sustainability and innovation in the hospitality industry. This cluster highlights the need for hotels and other hospitality businesses to focus on sustainable practices and the use of new technologies to improve customer satisfaction and experience.

Cluster 3 (blue), titled "Sustainable Tourism and Marketing", contains keywords related to sustainable tourism and marketing in the context of the hotel industry. The keywords "hotel", "marketing", "sustainable tourism", "tourism", and "virtual reality" all relate to the growing importance of sustainable practices and innovative marketing strategies in the hotel industry. This cluster highlights the need for hotels to focus on sustainable practices and the use of new technologies, such as virtual reality, in their marketing efforts to attract customers.

Cluster 4 (yellow), titled "Technology and the Hotel Industry in the Era of COVID-19", contains keywords related to the impact of technology and the ongoing COVID-19 pandemic on the hotel industry. The keywords "artificial intelligence", "COVID-19", "hotel industry", and "technology" all relate to the ongoing changes and challenges faced by the hotel industry in the wake of the COVID-19 pandemic and the increasing use of technology in the industry. This cluster highlights the need for hotels to adapt to the new technological and health-related challenges posed by the COVID-19 pandemic.

Cluster 5 (purple), titled "Digital Marketing and the Hospitality Industry", contains keywords related to digital marketing and the hospitality industry. The keywords "digital marketing", "hospitality industry", "hospitality services", and "social media" all relate to the use of digital marketing strategies and the growing importance of social media in the hospitality industry. This cluster highlights the need for hotels and other hospitality businesses to focus on digital marketing and social media in order to attract customers.

Cluster 6 (light blue), titled "Education and ICT in the Hospitality Industry", contains keywords related to education and the use of information and communication technology (ICT) in the hospitality industry. The keywords "education", "hospitality", and "ict" all relate to the importance of education and the use of technology in the hospitality industry. This cluster highlights the need for hotels and other hospitality businesses to focus on education and the use of technology in order to improve their operations and attract customers.

4. Discussion

The analysis performed has led to the identification of distinct groups of tools utilized in the global hotel industry. The application developed in this work falls within group 1, titled "Big Data and Customer Experience in the Sharing Economy", which is concerned with enhancing the overall experience of hotel guests. To achieve this objective, a categorization of the booking process into different stages was conducted, as illustrated in Figure 5 (Nelios, Athens, Greece) and supported by recent studies [33]. This approach allows the traveler to customize the booking process with a few clicks, resulting in a more personalized accommodation experience.

Figure 5. Stages of guest experience in the hotel industry: before arrival (**left**), during the stay (**center**), and after departure (**right**).

The first stage, before arrival, enables the guest to make choices such as early check-in, airport transportation, meal preferences, minibar contents, and pillow type. The second stage, during the stay, allows the guest to make reservations at various hotel departments (e.g., restaurants, spas, and gyms), order room service, and book activities outside the hotel. Finally, the third stage, after departure, invites the guest to provide feedback on their stay experience through a questionnaire and to share their thoughts on social media. All of this information is stored on the platform, allowing to provide a more personalized service during future stays and supporting actions such as email marketing.

The project structure employed in this study consists of three separate applications, each serving a specific purpose, with shared code libraries that allow for intercommunication and code reuse. The entire project is held within a monorepo and written in TypeScript. One of the applications is a Node.Js server, responsible for serving as a common API and database access point for the other two React-based applications. The first React app is designed to be utilized by the hotel for data entry and order management purposes, while the other app is aimed at providing a convenient interface for clients. Communication between the Node server and the React apps is established via GraphQL, enabling seamless data exchange between the different components of the system. The shared code libraries contain type definitions, which are utilized across all applications and ensure consistency and compatibility of code. Requests to the Node server are authenticated using JWT, ensuring in this way secure access to the data stored in the system, as shown in Figure 6.

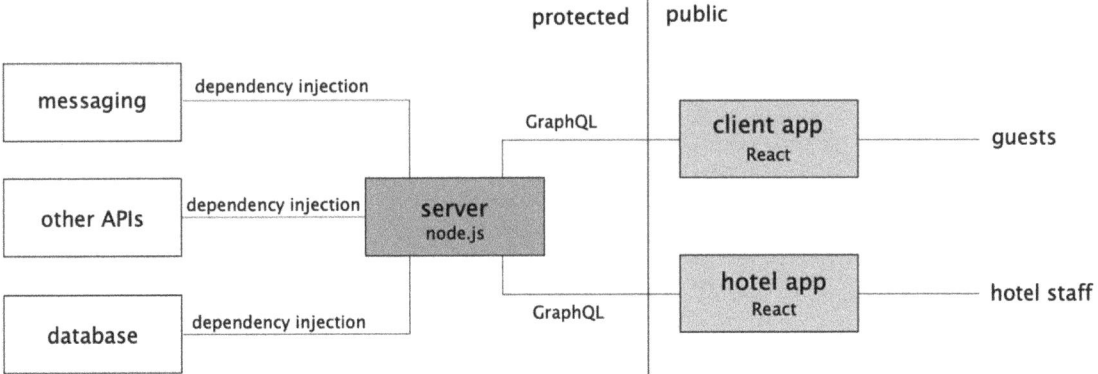

Figure 6. The architecture of the software.

The server-side application of the system is developed using the Nest.JS framework, which leverages the benefits of dependency injection. The architecture of the Node server is modular, with each module corresponding to a distinct entity within the system. There are modules for the three different types of services offered and a module for unifying these services into common lists. Similarly, there are modules for the orders accepted by each of the service modules and an additional module for aggregating all orders. The system also includes modules for managing hotel employees and guests, hotel departments, and other content entities such as offers and experiences. Finally, there are modules dedicated to internal functionalities such as authentication and file management.

By utilizing dependency injection, the system allows for flexible modularity, enabling any individual module to be altered without affecting the rest of the code. Within each module, the same principles apply, with database access solely managed through repository classes that are subsequently injected into the rest of the code. Each module exposes GraphQL resolvers that complement the GraphQL schema and, if necessary, service classes that can be utilized by other modules.

The architecture of the two React applications is broadly similar and leverages Next.JS as its underlying framework. Both apps have implemented a similar pattern for authentication and context management, following a modular approach. However, in this scenario, the use of dependency injection is not feasible and a simple folder structure with organized imports is adopted instead. Each module only exposes the components responsible for rendering the relevant pages, with other logic and components either being kept within the module or extracted to libraries if needed by multiple modules.

There is no direct communication between the two React applications at any point. They only interact with the server app and share a substantial amount of standard code such as interfaces, helper functions, unstyled components, and constants, which are housed in separate libraries that both apps can import.

The server app is deployed once for the entire application and functions as a multi-tenant app, able to accept requests from all hotels through different subdomains. The hotel ID is included in all requests and is utilized throughout the app to manage and process the requests. The two React apps are deployed individually for each hotel, utilizing the same code but with distinct environment variables. This allows for greater customization of the apps for each hotel, as well as facilitating integration with other hotel services and the use of different domains.

5. Conclusions

The study provides an overview of the literature on the technology and tools used in the hospitality sector through a bibliometric analysis. The analysis revealed a growing body of research in this field, with increasing trends in publications and citations over the years. The key actors, institutions, and research trends in the field were identified, highlighting the various ways in which technology and data are being utilized in the hospitality industry to enhance customer experience, improve operational efficiency, and promote sustainability. Additionally, a novel application was presented that falls under the umbrella of big data and the customer experience in the sharing economy. The study also discussed the limitations of bibliometric research and provided suggestions for future research, including expanding the range of keywords used in the search process and exploring other academic databases, such as WoS, to improve the accuracy and comprehensiveness of future research.

5.1. Contribution to the Theory

The results show a growing body of research in this field, with an increasing trend in both publications and citations over the years of examination. The majority of sources were articles and conference papers, comprising 62.76% and 20.45% of the dataset, respectively, suggesting a broad and representative sample of the literature in this field. The study also identified key actors, institutions, and research trends in the field, including significant contributions from organizations such as Cardiff Metropolitan University and Rosen College of Hospitality Management, and countries such as the United States and the United Kingdom. The co-authorship analysis revealed patterns of collaboration among countries, with clusters of countries showing varying degrees of collaboration.

Additionally, the analysis identified six key clusters in the literature on technology and tools in the hospitality sector, which highlights the various ways in which technology and data are being utilized in the hospitality industry to enhance customer experience, improve operational efficiency, and promote sustainability. Cluster 1, "Big Data and Customer Experience in the Sharing Economy", highlights the growing importance of utilizing big data and advanced technologies such as machine learning in understanding and improving customer experiences in the sharing economy, specifically in the context of companies such as Airbnb and TripAdvisor. Cluster 2, "Innovations in Hospitality Management and Sustainability", emphasizes the need for hotels and other hospitality businesses to focus on sustainable practices and the use of new technologies to improve customer satisfaction and experience. Cluster 3, "Sustainable Tourism and Marketing", highlights the need for hotels to focus on sustainable practices and the use of new technologies, such as virtual reality, in their marketing efforts to attract customers. Cluster 4, "Technology and the Hotel Industry in the Era of COVID-19", highlights the need for hotels to adapt to the new technological and health-related challenges posed by the COVID-19 pandemic. Cluster 5, "Digital Marketing and the Hospitality Industry", emphasizes the need for hotels and other hospitality businesses to focus on digital marketing and social media to attract customers. Lastly, Cluster 6 "Education and ICT in the Hospitality Industry", highlights the importance of education and the use of technology in the hospitality industry to improve operations and attract customers.

5.2. Contribution to the Management Practice

In Section 4, a novel application was presented that falls under the umbrella of group 1, titled "Big Data and Customer Experience in the Sharing Economy". The goal of this application is to provide a cutting-edge platform to the international market and to be the first integrated Greek platform with advanced capabilities. This analysis significantly contributes to the identification of key academic players, enabling the identification of strategic partnerships that emphasize collaboration between academic institutions and private companies.

It is worth noting that the presented platform is highly customizable by hotels, and the developers have already identified the next steps to integrate it with other hotel platforms. The collaboration between the different stakeholders is a critical aspect of this application, as it highlights the importance of teamwork in creating a platform that meets the needs of the hotel industry worldwide. The focus is on establishing a mutually beneficial partnership that leverages the expertise of academic institutions and the resources of private companies to provide a platform that exceeds the expectations of both hotels and guests.

5.3. Limitations

The limitations of bibliometric research are that it is based on a limited set of data, such as publications and citations, which may not fully capture the breadth of research in a field, and that may be subject to biases, such as publication bias, language bias, and citation bias [20], as can be caused by the "Matthew effect in science", where researchers use references from colleagues and friends [34]. To overcome these limitations, it is essential to use bibliometric research in conjunction with other research methods, such as qualitative analysis, to gain a comprehensive understanding of the scientific landscape. Utilizing a wider range of academic databases, such as Web of Science and Scopus, can increase the number and diversity of sources included in the analysis. While the study focused solely on Scopus, it is essential to note that no single database is comprehensive or error-free, and each has its unique strengths and weaknesses. By including a more comprehensive range of databases in future research, researchers can gain a more complete and nuanced understanding of the literature in a given field.

Additionally, utilizing advanced features of bibliometric software, such as network mapping and co-occurrence analysis, can provide a more in-depth understanding of the relationships and trends within the literature. Overall, incorporating a multi-faceted approach that includes a wider range of keywords, databases, and software features can enhance the scope and precision of future research in the field of technology and tools in the hospitality sector.

5.4. Suggestions for Future Research

This study provides a comprehensive review of the current state of research on hospitality technology and tools and their impact on the hotel guest experience. By identifying gaps and trends in the literature, future studies can build upon these findings and develop a deeper understanding of how specific technology tools and strategies can improve the guest experience. Additionally, the study highlights the need for more research on certain areas, such as the impact of technology on sustainability in the hospitality industry. This can serve as a starting point for researchers who wish to address these gaps and expand the field of knowledge in this area.

To improve the accuracy and comprehensiveness of future research in the field of technology and tools in the hospitality sector, it is recommended to expand the range of keywords used in the search process and to explore other academic databases such as WoS. Utilizing the advanced features of the software used in this study, such as the Boolean operator "OR" to include synonyms of keywords, can also help to increase the number of search results. Additionally, it may be beneficial to consider using other bibliometric tools such as CiteSpace and to perform deeper analysis using software like VOSviewer and Gephi, which can provide additional insights into the literature.

Funding: This research was implemented under the action RESEARCH-CREATE-INNOVATE and co-funded by the European Regional Development Fund (ERDF) of the European Union and national resources through the Competitiveness, Entrepreneurship, and Innovation Programme (EPANEK), under project code T2EDK-03945. The funding was administered by the Managing Authority of the Operational Programme "Competitiveness, Entrepreneurship, and Innovation" (MIS 5075101) and the Ministry of Development and Investments of Greece (No. Accession Protocol 5567).

Data Availability Statement: The data presented in this study are not publicly available, but can be obtained upon request from the corresponding author. The main script of the paper is presented in Table 1, which can be used to search for the examined database on Scopus.

Conflicts of Interest: The authors declare no conflict of interest.

References

1. Buhalis, D.; Lin, M.S.; Leung, D. Metaverse as a driver for customer experience and value co-creation: Implications for hospitality and tourism management and marketing. *Int. J. Contemp. Hosp. Manag.* **2022**, *35*, 701–716. [CrossRef]
2. Bulchand-Gidumal, J.M.; Sigala, R.; Thelwall, R.M. Big Data and Innovation in Tourism, Travel, and Hospitality. Managerial Approaches, Techniques, and Applications. *Z. Tour.* **2021**, *13*, 309–310. [CrossRef]
3. Gössling, S. Technology, ICT and tourism: From big data to the big picture. *J. Sustain. Tour.* **2021**, *29*, 849–858. [CrossRef]
4. Buhalis, D.; O'Connor, P.; Leung, R. Smart hospitality: From smart cities and smart tourism towards agile business ecosystems in networked destinations. *Int. J. Contemp. Hosp. Manag.* **2022**, *35*, 369–393. [CrossRef]
5. Kim, Y.R.; Liu, A.; Williams, A.M. Competitiveness in the visitor economy: A systematic literature review. *Tour. Econ.* **2022**, *28*, 817–842. [CrossRef]
6. Krabokoukis, T.; Polyzos, S. Drawing an indicator of tourism competitiveness and examining its relationship with tourism seasonality for the Greek prefectures. *Reg. Sci. Inq.* **2022**, *14*, 55–70.
7. Tsiotas, D.; Krabokoukis, T.; Polyzos, S. Detecting Tourism Typologies of Regional Destinations Based on Their Spatio-Temporal and Socioeconomic Performance: A Correlation-Based Complex Network Approach for the Case of Greece. *Tour. Hosp.* **2021**, *2*, 113–139. [CrossRef]
8. Ivanov, S.H.; Webster, C.; Stoilova, E.; Slobodskoy, D. Biosecurity, crisis management, automation technologies and economic performance of travel, tourism and hospitality companies—A conceptual framework. *Tour. Econ.* **2022**, *28*, 3–26. [CrossRef]
9. Günaydın, Y.; Kozak, M. Managing Crisis in the Tourism Industry: How Pessimism Has Changed to Optimism? *Tourism* **2022**, *70*, 317–330. [CrossRef]
10. Kansakar, P.; Munir, A.; Shabani, N. Technology in the Hospitality Industry: Prospects and Challenges. *IEEE Consum. Electron. Mag.* **2019**, *8*, 60–65. [CrossRef]
11. Buhalis, D.; Moldavska, I. Voice assistants in hospitality: Using artificial intelligence for customer service. *J. Hosp. Tour. Technol.* **2022**, *13*, 386–403. [CrossRef]
12. Bornmann, L.; Leydesdorff, L. Scientometrics in a changing research landscape: Bibliometrics has become an in-tegral part of research quality evaluation and has been changing the practice of research. *EMBO Rep.* **2014**, *15*, 1228–1232. [CrossRef]
13. Wang, J. Citation time window choice for research impact evaluation. *Scientometrics* **2013**, *94*, 851–872. [CrossRef]
14. Ali, J.; Jusoh, A.; Idris, N.; Abbas, A.F.; Alsharif, A.H. Nine Years of Mobile Healthcare Research: A Bibliometric Analysis. *Int. J. Online Biomed. Eng. (iJOE)* **2021**, *17*, 144–159. [CrossRef]
15. Alsharif, A.H.; Salleh, N.Z.M.; Baharun, R.; Hashem, E.A.R. Neuromarketing research in the last five years: A bibliometric analysis. *Cogent Bus. Manag.* **2021**, *8*, 1978620. [CrossRef]
16. Pilelienė, L.; Alsharif, A.H.; Alharbi, I.B. Scientometric Analysis of Scientific Literature on Neuromarketing Tools in Advertising. *Balt. J. Econ. Stud.* **2022**, *8*, 1–12. [CrossRef]
17. Leydesdorff, L. How are new citation-based journal indicators adding to the bibliometric toolbox? *J. Am. Soc. Inf. Sci. Technol.* **2009**, *60*, 1327–1336. [CrossRef]
18. Van Eck, N.J.; Waltman, L. Software survey: VOSviewer, a computer program for bibliometric mapping. *Scientometrics* **2010**, *84*, 523–538. [CrossRef]

19. Donthu, N.; Kumar, S.; Mukherjee, D.; Pandey, N.; Lim, W.M. How to conduct a bibliometric analysis: An overview and guidelines. *J. Bus. Res.* **2021**, *133*, 285–296. [CrossRef]
20. Majeed, S.; Uzair, M.; Qamar, U.; Farooq, A. Social Network Analysis Visualization Tools: A Comparative Review. In Proceedings of the IEEE 23rd International Multitopic Conference (INMIC), Bahawalpur, Pakistan, 5–7 November 2020; pp. 1–6. [CrossRef]
21. Mingers, J.; Leydesdorff, L. A review of theory and practice in scientometrics. *Eur. J. Oper. Res.* **2015**, *246*, 1–19. [CrossRef]
22. Glänzel, W.; Chi, P.-S.; Debackere, K. 3.1 Measuring the Impact. In *Handbook Bibliometrics*; Ball, R., Ed.; De Gruyter: Berlin, Germany, 2021; pp. 135–148. [CrossRef]
23. Xiang, Z.; Schwartz, Z.; Gerdes, J.H.; Uysal, M. What can big data and text analytics tell us about hotel guest experience and satisfaction? *Int. J. Hosp. Manag.* **2015**, *44*, 120–130. [CrossRef]
24. So KK, F.; King, C.; Sparks, B. Customer Engagement With Tourism Brands: Scale Development and Validation. *J. Hosp. Tour. Res.* **2014**, *38*, 304–329. [CrossRef]
25. Buhalis, D.; Harwood, T.; Bogicevic, V.; Viglia, G.; Beldona, S.; Hofacker, C. Technological disruptions in services: Lessons from tourism and hospitality. *J. Serv. Manag.* **2019**, *30*, 484–506. [CrossRef]
26. Skogland, I.; Siguaw, J.A. Are Your Satisfied Customers Loyal? *Cornell Hotel. Restaur. Adm. Q.* **2004**, *45*, 221–234. [CrossRef]
27. Walls, A.; Okumus, F.; Wang, Y.; Kwun, D.J.-W. Understanding the Consumer Experience: An Exploratory Study of Luxury Hotels. *J. Hosp. Mark. Manag.* **2011**, *20*, 166–197. [CrossRef]
28. Gilmore, J. Differentiating hospitality operations via experiences: Why selling services is not enough. *Cornell Hotel. Restaur. Adm. Q.* **2002**, *43*, 87–96. [CrossRef]
29. Mody, M.A.; Suess, C.; Lehto, X. The accommodation experiencescape: A comparative assessment of hotels and Airbnb. *Int. J. Contemp. Hosp. Manag.* **2017**, *29*, 2377–2404. [CrossRef]
30. Gao, Y.; Mattila, A.S. Improving consumer satisfaction in green hotels: The roles of perceived warmth, perceived competence, and CSR motive. *Int. J. Hosp. Manag.* **2014**, *42*, 20–31. [CrossRef]
31. Huang, Y.-C.; Backman, S.J.; Backman, K.F.; Moore, D. Exploring user acceptance of 3D virtual worlds in travel and tourism marketing. *Tour. Manag.* **2013**, *36*, 490–501. [CrossRef]
32. Ayuso, S. Adoption of voluntary environmental tools for sustainable tourism: Analysing the experience of Spanish hotels. *Corp. Soc. Responsib. Environ. Manag.* **2006**, *13*, 207–220. [CrossRef]
33. Buhalis, D.; Leung, D.; Lin, M. Metaverse as a disruptive technology revolutionising tourism management and marketing. *Tour. Manag.* **2023**, *97*, 104724. [CrossRef]
34. Lehmann, E.E.; Stockinger, S.A.E. Entrepreneurship in Higher Education: The impact of competition-based policy programmes exemplified by the German Excellence Initiative. *High. Educ. Q.* **2019**, *73*, 70–84. [CrossRef]

Disclaimer/Publisher's Note: The statements, opinions and data contained in all publications are solely those of the individual author(s) and contributor(s) and not of MDPI and/or the editor(s). MDPI and/or the editor(s) disclaim responsibility for any injury to people or property resulting from any ideas, methods, instructions or products referred to in the content.

Article

Decision-Making Approach for an IoRT-Aware Business Process Outsourcing

Najla Fattouch [1,*,†], **Imen Ben Lahmar** [2,†], **Mouna Rekik** [3,†] **and Khouloud Boukadi** [1,†]

1. FSEG Sfax, MIRACL Laboratory, Sfax University, Sfax 3029, Tunisia
2. ISIM Sfax, ReDCAD Laboratory, Sfax University, Sfax 3029, Tunisia
3. ISTLS Sousse, MIRACL Laboratory, Sousse University, Sousse 4003, Tunisia
* Correspondence: fattouchnajla@gmail.com; Tel.: +216-23812764
† These authors contributed equally to this work.

Abstract: In the context of Industry 4.0, IoRT-aware BPs represent an attractive paradigm that aims to automate the classic business process (BP) using the internet of robotics things (IoRT). Nonetheless, the execution of these processes within the enterprises may be costly due to the consumed resources, recruitment cost, etc. To bridge these gaps, the business process outsourcing (BPO) strategy can be applied to outsource partially or totally a process to external service suppliers. Despite the various advantages of BPO, it is not a trivial task for enterprises to determine which part of the process should be outsourced and which environment would be selected to deploy it. This paper deals with the decision-making outsourcing of an IoRT-aware BP to the fog and/or cloud environments. The fog environment includes devices at the edge of the network which will ensure the latency requirements of some latency-sensitive applications. However, relying on cloud, the availability and computational requirements of applications can be met. Toward these objectives, we realized an in-depth analysis of the enterprise requirements, where we identified a set of relevant criteria that may impact the outsourcing decision. Then, we applied the method based on the removal effects of criteria (MEREC) to automatically generate the weights of the identified criteria. Using these weights, we performed the selection of the suitable execution environment by using the ELECTRE IS method. As an approach evaluation, we sought help from an expert to estimate the precision, recall, and F-score of our approach. The obtained results show that our approach is the most similar to the expert result, and it has acceptable values.

Keywords: IoRT-aware BP; fog; cloud; MEREC; MCDM; ELECTRE IS

1. Introduction

In the last years, the world has seen a trend toward the incorporation of some emerging technologies, such as the IoT and robotics. In fact, this incorporation gives birth to the newest technology called the internet of robotic things (IoRT). The IoRT is defined as a cooperation between IoT and robotic technologies to increase the automation level. This technology has several advantages, noted as, for example, the machine-to-machine (M2M) communication. It managed to sweep several fields, such as the business process (BP). Thus, the business managers try to take advantage of the IoRT via its integration within the classic BP, which gives a new process generation called IoRT-aware business processes (IoRT-aware BPs) [1]. This integration will allow business managers to automate their process.

However, the IoRT-aware BPs need costly execution due to the high amount of data to be transferred in the network. Toward these issues, the enterprises attempt to apply a variety of process strategies and solutions. The outsourcing of the (BPs) called business process outsourcing (BPO) is one among the relevant existing strategies that aim to save cost, speed up production, and enhance the enterprise performance. This explains the increasing number of enterprises that have adopted the outsourcing strategy using different environments.

Among the externalized environments, the cloud is considered the most adopting one. According to the National Institute of standards and Technology (NIST) [2], the cloud is defined as a pay-as-you-go model that allows on-demand network access to a set of computing resources. It is characterized by its higher storage capacity and availability [3]. Moreover, it allows the enterprises to scale their services, which are gradually done, according to customer demand. Therefore, outsourcing processes to the cloud is a reasonable choice.

Despite its advantages, the cloud is not recommended for latency-sensitive applications, such as IoT applications (e.g., health care, smart home, and smart agriculture). This is due to the high latency added by network connections to data centers [4]. Toward this issue, fog computing emerged as a new paradigm to perform latency-sensitive applications. As defined by the OpenFog Consortium (OFC) (https://www.iiconsortium.org/pdf/OpenFog_Reference_Architecture_2_09_17.pdf, accessed on 5 May 2022), fog computing extends the cloud capabilities at the edge of the network. It includes devices, located in close proximity to the end devices, which are responsible for intermediate computation and storage between IoT and the cloud [5]. In the context of outsourcing IoRT-aware BPs, the fog provides interesting external service suppliers.

During the outsourcing of an IoRT-aware BP to the fog and/or cloud environments, the business experts must address several issues to correctly choose which parts of the processes are dedicated to be outsourcing and which adequate environment should be selected. This explains why the decision-makers within the enterprises spend about 80% of their time to decide on the suitability process parts that should be outsourced and its adequate environment [6]. Consequently, to make a properly outsourcing decision, the business experts must identify a set of criteria related to the outsourcing decision of each process part.

Our extensive literature exercise revealed that most of the existing approaches deal mainly with the decision-making of traditional BPs, such as [7–13]. Some recent works have addressed the decision-making of the BPs that embedded only the IoT technology (e.g., [14–16]). More research on the outsourcing of IoRT-aware BPs, on the other hand, is required. In addition, most existing approaches use the task as a unit to make their decision, which takes more time. Additionally, the literature review shows that most current approaches use fuzzy as an MCDM method, even though their results could be better because the fuzzy method relies heavily on inaccurate inputs. Based on the studied works, we note that in most cases, the approaches do not consider methods to generate the feature weights. In fact, the automatic generation weights allow the experts and decision-makers to increase the robustness of their MCDM method results following an automatic, logical, and systematic weight calculation. Furthermore, most outsourcing solutions consider the cloud environment to externalize business activities. However, few of them propose outsourcing the process to the fog environment despite its relevance.

Therefore, to close these gaps, we propose a decision-making approach for the BPs that integrates both IoT and robots in addition to classic BPs. In our approach, we consider fog and cloud environments to take advantage of their benefits, especially for the processes that are sensitive to latency. During this work, we looked at the main parts of BPO and came up with a list of criteria that must be looked at when an IoRT-aware BP is outsourced. This identification takes into account process, fog, and cloud requirements. Furthermore, we use single entry single exit (SESE) (https://eprints.qut.edu.au/70726/7/70726.pdf, accessed on 7 May 2022), rather than the task, to accelerate the outsourcing decision. Moreover, we applied the method based on the removal effects of criteria (MEREC) to automatically generate the identified criteria weights. ELECTRE IS uses the generated weights to select the adequate environment for the process outsourcing goal.

The remainder of the paper is organized as follows: Section 2 depicts the related work. Section 3 details our approach. The implementation, assessment, and result of the proposed approach are illustrated in Section 4. Section 5 targets the validation and robustness of our proposal. Finally, Section 6 summarizes our work and highlights its future directions.

2. Related Work

In the BP context, the outsourcing of a process allows business managers to enhance the performance of their enterprises, speed, and reduce production costs. Consequently, several researchers seek to outsource the process to external suppliers. We intend, in this section, to overview some of the existing approaches that deal with the process outsourcing.

To perform the review of the existing approaches, we considered a set of relevant criteria, as they are detailed in what follows:

- Business type: Presents the type of the outsourced BP. This criterion lets us distinguish the most considered process type that is used in the outsourcing operation. A process can be a classic BP or a process that is automated via the embedding of one or more technologies, such as IoT, robots, and so forth.
- MCDM method: Designates the multi-criteria decision-making method used to achieve the process-outsourcing decision. This criterion allows us to identify the most considered method to accomplish the process-outsourcing goal.
- Granularity: Gives the processing granularity (unit) that is considered during the process outsourcing. Indeed, it can be a task, a SESE (sub-process), and so forth. The task presents the smallest unit that can be taken into account during the process of outsourcing, while the SESE presents a set of tasks.
- Externalized environment: Refers to external suppliers that are used to execute such process task/SESE fragments to allow the enterprises to gain in productivity, costs, and performance. We are interested in this work in the cloud environment that is characterized by its storage capacity and availability. Moreover, the fog environment provides relevant capabilities to execute latency-sensitive applications.
- Weight method: A MCDM aims, generally, to evaluate a set of alternatives regarding a set of criteria. This evaluation is based on weights which allow the decision-makers to express their preference in terms of the importance of criteria. This criterion refers to the methods that are used to generate the weight used for the MCDM methods.
- Used properties: Presents a set of properties that are considered to achieve the process outsourcing decision. In this work, we realized an in-depth overview of the literature to identify the most considered proprieties for the outsourcing of a BP. Therefore, we distinguished the cost, security, availability, and latency proprieties. Indeed, the cost presents an ascertainment of the cost savings of the business managers. Security is among the most prominent proprieties that may prohibit enterprises from outsourcing to an external provider. This is caused by the fact that the supplier's service has to control outsourced activities, particularly those that deal with customers' personal information [6]. The availability propriety designates the time for which the task/SESE needs to be executed. However, latency is among the considered proprieties that correspond to the needed time to transfer data from the source to the external environment execution via the network.

Tables 1 and 2 classify some of the surveyed works that deal with the process outsourcing, according to the different identified criteria.

Table 1. Comparison of the studied approaches based on a set of criteria (Part 1).

Year	Paper	Externalized Environment		BP Type	MCDM Method	Weight Method
		Cloud	Fog			
2019	[7]	✓	-	Classic BP	-	-
2021	[8]	✓	-	Classic BP	-	-
2019	[9]	✓	-	Classic BP	AHP	-
2021	[14]	✓	✓	IoT-aware BP	-	-
2019	[15]	✓	✓	IoT-aware BP	-	-
2020	[16]	✓	✓	IoT workflow	fuzzy logic	-
2021	[17]	-	-	Classic BP	-	-
2021	[10]	-	-	Classic BP	-	-
2021	[11]	-	-	Classic BP	-	-
2021	[18]	✓	-	Classic BP	-	-
2020	[19]	✓	-	Classic BP	-	-
2020	[12]	✓	✓	Classic BP	-	-
2019	[13]	✓	-	Classic BP	-	-
2021	[20]	✓	-	Classic BP	-	-
2022	[21]	✓	-	Classic BP	-	-
2021	[22]	-	-	-	fuzzy set	-
2021	[23]	-	-	-	fuzzy set	-
2019	[24]	-	-	-	fuzzy set	-
2022	[25]	-	-	-	fuzzy set	-
2019	[26]	-	-	-	fuzzy set	-

Table 2. Comparison of the studied approaches based on a set of criteria (Part 2).

Paper	Used Properties				Granularity
	Cost	Security	Availability	Latency	
[7]	✓	✓	✓	-	Task
[8]	✓	-	-	-	Task
[9]	✓	✓	-	-	Task
[14]	✓	✓	-	-	Task
[15]	✓	-	-	-	Task
[16]	-	-	-	-	-
[17]	✓	-	-	-	Task
[10]	✓	-	-	-	Task
[11]	✓	-	-	-	Task
[18]	✓	-	-	-	Task
[19]	✓	-	-	-	Task
[12]	✓	-	-	-	-
[13]	-	-	-	-	Task
[20]	-	-	-	-	SESE
[21]	✓	-	✓	-	Task
[22]	✓	-	-	-	-
[23]	✓	-	-	-	-
[24]	✓	-	-	-	-
[25]	✓	-	-	-	-
[26]	-	-	-	-	-

Back to Table 1, we note that most of the studied approaches deal with the outsourcing of the classic BP. Nonetheless, new paradigms, such as IoT and robots, seem to be relevant for automating the BP via the elimination of human intervention. For example, Refs. [14,15] propose an architecture to support the outsourcing of the IoT-aware BP. Furthermore, we notice, from Table 1, that several of the studied approaches [7–9,13,18,20,21] are limited to the cloud environment to ensure the outsourcing of the process. However, the cloud is not recommended for latency-sensitive applications, such as IoT applications (e.g., health care, smart home, and smart agriculture). This is due to the high latency added by network connections to data centers [4]. We also notice that there is a lack of approaches that deal with the MCDM methods, despite their ability to decide on a set of alternatives according to a set of criteria. Moreover, we notice from this table that in most cases, the approaches that deal with the MCDM methods [9,15,16] do not take into account the weight generation method to automatically generate weights.

Back to Table 2, we note that most of the existing approaches (e.g., [7–9,21]) outsource the BP at the task level. However, in [20], the authors target the process outsourcing via the outsourcing of a set of sub-process (SESE) fragments rather than a task. Indeed, outsourcing the BP based on its sub-processes fragments allows, on one hand, to accelerate the outsourcing operation, and on the other hand, it allows to save the process workflow between tasks.

In summary, we denote from this comparison that the studied approaches deal mainly with the outsourcing of the classic BPs. Among these approaches, there are those that are limited to the cloud environment for outsourcing BPs. Moreover, applying the outsourcing in the smallest unit, which is the task, may be costly for the outsourcing operation and it cannot preserve as much of the process workflow between tasks. Furthermore, several of the studied approaches do not consider the MCDM during the process outsourcing decision, despite its ability to evaluate a set of alternatives regarding a set of criteria. The MCDM process can support decision-making by helping to structure the problem and offering all involved actors a common language for discussing and learning about the problem [27]. It has also the potential to enhance transparency and the analytic rigor of decisions regarding other optimization methods. Otherwise, the approaches that deal with the outsourcing of the BP using the MCDM techniques do not consider methods for the automatic generation of weights for the used criteria. Indeed, the weights allow the decision-makers to express their preference in terms of the importance of criteria during the evaluation of a set of alternatives.

To close the gaps mentioned above, we propose a decision-making approach for outsourcing the IoRT-aware business process divided into a set of SESE fragments. The SESE deals with a closed block that groups one or more tasks, and it is characterized by its properties, inputs, and outputs. It guarantees the speed of the outsourcing operation and allows the business managers to preserve the process workflow within the process as much as possible. Furthermore, we seek to benefit from the fog and cloud environments to outsource these fragments if they are sensitive to latency or require high computing capacity. During our proposal, we chose ELECTRE IS as a MCDM method to achieve our goal. It is one of the widespread MCDM selection methods characterized by its ability to manage the heterogeneity of types of criteria (e.g., cost and latency). Moreover, our approach is based on the automation of the values of the weights using the MEREC method, which shows its ability, reliability, and relative effectiveness.

3. Outsourcing of IoRT-Aware Business Process

In this section, we start with the identification of a set of criteria that are useful for making the right outsourcing decision. After that, we present the used environment to accomplish the outsourcing goal. Finally, we detail the used method for the proposed outsourcing approach.

3.1. Outsourcing Criteria

Our approach allows the outsourcing of some parts of the IoRT-aware BP, either to fog and/or cloud environments as an external supplier. To decompose the process to a set of parts (sub-processes), we applied the RPST (refined process structure tree) method that divides a process to a set of fragments named single entry single exit (SESE) fragments, preserving as far as possible the workflows of the BP. To properly outsource the SESE fragments, it is useful to specify their requirements that are considered input for the outsourcing decision. In this setting, we identified a set of criteria that seem to be relevant for the BP outsourcing for both fog and cloud. In what follows, we detailed these criteria.

3.1.1. Cost

Saving cost is among the attractive factors that encouraged the enterprises to outsource their process to external providers. In [6], the authors argued that process outsourcing is guided mainly by overhead costs, where the processes are selected by ascertaining how much money they may save. In this setting, we aim to consider the cost of the SESE fragments that relies on the estimation of process task cost $Cost(a_i)$ (see Equation (4)). This latter is calculated according to its execution cost (EC), storage cost (SC), and transfer cost (TC) (see Equations (1)–(3)). Equation (7) estimates the cost of a SESE, which is expressed on percentage. The $spec\_cost(SESE)$ represents the business manager's expected cost for a SESE. Indeed, $Cost1(SESE)$ presents the cost of SESE tasks that are inserted on a sequence, parallel (AND), and inclusive (OR) patterns (see Equation (5)). In fact, a sequence pattern shows the order of flow elements within the process where each element has one input and one output (https://www.omg.org/spec/BPMN/2.0/PDF, accessed on 13 June 2022). The parallel pattern is used to synchronize and create parallel flows within a process. However, the inclusive pattern presents both parallel and alternative paths within the process. These patterns directly influence the process cost estimation, where we suggest, in our proposal, to additionally calculate how much those patterns tasks cost. However, $Cost2(SESE)$ gives the cost of SESE tasks that are inserted on an exclusive (XOR) pattern. This pattern presents alternative paths within a process flow. For this pattern kind, we consider the minimum cost to estimate the SESE cost (see Equation (6)).

$$Ex\_Cost(a_i) = [EC(P_{a_i}) \times size(a_i)] \times loopMax(a_i) \qquad (1)$$

$$St\_Cost(a_i) = [SC(P_{a_i}) \times size(a_i)] \times loopMax(a_i) \qquad (2)$$

$$Tr\_Cost(a_i) = [TC(P_{a_i}) \times size(a_i)] \times loopMax(a_i) \qquad (3)$$

$$Cost(a_i) = (Ex\_Cost(a_i) + St\_Cost(a_i) + Tr\_Cost(a_i)) \qquad (4)$$

$$Cost1(SESE) = \sum_{a_i \in SESE\ Pattern\{seq, AND, OR\}} (\sum Cost(a_i)) \qquad (5)$$

$$Cost2(SESE) = \sum_{a_i \in SESE\ Pattern\{XOR\},} (\sum_{p=1}^{p=nb\_pattern} min(\sum_{k=1}^{n} Cost(a_{ipk}))) \qquad (6)$$

$$Cost(SESE) = [(Cost1(SESE) + Cost2(SESE)) \times 100]/spec\_cost(SESE) \qquad (7)$$

3.1.2. Security

Implies the security level which is required for a SESE to accomplish its execution. According to [6], security is among the most prominent criteria that may prohibit enterprises from outsourcing to an external provider. This is caused by the fact that the supplier's service has to control outsourced activities, particularly those that deal with customers' personal information. To identify the threats, we used the Cloud Security Alliance (CSA) that allows the identification of the critical security cloud threats. These threats may also concern the fog environment. To estimate the security value of a SESE fragment, we start first at the estimation of the security value for a process task $Sec(a_i)$ (see Equation (10)) that is calculated according to the number of the environment Env protection $nb\_CorrectedTH$ and the number of the threats thr that exist $nb\_ExistenceTH$ (see Equations (8) and (9)). Based on the $Sec(a_i)$ of tasks values that constitute a SESE, we proposed Equation (11) to estimate the SESE security value $Sec(SESE)$, which is expressed in percentage.

$$ExistenceTH(thr_k, a_i) \longrightarrow \{0,1\} \tag{8}$$

$$CorrectedTH(Env_j, thr_k) \longrightarrow \{0,1\} \tag{9}$$

$$Sec(a_i) = (nb\_CorrectedTH(a_i) * 100) / nb\_ExistenceTH(a_i) \tag{10}$$

$$Sec(SESE) = max(Sec(SESE(a_i))) \tag{11}$$

3.1.3. Availability

Relying on the time for which IoRT-aware BP tasks need to be executed (i.e, $Uptime(a_i)$) and the $Downtime(a_i)$ that implies the execution of a task. Several tasks require being available for a long period, which promotes its outsourcing to an environment that ensures a higher availability value, such as the cloud. Toward the estimation of the availability value for a SESE fragment, we start by the estimation of the task availability value $Ava(a_i)$ using its $Uptime(a_i)$ and $Downtime(a_i)$ (see Equation (12)). Then, we proposed Equation (13) to achieve the availability value for a SESE $Ava(SESE)$.

$$Ava(a_i) = [Uptime(a_i) / (Uptime(a_i) + Downtime(a_i))] \times 100 \tag{12}$$

$$Ava(SESE) = max(Ava(SESE_{ai})) \tag{13}$$

3.1.4. Latency

Latency corresponds to the needed time to transfer data from the source to the external environment execution, via the network. It is worthy to consider the latency as one among the IoRT-aware BP outsourcing criteria since this process is constituted by the IoT and robotic technologies that are sensitive to latency. In this work, we performed a thorough literature study, where we noticed that the latency of a task $Lty(a_i)$ is calculated using its size $size(a_i)$ and the bandwidth (b) value (see Equation (14)). However, to estimate the latency value for a SESE $Lty(SESE)$, we propose Equation (17). It is based, on one hand, on the latency value for the SESE tasks that are inserted on a sequence, AND, and OR patterns (see Equation (15)), and on the other hand, on the latency value of the tasks that are inserted on a XOR pattern (see Equation (16)).

$$Lty(a_i) = size(a_i) / b \tag{14}$$

$$Lty1(SESE) = \sum_{\substack{a_i \in SESE \\ Pattern\{seq, \\ AND, OR\}}} (Lty(a_i) \times loopMax(a_i)) \tag{15}$$

$$Lty2(SESE) = \sum_{\substack{a_i \in SESE \\ Pattern\{XOR\}, \\ p=1}}^{p=nb\_pattern} min(\sum_{k=1}^{n} Lty(a_{ipk}) \times loopMax(a_{ipk})) \tag{16}$$

$$Lty(SESE) = [(Lty1(SESE) + Lty2(SESE)) \times 100] / business\_lty(SESE) \tag{17}$$

3.2. Characteristics of Fog and Cloud Environments

To make an appropriate decision for the outsourcing of the IoRT-aware BP, there is a need for an in-depth analysis of fog and cloud environment characteristics. In this setting, we carried out a thorough study in the literature to determine the main features of these environments with respect to the identified criteria. According to [5], we note that the cloud environment is characterized by its highest availability thanks to its data centers. In addition, it has a low-security level and high latency due to the far distance between the end-user devices. The higher latency value can increase the transfer cost which increases the cost. The fog has a high-security level with the lowest latency value, thanks to its proximity to the end-user devices compared to the cloud. Hence, the lowest latency makes the process cost less expensive. We also noticed, in our study, that the fog has low availability value due to its dynamicity. Nonetheless, the duality of the fog and cloud environments has medium security, availability, latency, and cost values. Moreover, it is necessary to note that during the outsourcing of an IoRT-aware BP, the business managers may choose to keep the core of their process without outsourcing if the process tasks require a higher security level.

3.3. Outsourcing Decision-Making

We presented in an earlier sub-section, the main criteria for the outsourcing of the IoRT-aware BP to the fog and/or cloud environments, which are considered an input of our outsourcing decision-making approach. We present in this sub-section the adopted method to generate weights for the used criteria and for the outsourcing of decision-dmaking.

3.3.1. Automatic Generation of Weights

Multi-criteria decision-making (MCDM) is a branch of operations research (OR) that aims, generally, to evaluate a set of alternatives regarding a set of criteria. This evaluation is based on weights which allow the decision-makers to express their preference in terms of the importance of criteria. During our proposal, we aim to avail from the MCDM methods to propose a decision-making approach for the outsourcing of an IoRT-aware BP to the fog and/or cloud environments. In this setting, we use the method based on the removal effects of criteria (MEREC) to generate the weights of our identified criteria [28]. This method helps the experts and decision-makers to raise the robustness of their MCDM method results following an automatic, logical, and methodical weights calculation [28]. In addition, MEREC shows its stability, reliability, and relative effectiveness in differentiating criteria weights compared to other weight-calculation methods, such as CRITIC (criteria importance through inter-criteria correlation) [28].

3.3.2. Multi Criteria Decision Method

Our approach aims to select for each SESE the suitable execution environment. In this setting, we avail from the ELECTRE IS method to achieve our goal. It is among the widespread MCDM selection method which is characterized by its ability to manage the heterogeneity type of criteria (e.g., cost and latency) [29]. It is qualified by its ability to scale the criteria heterogeneity, where it does not require data normalization [29]. Moreover, among the attractive benefits of the ELECTRE IS, we cite its introduced thresholds, which are respectively the indifference threshold (Q), preference threshold (P), and veto threshold (V) that aim to improve the selection results regarding other selection methods. These thresholds respect the condition presented in Equation (18).

$$V \geq P \geq Q \qquad (18)$$

ELECTRE IS is based on the concordance C between alternatives (see Equation (19)), where k presents the sum of the criteria weights and c presents the local concordance index for a criterion.

$$C(a,b) = \begin{cases} 0, \text{if } \exists |g_j(bj) - g_j(a_i)| \geq V_j \\ \sum_{1 \leq j \leq n} k_j c_j(a,b) / \sum_{1 \leq j \leq n} k_j, \text{otherwise} \end{cases} \qquad (19)$$

4. Implementation, Experimentation and Results

In this section, we intend to implement and experiment with the proposed IoRT-aware BP outsourcing decision-making method. During the implementation of our approach, we used the Java environment to develop both the MEREC and ELECTRE IS methods. However, during the experimentation of our proposal, we used an IoRT-aware BP on the agriculture field that we developed under the eclipse modeling framework (EMF) using the BPMN 2.0 modeler plug-in which is an open-source eclipse editor [30]. In what follows, we detail our decision-making approach implementation. Afterward, we present the proposed experimentation.

4.1. Implementation

During the implementation of our decision-making approach, we start with the weights generation using the MEREC method. The MEREC method is based, initially, on a decision matrix that shows the scores of each execution environment (alternative) regarding the identified property as presented in Table 3. For the cost, security, and availability properties, we use 1, 0.8, 0.5, and 0.1 to express respectively the very high, high, medium, and low scores. Nonetheless, for the latency property, we use 1, 0.5, 0.2, and 0.1 to designate, respectively, high, medium, low, and not applied scores. To achieve the MEREC implementation goal, we used the eclipse tool, which is an open-source software development project. This implementation gives 0.22 as a weight value for the cost property, 0.22 for the security property weight. As well, we obtain 0.22 and 0.34 as weight values, respectively, for availability and latency properties (see Figure 1).

Table 3. Proposed decision matrix for MEREC method.

	Cost	Security	Availability	Latency
Cloud	1	0.1	1	1
Fog	0.5	0.8	0.5	0.2
Cloud&Fog	0.8	0.5	0.8	0.5
Local	0.1	1	0.1	0.1

To select the suitable environment execution for a SESE that has its specific cost, security, availability, and latency values, we implemented an interface that is depicted in Figure 1 using the eclipse tool. This interface allows the users to express the SESE requirements in the intention to select its adopted environment execution.

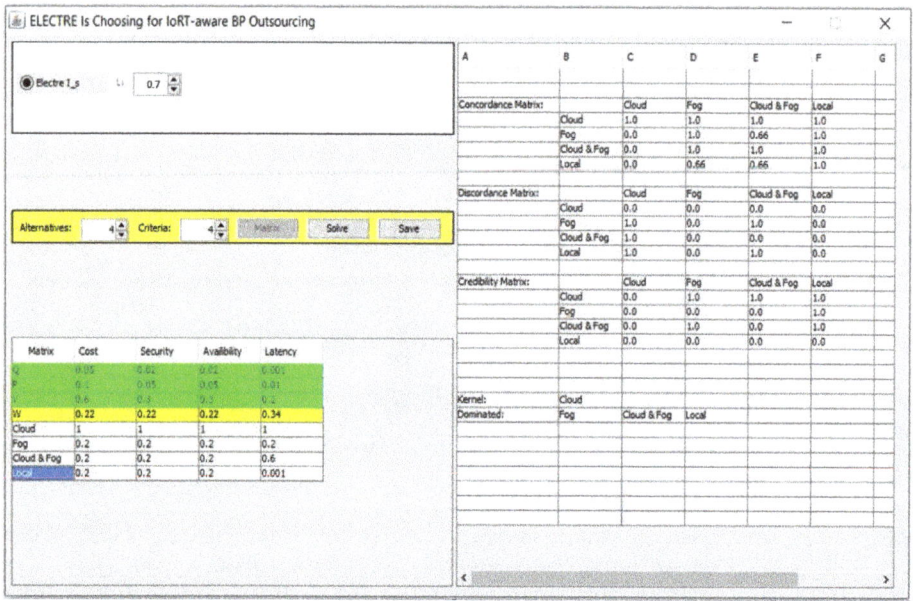

Figure 1. IoRT-aware BP outsourcing interface using ELECTRE IS.

4.2. Experimentation and Results

To better test our approach functionality, we conducted two experiments applied to an IoRT-aware BP in the agriculture field (see Figure 2). The used process presents an example of an IoRT-aware BP of a smart irrigation management system that intends to boost nutrient and water-use efficiency. Indeed, the process starts with the capture of temperature and soil moisture values using two sensors: capture temperature, and capture soil moisture. The captured values are stored using storage temperature value, and storage soil moisture value. Afterward, irrigation and grep decision-making is made through make irrigation and grep decision. In this setting, the process was finished either if there is no need for irrigation; otherwise, an irrigation request is launched called request launch irrigation, which activates an actuator to start the irrigation launch irrigation. Simultaneously, request picking weeds is launched, where it activates the robot to start the picking of weeds with launch picking weeds.

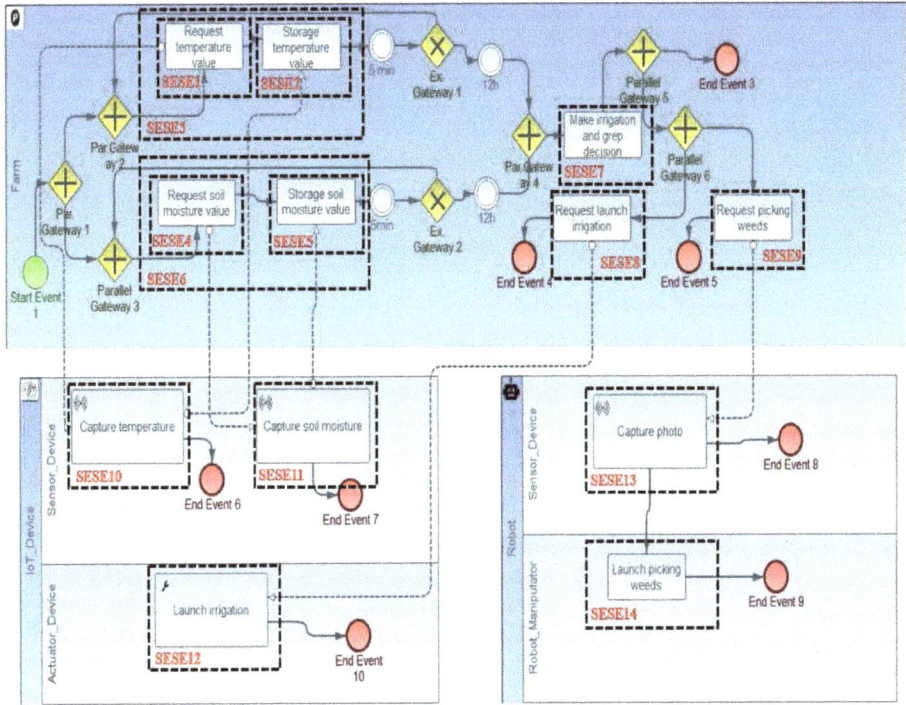

Figure 2. IoRT-aware business process on agriculture field composed by 14 SESE fragments.

Using the RPST technique, we divided the process into a set of SESE fragments, where each SESE has its own requirements in terms of cost, availability, security, and latency.

During our work, we dealt with the process presented in Figure 2, where we used it in two different scenarios that have their specific SESE property values. The first one is based on the property values that are presented in Table 4, whereas the second is based on the SESE property values detailed in Table 5. In addition, these tables give an expert outsourcing result for each SESE. The expert has high expertise that allows it to assess the outsourcing of the SESE according to its cost, security, availability, and latency values.

Table 4. Expert results for the outsourcing of each SESE according to cost, security, availability, and latency values for the first IoRT-aware BP scenario.

SESE Fragments	Properties Values	Expert Result
SESE1	Cost: 69%, Sec: 24%, Ava: 53%, Lty: 12%	Cloud&Fog, Cloud, Fog
SESE2	Cost: 55%, Sec: 21.7%, Ava: 45%, Lty: 19%	Cloud&Fog, Cloud, Fog
SESE3	Cost:32%, Sec: 18.7%, Ava: 35%, Lty: 11.8%	Cloud&Fog, Cloud, Fog
SESE4	Cost: 50%, Sec: 9%, Ava: 58%, lty: 25%	Cloud&Fog, Cloud
SESE5	Cost: 45%, Sec: 25%, Ava: 13.4%, lty: 17.99%	Cloud&Fog, Fog
SESE6	Cost: 30.2%, Sec: 13.1%, Ava: 39.8%, Lty: 14%	Cloud&Fog, Cloud, Fog
SESE7	Cost: 27.82%, Sec: 55.8%, Ava: 0.002%, Lty : 10.02%	Fog
SESE8	Cost: 71%, Sec: 10%, Ava: 72.3%, lty: 44%	Cloud
SESE9	Cost: 72%, Sec: 19.3%, Ava: 75%, lty: 31.2%	Cloud
SESE10	Cost: 21.2%, Sec: 69%, Ava: 0.009%, Lty: 12%	Fog
SESE11	Cost: 13%, Sec: 45.7%, Ava: 10.1%, Lty: 29%	Fog
SESE12	Cost: 2%, Sec: 71%, Ava: 9.9%, Lty: 0.001%	Local
SESE13	Cost: 10.01%, Sec: 52.8%, Ava: 29.8%, Lty: 29.9%	Fog
SESE14	Cost: 2%, Sec: 27%, Ava: 9.9%, Lty: 0.001%	Local

Table 5. Expert results for the outsourcing of each SESE according to cost, security, availability, and latency values for the second IoRT-aware BP scenario.

SESE Fragments	Properties Values	Expert Result
SESE1	Cost: 80%, Sec: 45%, Ava: 70%, Lty: 10%	Cloud
SESE2	Cost: 90%, Sec: 80%, Ava: 30%, Lty: 12%	Cloud
SESE3	Cost:40%, Sec: 18.6%, Ava: 33%, Lty: 10%	Cloud&Fog, Cloud, Fog
SESE4	Cost: 90%, Sec: 10%, Ava: 50%, lty: 30%	Cloud&Fog, Cloud
SESE5	Cost: 20%, Sec: 50%, Ava: 0.8%, lty: 8%	Fog
SESE6	Cost: 21%, Sec: 45%, Ava: 2%, Lty: 30%	Fog
SESE7	Cost: 54%, Sec: 25%, Ava: 17%, Lty : 15%	Cloud&Fog
SESE8	Cost: 70%, Sec: 65.8%, Ava: 80%, lty: 20 %	Cloud
SESE9	Cost: 92%, Sec: 33%, Ava: 87%, lty: 27.9%	Cloud
SESE10	Cost: 87.6%, Sec: 45%, Ava: 60%, Lty: 12%	Cloud
SESE11	Cost: 27.7%, Sec: 12%, Ava: 40%, Lty: 12%	Cloud&Fog, Cloud, Fog
SESE12	Cost: 2%, Sec: 79%, Ava: 92%, Lty: 0%	Local
SESE13	Cost: 8%, Sec: 83%, Ava: 75%, Lty: 0.1%	Local
SESE14	Cost: 12%, Sec: 55.6%, Ava: 27%, Lty: 12%	Fog

4.2.1. Experimentation 1

Our first experimentation aims to compare the effectiveness of our proposed approach regarding other selecting methods. To achieve this end, we chose to compare our method regarding ELECTRE I, ELECTRE Iv, and PROMETHEE I. ELECTRE I, applied only on numerical properties. ELECTRE Iv is presented as an improvement of ELECTRE I by adding the Veto threshold [29]. However, PROMETHEE I is based exclusively on a concordance analysis [29]. During this experimentation, we involved an expert to compare the correspondence between the approach's results and the expert one. In this setting, we used the Jaccard measure [31], which is calculated using Equation (20).

$$(x,y) = \frac{|x \cap y|}{|x \cup y|} \qquad (20)$$

Figure 3 displays the comparison result of our proposed method regarding other selection methods, based on the property values that are presented in Table 4. We denote from this figure that our proposed method has the closest result to the expert one, regarding ELECTRE I, ELECTRE Iv, and PROMETHEE I methods. In other words, the result generated by our method is the most similar to the expert result. This is explained, on one hand, by the use of indifference, preference, and veto thresholds that aim to improve the selection results. On other hand, our proposed approach is based on the use of an automatically generated weight method. Indeed, the use of the MEREC method to generate the properties' weight raises the robustness of our proposed method to generate correct results.

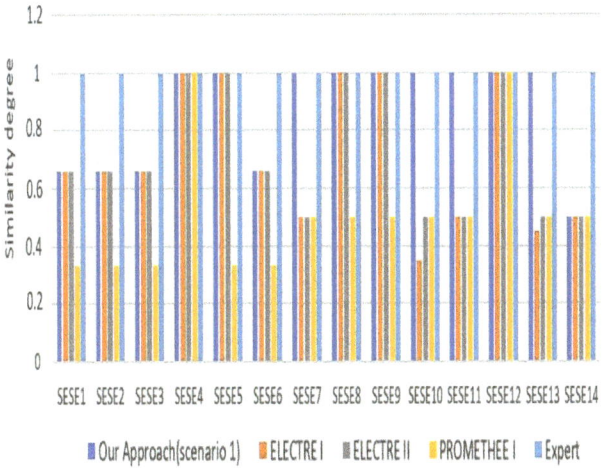

Figure 3. Distance of our approach result compared to other approaches results and expert one (scenario 1).

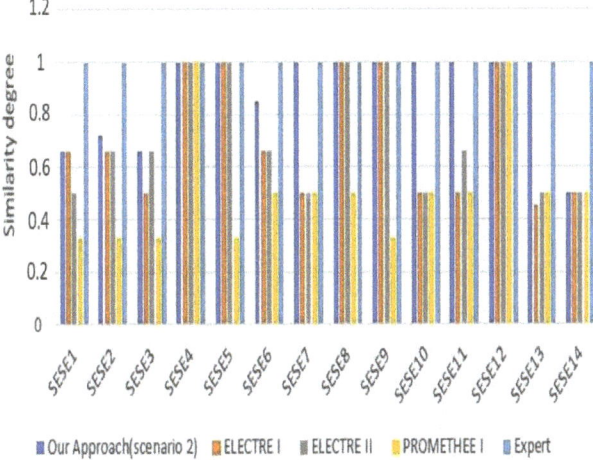

Figure 4. Distance of our approach result compared to other approaches' and expert results (Case 2).

Nonetheless, Figure 4 displays the comparison result of our proposed approach regarding other selection methods, based on the property values that are presented in Table 5, we notice from this figure that our approach gives the closest result to the expert one rather than the other ELECTRE I, ELECTRE Iv, and PROMETHEE I methods. Therefore, this result boosts the fact of the used thresholds and the MEREC method.

4.2.2. Experimentation 2

During the second evaluation, we intend to compare the results of our approach based on MEREC weights with the use of some other weight values (see Table 6). More precisely, we intend, in this experimentation, to compare our approach based on the MEREC method regarding weight values presented in cases 1, 2, and 3 (see Table 6), where each case specifies the values of the weights for the used criteria. This comparison is based on the estimation of precision, recall, and F-score values of the first scenario (see Figure 5) and the second one (see Figure 6).

Table 6. Cost, security, availability, and latency weight values.

Properties' Weight	Our Approach	Case 2	Case 3	Case 4
Cost weight	0.22	0.01	0.08	0.1
Security weight	0.22	0.65	0.15	0.5
Availability weight	0.22	0.13	0.4	0.3
Latency weight	0.34	0.21	0.37	0.1

Figure 5 illustrates the estimation of the precision, recall, and F-score values of our approach for the first scenario. During this scenario, we notice that the precision of our approach reaches 0.87%, and the recall is equal to 0.96%, while the F-score estimates 0.91%. However, in the second scenario (see Figure 6), our approach reaches 0.89%, 0.94%, and 0.91% as the precision, recall, and F-score values, respectively.

We denote from Figures 5 and 6 that our approach based on the MEREC method has the highest precision and recall values for both scenarios. Therefore, these figures show the reliability and the relative effectiveness of our approach in differentiating properties compared to other weight values.

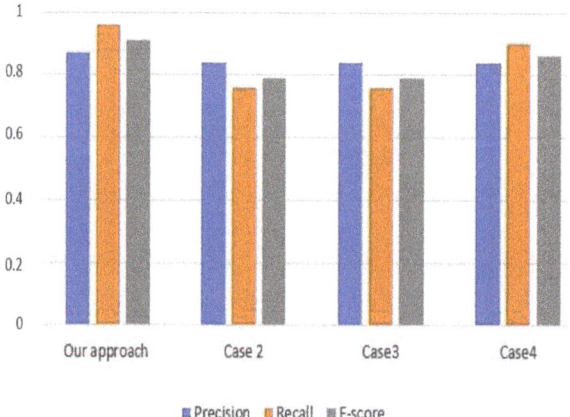

Figure 5. Precision, Recall, and F-score estimation metrics based on criteria values of Table 4.

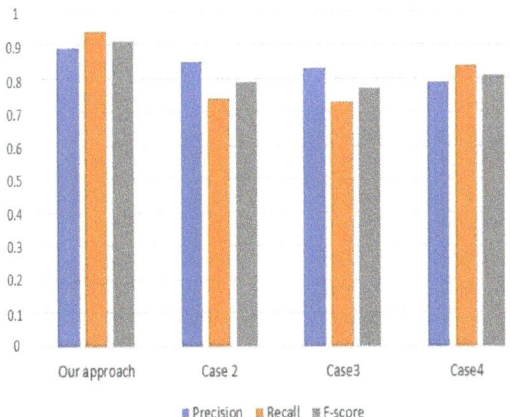

Figure 6. Precision, Recall, and F-score estimation metrics based on property values of Table 5.

5. Validation and Robustness

This section is dedicated to appreciating the validation and robustness of the proposed IoRT-aware BP outsourcing approach based on the ELECTRE IS method. Therefore, to perform this goal, we choose to compare our approach regarding the outsourcing method published in [16]. In their proposal, the authors took into account a set of six criteria, which are frequency, sensitivity, freshness, time, volume, and criticality, to perform the outsourcing of a goal of a thing to the fog and cloud (see Table 7). The frequency criterion refers to the data transfer rate from the thing to fog/cloud nodes, while the sensitivity refers to the nature of data exchanged between things and fog/cloud nodes. The freshness means how important data exchanged between things and fog/cloud nodes should be recent. The time criterion represents the latency delay that results from processing data at the thing until they are transferred to fog/cloud nodes. The volume criterion refers to the amount of data that tasks produce and outsource to fog/cloud nodes. However, the criticality criterion implies how important data tasks are concerning fog/cloud nodes' demands. In summary, the considered criteria focus on the data outsourcing from the thing to the fog and/or cloud nodes concerning different aspects (e.g., location, time, and application needs).

During their proposal, the authors adopted fuzzy logic as one of the MCDM techniques to select the adequate data recipient (e.g., fog only, cloud only, and fog/cloud). The authors justified their choice by the ability of fuzzy logic to handle the conflicting variables and the uncertainty degree of some criteria.

Throughout this section, we intend to compare the results of our approach based on the ELECTRE IS method to the proposal in [16]. Therefore, we applied their approach to the agriculture scenario presented above (see Figure 2), which constitutes a set of tasks. Based on their proposal, the result of the outsourcing is illustrated in Table 8. The table shows a mismatch between an expert's expected results and the obtained ones in most cases. For instance, the task 10 approach, which has a regular stream with short gap frequency, very high sensitivity, low freshness, and real-time streaming with a very low volume and criticality, gives fog and fog/cloud as a result. At the same time, the expert estimates to keep this task locally.

Table 7. Data-recipient selection criteria and interaction forms (HR: highly recommended, R: recommended, NR: not recommended, NA: not applicable) [16].

Criterion	Features	T → C	T → F	T → C/F	T → C → F	T → F → C
Frequency	Continuous stream	NR	HR	NA	NR	R
	Regular stream					
	Short gaps	NR	HR	NA	NR	HR
	Long gaps	R	R	R	R	R
Sensitivity	High	NR	HR	NA	NR	HR
	low	R	R	R	R	R
Freshness	Highly important	NR	HR	NA	NR	R
	lowly important	R	R	R	R	R
Time	Real-time	NR	HR	NA	NR	HR
	Near real-time	R	HR	HR	R	HR
	Batch-processing	HR	NR	NA	R	NR
Volume	High	HR	HR	NA	NR	R
	Low	NR	HR	NA	NR	R
Criticality	Highly important	HR	HR	HR	HR	R
	Lowly important	NR	HR	NA	NR	HR

To perform the comparison goal, we estimated the precision, recall, and F-score values using the details presented in Table 8 and the IoRT-aware BP scenario details presented in Table 4. The precision is the percentage of correctly classified predictive positive task samples. The recall refers to the rate of positive task samples that are correctly classified, while the F-score presents a measure that combines precision and recall [32].

Table 8. Comparison between expert's expected results and the obtained ones for the outsourcing of an IoRT-aware BP using the approach in [16].

Fragments	Frequency	Sensitivity	Freshness	Time	Volume	Criticality	Approach Result	Expert Result
Task1	Regular stream long gaps	Medium	low	Near real time	high	high	Cloud, Fog, Fog/Cloud	Cloud, Fog/Cloud
Task2	Regular stream long gaps	Medium	low	Near real time	around medium and high	high	Cloud, Fog, Fog/Cloud	Cloud, Fog/Cloud
Task3	Regular stream long gaps	very low	very low	Real time	very high	high	Cloud, Fog, Fog/Cloud	Fog, Cloud, Fog/Cloud
Task4	Regular stream long gaps	Medium	very high	Real time	Low	Low	Fog, Fog/Cloud	Fog
Task5	Regular stream short gaps	high	Very high	Real time	High	Very low	Fog, Fog/Cloud	Cloud, Fog/Cloud
Task6	Regular stream short gaps	very low	Very low	Real time	Very low	Very high	Fog, Fog/Cloud	Fog, Cloud
Task7	Regular stream short gaps	Medium	low	Near real time	Low	Very low	Cloud, Fog, Fog/Cloud	Fog/Cloud
Task8	Regular stream short gaps	high	Medium	Real time	Low	Very low	Cloud, Fog, Fog/Cloud	Fog
Task9	Regular stream long gaps	high	Medium	Near Real time	Very high	Medium	Cloud, Fog	Fog/Cloud, Cloud
Task10	Regular stream short gaps	Very high	Low	Real time	Very low	Very low	Fog, Fog/Cloud	Local
Task11	Regular stream short gaps	high	High	Near Real time	Very low	Medium	Fog, Fog/Cloud	Local, Fog
Task12	Regular stream long gaps	Medium	High	Real time	Medium	Low	Fog, Fog/Cloud	Fog

During this evaluation, we notice that the precision value reaches 0.75%, and the recall is equal to 0.51%, while the F-score estimates 0.60% (see Table 9). Therefore, we deduce from this comparison that our proposal is more robust and relatively effective compared to their approach. The precision value of our approach reaches 0.87%, the recall is estimated to be 0.96%, and the F-score is equal to 0.91% (see Figure 5). The disparity obtained at the precision, recall, and F-score values can be explained by the set of the considered criteria for each approach, where the approach published in [16], focused on the data exchange and did not consider the cost and security requirements of fog/cloud nodes.

On the other hand, we are aware that our proposal has some flaws that should be fixed in future work. Our proposal needs to consider the human side involved in the administration and commitment processes. Each business depends mainly on the knowledge of its staff. Its employees' capacity to meet its needs and accomplish its strategic goals determines whether the company succeeds or fails. Moreover, our proposed outsourcing approach is limited to design time execution. However, a business process is likely to be modified at runtime due to the dynamicity of IoT and robot devices. Therefore, it seems to be relevant to consider the scheduling of the process outsourcing. Indeed, the scheduling consists of planning the process outsourcing to allow the business managers to achieve their goals whenever the fog/cloud is available.

Table 9. Precision, recall, and F-score estimated values for the tasks of the first IoRT-aware BP scenario using the approach in [16].

Fragments	Precision	Recall	F-Score
Task1	1	0.66	0.79
Task2	1	0.66	0.79
Task3	1	1	1
Task4	1	0.5	0.66
Task5	0.5	0.5	0.66
Task6	0.5	0.5	0.5
Task7	1	0.5	0.66
Task8	1	0.33	0.49
Task9	0.5	0.5	0.5
Task10	0	0	0
Task11	0.5	0.5	0.5
Task12	1	0.5	0.66
Whole IoRT-aware BP	0.75	0.51	0.60

6. Conclusions

The outsourcing of an IoRT-aware BP to the fog and/or cloud environments presents several advantages to the enterprises, as it allows them to save their cost, and focus on their core competence. It consists of deploying partially or totally the process in an external execution environment. Despite these advantages, the outsourcing of an IoRT-aware BP is not a trivial task. Therefore, there is a crucial need in the decision-making outsourcing to determine which part of the process should be outsourced and which environment would be selected to deploy it. Toward these objectives, we identified in this paper a set of criteria for the IoRT-aware BP outsourcing in fog and/or cloud environments. In addition, we used the ELECTRE IS method based on the MEREC method for the weight generation to select the suitable environment for each SESE.

We also aim to propose a framework to take into account the human side involved in the administration and commitment process for the outsourcing decision of a BP. Moreover, we seek, in the future, to enhance our proposal by scheduling the process outsourcing to consider the dynamic changes of the IoT and/or robot devices, thereby allowing the business managers to achieve their goals in time.

Author Contributions: Conceptualization, N.F., I.B.L., M.R. and K.B.; methodology, N.F., I.B.L., M.R. and K.B.; software, N.F., I.B.L., M.R. and K.B.; validation, N.F., I.B.L., M.R. and K.B.; formal analysis, N.F., I.B.L., M.R. and K.B.; investigation, N.F., I.B.L., M.R. and K.B.; resources, N.F., I.B.L., M.R. and K.B.; data curation, N.F., I.B.L., M.R. and K.B.; writing—original draft preparation, N.F., I.B.L., M.R. and K.B.; writing—review and editing, N.F., I.B.L., M.R. and K.B.; visualization, N.F., I.B.L., M.R. and K.B.; supervision, K.B. All authors have read and agreed to the published version of the manuscript.

Funding: This research has no external funding.

Institutional Review Board Statement: Not applicable.

Informed Consent Statement: Not applicable.

Data Availability Statement: Not applicable.

Conflicts of Interest: The authors declare no conflict of interest.

References

1. Fattouch, N.; Ben Lahmar, I.; Boukadi, K. A comprehensive architecture for an IoRT-aware Business Process outsourcing into Fog and Cloud computing. In Proceedings of the Tunisian-Algerian Joint Conference on Applied Computing (TACC), Tabarka, Tunisia, 18–20 December 2021; pp. 164–172.
2. Mell, P.; Grance, T. The NIST Definition of Cloud Computing. 2011. Available online: https://csrc.nist.gov/publications/detail/sp/800-145/final (accessed on 1 October 2022).
3. Abdulqadir, H.R.; Zeebaree, S.R.; Shukur, H.M.; Sadeeq, M.M.; Salim, B.W.; Salih, A.A.; Kak, S.F. A study of moving from cloud computing to fog computing. *Qubahan Acad. J.* **2021**, *1*, 60–70. [CrossRef]
4. Lahmar, I.B.; Boukadi, K. Resource Allocation in Fog Computing: A Systematic Mapping Study. In Proceedings of the 2020 Fifth International Conference on Fog and Mobile Edge Computing (FMEC), Paris, France, 20–23 April 2020; pp. 86–93.
5. Yousefpour, A.; Fung, C.; Nguyen, T.; Kadiyala, K.; Jalali, F.; Niakanlahiji, A.; Kong, J.; Jue, J.P. All one needs to know about fog computing and related edge computing paradigms: A complete survey. *J. Syst. Archit.* **2019**, *98*, 289–330. [CrossRef]
6. Govindan, K.; Agarwal, V.; Darbari, J.D.; Jha, P. An integrated decision making model for the selection of sustainable forward and reverse logistic providers. *Ann. Oper. Res.* **2019**, *273*, 607–650. [CrossRef]
7. Boukadi, K.; Grati, R.; Rekik, M.; Ben-Abdallah, H. Business process outsourcing to cloud containers: How to find the optimal deployment? *Future Gener. Comput. Syst.* **2019**, *97*, 397–408. [CrossRef]
8. Ben Halima, R.; Kallel, S.; Ahmed Nacer, M.; Gaaloul, W. Optimal business process deployment cost in cloud resources. *J. Supercomput.* **2021**, *77*, 1579–1611. [CrossRef]
9. Zarour, K.; Benmerzoug, D. A decision-making support for business process outsourcing to a multi-cloud environment. *Int. J. Decis. Support Syst. Technol. (IJDSST)* **2019**, *11*, 66–92. [CrossRef]
10. Suresh, S.; Ravichandran, T. Value gains in business process outsourcing: The vendor perspective. *Inf. Syst. Front.* **2022**, *24*, 677–690. [CrossRef]
11. Shi, Z.; Liu, S.; Wu, R. Incentive design with customer satisfaction for business process outsourcing: Multi-task vs. multi-agent. *RAIRO-Oper. Res.* **2021**, *55*, S401–S434. [CrossRef]
12. Gaaloul, W.; Zhou, Z.; Panetto, H.; Zhang, L. Special issue on fog and cloud computing for cooperative information system management. *Future Gener. Comput. Syst.* **2020**, *109*, 704–705. [CrossRef]
13. Asatiani, A.; Apte, U.; Penttinen, E.; Rönkkö, M.; Saarinen, T. Impact of accounting process characteristics on accounting outsourcing-Comparison of users and non-users of cloud-based accounting information systems. *Int. J. Account. Inf. Syst.* **2019**, *34*, 100419. [CrossRef]
14. Kallel, A.; Rekik, M.; Khemakhem, M. IoT-fog-cloud based architecture for smart systems: Prototypes of autism and COVID-19 monitoring systems. *Softw. Pract. Exp.* **2021**, *51*, 91–116. [CrossRef]
15. Stavrinides, G.L.; Karatza, H.D. A hybrid approach to scheduling real-time IoT workflows in fog and cloud environments. *Multimed. Tools Appl.* **2019**, *78*, 24639–24655. [CrossRef]
16. Yahya, F.; Maamar, Z.; Boukadi, K. A multi-criteria decision making approach for cloud-fog coordination. In *Advanced Information Networking and Applications, Proceedings of the International Conference on Advanced Information Networking and Applications, Caserta, Italy, 15–17 April 2020*; Springer: Cham, Switzerland, 2020; pp. 1150–1161.
17. Ge, L.; Wang, X.; Yang, Z. The strategic choice of contract types in business process outsourcing. *Bus. Process. Manag. J.* **2021**, *27*, 1569–1589. [CrossRef]
18. Wakrime, A.A.; Boubaker, S.; Kallel, S.; Guermazi, E.; Gaaloul, W. A Formal Model for Configurable Business Process with Optimal Cloud Resource Allocation. *J. Univ. Comput. Sci.* **2021**, *27*, 693–713. [CrossRef]

19. Halima, R.B.; Kallel, S.; Gaaloul, W.; Maamar, Z.; Jmaiel, M. Toward a correct and optimal time-aware cloud resource allocation to business processes. *Future Gener. Comput. Syst.* **2020**, *112*, 751–766. [CrossRef]
20. Rekik, M.; Fourati, M.; Boukadi, K. Business process implementation through SaaS services composition. In Proceedings of the Tunisian Algerian Conference on Applied Computing (TACC 2021), Tabarka, Tunisia, 18–20 December 2021; pp. 37–48.
21. Hadded, L.; Hamrouni, T. Optimal autonomic management of service-based business processes in the cloud. *Soft Comput.* **2022**, *26*, 7279–7291. [CrossRef]
22. Jana, C.; Pal, M. A dynamical hybrid method to design decision making process based on GRA approach for multiple attributes problem. *Eng. Appl. Artif. Intell.* **2021**, *100*, 104203. [CrossRef]
23. Jana, C.; Muhiuddin, G.; Pal, M.; Al-Kadi, D. Intuitionistic fuzzy dombi hybrid decision-making method and their applications to enterprise financial performance evaluation. *Math. Probl. Eng.* **2021**, *2021*, 3218133. [CrossRef]
24. Jana, C.; Pal, M.; Wang, J. A robust aggregation operator for multi-criteria decision-making method with bipolar fuzzy soft environment. *Iran. J. Fuzzy Syst.* **2019**, *16*, 1–16.
25. Jana, C.; Garg, H.; Pal, M. Multi-attribute decision making for power Dombi operators under Pythagorean fuzzy information with MABAC method. *J. Ambient. Intell. Humaniz. Comput.* **2022**, 1–18. [CrossRef]
26. Jana, C.; Pal, M. Assessment of enterprise performance based on picture fuzzy Hamacher aggregation operators. *Symmetry* **2019**, *11*, 75. [CrossRef]
27. Köhler, B.; Ruud, A.; Aas, Ø.; Barton, D.N. Decision making for sustainable natural resource management under political constraints—The case of revising hydropower licenses in Norwegian watercourses. *Civ. Eng. Environ. Syst.* **2019**, *36*, 17–31. [CrossRef]
28. Keshavarz-Ghorabaee, M.; Amiri, M.; Zavadskas, E.K.; Turskis, Z.; Antucheviciene, J. Determination of objective weights using a new method based on the removal effects of criteria (MEREC). *Symmetry* **2021**, *13*, 525. [CrossRef]
29. Sałabun, W.; Wątróbski, J.; Shekhovtsov, A. Are mcda methods benchmarkable? a comparative study of topsis, vikor, copras, and promethee ii methods. *Symmetry* **2020**, *12*, 1549. [CrossRef]
30. Fattouch, N.; Lahmar, I.B.; Boukadi, K. Towards a Meta-Modeling Approach for an IoRT-Aware Business Process. *Commun. ECMS* **2022**, *36*, 29–35.
31. Lu, Y.; Huang, X.; Dai, Y.; Maharjan, S.; Zhang, Y. Blockchain and federated learning for privacy-preserved data sharing in industrial IoT. *IEEE Trans. Ind. Inform.* **2019**, *16*, 4177–4186. [CrossRef]
32. Miao, J.; Zhu, W. Precision–recall curve (PRC) classification trees. *Evol. Intell.* **2022**, *15*, 1545–1569. [CrossRef]

Article

Significance of Machine Learning for Detection of Malicious Websites on an Unbalanced Dataset

Ietezaz Ul Hassan [1], Raja Hashim Ali [1,*], Zain Ul Abideen [1], Talha Ali Khan [2,*] and Rand Kouatly [2]

[1] Faculty of Computer Science and Engineering, Ghulam Ishaq Khan Institute of Engineering Sciences and Technology, Topi 23460, Pakistan
[2] Faculty of Tech and Software Engineering, University of Europe of Applied Sciences, 14469 Potsdam, Germany
* Correspondence: hashim.ali@giki.edu.pk (R.H.A.); talhaali.khan@ue-germany.de (T.A.K.)

Abstract: It is hard to trust any data entry on online websites as some websites may be malicious, and gather data for illegal or unintended use. For example, bank login and credit card information can be misused for financial theft. To make users aware of the digital safety of websites, we have tried to identify and learn the pattern on a dataset consisting of features of malicious and benign websites. We treated the problem of differentiation between malicious and benign websites as a classification problem and applied several machine learning techniques, for example, random forest, decision tree, logistic regression, and support vector machines to this data. Several evaluation metrics such as accuracy, precision, recall, F1 score, and false positive rate, were used to evaluate the performance of each classification technique. Since the dataset was imbalanced, the machine learning models developed a bias during training toward a specific class of websites. Multiple data balancing techniques, for example, undersampling, oversampling, and SMOTE, were applied for balancing the dataset and removing the bias. Our experiments showed that after balancing the data, the random forest algorithm using the oversampling technique showed the best results in all evaluation metrics for the benign and malicious website feature dataset.

Keywords: machine learning; malicious website; benign website detection

1. Introduction

Digital security has gained paramount importance in recent times with the exponential growth in the number of applications and users, and rapid evolution in the field of Information Technology. Easy access to the internet from across the globe, the availability of high-speed Internet, and technological advances through the availability of 4G and 5G technology, have significantly increased usage of the Internet around the world [1]. Specifically, due to the recent waves of COVID-19 pandemic, several companies and businesses shifted their business models from the physical domain to the digital domain, using web applications and mobile applications to reduce physical contact [2,3]. However, with the opportunity to grow significantly and be open and accessible to the world, there is a significant security threat as well—the leaking of private or insecure data. Some recent major data leaks involve large volumes and variety of compromised data and have impacted millions of online users (as summarized in Table 1).

The openness and ease of access to the Internet has significantly increased the digital visibility of a person, which leads to opportunities for hackers and digital thieves to gain access to private credentials and data. This is a severe breach of security, leading to financial loss and deep mental pressure at times. One way to gather private data from unsuspecting internet users is through malicious websites. The malicious websites typically look like ordinary benign websites and ask for private data, for example, credit card information, or usernames and passwords to gain access to private pictures, or other important information. This information is kept stored in a database and can then be used online for any malicious purpose, for example, for online shopping, the illegal transfer of money, or for blackmailing or harassing the person. One of the simplest techniques to steal digital information is using identical-looking fake pages to the original web pages [4].

Table 1. Table displaying the recent large data breach attacks, their impact, and their cause. Digital security, especially for online users and businesses, is a significant cause of concern.

Breach Name	Date of Data Breach	Impact	Caused by
Ronin (Ethereum sidechain to power Axie Infinity) Breach	March 2022	Looted over 540 million USD	Hackers (Lazarus Group, North Korea)
0ktapus	August 2022	Compromised at least 130 companies (including Cloudflare, Doordash, Mailchimp)	Extended Phishing Campaign
Uber Total Compromise	August 2022	Complete access to Uber's source code, internal databases, and more information by a hacker under the alias "teapotuberhacker"	Hacker with ties to Lapsus$ using purchased credentials and MFA fatigue attack
Lapsus$ hacking spree	February–March 2022	Looted a terabyte of proprietary data (Nvidia) and blackmail the company. Leaked source codes and algorithms from Samsung. Temporarily brought down Ubisoft's online gaming services. Partial source code released for Bing and Cortana, breaching Microsoft Inc.	Method not known
Neopets Breach	19 July 2022	Personal data of 69 million Neopets users including username, email addresses, date of birth, zip codes was released	Phishing attack

One way to ensure the security of the user is to identify if the accessed website is malicious or not, using classification techniques [5,6]. An accurate classification ensures that the user will be warned not to enter data on the suspicious website [7,8]. Machine learning techniques have recently shown excellent results when used for the classification of data [9,10]. They are not only limited to the field of malicious attacks but have been used for many prediction and identification tasks in multiple fields including image processing [11], weather prediction [12], price prediction [13], stock prediction [14], and other topics. With the availability of large amounts of data, improvement in computing power, and the development of advanced models of computation, the field of machine learning has shown a lot of promise and progress. In traditional machine learning approaches, a new model is developed first and its architecture and parameters are initialized. It is then trained using the training dataset so that the model learns the mapping between the input features and the expected output. After learning the intrinsic general mapping between the input feature set and the output labels, the model can then be used for the classification of the unseen dataset with a similar feature set. This phase is called the validation phase, where the model is validated during training by measuring its performance on unseen data. A trained model can then be applied to unseen data and the results are measured to evaluate the performance. Some of the popular machine learning algorithms are K-Nearest Neighbors (KNN) [15], Support Vector Machine (SVM) [16], Decision Tree [17], Logistic Regression [18], and Naïve Bayes [19].

Several evaluation metrics, e.g., accuracy, precision, and recall, are used in the literature to measure the performance of a machine learning model [20]. All these metrics are typically derived from the confusion matrix, where the idea is to count true positives, true negatives, false positives, and false negatives. Then, a specific formula based on these four counts and their ratio can be used to evaluate the performance of an algorithm on a given dataset. Since the false positives or false negatives are both measures meant for counting the incorrect classification of data, while the true positives or the true negatives are measures for counting the correct classification of data, all ratios generally tend to improve the true positives or the true negatives, or both, while lowering the count of false positives or false negatives or both.

However, one of the major issues faced during the classification of data is the imbalanced dataset [21,22]. In an unbalanced dataset, a single class or a selected group of classes contained the most samples and dominated the data. This means that if a method gets biased toward a certain class or group of classes with the most data, then it will give good results for that class and simply ignore other classes. Several strategies for data balancing are proposed in the literature. SMOTE, undersampling, and oversampling are some of the popular methods that have been deployed for data balancing [23].

In this study, machine learning techniques were deployed for the identification of malicious and benign websites. We used the "Malicious Website" data set that is publicly available on Kaggle. The dataset consists of features of websites that can be used to determine if the website is malicious or benign. We trained five different machine learning models on this dataset. The goal of machine learning models is to capture the underlying structure of the data. When the underlying structure of the data has been captured and a new unseen record is presented to the model, the machine learning model can determine whether the new set of features should be labelled malicious or benign.

Note that the "Malicious Website" dataset is imbalanced; when the model is trained on such data, it is biased towards the class whose records are in a majority because it is rewarded to classify all data as members of that class. So, for resolving the issue of data imbalance and the skew toward malicious websites, data balancing techniques including undersampling, oversampling, and SMOTE were used in this study to improve the performance of the model [21].

As discussed earlier, the machine learning model had two phases, a training and validation phase, followed by a test phase, where the dataset is divided into training data for training and validating the model and test data for measuring the performance of the model. The model is trained on training data and then its performance is tested on the test data. Note that fixing the datasets into a fixed test and train dataset sometimes causes issues for a particular division of the data, for example, when all classes are not evenly distributed among the two subsets. Hence, k-fold cross-validation is generally recommended to counter these complications with continuous changing of validation and training data samples in each iteration of training.

A 10-fold cross-validation of the dataset for training and validation was deployed in this study. We evaluated the model performance based on the five most common metrics including accuracy, precision, recall, F1-score, and true positive rate. After checking the performance of classifiers on the dataset, the study recommends that deploying the random forest technique when used with oversampling for balancing the dataset gave the best results for all metrics.

2. Related Work

Singhal et al. [24] used several supervised machine learning classifiers, such as random forest, gradient boosting, decision trees, and deep neural networks, for the classification of malicious and benign websites. First, URLs were collected. From each of the malicious and benign websites, the authors extract lexical-based, host-based, and content-based features for the website, which served as input for the machine learning models. The lexical-based features selected by the authors are URL length, host length, host token count, path length, and several symbols. Similarly, the host-based features extracted from the URL are location and autonomous system number (ASN). The content-based features selected by the author are HTTPS-enabled, applet count, Eval() function, XMLHttpRequest (XHR), popups, redirection, and unescaped() function. The authors collected the benign website from the public blacklist provided by PhishTank. There are a total of eighty thousand unique URLs in this dataset and the dataset is balanced. After collecting the data, the features are extracted. The evaluation metrics used for measuring classifier performance on this dataset are accuracy, precision, and recall for comparing various classifiers. The paper achieved the best result of 96.4% accuracy by using the gradient boosting technique.

Patil et al. [25] designed their algorithm, called kAYO, for distinguishing between malicious and benign mobile webpages. Their method uses the static features of a webpage for classification. The authors also applied their method to a large, labelled dataset, made up of 350,000 malicious and benign mobile webpages, on which the authors achieved an accuracy of 90 per cent. The authors also developed their browser extension. At the backend of the browser extension, kAYO is running for identifying whether the selected webpage is malicious or benign.

Iv et al. [26] explored the relationship between the number of extracted features from the HTTP header and the chance of detecting malicious websites. They analyzed HTTP headers of 6021 malicious and 39,853 benign websites. From these websites, the authors extracted 672 features and identified 22 features for further analysis, of which 11 features were studied in prior research while the remaining 11 features were identified in their work. Of these 22 features, three features accounted for 80% of the total importance of all the features. The authors observed that instead of using only 11 features as was performed initially, a better result is observed if all 22 features are used. Furthermore, the authors also applied two dimensionality reduction techniques, in which it was observed that the application of principal component analysis (PCA) on the identified features increases the detection. The authors used eight supervised machine learning classifiers in this work.

Patil et al. [27] used a hybrid methodology for the detection of malicious URLs. The hybrid methodology stands for a combination of static and dynamic approaches, in which some features were extracted using a static approach and some were extracted using a dynamic approach. The authors extracted a total of 117 features, of which 44 were new features. The dataset used in this paper consisted of 52,082 samples. The training data consisted of 40,082 samples out of which 20,041 were malicious and 20,041 were benign. This shows that the dataset used by the authors in this study was balanced. For the effective detection of malicious website URLs, the authors built their classifier using a majority voting classification scheme. The authors evaluated their method using six decision tree classifiers including the J48 decision tree, Simple CART, random forest, random tree, ADTree, and REPTree. The authors used accuracy, false-positive rate, and false-negative rate for evaluation. By using their majority-voting classification method, the authors were able to achieve an accuracy of 99.29% with a low false positive rate and a low false negative rate. The authors showed that with decision tree-based classification, the authors achieved an accuracy between 98 to 99 per cent. The authors have also compared their results with 18 anti-virus and anti-malware solutions, and show promising results for their proposed methodology.

Al-milli et al. [28] proposed a one-dimensional convolutional neural network (1D-CNN) model for the identification of illegitimate URLs. The authors used benchmark datasets and two evaluation metrics (accuracy and receiver operating characteristic ROC curve) for their experiment. Their proposed model achieved an accuracy of 94.31% and an area under curve (AUC) value of 91.23%. Sixty-four filters, having a kernel size of 16 each, were applied in the proposed CNN architecture. The authors used the rectified linear unit (ReLU) activation function that was followed by a max-pooling layer. The final layer was fully connected where there was only one neuron and used sigmoid as the activation function. In their dataset, there were a total of 2456 records having 30 features. In the dataset, there were three output classes which were false URL, true URL, and suspicious. The authors also considered the suspicious and false URLs in the same category. They used 70 per cent of the dataset for training and 30 per cent of the dataset for testing. They used 500 and 2000 epochs. By increasing the epochs, their results were improved by a rate of 11.31 per cent.

Jayakanthan et al. [29] proposed a method for the detection of malicious URLs in two steps. The first step is the enhanced probing classification (EPCMU) algorithm to detect a malicious URL. The second step is the naïve bayes. Detection is performed in the first step and classification is performed in the second step. The EPCMU checks the input URL with very deep details. If any feature of a malicious website is found, or it is found in the list of the blacklisted profile of the system, it then reports this URL as malicious. Otherwise, it checks in depth further. In the classification step, the naïve bayes algorithm takes input from the EMPCU, which is a set of URLs. It checks whether the URL set is malicious or genuine.

Assefa et al. [30] proposed an auto-encoder for differentiating between a malicious and benign website. The data for phishing websites was collected from Phish Tank, an open-source dataset, and the data for genuine websites was collected from the Canadian Institute for Cybersecurity dataset. The final dataset consisted of 10,000 samples with 16 features in total. Features are initially extracted from the data and it is then preprocessed to remove incomplete data. Autoencoders are trained only on URLs of legitimate websites so that when an unseen validation URL is encountered, it will be classified based on the amount of deviation from the typical characteristics of a benign website. The autoencoder was made up of three layers namely input, hidden, and output layers. The authors compared the performance of their model with the SVM and decision trees. Their model, based on autoencoders, gives an accuracy of 91.24%. While the SVM and decision tree algorithms give an accuracy of 88.4% and 86.1%, respectively, the accuracy of both traditional machine learning algorithms is significantly lower than that of the autoencoder.

Table 2 displays the literature review in terms of the different research works that have worked on separating benign websites from malicious websites.

Table 2. Table displaying the literature review for important research works in the field of malicious and benign website identification and their contribution to the field.

Author Name	Balanced Dataset	Model	Metric	Metric Value (Accuracy)
Singhal et al. [24]	Yes	Random forest, Gradient boosting, Decision trees, Deep neural networks.	Accuracy, Precision, Recall.	96.4%
Patil et al. [25]		kAYO (self-Proposed)	Accuracy.	90 %
Iv et al. [26]	No (SMOTE)	Adaptive Boosting, Extra Trees, Random Forest, Gradient Boosting, Bagging Classifier, Logistic Regression, K-Nearest Neighbors.	Accuracy, False positive rate, False negative rate, AUC.	89%
Patil et al. [27]	Yes	J48 decision tree, Simple CART, Random forest, Random tree, ADTree, REPTree.	Accuracy, False-positive rate, False-negative rate.	99.29%
Al-milli et al. [28]		One-dimensional Convolutional Neural Network (1D-CNN)	Accuracy, ROC curve.	94.31%
Jayakanthan et al. [29]		Enhanced Probing Classification (EPCMU) for detection, Naïve Bayes.		
Assefa et al. [30]		Auto-encoder, SVM, Decision trees.	Accuracy.	91.24%
Vinayakumar et al. [31]		Deep Learning.	Accuracy.	99.96%
Vazhayil et al. [32]		CNN-LSTM.	Accuracy.	98%

3. Methodology

In this study, we used the publicly available "Malicious Websites" dataset on the Kaggle website. The original dataset is imbalanced with a strong bias towards malicious websites. For solving the imbalanced dataset problem, we applied the three data balancing techniques—undersampling, oversampling and SMOTE. After making the dataset balanced, the K Fold cross-validation technique was then applied for evaluating the performance of the model. In this paper, we used five machine learning classifiers including decision trees, random forest, the support vector machine (SVM), logistic regression, and stochastic gradient descent. The complete methodology and workflow of our contribution are discussed in Figure 1.

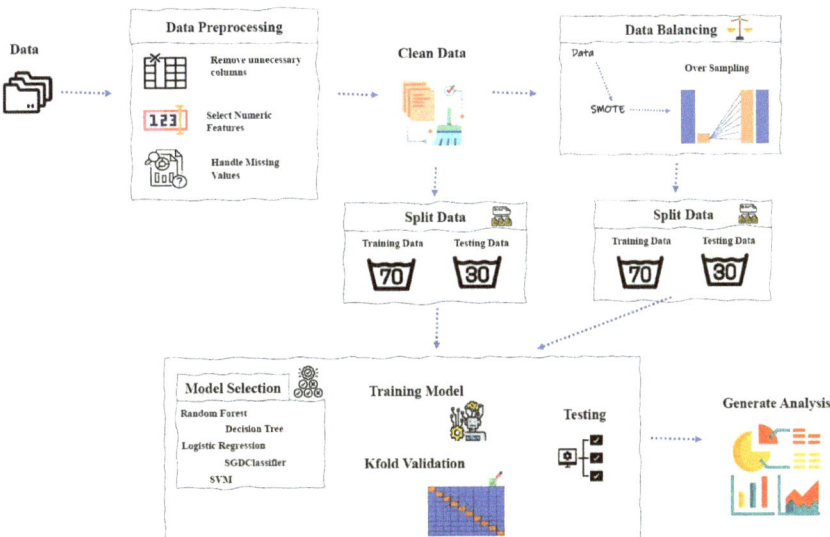

Figure 1. The overall working of the proposed solution.

3.1. Dataset Description

The dataset used in this study consists of 1781 records of malicious and benign website data with 13 features (independent variables), while the target label column 'Type' indicates whether the sample website is malicious or not. Features used for predicting whether the website is malicious or benign are 'length of URL', 'special character number', 'content-length', 'TCP conversation exchange', 'destination remote TCP port', 'remote IPS', 'APP bytes', 'source app packets', 'remote app packets', 'source app bytes', 'remote app bytes', 'App packets', and 'DNS query time'. The different characteristic features of the dataset are shown in Figure 2.

3.2. Data Balancing Technique

In the "Malicious Website" dataset, there are a total of 1781 samples, of which there are 1565 samples that correspond to the malicious class and the remaining 216 samples belong to the benign class. The pie chart in Figure 3 displays the data distribution based on whether the sample belongs to the malicious website class or the benign website class.

From Figure 3, it can be observed that the data is imbalanced and heavily biased toward malicious websites. So, for addressing the imbalanced dataset, three data balancing techniques, namely undersampling, oversampling and the SMOTE, are used to handle the imbalance in the data. Each of these techniques are discussed below.

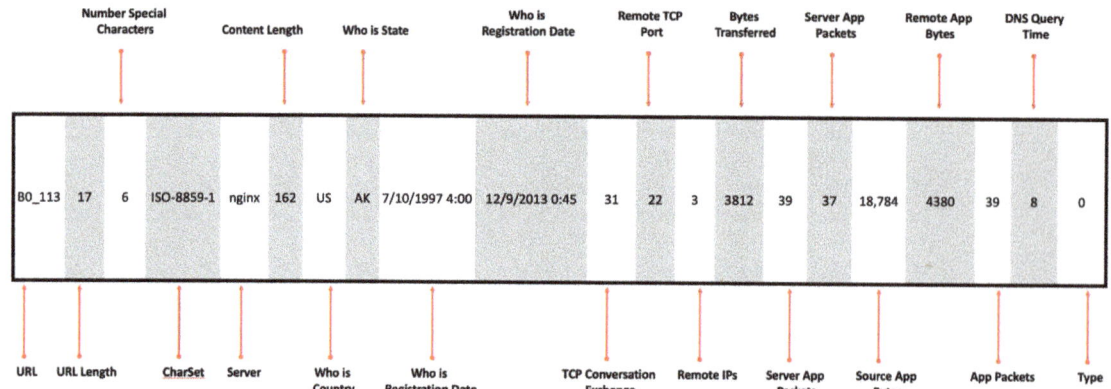

Figure 2. Figure showing a sample row of the data and their column labels.

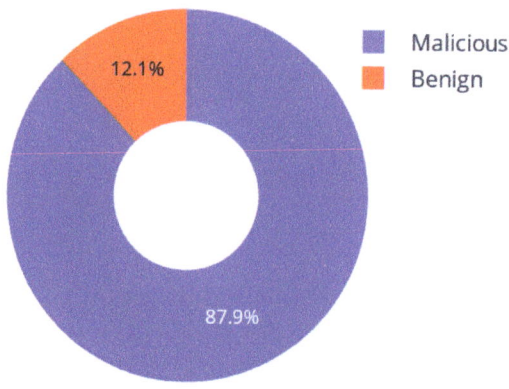

Figure 3. Pie chart showing the distribution of malicious and benign website samples in the "Malicious Websites" Kaggle dataset.

3.2.1. Random Undersampling Technique

In undersampling, the dataset is balanced by reducing the size of the majority class to make it equal to the minority class. As the minority class in this dataset contained 216 records, the majority class (samples corresponding to the malicious data) were reduced to 216 from 1565 by randomly choosing values. The new dataset consists of 432 samples only, of which 216 samples are labelled as malicious and the remaining 216 samples belong to the benign class.

3.2.2. Random Oversampling Technique

In oversampling, the dataset is balanced by duplicating the samples of the minority class, so that it becomes equal to the number of samples in the majority class. Therefore, the number of samples in the benign class was duplicated so that the 216 benign class samples became 1565. The samples to be duplicated were randomly selected from the original 216 samples, and a duplicate for each selected sample was added to the dataset. After the oversampling operation, the dataset contains a total of 3130 samples with 1565 samples labelled as malicious websites and 1565 samples belonging to the benign class.

3.2.3. Synthetic Minority Oversampling Technique (SMOTE)

The synthetic minority oversampling technique (SMOTE) is an oversampling technique that begins by randomly selecting a minority class instance and locating its k-nearest minority class neighbors. The synthetic instance is then constructed by selecting one of the k nearest neighbors b at random and connecting a and b in the feature space to form a line segment. The synthetic instances are created by convexly combining the two selected examples a and b. After applying the SMOTE, our dataset contains 3128 records, of which 1564 records belong to the malicious class and 1564 records belong to the benign class.

3.3. Classifiers

Since this work is based on a machine learning-based classification mechanism, several classifiers were tested to identify the best-performing classifier. The following sections give a brief introduction to the various classification techniques commonly used in the field of classification.

3.3.1. Decision Trees

Decision trees belong to the family of supervised learning algorithms. Unlike other supervised learning algorithms, the decision tree algorithm can also be used to solve regression and classification problems [33]. The goal of using a decision tree is to build a training model that can predict the class or value of a target variable by learning simple decision rules from prior data (training data). To predict a class label for a record in decision trees, we start at the root of the tree. We compare the values of the root attribute and the record attribute. Based on the comparison, we proceed to the next node by following the branch corresponding to that value. Decision trees classify examples by descending the tree from the root to some leaf/terminal node, with the classification provided by the leaf/terminal node. Each node in the tree represents a test case for some attribute, and each edge descending from the node represents one of the possible answers to the test case. This recursive process is repeated for each new node-rooted subtree.

3.3.2. Random Forest

Random forest is a popular supervised machine learning algorithm for classification and regression problems. It builds decision trees from various samples and classifies them based on their majority vote. The random forest algorithm's ability to handle data sets with both continuous and categorical variables, as in regression and classification, is one of its most important features. In classification problems, it outperforms other algorithms [34]. The following are some of the steps involved in the random forest:

- Random forest selects n random records at random from a data set of k records.
- A distinct decision tree is constructed for each sample.
- Each decision tree yields a result.
- In classification, the final result is determined by majority voting.

Figure 4 illustrates the working of the random forest algorithm on the test dataset.

3.3.3. Logistic Regression

Logistic regression, a probabilistic statistical method, is a popular supervised machine learning algorithm used for classification and optimization problems [35]. The algorithm has shown great performance for a variety of common applications such as email spam detection, diabetes prediction, cancer detection, etc. In logistic regression, the sigmoid function (also called the logistic function) and a threshold are used to calculate the likelihood of a label.

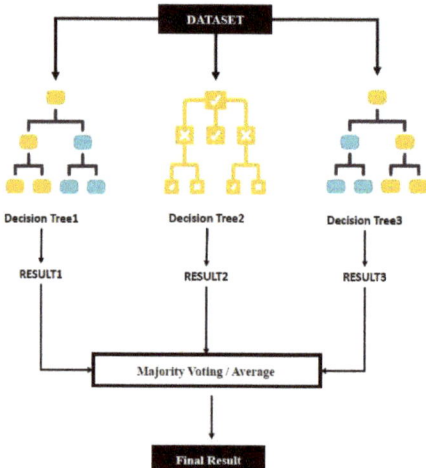

Figure 4. An illustration of how random forest works as a classification technique.

Logistic regression differs from linear regression in multiple ways. Linear regression assumes a linear relationship between the dependent and independent variables. The best fit line describes two or more variables in linear regression. Moreover, linear regression attempts to predict the outcome of a continuous dependent variable with high accuracy. On the other hand, logistic regression predicts the likelihood of an event or class that is dependent on other factors. Logistic regression estimates the likelihood of each label for the test sample and is typically deployed for predicting the target value with categorical dependent variables, for example, with binary labels ('true' or 'false', 'yes' or 'no'). Since the prediction of logistic regression is a likelihood value, it forms an "S" shape when plotted on a graph due to likelihood ranged between 0 and 1. The working of the logistic regression model is shown schematically in Figure 5.

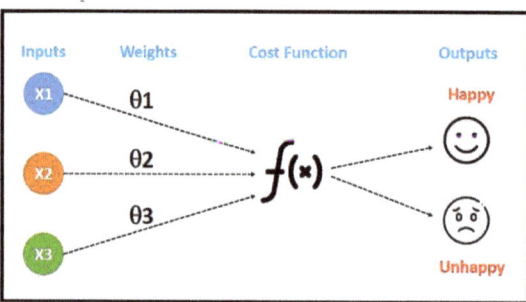

Figure 5. An illustration of how the logistic regression algorithm works as a classification technique.

3.3.4. Support Vector Machine

The support vector machine algorithm's goal is to find a hyperplane in an N-dimensional space. To separate the two types of data points, a variety of hyperplanes could be used. The SVM looks for the plane with the smallest margin of error. The margin is the difference in distance between two groups of data points. Increasing the margin distance provides some reinforcement, making future data points more confidently classified. Hyperplanes are decision boundaries that aid in the classification of data points. Data points on either side of the hyperplane can be classified in a variety of ways. Furthermore, the number of features determines the hyperplane's size. When only two input features are present, the hyperplane is simply a line. When the number of input features reaches three, the hyperplane transforms into a two-dimensional plane. When the number of features exceeds three, it becomes difficult to imagine. Support vectors are data points that are closer to the hyperplane and have an effect on its position and orientation. Using these support vectors, we maximize the classifier's margin. The position of the hyperplane will change if the support vectors are removed. These are the considerations that will aid in the development of the SVM model [36]. The working of the SVM is shown schematically in Figure 6.

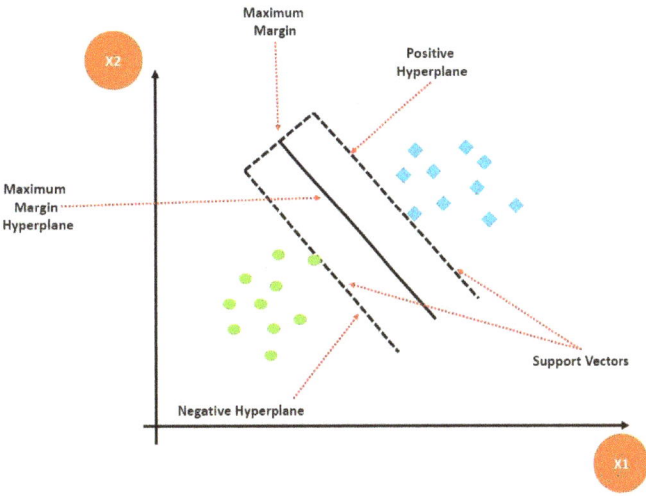

Figure 6. An illustration of how support vector machine (SVM) works as a classification technique.

3.3.5. Stochastic Gradient Descent

Gradient descent is a popular algorithm used in artificial neural networks to back-propagate errors during the training of neural networks. It is one of the most commonly used algorithms that minimizes error functions. The gradient descent starts an iterative process with an initial set of parameters and iteratively moves towards a set of parameter values that tend to find the local minima of an error function. Gradient descent is based on the derivatives of gradients that can help reach the global minimum. However, note that the gradient descent algorithm is extremely slow on very large networks and can lead to vanishing gradient problems for large networks. For each iteration of the gradient descent algorithm, a prediction of each instance in the training dataset is required. The procedure could take a long time when dealing with millions of samples and a billion data points per sample. Stochastic gradient descent differs significantly from gradient descent because the coefficient update for the algorithm occurs only during the execution of the training process. Note that the update procedure for the coefficient remains the same as that of the gradient descent algorithm, except for the custom, which is summed for one training sample instead of overall samples. This is the main difference between gradient descent and stochastic gradient descent for classification [37]. The working of the stochastic gradient descent algorithm in searching the solution space and converging to a solution is shown schematically in Figure 7.

3.4. K-Fold Cross-Validation

The cross-validation approach is a resampling strategy for testing machine learning models on a small dataset and estimating their efficacy. The technique of cross-validation is used to determine the accuracy of an untested machine learning model, i.e., the test and training data are continuously swapped in each iteration. The concept of swapping the validation data continuously helps in evaluating how well the model learns the general characteristics of the data. The procedure takes one input, k, which specifies how many subsets of the original data set are to be created. Accordingly, the process is sometimes referred to as k-fold cross-validation. For example, k = 10 denotes a "10-fold cross-validation," where k is the number of folds. The general mechanism of k-fold cross-validation is shown schematically in Figure 8.

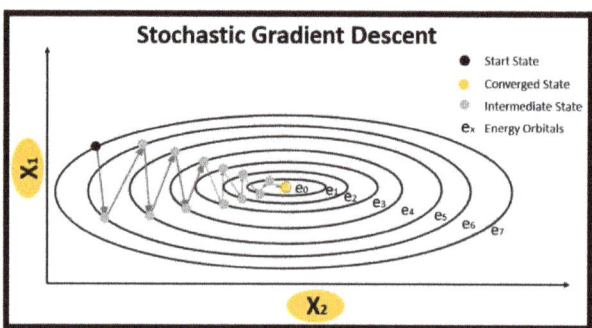

Figure 7. An illustration of how stochastic gradient descent works as an optimization strategy for reaching global optima.

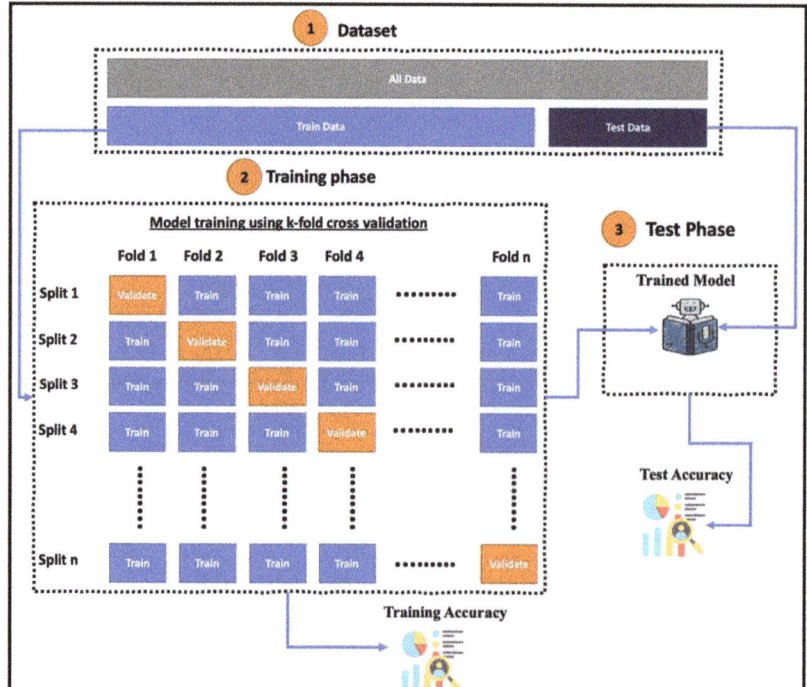

Figure 8. An illustration of how the data is divided into n folds during k-fold cross-validation.

3.5. Overall Methodology

In this study, we tested five different classifiers with no data balancing, the SMOTE, oversampling, and undersampling strategies for removing bias from each class, if any. We deployed a 70/30 split for training and test data. From the training data, we used a stratified 10-fold validation scheme. Nine folds from the training data were used to train the classifier, while the tenth fold of the training data was used to validate the training progress. After the training was complete, the results were then verified on the processed and balanced test data. The overall process of 10-fold cross validation technique deployed for training is shown in Figure 9.

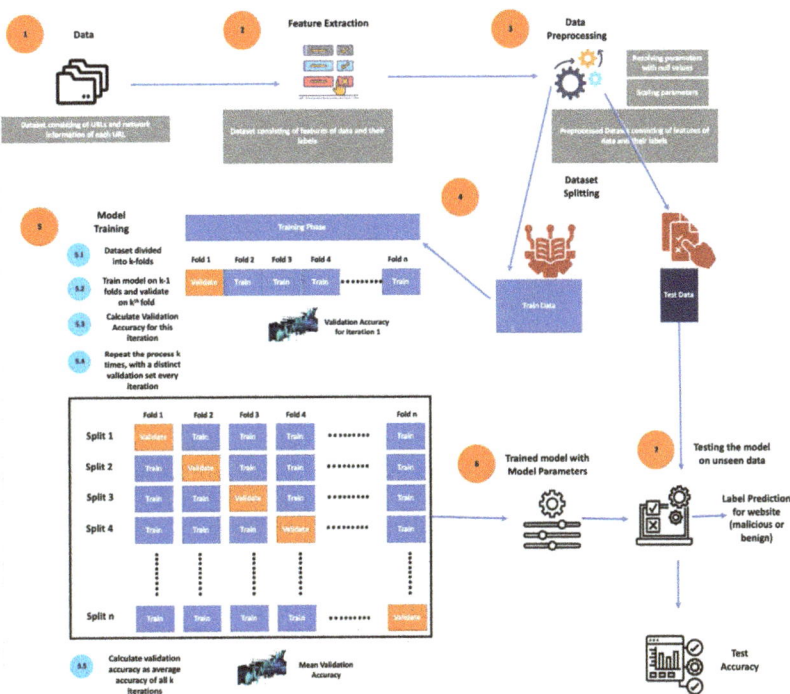

Figure 9. The treatment of data and model training and validation in the current study, using 10-fold cross-validation and different data balancing techniques with various classifiers.

3.6. Evaluation Metrics

Five metrics have been used in this study to gauge the results and compare different methods. The metrics are calculated using the confusion matrix, where true positives (TPs—number of malicious websites identified correctly as malicious by the classifier), true negatives (TNs—number of benign website records identified correctly as benign by the classifier), false positives (FPs—number of benign websites identified incorrectly as malicious by the classifier), and false negatives (FNs—number of malicious websites incorrectly as benign by the classifier) are used to calculate accuracy, precision, recall, F1-score, and false positive rate (FPR) for each classifier.

3.6.1. Accuracy

Accuracy is the ratio of a correct prediction made by the classifier to the total prediction made by the classifier:

$$Accuracy = \frac{TP + TN}{TP + FP + TN + FN} \quad (1)$$

3.6.2. Precision

In precision, we consider the predictions made by our classifier as our baseline:

$$Precision = \frac{TP}{TP + FP} \quad (2)$$

3.6.3. Recall

Recall considers the truth as the baseline and is the ratio of true positives and the total number of positives in the dataset:

$$Recall = \frac{TP}{TP + FN} \quad (3)$$

3.6.4. F1-Score

F1-score is the harmonic mean of the precision and recall:

$$F1 - Score = 2 \times \frac{Precision \times Recall}{Precision + Recall} \quad (4)$$

3.6.5. False Positive Rate (FPR)

The false positive rate (FPR) is the ratio of false positives, and the total negatives present in the dataset:

$$FPR = \frac{FP}{FP + TN} \quad (5)$$

4. Results

This study compares the performance of various classifiers on the "Malicious Websites" dataset to classify which websites are malicious and which are not. The performance of different classifiers was measured using multiple evaluation metrics including accuracy, precision, recall, F1 score, and false positive rate. Since the data was imbalanced, several techniques such as random undersampling, random oversampling, and the SMOTE, were applied to the data for balancing the number of samples for malicious and for benign websites. The results of various classifiers were then computed on balanced and imbalanced data.

4.1. Exploratory Data Analysis

The exploratory data analysis on the "Malicious Websites" dataset revealed some interesting insights about the data. Correlation, which describes the relationship between two or more variables, was utilized to determine the relevant features in the feature set that influence the "Type" variable the most; for example, "APP BYTES" or "REMOTE APP" appear to have little influence on the results since they have a low correlation with the target column [38]. On the other hand, "NUMBER SPECIAL" and "URL LENGTH" appear to have a huge influence on the malicious nature of the websites. The correlation plot for each variable with the target variable "Type" is shown in Figure 10.

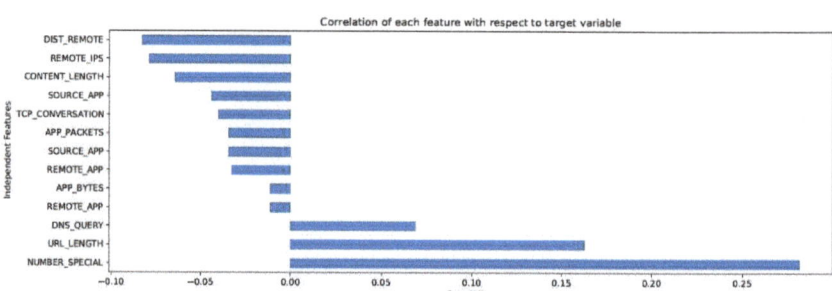

Figure 10. A figure displaying the correlation histogram between different input features and the target "Type" variable.

4.2. Confusion Matrix

The number of true positives, true negatives, false positives, and false negatives are an important indicator of how good the method is performing in various evaluation metrics. Although the ratio is shown via the accuracy, precision, or recall, the raw numbers are also interesting to view. Table 3 displays the count of TPs, TNs, FPs, and FNs.

Table 3. Table displaying the number of true positives (TPs—malicious websites identified as malicious), true negatives (TNs—benign websites identified as benign), false positives (FPs—benign websites identified as malicious), and false negatives (FNs—malicious websites identified as benign by the classifier).

	Imbalanced Data				SMOTE			
Model Name	**TP**	**FP**	**FN**	**TN**	**TP**	**FP**	**FN**	**TN**
Decision Tree	440	20	**23**	51	396	36	21	486
Random Forest	454	6	25	49	407	25	7	**500**
SVC	**460**	0	74	0	281	151	277	230
Logistic Regression	449	0	50	24	**454**	6	74	0
Stochastic Gradient Decent	454	6	74	0	258	174	324	183
	Random Under Sampling				**Random Over Sampling**			
Model Name	**TP**	**FP**	**FN**	**TN**	**TP**	**FP**	**FN**	**TN**
Decision Tree	66	5	9	50	420	20	0	499
Random Forest	**67**	**4**	10	49	**428**	**12**	0	**499**
SVC	30	41	12	47	122	318	66	433
Logistic Regression	48	23	6	53	287	153	42	457
Stochastic Gradient Decent	0	71	**0**	59	202	238	221	278

4.3. Accuracy

Among all the classifiers, random forest shows the highest accuracy, which is 0.97 when data was balanced after applying the oversampling technique. The accuracy scores of different classifiers along with different methods for making the data to be balanced as well as the imbalanced data are shown in Figure 11.

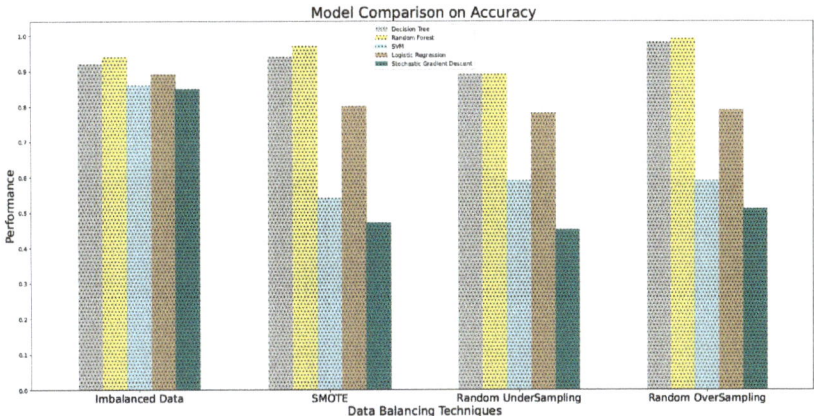

Figure 11. An illustration of performance comparison of different machine learning models on various data balancing techniques using accuracy as the evaluation metric.

4.4. Precision

The highest precision of 0.99 can be achieved by random forest when the oversampling technique for making the data balance is applied. The results of another classifier on different methods including imbalanced data, and data balancing techniques including undersampling, oversampling, and the SMOTE are shown in Figure 12.

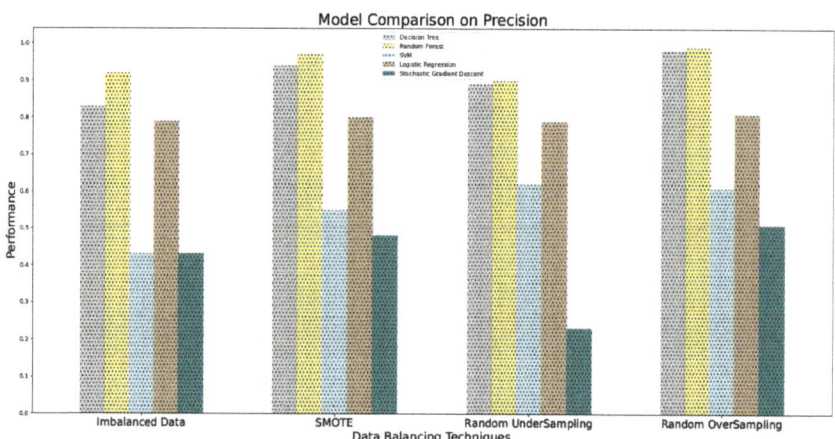

Figure 12. An illustration of performance comparison of different machine learning models on various data balancing techniques using precision as the evaluation metric.

4.5. Recall

Among all of the models, random forest and decision tree give better recall, which is 1 when data was balanced after applying the oversampling. The result of different classifiers on imbalanced data, undersampling, oversampling, and the SMOTE are shown in Figure 13.

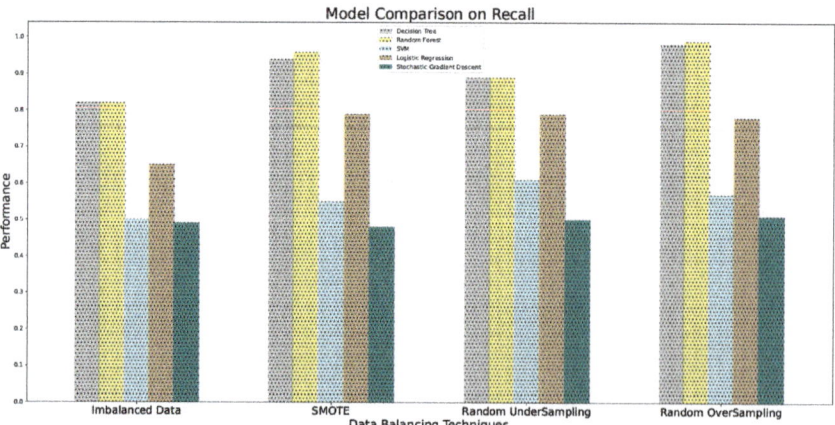

Figure 13. An illustration of performance comparison of different machine learning models on various data balancing techniques using recall as the evaluation metric.

4.6. F1-Score

The highest F1-score can be achieved from random forest when trained on balanced data using the oversampling technique. While the F1-score results of other classifiers along with imbalanced data, and balanced data using undersampling, oversampling, and the SMOTE are mentioned in Figure 14.

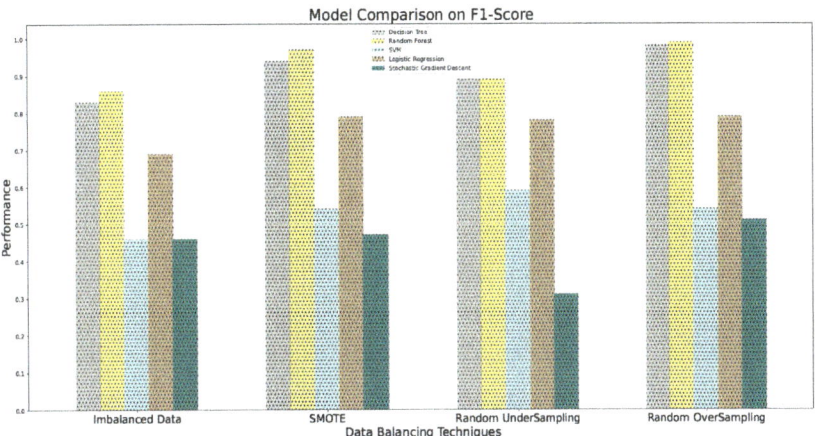

Figure 14. An illustration of performance comparison of different machine learning models on various data balancing techniques using F1-score as the evaluation metric.

4.7. False Positive Rate (FPR)

The FPR is the likelihood of a false alarm being raised: that a positive result will be returned when the true value is negative. So, a lower value of the FPR is always preferred. The logistic regression gives the lowest false positive rate of 0.01 when trained on the imbalanced dataset. However, random forest and stochastic gradient descent give a second lowest false positive rate of 0.05. However, random forest also gives the lowest false error rate of 0.05, when trained on the balanced dataset using the oversampling technique. Figure 15 shows the performance of various classifiers based on the false positive rate (FPR).

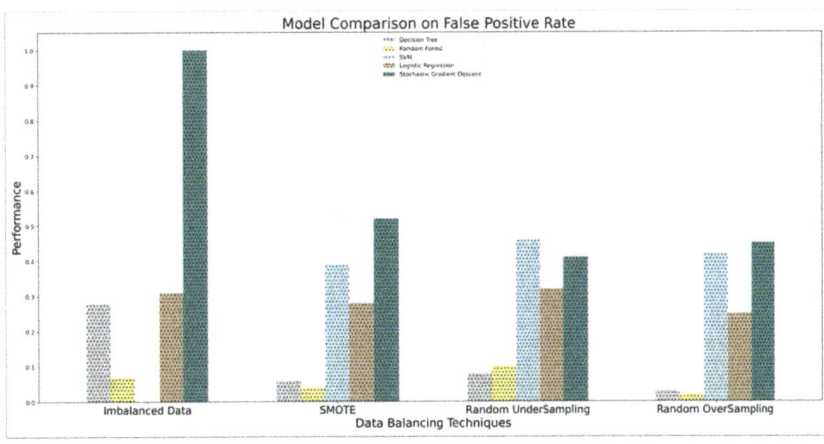

Figure 15. An illustration of performance comparison of different machine learning models on various data balancing techniques using the false positive rate as the evaluation metric.

5. Discussion

This study tested multiple classifiers with a 70/30 training split and 10-fold cross validation for validating the trained models. We first conducted exploratory data analysis to estimate the best features and parameter settings for the machine learning classifiers used in this study. This ensured that the most optimized set of parameters were deployed, and the performance of the current methodology was optimized for the given data set. Multiple machine learning classifiers were also used in this study.

5.1. Using 10-Fold Cross Validation

Using a 10-fold cross-validation approach ensured that the training data and validation data were continually mixed and re-used in training. Hence, the validation took place on the whole data. The final training accuracy is the average accuracy across all validation samples. However, a possible drawback is that the data used for validation is not completely unseen and may not agree with the results when checked on completely unseen data, for example, with the test data. Hence, typically separate test data is always required in the case of the k-fold cross-validation method.

5.2. Using Multiple Data Balancing Techniques

We also tested multiple data balancing techniques to assure that the model does not learn any bias towards a certain class. It also helped us verify the results of various data balancing techniques for the malicious and benign website dataset. The data balancing techniques play an essential role in identifying and removing bias, as otherwise a class that has the greatest number of samples, may dominate the model training. If the model learns best to classify just the majority class, it will by default perform better than a random method, but does not have the ability to work for any other class. This means that the results and performance will be heavily biased towards the majority class only. Hence, to ensure a fair judgement of method performance, data balancing is necessary.

5.3. Evaluation with Multiple Evaluation Metrics

Using multiple evaluation metrics also ensures that the models were evaluated based not only on performance in a specific criterion, but on the overall performance across categories. It also reflected if a particular measure or a particular class affected the results. For example, the accuracy is a measure that consists of ratio of correctly identified malicious and non-malicious websites with the total number of websites. While accuracy alone is an excellent measure of correct classification, note that if the number of malicious websites in the dataset are too few, as compared to the number of benign websites, the accuracy will be dependent on the performance in the negatives mainly. In such a case, a false positive rate (FPR) is a true reflection of system performance. Therefore, we showed performance of each classifier in all five parameters. Each evaluator indicates how the model performs w.r.t. different performance criteria. As is apparent from Figures 11–15, random forest with the SMOTE data balancing technique gives the best results across all five indicators.

5.4. Overall Prospects

Using a completely isolated test dataset, as well as utilizing k-fold cross-validation and data balancing techniques, ensured that overfitting was avoided, and minimum bias towards a specific class was introduced. The method achieved good training and testing accuracy, where the testing accuracy was slightly lower than the training accuracy as expected, since the test dataset is completely unseen for the model while it is somewhat seen for the validation during the training phase.

6. Conclusions

Digital security is one of the paramount concerns in today's digital world, where billions of dollars are lost to digital theft every year. In that aspect, malicious websites are the most common source of digital theft and accurate differentiation between malicious and benign websites is desired. We have used several machine learning algorithms in this study and measured the performance of each algorithm using several evaluation metrics such as F1-score, precision, recall, accuracy, and false positive rate. The machine learning algorithms demonstrated in this work included decision trees, random forest, the SVMs, logistic regression, and stochastic gradient descent. The "Malicious Website" data used in this study is imbalanced and heavily biased toward malicious websites. Therefore, several data balancing techniques were also evaluated in this study to measure their effectiveness. A 10-fold cross-validation technique was used during the training phase to remove any effects of poor sampling. Out of all the machine learning algorithms studied in this work, and with all the data balancing techniques, random forest showed the best results when trained on the dataset after balancing it using the random oversampling technique. It was closely followed by random forest with a balanced dataset using the SMOTE technique. In short, the study demonstrates that the performance of machine learning algorithms is vastly influenced by the data and its properties, and random forest offers a significant performance advantage when used with a balanced dataset.

Author Contributions: Conceptualization, R.H.A.; formal analysis, I.U.H.; investigation, T.A.K.; methodology, R.K.; software, Z.U.A.; writing—original draft preparation, I.U.H.; writing—review and editing, R.H.A. and T.A.K.; visualization, Z.U.A.; supervision, R.K.; project administration, R.K. All authors have read and agreed to the published version of the manuscript.

Funding: This research received no external funding.

Institutional Review Board Statement: Not applicable.

Informed Consent Statement: Not applicable.

Data Availability Statement: The data is publicly available and can be found at the Kaggle website https://www.kaggle.com/code/angadchau/maliciousurldetection/data (accessed on 31 August 2022).

Conflicts of Interest: The authors declare no conflict of interest.

References

1. Gopal, B.G.; Kuppusamy, P.G. A comparative study on 4G and 5G technology for wireless applications. *IOSR J. Electron. Commun. Eng.* **2015**, *10*, 2278–2834.
2. Piroșcă, G.I.; Șerban-Oprescu, G.L.; Badea, L.; Stanef-Puică, M.-R.; Valdebenito, C.R. Digitalization and labor market—A perspective within the framework of pandemic crisis. *J. Theor. Appl. Electron. Commer. Res.* **2021**, *16*, 2843–2857. [CrossRef]
3. Pandey, N.; Pal, A. Impact of digital surge during COVID-19 pandemic: A viewpoint on research and practice. *Int. J. Inf. Manag.* **2020**, *55*, 102171.
4. Desolda, G.; Ferro, L.S.; Marrella, A.; Catarci, T.; Costabile, M.F. Human factors in phishing attacks: A systematic literature review. *ACM Comput. Surv. (CSUR)* **2021**, *54*, 1–35. [CrossRef]
5. Rupa, C.; Srivastava, G.; Bhattacharya, S.; Reddy, P.; Gadekallu, T.R. A machine learning driven threat intelligence system for malicious url detection. In Proceedings of the 16th International Conference on Availability, Reliability and Security, Vienna, Austria, 17–20 August 2021; pp. 1–7.
6. Aksu, D.; Turgut, Z.; Üstebay, S.; Aydin, M.A. Phishing analysis of websites using classification techniques. In Proceedings of the ITelCon 2017, Istanbul, Turkey, 28–29 December 2017; Springer: Singapore, 2019; pp. 251–258.
7. Naveen, I.N.V.D.; Manamohana, K.; Verma, R. Detection of malicious URLs using machine learning techniques. *Int. J. Innov. Technol. Explor. Eng.* **2019**, *8*, 389–393.
8. Vanitha, N.; Vinodhini, V. Malicious-url detection using logistic regression technique. *Int. J. Eng. Manag. Res.* **2019**, *9*, 108–113.
9. Kaddoura, S. Classification of malicious and benign websites by network features using supervised machine learning algorithms. In Proceedings of the 2021 5th Cyber Security in Networking Conference (CSNet), Abu Dhabi, United Arab Emirates, 12–14 October 2021; pp. 36–40.
10. Odeh, A.; Keshta, I.; Abdelfattah, E. Machine learningtechniquesfor detection of website phishing: A review for promises and challenges. In Proceedings of the 2021 IEEE 11th Annual Computing and Communication Workshop and Conference (CCWC), Virtual, 27–30 January 2021; pp. 813–818.
11. Chaganti, S.Y.; Nanda, I.; Pandi, K.R.; Prudhvith, T.G.; Kumar, N. Image classification using SVM and CNN. In Proceedings of the 2020 International Conference on Computer Science, Engineering and Applications (ICCSEA), Gunupur, India, 13–14 March 2020; pp. 1–5.
12. Singh, N.; Chaturvedi, S.; Akhter, S. Weather forecasting using machine learning algorithm. In Proceedings of the 2019 International Conference on Signal Processing and Communication (ICSC), Noida, India, 7–9 March 2019; pp. 171–174.
13. Gegic, E.; Isakovic, B.; Keco, D.; Masetic, Z.; Kevric, J. Car price prediction using machine learning techniques. *TEM J.* **2019**, *8*, 113.
14. Vijh, M.; Chandola, D.; Tikkiwal, V.A.; Kumar, A. Stock closing price prediction using machine learning techniques. *Procedia Comput. Sci.* **2020**, *167*, 599–606. [CrossRef]
15. Alfeilat, H.A.A.; Hassanat, A.B.A.; Lasassmeh, O.; Tarawneh, A.S.; Alhasanat, M.B.; Salman, H.S.E.; Prasath, V.B.S. Effects of distance measure choice on k-nearest neighbor classifier performance: A review. *Big Data* **2019**, *7*, 221–248. [CrossRef]
16. Zendehboudi, A.; Baseer, M.A.; Saidur, R. Application of support vector machine models for forecasting solar and wind energy resources: A review. *J. Clean. Prod.* **2018**, *199*, 272–285. [CrossRef]
17. Charbuty, B.; Abdulazeez, A. Classification based on decision tree algorithm for machine learning. *J. Appl. Sci. Technol. Trends* **2021**, *2*, 20–28. [CrossRef]

18. Christodoulou, E.; Ma, J.; Collins, G.S.; Steyerberg, E.W.; Verbakel, J.Y.; van Calster, B. A systematic review shows no performance benefit of machine learning over logistic regression for clinical prediction models. *J. Clin. Epidemiol.* **2019**, *110*, 12–22. [CrossRef] [PubMed]
19. Halimaa, A.; Sundarakantham, K. Machine learning based intrusion detection system. In Proceedings of the 2019 3rd International Conference on Trends in Electronics and Informatics (ICOEI), Tirunelveli, India, 23–25 April 2019; pp. 916–920.
20. Hossin, M.; Sulaiman, M.N. A review on evaluation metrics for data classification evaluations. *Int. J. Data Min. Knowl. Manag. Process* **2015**, *5*, 1.
21. Kaur, H.; Pannu, H.S.; Malhi, A.K. A systematic review on imbalanced data challenges in machine learning: Applications and solutions. *ACM Comput. Surv. (CSUR)* **2019**, *52*, 1–36. [CrossRef]
22. Fernández, A.; García, S.; Galar, M.; Prati, R.C.; Krawczyk, B.; Herrera, F. *Learning from Imbalanced Data Sets*; Springer: Cham, Switzerland, 2018; Volume 10.
23. Brandt, J.; Lanzén, E. A Comparative Review of SMOTE and ADASYN in Imbalanced Data Classification. Bachelor's Thesis, Uppsala University, Uppsala, Sweden, 2021.
24. Singhal, S.; Chawla, U. Machine learning & concept drift based approach for malicious website detection. In Proceedings of the 2020 International Conference on COMmunication Systems & NETworkS (COMSNETS), Bengaluru, India, 7–11 January 2020; pp. 2020–2023.
25. Amrutkar, C.; Kim, Y.S.; Traynor, P.; Member, S. Detecting mobile malicious webpages in real time. *IEEE Trans. Mob. Comput.* **2017**, *16*, 2184–2197. [CrossRef]
26. Iv, J.M. A comprehensive evaluation of HTTP header features for detecting malicious websites. In Proceedings of the 2019 15th European Dependable Computing Conference (EDCC), Naples, Italy, 17–20 September 2019. [CrossRef]
27. Patil, D.R.; Patil, J.B. Malicious URLs detection using decision tree classifiers and majority voting technique. *Cybern. Inf. Technol.* **2018**, *18*, 11–29. [CrossRef]
28. Al-milli, N. A Convolutional neural network model to detect illegitimate URLs. In Proceedings of the 2020 11th International Conference on Information and Communication Systems (ICICS), Irbid, Jordan, 7–9 April 2020; pp. 220–225.
29. Jayakanthan, N.; Ramani, A.V.; Ravichandran, M. Two phase classification model to detect malicious URLs. *Int. J. Appl. Eng. Res.* **2017**, *12*, 1893–1898.
30. Assefa, A.; Katarya, R. Intelligent phishing website detection using deep learning. In Proceedings of the 2022 8th International Conference on Advanced Computing and Communication Systems (ICACCS), Coimbatore, India, 25–26 March 2022; pp. 1741–1745.
31. Vinayakumar, R.; Soman, K.P.; Poornachandran, P. Evaluating deep learning approaches to characterize and classify malacious URL's. *J. Intell. Fuzzy Syst.* **2022**, *34*, 1333–1343. [CrossRef]
32. Vazhayil, A.; Vinayakumar, R.; Soman, K.P. Comparative study of the detection of malicious URLs using shallow and deep networks. In Proceedings of the 2018 9th International Conference on Computing, Communication and Networking Technologies (ICCCNT), Bengaluru, India, 10–12 July 2018; pp. 1–6.
33. Somvanshi, M.; Chavan, P.; Tambade, S.; Shinde, S.V. A review of machine learning techniques using decision tree and support vector machine. In Proceedings of the 2016 International Conference on Computing Communication Control and Automation (ICCUBEA), Pune, India, 12–13 August 2016; pp. 1–7.
34. More, A.S.; Rana, D.P. Review of random forest classification techniques to resolve data imbalance. In Proceedings of the 2017 1st International Conference on Intelligent Systems and Information Management (ICISIM), Aurangabad, India, 5–6 October 2017; pp. 72–78.
35. Wang, Y. A multinomial logistic regression modeling approach for anomaly intrusion detection. *Comput. Secur.* **2005**, *24*, 662–674. [CrossRef]
36. Cervantes, J.; Garcia-Lamont, F.; Rodríguez-Mazahua, L.; Lopez, A. A comprehensive survey on support vector machine classification: Applications, challenges and trends. *Neurocomputing* **2020**, *408*, 189–215. [CrossRef]
37. Deepa, N.; Prabadevi, B.; Maddikunta, P.K.; Gadekallu, T.R.; Baker, T.; Khan, M.A.; Tariq, U. An AI-based intelligent system for healthcare analysis using Ridge-Adaline Stochastic Gradient Descent Classifier. *J. Supercomput.* **2021**, *77*, 1998–2017. [CrossRef]
38. Kumar, S.; Chong, I. Correlation analysis to identify the effective data in machine learning: Prediction of depressive disorder and emotion states. *Int. J. Environ. Res. Public Health* **2018**, *15*, 2907. [CrossRef] [PubMed]

Article
Explicit and Implicit Trust Modeling for Recommendation [†]

Utku Demirci and Pinar Karagoz *

Department of Computer Engineering, Middle East Technical University (METU), Ankara 06800, Turkey; utku.demirci@ceng.metu.edu.tr
* Correspondence: karagoz@ceng.metu.edu.tr; Tel.: +90-312-210-5518
† This paper is an extended version of our paper published in Demirci, U.; Karagoz, P. Trust Modeling in Recommendation: Explicit and Implicit Trust Model Compatibility and Explicit Trust Prediction. In Proceedings of the 13th International Conference on Management of Digital EcoSystems (MEDES'21), Hammamet, Tunisia, 1–3 November 2021.

Citation: Demirci, U.; Karagoz, P. Explicit and Implicit Trust Modeling for Recommendation. *Digital* 2022, 2, 444–462. https://doi.org/10.3390/digital2040024

Academic Editors: Yannis Manolopoulos, Mirjana Ivanović and Richard Chbeir

Received: 3 August 2022
Accepted: 24 September 2022
Published: 29 September 2022

Publisher's Note: MDPI stays neutral with regard to jurisdictional claims in published maps and institutional affiliations.

Copyright: © 2022 by the authors. Licensee MDPI, Basel, Switzerland. This article is an open access article distributed under the terms and conditions of the Creative Commons Attribution (CC BY) license (https://creativecommons.org/licenses/by/4.0/).

Abstract: Recommendation has become an inseparable component of many software applications, such as e-commerce, social media and gaming platforms. Particularly in collaborative filtering-based recommendation solutions, the preferences of other users are considered heavily. At this point, *trust* among the users comes into the scene as an important concept to improve the recommendation performance. Trust describes the nature and the strength of ties between individuals and hence provides useful information to improve the recommendation accuracy, particularly against *data sparsity* and *cold start* problems. The *Trust* notion helps alleviate the effect of these problems by providing additional reliable relationships between the users. However, trust information, specifically *explicit trust*, is not straightforward to collect and is only scarcely available. Therefore, *implicit* trust models have been proposed to fill in the gap. The literature includes a variety of studies proposing the use of trust for recommendation. In this work, two specific sub-problems are elaborated on: the relationship between explicit and implicit trust scores, and the construction of a machine learning model for explicit trust. For the first sub-problem, an implicit trust model is devised and the compatibility of implicit trust scores with explicit scores is analyzed. For the second sub-problem, two different explicit trust models are proposed: Explicit trust modeling through users' rating behavior and explicit trust modeling as a link prediction problem. The performances of the prediction models are analyzed on a set of benchmark data sets. It is observed that explicit and implicit trust models have different natures, and are to be used in a complementary way for recommendation. Another important result is that the accuracy of the machine learning models for explicit trust is promising and depends on the availability of data.

Keywords: trust modeling; implicit trust; explicit trust; recommendation; recommender systems; supervised learning; one class classification

1. Introduction

Recommendation has become an indispensable part of software systems, particularly e-commerce and online streaming applications such as Spotify (spotify.com) and Netflix (netflix.com), alleviating the load of search for users in a vast item collection and positively affecting the perception of the users about the applications through improved user experience [1]. Recommender systems process user history to generate recommendations. One way of obtaining a user' previous experience on an item is through explicit ratings. As an alternative way, implicit rating indirectly provides information about the user's opinion on an item, based on activities of the user such as clicking, searching some keywords, purchases, etc., and gives hints for the user's intent and interest [2]. The Collaborative Filtering (CF) method [3], being a popular recommendation technique, uses the similarity between past preferences of users. However, CF suffers from well-known *data sparsity* and *cold start* problems. In order to overcome the performance degrading due to such problems, recommender systems employ a variety of auxiliary information including product details of the items, social network of users or external contextual information such as weather or currency rate [4].

In social relationships, concepts such as *trust* and *loyalty* are important and useful to describe and quantify the nature of the relationship between users [1]. Loyalty expresses the strength of the tie between a user and an object or environment, whereas trust is merely about the relationship between the users in an environment, such as a social network. In recommendation methods, specifically in CF, these concepts provide valuable information to improve recommendation performance, and hence it has been used within recommender systems in the literature mostly to overcome the aforementioned issues of CF. Particularly, trust information helps to reduce the data sparsity through enrichment with the ratings of trusted neighbors. It is also useful against the cold start problem as the preferences of trusted neighbors or trusted users, in general, can provide a basis for recommendation.

In trust-aware recommendation studies, two types of trust data are used: *explicit* and *implicit trust*. Explicit trust is obtained through user feedback on other users. A well-known example is Epinions (http://www.epinions.com/help/faq/?show=faq_wot, accessed on 3 August 2022), which is a website of product reviews. It uses a trust system such that users can define their *web of Trust*, which is a set of reviewers whose reviews and ratings are consistently found to be useful, and their *block list*, which includes reviewers that a user consistently finds inaccurate or not useful (http://www.trustlet.org/epinions.html, accessed on 3 August 2022). The data set crawled from The Epinions website, namely *epinions data set*, has been popularly used as explicit trust data in various studies [5–8]. Explicit trust networks can be *unsigned*, including only positive trust links, or *signed*, where both negative and positive trust links are available.

On the other hand, *implicit trust* provides information about the trust relationship between users indirectly, generally through activities and behavior of users [5,9]. Since explicit trust information is scarcely available, and it is mostly sparse, several studies focus on generating implicit trust by using other data sources such as the rating data and social connection of users [10]. For example, in [11], interest similarity is used for inferring trust between two users, whereas in [9], trust propagation over a social network is employed for constructing the trust network of a given user.

Research Questions. Trust information has been used in a variety of recommendation studies both in explicit and implicit form and it has been shown that it improves recommendation accuracy [9,12,13]. In this work, focusing on a different aspect of trust-aware recommendation, the following two sub-problems of explicit and implicit trust are analyzed in the recommendation setting:

- What is the relationship between explicit and implicit trust scores? Are they replaceable?
- Would it be possible to construct a machine learning model of the explicit trust in a trust network feasibly?

The first one is about examining the compatibility between explicit and implicit trust scores. For this analysis, an implicit trust model is devised, and by using this implicit trust model, the matching between implicit and explicit trust scores is analyzed. This analysis is crucial for understanding the nature of implicit and explicit trust and using them in either a complementary way or as a replacement.

The second sub-problem is about constructing a machine learning model for explicit trust in order to predict missing trust relationships in a trust network. In this way, the data sparsity in explicit trust information can be reduced. There are two types of explicit trust networks: an *unsigned* network with only positive links and a *signed* trust network with negative and positive links. In an unsigned trust matrix, trust information is explicitly expressed as 1 to denote trust. However, 0 as the trust value may indicate either a neutral or unknown trust relationship. For this, two different explicit trust models are generated. In the first model, users' rating behavior is exploited for explicit trust modeling. A trust graph is generated in the second approach, and the problem is specified as a link prediction problem. In the graph model, trust value 1 in the matrix denotes a link, whereas trust value 0 shows that there is no edge between the given nodes (i.e., users). It is aimed to predict the missing trust relationships in the trust graph by constructing an explicit trust model. The effect of augmenting the trust matrix through the proposed approach is analyzed through trust-based recommendation methods in the literature.

Contributions. A preliminary version of the study is published in [14]. In this paper, the study is extended both with more detailed explanations and discussions, and additional machine learning models, algorithms and their analysis. For the explicit and implicit trust model comparison part, the approach and analyses are described in more detail. Similarly, in explicit trust modeling, descriptions of the proposed approaches are given with additional explanations. As a new modeling approach in this paper, unsupervised machine learning algorithms are applied for explicit trust modeling, and an outlier detection-based model is developed based on Isolation Forest and One-Class Support Vector Machine (SVM). Additionally, the explicit trust model is constructed by SVM in addition to Random Forest and Naive Bayes classifier. For all the experiments, the results are further discussed and elaborated on.

The contributions of this study can be summarized as follows:

- An implicit trust model is devised, which is adapted from the consistency model for reputation scores of users in [15]. This model is used for compatibility analysis of implicit and explicit scores.
- The implicit trust model generates a single score per user. In contrast, the available explicit trust data sets inform about the trust relationship between two users. To overcome this incompatibility, a mapping schema is proposed such that an explicit trust score per user is generated by using the explicit trust graph.
- A supervised learning model is constructed for explicit trust score prediction by using the ratings that users give to model explicit trust data. This method is used for both signed and unsigned trust data.
- Another explicit trust score prediction model is constructed such that finding an explicit trust between two users is considered an edge prediction problem and a supervised learning model is generated to predict unknown trust values. The effectiveness of an augmented trust network is analyzed through recommendation performance.

Organization. The rest of the paper is organized as follows. In Section 2, related studies in the literature are summarized. The methods proposed and employed in this study are presented in Section 3. The experiments and results are presented in Section 4. Finally, Section 5 concludes the paper with an overview and future work.

2. Literature Review

Trust-aware recommendation is a challenging research problem and there is a variety of solutions that focus on the use of the trust information to improve the accuracy of recommendations, particularly alleviating cold start and rating data sparsity problems.

As one of the initial trust-based studies, in [11], Htun and Tar consider trust as a solution to cold-start problems in recommender systems. To this aim, explicit trust ratings are used for neighbor formation. Since reliable explicit trust data is rarely available, the authors propose a method to derive implicit trust relationships based on the similarity of user interests. Trust between users is measured according to the following similarity measures: user interest similarity, resource item similarity, and interest similarity on resource items. The resulting trust metric is incorporated into the recommender system. The performance of the proposed approach is reported to outperform traditional CF.

In [16], Chen et al. propose a cold start recommendation method that integrates the user model with trust and distrust for each new user. With the proposed approach, trustworthy users can be identified by analyzing the web of trust of experienced users. In the proposed method, a user model is constructed by using a clustering algorithm to group experienced users into clusters. Each cluster is formed with users that have similar item preferences. A web of trust is constructed for each cluster and the PageRank algorithm is used for finding experienced users in the cluster. The authors use distrust networks to find unreliable users in a similar way. Following this, the most closely related cluster is identified for a cold start new user to predict an unrated item's possible rating. Previously identified experienced users in the cluster are exploited to recommend new cold-start users. Moreover, the proposed method identifies implicit trust links between users by exploiting the given rating.

In another study [13], Guo et al. propose three factored similarity models that use social trust based on implicit user feedback. The proposed trust-based recommendation approach generates top-N item recommendations based on social trust relationships between users. In [17], the authors develop another trust-based recommender that uses explicitly specified social trust information for generating recommendations. The method merges the ratings of a user's trusted neighbors in order to find similar users.

In [12], Yang et al. propose TrustMF, a matrix factorization-based method that fuses rating and trust information. TrustMF defines two models: the *truster* model which denotes how others will affect user u's preferences and the *trustee* model which denotes how user u will affect others' preferences. The main motivation for the use of truster and trustee models is to link ratings and trust information.

In order to overcome accuracy issues due to cold start and data sparsity, in [9], Li et al. propose an implicit trust recommendation approach (ITRA) that utilizes implicit user information. The method generates a set of trusted neighbors of a given user by exploiting the social network and trust diffusion features in a trust network. After finding the trust neighbor set, trust values are determined by computing the shortest distance between a user and inferred trusted neighbor.

In [18], Wang et al. introduce TeCF, a trust-enhanced collaborative filtering method that integrates user-based, item-based, and trust-based techniques to predict unrated items. The conducted experiments show that the proposed approach significantly reduces the effects of data sparsity by making the rating matrix denser.

The trust model of the SSL-SVD method in [5] incorporates social trust (explicit trust) and sparse trust (implicit trust) information to improve recommendation accuracy. In the study, Hu et al. report that social trust is influenced by many social factors and has a limited effect on improving the accuracy of recommendations.

In recent studies, neural network-based solutions are also employed in trust-aware recommender systems. In [19], a trust network is used in order to determine reliable implicit ratings of users. Once the rating profile of a user is augmented with such ratings, latent features of users are derived by using a deep representation model. The recommendation is generated based on the similarity of users through their latent feature representations.

As seen in the above-mentioned studies, the nature of trust information used in the recommendation and how it is incorporated varies; however, it is reported that overall the use of trust information has a positive effect on recommendation performance. In this study, another aspect of the use of trust modeling in the recommendation is focused on. The nature of implicit and explicit trust modeling and their compatibility are analyzed to further increase this positive effect.

3. Proposed Methods for Trust Modeling and Comparison

In this section, the compatibility analysis of explicit and implicit trust models, and generating explicit trust prediction models are described in detail. The symbols used in the formulas are given in Table 1.

Table 1. The list of symbols.

Notation	Explanation
u	User
r	Rating
m	Item
R_u	Set of ratings by user u
r_m	Average rating of item m
r_u	Average of the ratings given by user u
$r_u m$	The rating given by user u to item m
O_u	Conformity of user u
$O_{r_{um}}$	Conformity of rating r by user u for item m
C_u	Consistency of user u
s_m	Standard deviation of ratings for item m

3.1. Compatibility Analysis of Explicit and Implicit Trust Models

In the literature, trust information is reported to improve the quality of recommendation accuracy [20]. However, explicit trust data is scarcely available. Therefore, there are studies inferring implicit trust between the users and the trust value of a user from other sources, such as the behavior of the user. However, the relationship between explicit and implicit trust is not always clear and the number of studies focusing on such analysis is limited [5]. Thus, in this work, it is investigated how compatible implicit and explicit trust scores are. This analysis is crucial to be able to understand whether these two models have an overlapping or complementary nature.

The overview of the proposed approach for the compatibility analysis is shown in Figure 1. As the first step, the implicit trust score model is constructed using the rating data of users, and implicit trust scores are generated for each user with this model. In parallel, explicit trust scores are generated for each user based on explicit trust data. Finally, the top-k elements of both lists are compared for the compatibility check.

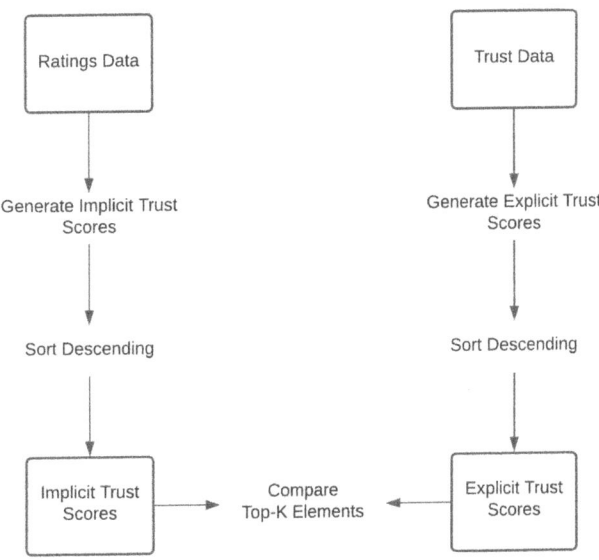

Figure 1. Overview of the process of analyzing the compatibility of the implicit and explicit scores.

3.1.1. Implicit Trust Model

Trust and reputation are important concepts in social network analysis, as in recommendation. In [15], Oh and Kim introduce the mathematical models for *activity*, *objectivity*, and *consistency* of social media users. These are used for calculating the reputation scores of users.

In this work, the features presented in [15] are adapted for generating the implicit trust scores of users (a similar adaptation of Oh and Kim's features in [15] for calculation of implicit trust scores for location-based social networks is also presented in [21]. In this study, these mathematical models are adapted for rating data). In the proposed implicit trust model, users with a high count of ratings (above a given threshold) are considered as *active* users. The conformity of a rating, $O_{r_{um}}$, is a measure of whether a rating r by user u on item m differs from the average rating on item m (denoted as $\bar{r}_m$). s_m denotes the standard deviation of the ratings on item m. Conformity of a given rating increases as $O_{r_{um}}$ approaches zero (Equation (1)).

$$O_{r_{um}} = \left| \frac{r_{um} - \bar{r}_m}{s_m} \right| \tag{1}$$

The conformity of user, O_u, is the average of ratings, $O_{r_{um}}$, by user u. As in the rating conformity, as the value gets closer to zero, the conformity of the user is considered to be higher (Equation (2)). Here, R_u denotes the number of ratings by user u.

$$O_u = \frac{1}{|R_u|} \sum O_{r_{um}} \tag{2}$$

If the user u behaves similarly to other users in the system, it can be inferred that the user's behavior is consistent. The consistency of a user, C_u, is defined as the variation in conformity of her/his own evaluations (Equation (3)). In the proposed approach, the C_u score of a user u is used as the *implicit trust score*.

$$C_u = \frac{1}{|R_u|} \sum_{r \in R_u} (O_r - O_u)^2 \tag{3}$$

3.1.2. Construction of Explicit Trust Score per User

The implicit trust model generates a trust score per user. On the other hand, explicit trust in the network is not a per-user score, it rather indicates the trust relationship between two users. To provide compatibility between implicit and explicit trust models, a mapping schema is defined that generates an explicit trust score per user from the explicit trust graph.

The proposed mapping schema is as follows: given a user in an *unsigned* trust network, the number of incoming trust edges is determined as the explicit trust score per user. For *signed* networks, the number of incoming edges with weight 1 denotes the trust score per user. Similarly, the number of incoming edges with weight −1 is the *distrust score* of the user. For example, for an unsigned trust network, if the node of *usera* has 10 incoming edges, this denotes that 10 users trust this user. Then, the explicit trust score of *usera* is set as 10.

As an alternative mapping schema, the well-known PageRank algorithm [22] is used. In order to generate a trust score per user, the PageRank algorithm is applied to the trust network. This scoring also gives the ranking of the users in the trust network, which is used for comparison with implicit trust score ranking. Although there are several other personalized node ranking algorithms proposed for signed networks in the literature [23], in this study, the conventional PageRank algorithm is used for both unsigned and signed trust networks.

3.1.3. Comparison of Explicit and Implicit Trust Scores

After generating the implicit and explicit trust scores per user, a comparison schema is applied to them. Each set of scores is sorted separately in descending order. The compatibility of the implicit and explicit scores is analyzed as the overlapping of users on top-k% items between the sorted implicit and explicit trust scores. The analysis results conducted on three data sets are presented and discussed in Section 4.3.

3.2. Explicit Trust Modeling

The basic motivation for constructing a supervised explicit trust model is to be able to estimate the unknown values in the explicit trust matrix and augment the trust graph, thus increasing the accuracy of trust-based recommendation. Two different approaches are proposed for explicit trust modeling. In the first one, explicit trust is modeled by using rating behavior. In the second approach, an explicit trust network is created, and missing links between users are aimed to be determined with link prediction.

3.2.1. Explicit Trust Modeling through Rating Behavior

The proposed approach aims to construct a supervised learning model to predict explicit trust scores by using rating information-based features. The explicit trust predictions are used for augmenting the available explicit trust data. The overview of the proposed approach is shown in Figure 2.

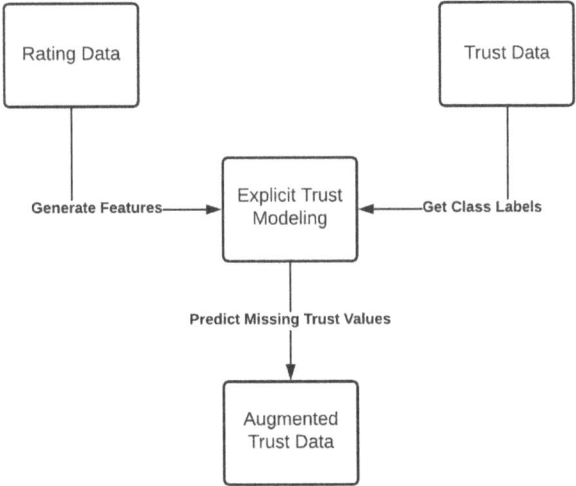

Figure 2. Overview of the process of explicit trust modeling through user's rating behavior.

In this approach, the problem is considered a classification task. Therefore, a set of features are generated for each explicit trust relationship by using the ratings given by the users. While generating those features, the concepts of *liked item* and *disliked item* are considered. The definition of these concepts is given in Equation (4). Here, r_{um} denotes the rating of the user u for item m, and r_u denotes the average rating for user u.

$$isItemLiked = \begin{cases} True, & \text{if } r_{um} \geq r_u \\ False, & \text{otherwise} \end{cases} \quad (4)$$

As reflected in the equation, an average rating score is created for each user by checking the ratings given by the user. Then, the rating given to an item by the target user and the average rating score of the user is compared. If the rating given to the item is greater than or equal to the average rating score of the user, the item is considered to be a *liked item*, otherwise, it is considered as a *disliked item*. The procedure is described in Algorithm 1. For instance, suppose a user gives the ratings of 1.0, 2.0, 5.0 to the movies a, b, and c, respectively. Since the average rating of the user is 3.0, it is considered that the user disliked movies a and b and liked the movie c.

Algorithm 1 Discovering Liked and Disliked Items for Each User

U: a set of users
R: a set of ratings
procedure DISCOVERLIKEDANDDISLIKEDITEMS(U, R)
    Build R_u, a list of ratings given by each user u using U and R
    for each user u in R **do**
        Calculate average rating a_u for u
        for each rating r in R_u **do**
            if $r \geq a_u$ **then**
                rated item is a liked item for user u
            else
                rated item is a disliked item for user u
            end if
        end for
    end for
end procedure

Given two users, the target model aims to predict the nature of the trust between them. Given two users, trustor and trustee, the features constructed over them for the supervised learning model are as follows:

- The number of mutual rated items;
- The number of mutual liked items;
- The number of mutual disliked items;
- The average of the ratings given by the trustor;
- The number of the ratings given by the trustor;
- The average of the ratings given by the trustee;
- The number of the ratings given by the trustee.

For each user, separate lists are created for the rated items, liked items, and disliked items. By scanning these lists, the intersection of rated, liked, and disliked items between two users can be found easily.

The explicit trust value between two users is the class label in each trust relationship. However, the value of the class label varies depending on whether the trust network is signed or unsigned. Hence, the model construction follows two different mechanisms:

- For the signed trust network, the class labels are 1 and -1. In this case, the problem can be considered a binary classification problem. For modeling signed explicit trust data, SVM, Random Forest, and Naive Bayes classifier algorithms are used. These supervised learning algorithms are preferred since they have been successfully applied for prediction problems in a variety of domains.
- The class labels are slightly different for unsigned trust networks. Since there is no distrust information in such data, every relationship in the network is expressed with 1. In this case, the problem is considered an outlier/novelty detection or a one-class classification problem. Isolation Forest and One-class SVM algorithms are used for modeling unsigned explicit trust data.

In both of the cases, new trust relationships are predicted with these models, and the explicit trust network is updated with the predicted trust relationships. The effect of updated/augmented trust networks is analyzed through various trust-based recommendation algorithms. The related experiments are described in Section 4.4.

3.2.2. Trust Prediction Modeling as a Link Prediction Problem

For explicit trust modeling, another approach is also devised such that the problem is considered as an edge (link) prediction task on the directed trust network. More specifically, a supervised learning model is built for the *inference of explicit trust* between users by using features extracted from the trust network. The process is visualized in Figure 3.

In this classification task, the edges correspond to class labels. For unsigned trust networks, an edge denotes a trust relationship, and it is represented with *class label 1*. The rest of the (non-existing) edges in the graph are assumed to correspond to *class label 0*. For signed trust networks, the setting has a slight difference such that the edges are labeled (signed) as either 1 or −1, denoting trust or distrust, respectively.

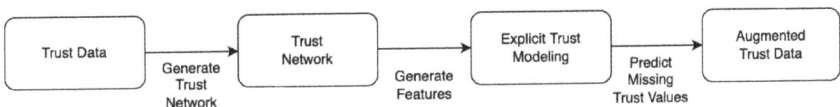

Figure 3. Overview of the process of trust prediction modeling as a link prediction problem.

To determine a balanced set of training instances, links with 0 labels are randomly included in as many as the number of trust links. On the unsigned trust graph, for each edge, the following features are extracted:

- Jaccard similarity for destination (trustee) and source (trustor) nodes;
- Cosine similarity for destination and source nodes;
- Katz centrality for destination and source nodes;
- Adar Index [24] for destination and source nodes;
- Number of nodes that trust the source node;
- Number of nodes that trust the destination node;
- Number of nodes that the source node trusts;
- Number of nodes that the destination node trusts;
- Intersection of the nodes that trust source and destination nodes;
- Intersection of the nodes that both source and destination nodes trust;
- Trust back;
- The shortest trust path between nodes.

As given in the list, a total of 12 features are extracted from the trust graph. Among the features given above, *Adar Index* is a measure to predict links in a network by using the shared links between two nodes. *Trust back* is a binary field that denotes whether the destination node trusts the source node back or not. For calculating the shortest trust path between nodes, firstly, if they have been already connected, the link between them is deleted. Then, the shortest path between the nodes is computed.

Before constructing the supervised learning model, feature elimination is applied by using Extra-Trees Classifier [25] and Jaccard similarity, Cosine similarity, Katz centrality, and Adar Index features are filtered out. As the supervised learning algorithms, Random Forest Classifier and SVM Classifier are employed [25] to construct the explicit trust model.

4. Experiments

4.1. Data Sets and Experiment Environment

The experiments are conducted on MacOS Catalina, Intel(R) Core(TM) i5 CPU @1.4 GHz, 16 GB of RAM. The proposed methods are coded in Python programming language by using scikit-learn [25], and RecQ [26] frameworks.

For the analysis, Epinions (Unsigned) [27], Epinions (Signed) [28], FilmTrust [29], and Ciao [30] data sets are used. All of those data sets are frequently used for recommendation systems analysis, specifically in trust-based systems. The statistical details about the data sets are given in Table 2. FilmTrust is a platform that allows its users to evaluate the movies they watch. Epinions is a social networking site where users can share their opinions about various products and express their trust network. Ciao is a product review and online shopping portal that contains trust relationships between users.

Table 2. Statistics on the data sets.

	# of Users	# of Items	# of Ratings
FilmTrust	1508	2071	35,497
Epinions (Unsigned)	75,888	29,000	681,213
Epinions (Signed)	132,492	755,760	13,668,320
Ciao	7375	105,114	284,086

4.2. Evaluation Metrics

In this study, the following metrics are used for measuring prediction performance.

Accuracy measures the proportion of correct predictions among the total number of predictions (Equation (5)).

$$Accuracy = \frac{True\ Positive + True\ Negative}{All\ Predictions} \quad (5)$$

Precision measures the number of positive class predictions that actually belong to the positive class (Equation (6)).

$$Precision = \frac{True\ Positive}{True\ Positive + False\ Positive} \quad (6)$$

Recall measures the number of positive class predictions made from all positive samples (Equation (7)).

$$Recall = \frac{True\ Positive}{True\ Positive + False\ Negative} \quad (7)$$

F1-score provides a single score that balances both precision and recall as their harmonic mean in one score (Equation (8)).

$$F1 = 2 * \frac{Precision * Recall}{Precision + Recall} \quad (8)$$

Outlier Ratio shows how many samples in the test data are determined as outliers (Equation (9)).

$$Outlier\ Ratio = \frac{Number\ Of\ Outliers}{Number\ Of\ Test\ Samples} \quad (9)$$

4.3. Implicit and Explicit Trust Models Compatibility Analysis Results

In explicit and implicit trust model comparison, the implicit trust scores are generated as described in Section 3.1 in various configurations by filtering users according to the number of activities. The users are filtered with respect to the number of ratings given and the values 3, 5 and 10 are used as the minimum rating count threshold. As a result, two rankings of users are obtained with respect to implicit and explicit trust scores, respectively, and we measure how well the top k-percent elements match. In the experiments, 10 and 20 values are used as the k value. The results are given in Tables 3–5 on the data sets FilmTrust, Epinions and Ciao, respectively.

Table 3. Implicit vs. Explicit trust model comparison results (FilmTrust).

	min. 3 Ratings	min. 5 Ratings	min. 10 Ratings
Recall@10%	0.003	0.003	0.004
Precision@10%	0.025	0.025	0.038
Recall@20%	0.023	0.023	0.027
Precision@20%	0.106	0.106	0.125

Table 4. Implicit vs. Explicit trust model comparison results (Epinions).

	min. 3 Ratings	min. 5 Ratings	min. 10 Ratings
Recall@10%	0.000	0.000	0.000
Precision@10%	0.002	0.004	0.020
Recall@20%	0.000	0.000	0.001
Precision@20%	0.006	0.015	0.041

Table 5. Implicit vs. Explicit trust model comparison results (Ciao).

	min. 3 Ratings	min. 5 Ratings	min. 10 Ratings
Recall@10%	0.006	0.006	0.008
Precision@10%	0.064	0.064	0.080
Recall@20%	0.035	0.035	0.042
Precision@20%	0.173	0.173	0.214

The same comparison is applied between the implicit trust scores and PageRank scores on the explicit trust network. Similarly, the results are given in Tables 6–8 on the data sets FilmTrust, Epinions and Ciao, respectively.

Table 6. Implicit vs. PageRank model comparison results (FilmTrust).

	min. 3 Ratings	min. 5 Ratings	min. 10 Ratings
Recall@10%	0.003	0.005	0.006
Precision@10%	0.038	0.50	0.062
Recall@20%	0.025	0.024	0.027
Precision@20%	0.138	0.131	0.150

Table 7. Implicit vs. PageRank model comparison results (Epinions).

	min. 3 Ratings	min. 5 Ratings	min. 10 Ratings
Recall@10%	0.000	0.000	0.001
Precision@10%	0.004	0.008	0.022
Recall@20%	0.000	0.000	0.001
Precision@20%	0.009	0.019	0.042

Table 8. Implicit vs. PageRank model comparison results (Ciao).

	min. 3 Ratings	min. 5 Ratings	min. 10 Ratings
Recall@10%	0.006	0.006	0.007
Precision@10%	0.057	0.057	0.070
Recall@20%	0.035	0.035	0.040
Precision@20%	0.174	0.174	0.203

In the analysis, precision and recall metrics are used for measuring the overlap between the top elements of implicit and explicit trust score rankings, rather than any prediction accuracy. In the measurement, the ranking of the explicit trust model is considered as the basis and the results of implicit trust score results are compared against them to obtain precision and recall values. As given in the tables, the low precision and recall scores show that the matching between two rankings is very scarce. However, as the implicit modeling is performed among more active users, it is seen that the precision and recall scores in the amount of match between implicit and explicit scores slightly increase. For the results of the proposed matching schema and the PageRank-based scoring, there are slight differences in the matching scores; however, overall, both show very similar behavior. The decrease, particularly in the recall value in the PageRank-based scoring, could be due to the incompatibility between the network propagation nature of the PageRank algorithm and the trust propagation behavior.

Overall, the low precision and recall scores show that explicit and implicit trust models rank the users differently and hence they model different aspects of the trust relationship. In [5], it is reported that the combination of explicit and implicit trust models increases the accuracy of estimates compared to using them separately. In the same study, it is also noted that the explicit trust relationship is also related to the social ties between users, so this cannot be entirely determined only by ratings given by users. The results of our analyses are compatible with the findings given in [5].

4.4. Explicit Trust Modeling Results

4.4.1. Explicit Trust Modeling through User's Rating Behavior Results

Before creating the features to model the explicit trust data implicitly, data exploration is performed to observe which features are needed to be created. Firstly, a signed trust network is used to elaborate on the concepts of liked and disliked items, since there is no distrust in the unsigned data set, the contrast here cannot be fully seen in the data. When we examine Table 9, the values in positive and negative trust relationships are calculated separately for each feature to be created.

Table 9. The Mean of the Generated Features (Signed Epinions).

	Positive Trust	**Negative Trust**
# of mutually rated items	98.807	61.179
# of mutually liked items	83.241	49.783
# of mutually disliked items	5.607	3.819
avg of the ratings given by the trustor	4.637	4.417
# of the ratings given by the trustor	1310.380	6482.471
avg of the ratings given by the trustee	4.605	4.367
# of the ratings given by the trustee	5947.152	2434.528

In this exploratory analysis, significant findings of users in positive trust and negative trust relationships can be obtained. Users in a positive trust relationship rate more common items on average than those in a negative relationship. In addition, the positive trust relationship correlates with the number of common favorite items. Although the negative trust items appear to be fewer than the positive trust items in the number of common disliked items, after normalizing the value, the number of common disliked items is also correlated with a negative trust relationship.

In addition, when Table 9 is checked, it is observed that the total number of ratings given by users who give negative trust is higher than the total number of ratings given by users who give positive trust. It can be interpreted that more active users, who give higher ratings, are also more selective and evaluate other users accordingly.

Similar data exploration is also applied to the unsigned data sets. The summary of the analysis is shown in Table 10. According to the results, the number of commonly liked items in trust relationships established in all three unsigned trust data sets is higher than that of commonly disliked items. It shows that liked items and established trust relationships correlate in unsigned trust data sets as well as in signed trust data sets.

Table 10. The Mean of the Generated Features (Unsigned Data Sets).

	FilmTrust	Epinions	Ciao
# of mutually rated items	9.079	1.194	2.018
# of mutually liked items	3.287	0.481	0.761
# of mutually disliked items	1.818	0.292	0.397
avg of the ratings given by the trustor	3.033	4.064	4.174
# of the ratings given by the trustor	39.865	69.332	150.835
avg of the ratings given by the trustee	3.041	4.015	4.209
# of the ratings given by the trustee	38.670	108.083	83.771

The performance of the unsupervised model generated by the unsigned data set is presented in Table 11. According to the results, the Isolation Forest model classifies most of the randomly generated trust instances to be in the regular class, which does not reflect the outlier (edge label 1) ratio in the data set. On the other hand, it is shown that the one-class SVM model labels nearly 50% of the Epinions and Ciao data sets as outliers. Here, too, the prediction accuracy is limited. Only FilmTrust data shows an outlier ratio close to expected. This difference in the result could be due to the differences in the nature of the data sets. As an example, Table 10 shows that the number of mutually rated items by users in the FilmTrust data set is significantly higher. Considering that the FilmTrust data set is smaller than the others, the unsupervised model can construct a model separating the outlier from regular cases better.

Table 11. Outlier Ratio of the Unsigned Data Sets.

	Isolation Forest	One-Class SVM
FilmTrust	0.134	0.883
Epinions	0.098	0.512
Ciao	0.111	0.538

The outlier/novelty detection methods mentioned above are also applied to Epinions data, a signed trust network. For both the Isolation Forest classifier and One-class SVM classifier, predictions are obtained with the following models:

- The model trained with positive trust data and tested with positive instances;
- The model trained with positive trust data and tested with negative instances;
- The model trained with negative trust data and tested with negative instances;
- The model trained with negative trust data and tested with positive instances.

The aim of this analysis is to see how much positive and negative trust relationships differ using the created features and outlier/novelty detection methods or whether positive and negative trust relationships can be modeled consistently within themselves. Table 12 shows the results of the experiment. Based on the results here, one can say that the One-class SVM model does not perform well in distinguishing negative and positive trust relationships. On the other hand, the Isolation Forest model successfully models both positive and negative trust data within itself. However, it does not perform the same success level in distinguishing positive and negative trust. One reason could be that the created features may not be fitting for the outlier/novelty detection method. In Table 9, it is observed that although there are points where positive and negative trust differ, the users who have established these two relationships are also active users who have interacted with each other.

Table 12. Outlier Ratio of the Signed Epinions Data Set.

	Isolation Forest	One-Class SVM
Trained with positive, tested with positive	0.076	0.495
Trained with negative, tested with negative	0.077	0.501
Trained with positive, tested with negative	0.267	0.679
Trained with negative, tested with positive	0.114	0.526

Besides unsupervised outlier/novelty detection methods, Signed Epinions data is also modeled using multi-class classification algorithms. SVM, Random Forest, and Naive Bayes classifiers are used for model construction. The data is partitioned as training and test subsets with a ratio of 0.8 and 0.2. Table 13 shows the prediction performances of the models. When these results are examined, multi-class classification methods give more successful results than outlier/novelty detection methods. The reason is that both negative and positive trust relationships are used in the training phase. In addition, it can be seen that the Random Forest method gives the best results among these three classification methods. This can be considered an expected result since the Random Forest is a boosting-based method and it is reported to give successful prediction performance for a variety of domains.

Table 13. The Performance of Supervised Learning Models (Signed Epinions).

	Precision	Recall	F1-Score
SVM	0.780	0.743	0.747
Random Forest	0.873	0.865	0.868
Naive Bayes	0.744	0.723	0.726

In the next analysis, a trust network augmented with a multi-class classification model's predictions is used within trust-aware recommendation. The trust-aware recommendation algorithms used in the experiments are as follows:

- SBPR [31] is a ranking-based model that exploits social connections between users to build better prediction models. The model is based on the idea that users tend to give higher rankings to items that their connections prefer.
- SREE [32] is a social recommendation approach based on Euclidean Space. The idea behind this algorithm is to place users and items in a unified Euclidean space where users are close to both the items they want and their social friends.
- TBPR [33] classifies strong and weak ties in a social network and learns latent feature vectors for all users and items. It is an extension of the Bayesian Personalized Ranking model.

In the experiments, users who rate at least one mutual item are selected while choosing new trust relationships to be predicted. The results are given in Table 14. Precision and recall values are calculated by considering the top-10 item rankings in each recommendation algorithm. Judging by the results, performance gains have been observed in almost every case where augmented trust data is used. It can be said that the trust inference method is effective for improving recommendation accuracy.

Table 14. The effect of Modeled Explicit Trust Inference with SBPR, SREE and TBPR algorithms (Signed Epinions).

	w/o Trust Inference		With Trust Inference	
	Precision	Recall	Precision	Recall
SBPR [31]	0.005	0.016	0.009	0.027
SREE [32]	0.002	0.002	0.003	0.001
TBPR [33]	0.001	0.004	0.002	0.008

4.4.2. Trust Prediction Modeling as a Link Prediction Problem Results

In explicit trust modeling analysis, the basic idea is to construct a trust prediction model and to reduce data sparsity by filling in the trust matrix by using the predictions of the explicit trust model. In other words, a prediction is generated for the edge weights, which are 0 in the original network. The accuracy performances of the models generated with Random Forest and SVM classifiers for explicit trust prediction are given in Tables 15 and 16, respectively.

According to the results, the proposed explicit trust models can predict trust classes at a satisfactory rate, and an augmented matrix can be created effectively by inferring unknown trust links between users with the proposed modeling technique. It is also observed that the highest prediction accuracy is obtained on the Ciao data set, whereas the performance of the prediction on the unsigned Epinions data set is better than those on FilmTrust. FilmTrust is comparatively small in size, and hence the amount of trust information captured in the data is also comparatively limited. This possibly negatively affects the performance of the constructed prediction models. Moreover, according to the results, the Random Forest classifier performs better than the SVM method. For this reason, the output of the Random Forest model is used when creating the augmented trust network in the following experiment. Random Forest, being a boosting-based classifier, has been shown to be successful for a variety of prediction problems in the literature. Therefore, our observations are also in line with the literature in general.

Table 15. Accuracy results for explicit trust prediction (Random Forest).

Data Sets	Accuracy	Precision	Recall	F1-Score
FilmTrust	0.675	0.952	0.639	0.765
Epinions	0.930	0.979	0.879	0.926
Ciao	0.940	0.969	0.904	0.935

Table 16. Accuracy results for explicit trust prediction (SVM).

Data Sets	Accuracy	Precision	Recall	F1-Score
FilmTrust	0.819	0.891	0.728	0.801
Epinions	0.961	0.870	0.916	0.892
Ciao	0.901	0.955	0.843	0.895

To analyze the effect of explicit trust inference, the performance of the augmented trust matrix is compared against the original one by using a set of trust-based recommendation algorithms, SBPR, SREE, and TBPR on FilmTrust, unsigned Epinions, and Ciao data sets, given in Tables 17–19, respectively. The results indicate a minor increase in the recommendation performance with the inclusion of explicit trust inference. This result may be due to the fact that the trust values to be predicted do not have a significant change. Hence, the results hint at the possibility for improvement by carefully selecting the trust relationships to be predicted and updated.

Table 17. The effect of Explicit Trust Inference on Recommendation with SBPR, SREE and TBPR algorithms (FilmTrust).

	w/o Trust Inference		With Trust Inference	
	Precision	Recall	Precision	Recall
SBPR [31]	0.301	0.537	0.303	0.549
SREE [32]	0.310	0.402	0.306	0.397
TBPR [33]	0.294	0.472	0.287	0.471

Table 18. The effect of Explicit Trust Inference on Recommendation with SBPR, SREE and TBPR algorithms (Epinions).

	w/o Trust Inference		With Trust Inference	
	Precision	Recall	Precision	Recall
SBPR [31]	0.007	0.017	0.008	0.018
SREE [32]	0.007	0.013	0.007	0.013
TBPR [33]	0.001	0.003	0.002	0.004

Table 19. The effect of Explicit Trust Inference on Recommendation with SBPR, SREE and TBPR algorithms (Ciao).

	w/o Trust Inference		With Trust Inference	
	Precision	Recall	Precision	Recall
SBPR [31]	0.015	0.022	0.016	0.023
SREE [32]	0.004	0.003	0.005	0.004
TBPR [33]	0.003	0.004	0.004	0.005

5. Conclusions

In this work, trust modeling within the recommendation context is studied. More specifically, two sub-problems are focused on: (1) inferring the implicit trust information by examining the past user behaviors and analyzing the compatibility of implicit and explicit trust scores; (2) building an explicit trust model and predicting the missing explicit trust information.

For the first sub-problem, an implicit trust model is created. The implicit trust information is inferred by defining notions of conformity and consistency. After extracting implicit trust scores, the compatibility of implicit and explicit trust values is analyzed. The analysis of the approach reveals that there is no clear correlation between the implicit and explicit scores. The conducted experiments analyze how well the implicit and explicit scores match at the top-20% and top-10% of the trust scores. Under varying parameters, precision and recall scores are generally below 0.1. In addition, when the compatibility analysis is performed among more active users, it is seen that the precision increases above 0.1. The results hint at the effect of social ties in the trust relationship, and hence the implicit trust model cannot replace explicit trust but is merely helpful as complementary information.

For the second sub-problem, two different explicit models exhibit two different approaches. In the first approach, explicit trust is modeled by generating a set of new features containing liked and disliked items. While creating these features, users' rating behavior is used. Here, separate experiments are performed for signed and unsigned trust networks. Expected performance could not be achieved in models created with one-class classification. However, in the experiments conducted with the augmented trust data created with the multi-class classification model, the precision and recall values in the SBPR and TBPR algorithms are boosted approximately twice. Here, it is seen that trust-based recommendation accuracy can be increased by modeling the ratings and explicit trust given by the users together.

For explicit trust score prediction, another solution is devised using the trust network itself. After generating the augmented trust network with this method, the effect of the augmented network is analyzed using various trust-based algorithms. The results show that the augmented trust matrix leads to improvement in performance, but the effect is not very high. This can be due to the fact that the trust values to be predicted are selected randomly, and the predictions do not significantly change the edge labels. Hence, with a more detailed mechanism for selecting the unknown trust relationships to be predicted, the performance could be further improved.

The proposed analysis on trust modeling for recommendation can be extended in a variety of directions. As one of the future dimensions, the proposed explicit trust model created by using rating behavior can be modified to be used for recommendation environments without any explicit trust data. Since the trust data is generally only scarcely available, such a solution widens the applicability of trust-based recommendation. In another future study, hybrid machine learning models and deep learning methods can be investigated to construct explicit trust models. The number of available data sets incurs a limitation, particularly for data-hungry deep learning-based solutions. At this point, mechanisms to incentive explicit trust in social network environments will be helpful to increase the amount of publicly available explicit trust data. Similar mechanisms have been employed in e-commerce platforms to express the reliability of e-stores. These mechanisms can be adapted and extended to social networks.

Another future work direction is conducting studies to detect and prevent attacks that can manipulate trust-based systems and affect users' trust scores. Additionally, generating different implicit trust models and elaborating on their compatibility with explicit trust scores can be further studied. Another interesting direction could be developing an implicit trust model that produces a distrust score as well as trust value.

Author Contributions: Conceptualization, U.D. and P.K.; methodology, U.D. and P.K.; software, U.D.; validation, U.D. and P.K.; writing, U.D. and P.K.; project administration, P.K.; funding acquisition, P.K. All authors have read and agreed to the published version of the manuscript.

Funding: This research was funded by TUBITAK grant number 118E356.

Institutional Review Board Statement: Not applicable.

Informed Consent Statement: Not applicable.

Data Availability Statement: Data sets used in the study are publicly available through the related references. For the analysis, Epinions (Unsigned) [27], Epinions (Signed) [28], FilmTrust [29], and Ciao [30] data sets are used.

Conflicts of Interest: The authors declare no conflict of interest.

References

1. Raza, S.; Ding, C. News recommender system: A review of recent progress, challenges, and opportunities. *arXiv* **2021**, arXiv:2009.04964.
2. Dhelim, S.; Ning, H.; Aung, N. ComPath: User interest mining in heterogeneous signed social networks for Internet of people. *IEEE Internet Things J.* **2020**, *8*, 7024–7035. [CrossRef]
3. Herlocker, J.L.; Konstan, J.A.; Terveen, L.G.; Riedl, J.T. Evaluating Collaborative Filtering Recommender Systems. *ACM Trans. Inf. Syst.* **2004**, 5–53. [CrossRef]
4. Chae, D.K.; Kim, J.; Chau, D.H.; Kim, S.W. AR-CF: Augmenting Virtual Users and Items in Collaborative Filtering for Addressing Cold-Start Problems. In Proceedings of the 43rd International ACM SIGIR Conference on Research and Development in Information Retrieval, Xi'an, China, 25–30 July 2020; Association for Computing Machinery: New York, NY, USA, 2020; pp. 1251–1260.

5. Hu, Z.; Xu, G.; Zheng, X.; Liu, J.; Li, Z.; Sheng, Q.Z.; Lian, W.; Xian, H. SSL-SVD: Semi-Supervised Learning–Based Sparse Trust Recommendation. *ACM Trans. Internet Technol.* **2020**, *20*, 1–20. [CrossRef]
6. Khan, J.; Lee, S. Implicit user trust modeling based on user attributes and behavior in online social networks. *IEEE Access* **2019**, *7*, 142826–142842. [CrossRef]
7. Jamali, M.; Ester, M. A Matrix Factorization Technique with Trust Propagation for Recommendation in Social Networks. In Proceedings of the Fourth ACM Conference on Recommender Systems (RecSys'10), Barcelona, Spain, 26–30 September 2010; Association for Computing Machinery: New York, NY, USA, 2010;pp. 135–142.
8. Zhang, C.; Yu, L.; Wang, Y.; Shah, C.; Zhang, X. Collaborative User Network Embedding for Social Recommender Systems. In Proceedings of the 2017 SIAM International Conference on Data Mining (SDM), Houston, TX, USA, 27–29 April 2017; pp. 381–389.
9. Li, Y.; Liu, J.; Ren, J.; Chang, Y. A Novel Implicit Trust Recommendation Approach for Rating Prediction. *IEEE Access* **2020**, *8*, 98305–98315. [CrossRef]
10. Guo, G.; Zhang, J.; Thalmann, D.; Yorke-Smith, N. ETAF: An extended trust antecedents framework for trust prediction. In Proceedings of the 2014 IEEE/ACM International Conference on Advances in Social Networks Analysis and Mining (ASONAM 2014), Beijing, China, 17–20 August 2014; pp. 540–547.
11. Htun, Z.; Tar, P.P. A Trust-aware Recommender System Based on Implicit Trust Extraction. *Int. J. Innov. Eng. Technol. (IJIET) Technol. (IJIET)* **2013**, *2*, 271–276.
12. Yang, B.; Lei, Y.; Liu, J.; Li, W. Social Collaborative Filtering by Trust. *IEEE Trans. Pattern Anal. Mach. Intell.* **2017**, *39*, 1633–1647. [CrossRef] [PubMed]
13. Guo, G.; Zhang, J.; Zhu, F.; Wang, X. Factored similarity models with social trust for top-N item recommendation. *Knowl.-Based Syst.* **2017**, *122*, 17–25. [CrossRef]
14. Demirci, M.U.; Karagoz, P. Trust Modeling in Recommendation: Explicit and Implicit Trust Model Compatibility and Explicit Trust Prediction. In Proceedings of the 13th International Conference on Management of Digital EcoSystems, Virtual Event, Tunisia, 1–3 November 2021; Association for Computing Machinery: New York, NY, USA, 2021; pp. 8–14.
15. Oh, H.K.; Kim, S.W. Identifying and Exploiting Trustable Users with Robust Features in Online Rating Systems. *TIIS* **2017**, *11*, 2171–2195.
16. Chen, C.C.; Wan, Y.H.; Chung, M.C.; Sun, Y.C. An effective recommendation method for cold start new users using trust and distrust networks. *Inf. Sci.* **2013**, *224*, 19–36. [CrossRef]
17. Guo, G.; Zhang, J.; Thalmann, D. Merging trust in collaborative filtering to alleviate data sparsity and cold start. *Knowl.-Based Syst.* **2014**, *57*, 57–68. [CrossRef]
18. Wang, F.; Zhong, W.; Xu, X.; Rafique, W.; Zhou, Z.; Qi, L. Privacy-aware Cold-Start Recommendation based on Collaborative Filtering and Enhanced Trust. In Proceedings of the 2020 IEEE 7th International Conference on Data Science and Advanced Analytics (DSAA), Sydney, Australia, 6–9 October 2020; pp. 655–662.
19. Ahmadian, M.; Ahmadi, M.; Ahmadian, S. A reliable deep representation learning to improve trust-aware recommendation systems. *Expert Syst. Appl.* **2022**, *197*, 116697. [CrossRef]
20. Zahir, A.; Yuan, Y.; Moniz, K. AgreeRelTrust—A Simple Implicit Trust Inference Model for Memory-Based Collaborative Filtering Recommendation Systems. *Electronics* **2019**, *8*, 427. [CrossRef]
21. Canturk, D.; Karagoz, P. SgWalk: Location Recommendation by User Subgraph-Based Graph Embedding. *IEEE Access* **2021**, *9*, 134858–134873. [CrossRef]
22. Brin, S.; Page, L. The anatomy of a large-scale hypertextual web search engine. *Comput. Netw. ISDN Syst.* **1998**, *30*, 107–117. [CrossRef]
23. Lee, W.; Lee, Y.C.; Lee, D.; Kim, S.W. Look Before You Leap: Confirming Edge Signs in Random Walk with Restart for Personalized Node Ranking in Signed Networks. In Proceedings of the 44th International ACM SIGIR Conference on Research and Development in Information Retrieval, Virtual Event, Canada, 11–15 July 2021; Association for Computing Machinery: New York, NY, USA, 2021; pp. 143–152.
24. Adamic, L.A.; Adar, E. Friends and neighbors on the web. *Soc. Netw.* **2003**, *25*, 211–230. [CrossRef]
25. Pedregosa, F.; Varoquaux, G.; Gramfort, A.; Michel, V.; Thirion, B.; Grisel, O.; Blondel, M.; Prettenhofer, P.; Weiss, R.; Dubourg, V.; et al. Scikit-learn: Machine learning in Python. *J. Mach. Learn. Res.* **2011**, *12*, 2825–2830.
26. Yu, J.; Gao, M.; Yin, H.; Li, J.; Gao, C.; Wang, Q. Generating reliable friends via adversarial training to improve social recommendation. In Proceedings of the 2019 IEEE International Conference on Data Mining (ICDM), Beijing, China, 8–11 November 2019; pp. 768–777.
27. Richardson, M.; Agrawal, R.; Domingos, P. Trust management for the semantic web. In Proceedings of the International Semantic Web Conference, Sanibel Island, FL, USA, 20–23 October 2003; pp. 351–368.
28. Hamedani, M.R.; Ali, I.; Hong, J.; Kim, S.W. TrustRec: An effective approach to exploit implicit trust and distrust relationships along with explicitones for accurate recommendations. *Comput. Sci. Inf. Syst.* **2021**, *18*, 93–114. [CrossRef]
29. Golbeck, J.; Hendler, J. Filmtrust: Movie recommendations using trust in web-based social networks. In Proceedings of the IEEE Consumer Communications and Networking Conference, Las Vegas, NV, USA, 8–10 January 2006; Volume 96, pp. 282–286.
30. Tang, J.; Gao, H.; Liu, H.; Sarma, A.D. eTrust: Understanding Trust Evolution in an Online World. In Proceedings of the Eighteenth ACM SIGKDD International Conference on Knowledge Discovery and Data Mining, Beijing, China, 12–16 August 2012.

31. Zhao, T.; McAuley, J.; King, I. Leveraging social connections to improve personalized ranking for collaborative filtering. In Proceedings of the 23rd ACM International Conference on Conference on Information and Knowledge Management, Shanghai, China, 3–7 November 2014; pp. 261–270.
32. Li, W.; Gao, M.; Rong, W.; Wen, J.; Xiong, Q.; Jia, R.; Dou, T. Social recommendation using Euclidean embedding. In Proceedings of the 2017 International Joint Conference on Neural Networks (IJCNN), Anchorage, AK, USA, 14–19 May 2017; pp. 589–595.
33. Wang, X.; Lu, W.; Ester, M.; Wang, C.; Chen, C. Social recommendation with strong and weak ties. In Proceedings of the 25th ACM International on Conference on Information and Knowledge Management, Indianapolis, IN, USA, 24–28 October 2016; pp. 5–14.

Article

Data-Driven Decision Support for Adult Autism Diagnosis Using Machine Learning [†]

Sotirios Batsakis [1,2], Marios Adamou [3], Ilias Tachmazidis [2], Sarah Jones [3], Sofya Titarenko [4], Grigoris Antoniou [3,*] and Thanasis Kehagias [5]

[1] School of Production Engineering and Management, Technical University of Crete, 73100 Chania, Greece; s.batsakis@hud.ac.uk
[2] Department of Computer Science, School of Computing and Engineering, University of Huddersfield, Huddersfield HD1 3DH, UK; i.tachmazidis@hud.ac.uk
[3] South West Yorkshire Partnership NHS Foundation Trust, Wakefield WF1 3SP, UK; marios.adamou@swyt.nhs.uk (M.A.); sarah.jones1@swyt.nhs.uk (S.J.)
[4] School of Mathematics, University of Leeds, Leeds LS2 9JT, UK; s.titarenko@leeds.ac.uk
[5] Department of Electrical and Computer Engineering, Aristotle University, 54124 Thessaloniki, Greece; kehagiat@auth.gr
* Correspondence: g.antoniou@hud.ac.uk
[†] This paper is an extended version of our paper published in Batsakis, S.; Adamou, M.; Tachmazidis, I.; Antoniou, G.; Kehagias, T. Data-Driven Decision Support for Autism Diagnosis using Machine Learning. In Proceedings of the 13th International Conference on Management of Digital EcoSystems (MEDES'21), Hammamet, Tunisia, 1–3 November 2021.

Abstract: Adult referrals to specialist autism spectrum disorder diagnostic services have increased in recent years, placing strain on existing services and illustrating the need for the development of a reliable screening tool, in order to identify and prioritize patients most likely to receive an ASD diagnosis. In this work a detailed overview of existing approaches is presented and a data driven analysis using machine learning is applied on a dataset of adult autism cases consisting of 192 cases. Our results show initial promise, achieving total positive rate (i.e., correctly classified instances to all instances ratio) up to 88.5%, but also point to limitations of currently available data, opening up avenues for further research. The main direction of this research is the development of a novel autism screening tool for adults (ASTA) also introduced in this work and preliminary results indicate the ASTA is suitable for use as a screening tool for adult populations in clinical settings.

Keywords: machine learning; autism diagnosis; decision support

1. Introduction

Autism spectrum disorder (ASD) is a neurodevelopmental condition characterized by a pervasive impairment in reciprocal social interaction and communication, alongside restricted interests and repetitive behaviors [1,2]. Thus far, no biological markers are evident. It is estimated to affect 9.8 per 1000 adults in England [3]. ASD is usually diagnosed in childhood; however, it is recognized as a lifelong condition [4–8]. In recent years there has been a marked increase in the number of adults referred for autism assessment [9], consequently placing greater demands on health services. Because of this pressure, the time for diagnosis is lengthy with one report finding 29% of adults with autism and 46% of those with Asperger's disorder did not receive a diagnosis until adulthood [10].

NICE (National Institute for Health and Care Excellence, UK) guidelines recommend diagnosis of ASD in adulthood is reached on a consensus of expert opinion made by observations from a variety of assessments, including detailed history taking, current behavioral factors, and cognitive abilities [11]. This means that ASD diagnosis is expensive in time and resources; typically, assessments are lengthy, and subjective. Observations undertaken by multidisciplinary teams should be usual diagnostic procedure [12], which are comprised of evaluation of current functioning and behaviors, together with a detailed history taking [13]. This process can be complex as the ASD phenotype presents with a range of severities, language ability, and intellects [11]. Furthermore, pertinent to adult ASD populations, issues may occur due to (1) difficulties acquiring an accurate early history; (2) differentiating autistic symptoms from learned behavior or compensation strategies; and (3) differentiating from other conditions, or mental health disorders, specifically schizophrenia [14,15]. These factors may lead to misdiagnosis [12,14–23]. Diagnosing autism is resource intensive because of the quantity of information which is required, ideally from a variety of sources. If information from a caregiver is not available, it can be a challenge to obtain an accurate account of the neurodevelopmental period, as self-insight from the service user may be inaccurate [17,18].

There is a necessity to relieve the pressures on specialist diagnostic services by screening waiting lists to identify and prioritize referrals that are at a greater probability of receiving an autism diagnosis [24]. Employing screening tools can facilitate a timely and economical approach for specialist services if they can identify patients who are more likely to have autism, using a standardized method [24].

Whilst a varied collection of ASD screening measures is available for both developmental and adulthood populations, for ASD in adulthood, the most generally used screening measures for ASD is the autism questionnaire presented in [25], which forms the basis of the analysis in the first part of this work. The objective of this part of the work is to apply machine learning for analyzing autism questionnaire results and investigating the components of the assessment, in relation to diagnostic outcome in a clinical setting. In turn, analysis results can over insights for decision support for autism diagnosis. This is followed by the introduction of novel assessments tools: the first is completed by the clinician and the second is completed by the patient.

The remainder of this paper is organized as follows. Background and related work are presented in Section 2. Assessment data and analysis over current data is presented in Section 3. Novel screening tools are presented in Section 4 and conclusions and directions of future work are presented in Section 5.

2. Background and Related Work

Numerous screening tools are available for quantifying childhood and adulthood ASD [26–32], yet issues of validity are apparent. Recommended clinical screening measures for quantifying ASD in adulthood include the autism-spectrum quotient (AQ) [33] the Ritvo Autism and Asperger Diagnostic Scale-Revised (RAADS-R) [9,13,34]. The AQ was developed to quantify high functioning autism (HFA) and Asperger's syndrome (AS) in adult populations. It serves as a standardized measure which can aid clinicians to identify patients that would benefit from a full ASD assessment [25]. Generally, the AQ boasts high sensitivity and specificity [25,33–36]. However, clinically the AQ has shown to be problematic [37–40].

In a clinical sample of 132 patients referred for clinical diagnostic assessment, Kenny and Stansfield [37] reported no difference in scores on the AQ, regardless of ASD/non-ASD diagnosis after full assessment. More recently, Adamou et al. [39] explored the predictive efficacy of the AQ compared to final diagnostic formulation by an expert multidisciplinary team, in a sample of adults referred to a specialist diagnostic service. The AQ measured 74% sensitivity and 30.3% specificity, respectively. No significant association between scores on the AQ and diagnostic outcome was evident. Similar levels of sensitivity (77%) and specificity (29%) have been reported by Ashwood et al. [40] in an ASD sample of 476 patients. In a study which explored AQ scores in adults diagnosed with ASD with average and below average intelligence, only 17% of the sample scored above the diagnostic cutoff of the AQ which again indicates a significantly lower sensitivity than in the original study [41]. Furthermore, AQ scores have failed to correlate with other popular measures of ASD, such as the Autism Diagnostic Interview-Revised or Vineland scores [41].

In studies employing control samples, the AQ has shown discriminative ability between ASD profiles and neurotypical profiles [32,36,42–46], yet it remains uncertain as to how well the AQ performs in those who do not have a clinical diagnosis of ASD, but display ASD traits [46]. In a systematic review of screening tools for ASD populations it was concluded that even though the AQ is commonly utilized in clinics, it is considerably under researched, therefore no recommendations on its use could be put forth by the review [47].

Validation issues are also evident for different measures of ASD that are often used in clinics [48]. The Ritvo Autism Asperger's Diagnostic Scale-Revised (RAADS-R) was developed for adults, based on the ICD-10 and DSM-5 diagnostic criteria. It covers four areas of neurodevelopment (language, sensory motor, circumscribed interest, and social cognition). The RAADS assessment has a reported sensitivity of 97% and specificity of 100% [49,50]. However other studies have questioned its validity.

In a recent study, Jones et al. [51] found RAADS failed to differentiate between ASD/non-ASD patients after full clinical assessment. Levels of false positives were high, with the assessment only having a 3.03% chance of detecting the absence of ASD in the sample. Other studies have found the assessment (including RAADS-14 [52]) is likely to result in high levels of false positives [34], is unable to differentiate between ASD/non-ASD groups [53], and has significantly reduced specificity in psychiatric control groups [54]. Due to the high levels of false positives, it has been recommended the cut-off threshold score is too low to be clinically valuable [55], and that the assessment fails to cover a full range of behavioral issues, particularly those relevant to milder forms of ASD [56].

The concept of concurrent validity is appropriate here. The RAADS-R has shown a strong positive correlation with AQ scores [52,57] and with validity issues surrounding the AQ [37,39,40], this is problematic for both assessments. It is important to note that a potential justification for the low levels of specificity reported in these studies may be due to the high levels of comorbidity demonstrated in ASD profiles [6,58–63]. For instance, anxiety and depression, may imitate particular ASD symptoms [40,64] thereby leading to false positives. However, until these issues are fully resolved, such assessments are not reliable gauges of which patients should receive full ASD assessment as priority [65]. Notice also that extensive work has been done on ASD diagnosis for children using machine learning [66–70], but adult ASD diagnosis, which is the topic of this work, is a much less studied topic.

3. Data Analysis Using Machine Learning

The dataset used in the machine learning based analysis initially presented in [71] consists of autism assessment results for 192 patients, from Adult ADHD and Autism Service, South West Yorkshire Partnership NHS Foundation Trust, in the South and West Yorkshire geographical area, between 2017 and 2018. The Adult ADHD and Autism Service is a specialist Service in diagnosing ADHD and autism in adulthood. Patients are referred to the service by health care professionals, whom deem it appropriate based on patient's history and current difficulties. Inclusion criteria dictated that participants were over the age of 18 years (no cut of), had a good comprehension of the English language, and IQ within normal range. The assessment is designed to identify adults who may benefit from a full diagnostic assessment for autism spectrum disorder.

The assessment procedure adopts the procedure proposed in [25] and consists of two parts. The first part consists of a test that the examined individual completes based on AAA AQ and AAA EQ parts (the RAADS AQ, EQ, RQ questionnaires presented in Section 2). The second part (AAA RQ score) is the result of answers of persons familiar with the examined individual, typically close relatives. Related to the diagnosis are social aspects, communication, imagination and obsessions of the examined individual (these are features CLASS SOCIAL, CLASS OBSESSIONS, CLASS COMMUNICATION and CLASS IMAGINATION) and they are defined from responses to AAA AQ, EQ and RQ and clinician's input. These parts of the AAA examination in turn are the Autism-Spectrum Quotient (AQ) score [33] and the Empathy Quotient (EQ) score [25], in addition to Relatives

Quotient (RQ). Given the AAA AQ, AAA EQ and AAA RQ responses clinicians confirm answers (Yes = 1), which count towards CLASS classification. Thus, CLASS classification is a function of AAA responses and clinician's assessment. The last feature of the dataset is the diagnostic outcome which is a binary categorical feature that the machine learning model has to predict. Overall, the dataset is unbalanced with 28 out of 192 examined patients (14.58%) being diagnosed with autism after a full assessment is completed. Thus, in total the dataset consists of seven numerical input features (three consisting solely of questionnaire's results and four based on questionnaire's results and clinician's input) and an output categorical feature.

The objective of data analysis is to create a model for predicting the diagnostic outcome given the AAA test data [25] as input. Specifically, the input data are AAA test results consisting of AAA AQ, AAA EQ and AAA RQ scores. The AAA AQ has numerical values ranging from 4 to 50 with a mean 34.74 and a standard deviation 8.47, for EQ the corresponding values are 0, 80, 19.99 and 11.38 and for RQ the values are 0, 31, 18.21 and 6.31. In addition, the input data include the features CLASS SOCIAL, CLASS OBSESSIONS, CLASS COMMUNICATION and CLASS IMAGINATION derived from AAA test responses as defined in [34]. The CLASS SOCIAL values range from min = 0 to max = 11 with mean value 2.39 and standard deviation 1.46, for the CLASS OBSESSIONS the corresponding values are 0, 9, 2.30 and 1.22, for CLASS COMMUNICATION values are 0, 5, 2.17 and 1.32 and for CLASS IMAGINATION min, max, mean and standard deviation values are 0, 4, 1.05 and 0.87. The dataset consists of exam results of 192 individuals, with 85.24% of diagnostic outcomes being negative. In this work, various classification methods have been used for the analysis.

3.1. Analysis Using Weka

The first part of the analysis consisted of the application of six machine learning algorithms using Weka [72] over the dataset as presented in [71]. Three of the algorithms are non-interpretable and three are interpretable. The non-interpretable algorithms are multilayer perceptron (the neural network implementation in Weka), SMO (sequential minimal optimization algorithm for training a support vector classifier) and random forest. The interpretable algorithms are the decision tree (J48), logistic regression and semantic artificial neural networks (SANN) [73]. SANN is a variant of neural networks with labeled hidden layer nodes which can be interpreted as logistic regression over each layer given the previous one. In all experiments, pre-processing has been applied by replacing missing values with the average value, while performance estimation and model selection was based on 10-fold cross validation.

The results of experiments using the non-interpretable classification algorithms of Weka and the default hyperparameters are presented in Table 1 (optimal values as marked in bold). Although Table 1 presents some basic results using the non-interpretable algorithms, the imbalance of the dataset and the relative importance of the different diagnostic outcomes and corresponding consequences make the overall precision of algorithms one—but not the only—factor to take into account in the analysis. Thus, a detailed examination is required in order to assess the true usability of a data driven analysis in the decision process. Specifically, the cost of error varies given its type, typically it is a more serious error to predict a negative diagnostic outcome when it is actually positive resulting in the patient not receiving the needed treatment, compared to predicting a positive diagnosis when in fact it is negative with the cost being that of that of conducting a full assessment that eventually leads to a negative diagnosis. This observation in turn changes the use of a machine learning model in practice.

Typically, when each class is considered equally important and having similar costs for all types of errors a classifier selects the class having the higher probability. However, when classes have different importance and also different costs in case of classification errors, then the selection threshold of an algorithm must be adjusted accordingly. Data driven analysis may help making such policies more accurate and efficient. In practice, up to a certain degree, it is better to make an additional assessment of positive diagnosis to the patient rather than to select a negative diagnostic outcome (which could actually be positive).

Table 1. Classification results using non interpretable algorithms of Weka.

Model	Total Positive Rate	ROC Area
Multilayer Perceptron	**0.885**	0.805
SMO	0.854	0.500
Random Forest	0.859	**0.870**

After taking the above observations into account the detailed results for each algorithm are the following: SMO actually assigns all instances as having negative diagnostic outcome where the total positive rate is 0.854 (percentage of instances with negative diagnostic outcome) and the receiver operating characteristic (ROC) curve (or area under the curve—AUC) is 0.500, corresponding to a random classification, thus this model cannot be used in practice. Random forest achieved better results with total positive rate 0.859 and the ROC curve is 0.870. In this case, the classifier can be useful in practice. For example, given a policy that assigns much higher cost to a false negative error than to a false positive, the diagnostic outcome can be classified as positive even if the probability is low, in order to avoid false negative errors. Subsequently, if an assessment result is positive even if the probability of such outcome is according to classifier just 1% then all 28 positive cases will be classified correctly and so are 47 of the negative ones, with the cost of having to provide full assessment in the 117 remaining negative cases. Thus, the classifier can be used for making a decision for filtering out some cases, but also providing full assessment to all cases that have a positive diagnosis. By increasing the threshold to 2% the classification is correct for 26 out of the 28 positive cases and 69 out of the 164 negative cases (95 negative cases will still have full assessment). Thus, reduction of false positives is combined with increase of false negatives and the relative cost of errors is used for defining the proper threshold and decision policy rather than the threshold value that maximizes classification accuracy, that is reported in Table 1. In case of multilayer perceptron (neural network), the total positive rate is 0.885 and the ROC curve is 0.805, thus offering the possibility of implementing a selection policy minimizing the cost of errors, but without creating an interpretable model.

Even though non-interpretable algorithms can assist in decision making by producing models that can predict the probability (given the results of an assessment) of a specific diagnostic outcome, thus facilitating the definition of a decision policy given the relative costs of errors, interpretability of the prediction model is often an important issue. Compliance to legal requirements and regulations means that specific rules have been taken into account when applying an AI-based system and this in turn means that the system's functionality is transparent and interpretable. A proposed approach is to employ interpretable machine learning algorithms, such as logistic regression and decision trees [74]. These algorithms are often efficient but do not always perform as non-interpretable ones, such as support vector machines (SVM) and neural networks.

In the case of neural networks, using existing knowledge for building neural networks was first proposed in [75] and further developed in [76], introducing the knowledge-based artificial neural networks (KBANN). These networks are constructed based on knowledge represented using logic rules, and in [73] a variant of KBANN called semantic artificial neural networks (SANNs) is proposed. SANNs are neural networks with labeled hidden layer nodes as KBANNs, but the construction of such neural networks is based on knowledge graphs rather than rules. In this work the interpretable algorithms applied to the autism assessment dataset are: logistic regression, J48 decision tree and SANN. The SANN is constructed by introducing to the hidden layer nodes representing the AAA score (combining AAA AQ, AAA EQ and AAA RQ scores) and the CLASS score (combining the CLASS SOCIAL, CLASS OBSESSIONS, CLASS COMMUNICATION and CLASS IMAGINATION scores). The resulting network is presented in Figure 1.

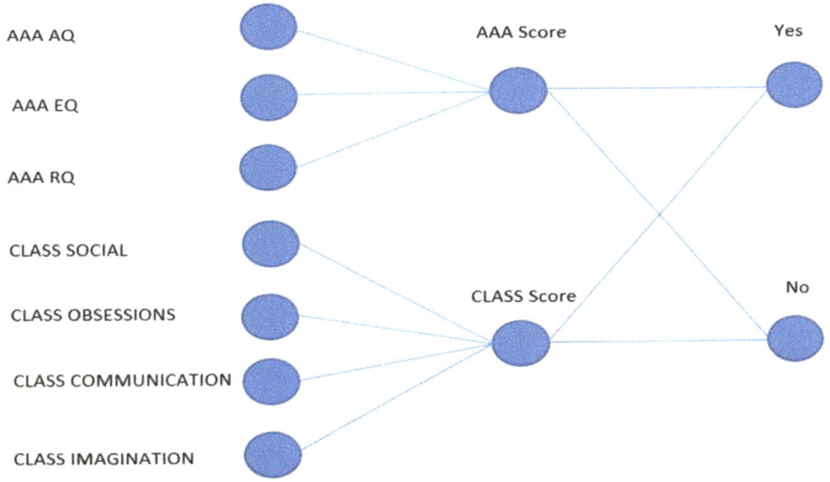

Figure 1. Semantic artificial neural network for classification on the autism dataset.

The results using the interpretable algorithms of Weka are presented in Table 2 (optimal values as marked in bold). In medical diagnosis, interpreting the models is significant for decision making, thus we choose to present the two categories of algorithms separately, since in case that interpretability is not an option but a strict requirement then only the corresponding algorithms can be used. Decision tree (J48) achieved a total positive rate of 0.870 and ROC curve of 0.775.

Table 2. Classification results using interpretable algorithms of Weka.

Model	Total Positive Rate	ROC Area
Logistic Regression	0.844	0.814
Decision Tree (J48)	0.870	0.775
SANN	**0.875**	**0.870**

In the case of logistic regression, the coefficients for predicting a negative diagnosis result are AAA AQ: 0.0381, AAA EQ: −0.0064, AAA RQ: −0.1282, CLASS SOCIAL: −0.585, CLASS OBSESSIONS: −0.2791, CLASS COMMUNICATION: −0.371, CLASS IMAGINATION: −0.6105 and Intercept: 7.344. These coefficients indicate factors correlated positively or negatively with negative diagnosis and the degree of this correlation (with CLASS features and AAA RQ having more weight).

The third algorithm, SANN, (using the network of Figure 1) achieved a total positive rate of 0.875 and ROC curve of 0.870, outperforming the other two interpretable algorithms. There are two hidden layer nodes in the SANN, the AAA Score node representing the cumulative AAA score and CLASS Score node representing cumulative CLASS score. The output node representing negative diagnostic output has weights of 3.21 at input from the AAA Score node and 4.84 at input from CLASS Score node, while the corresponding weights at positive diagnostic outcome node are −3.21 and −4.48, respectively. Thus, the positive diagnostic outcome has lower probability when cumulative AAA and CLASS scores are higher. The AAA Score in turn has weights of 5.07 from AAA AQ input, −10.10 from AAA EQ and −12.39 from AAA RQ indicating that overall the higher the AAA AQ the lower the probability of a positive diagnosis and that lower AAA EQ and AAA RQ scores increase the probability of positive diagnostic outcome. Furthermore, AAA

EQ and AAA RQ scores have more weight than AAA AQ. The corresponding weights for the cumulative CLASS Score are for CLASS SOCIAL: −12.70, CLASS OBSESSIONS: −3.24, CLASS COMMUNICATION: −3.81 and CLASS IMAGINATION: −2.81 indicating that lower CLASS scores increase probability of positive diagnostic outcome.

Depending on the relative cost of classification errors, by setting a low threshold for accepting a positive diagnosis, the created model can be used to filter out cases which have a negative diagnostic outcome with very high probability. For example, when setting a threshold for classifying a case as positive to 1% then 26 out of 28 positive cases are classified correctly and so are 86 out of 164 negative cases (thus a full assessment is applied for 78 negative cases). Thus, practically more than half of negative cases can be exempted from further examination while keeping almost all of positive cases. This is actually similar to the clinical assessment practice. For example, in this dataset, out of the 192 cases, 28 are positive and 164 are negative. In the screening process, 125 cases went through full assessment and 67 did not. Finally, of these 125 cases, 26 were positive and 99 were negative. Out of the 67 cases, not further assessed, 65 were negative and 2 were positive. Thus, the policy adopted in clinical practice corresponds to that of applying a low threshold classifier, minimizing false negatives for the positive diagnosis class. Notice that, although SANN achieved high performance and is interpretable, a disadvantage of this method is that the construction of network topology must be done manually, thus this algorithm is incompatible with a fully automated data analysis process.

3.2. Analysis Using JADBio

Even though tools such as Weka can be used whether interpretability is required or not, when using a tool such as Weka there are two disadvantages; first the user must be familiar with machine learning which is not always the case in an environment such as the medical domain and second the analyst must apply various algorithms and also has to tune their hyperparameters in order to achieve optimal results. Overall, this is a time-consuming process, and in addition to this it is also uncertain, especially in the case of a large search space for hyperparameter's values, with respect to the optimal selection of hyperparameters. This is the reason why systems automating machine learning are very important for wide scale adoption of machine learning for data analysis and decision support in the medical domain.

In this work, in addition to the analysis done manually using Weka, the automated analysis tool called JADBio [77] was used as well as in [71]. By using JADBio, users simply upload their data and provide their preferences, subsequently the system selects the optimal model. In an application domain such as medical diagnosis where expertise on machine learning may not be available and a series of trials with many algorithms and their hyperparameters may not be an option due to limitations over resources such as time, the use of tools that automate machine learning tasks is expected to be widespread. JADBio allows for setting user preferences related to feature selection (optional or required), interpretability (optional or required) and time preference (preliminary, typical and extensive). Results using the above preferences are summarized in Table 3.

Table 3. Area under the curve (AUC) results using JADBio.

Analysis Type	Interpretability Required		Interpretability Not Required	
	Feature Selection	No Feature Selection	Feature Selection	No Feature Selection
Preliminary	0.756	0.794	0.750	0.833
Typical	0.778	0.807	0.798	0.830
Extensive	0.794	0.806	0.833	0.823

When using the JADBio system, in the case that interpretability is not required, a support vector machine (SVM) is the optimal model selected when combined with feature selection (and extensive time preference) and classification random forests training 100 trees is the optimal algorithm when feature selection is not applied. In case the algorithm must be interpretable then ridge logistic regression is the best performing algorithm when combined with feature selection (and extensive time preference) and without feature selection (and typical time preference). Feature selection, pre-processing and hyperparameter selection is performed automatically by the JADBio system and results are presented below.

Specifically, after examining various possible settings the JADBio system applied in pre-processing is constant removal and standardization. Then in feature selection the algorithm applied is the statistically equivalent signature (SES) algorithm with hyper-parameters: maxK = 2 (i.e., the maximum conditioning set to use in the conditional independent sets), and alpha = 0.1 (i.e., threshold for assessing *p*-value significance). JADBio selected three out of the total number of features in the original dataset: CLASS SOCIAL, AAA RQ and CLASS COMMUNICATION. Performance when using all features instead of only these three remained almost identical. The feature selection was applied by estimating the performance decrease when the feature was removed.

The best predictive model was support vector machines (SVM) of type C-SVC with polynomial kernel and hyper-parameters: cost = 0.001 (cost parameter trades off correct classification of training examples against maximization of the decision function's margin), gamma = 10.0 (gamma parameter defines the degree of the influence of a single training example), degree = 3 (degree of the polynomial that SVM returns) having an area under the curve (AUC) of 0.833. Notice that the corresponding algorithm using Weka (SMO) has lower performance because of the different hyperparameter selection. The ROC curve of the best performing model using JADBio is presented in Figure 2. Using the diagram, the user can specify the true positive rate for a specific class (in the case its class 2 indicating a positive diagnostic outcome) given the threshold selected.

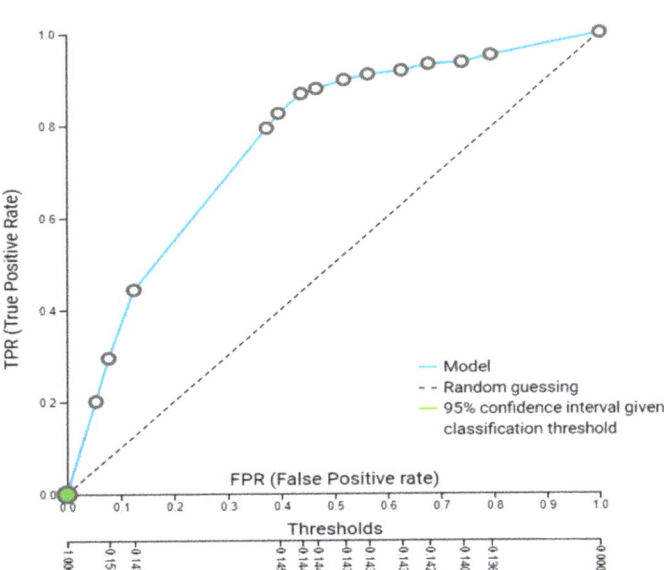

Figure 2. ROC curve of best performing model using JADBio.

The best interpretable model with feature selection was ridge logistic regression with penalty hyper-parameter lambda = 100.0 (lambda defines the amount of regularization used in the model produced by the algorithm), with AUC (ROC) 0.794. The ROC curve for ridge logistic regression is presented in Figure 3. Based on the curve, we can see that when setting the threshold to 9.4%, the true positive rate for the positive diagnostic outcome class is 0.969 and false negatives rate is 0.005. Taking into account the trade-off between false positive error rate and false negative error rate and the corresponding costs the optimal threshold can be defined for cost minimization.

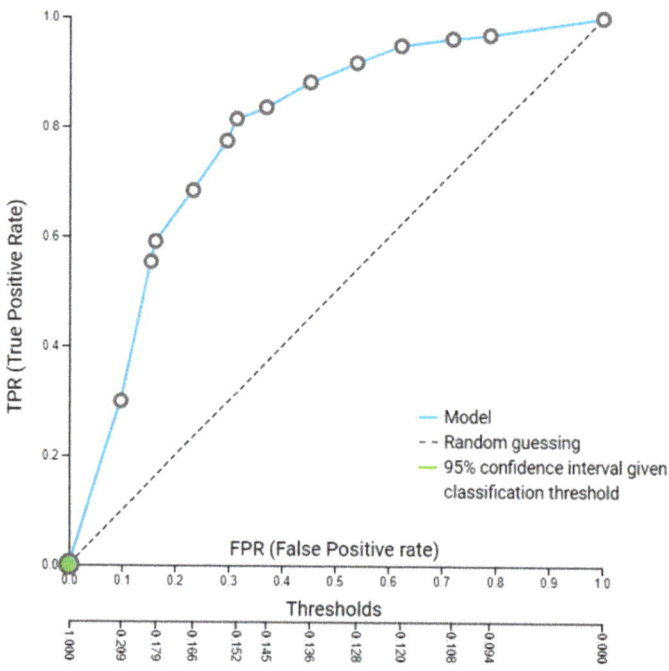

Figure 3. ROC curve of best performing interpretable model with feature selection using JAD-Bio.

Notice that JADBio adopts the bootstrap corrected cross validation performance estimation protocol presented in [78]. The objective of bootstrap corrected cross validation is to overcome the optimistic bias of cross validation, that is the typical method for performance estimation and model selection in machine learning (notice that 10-fold cross validation was used as performance metric in the experiments using Weka). The performance estimation is a task both difficult and critical, especially in medical applications where the reliability of the prediction model is a crucial parameter in decision making. This means that the performance metric of JADBio is less optimistic than that of Weka, but this stricter performance evaluation is also desirable in critical applications.

Overall, the JADBio system produced models (including interpretable models) that offered high performance in addition to fully automating the analysis process which is a great advantage over traditional systems such as Weka. Although the dataset was not balanced and the two classes were difficult to separate (this is illustrated by the poor performance of SMO algorithm using Weka), by carefully selecting the threshold value of the classification model, after taking into account corresponding costs, the performed analysis can assist the decision-making process. Notice also that depending on the cost estimation, a cost benefit analysis, when combined with an examination of the classification models, may lead to a decision to revise the assessment or even discontinue it in case there is no benefit of applying this assessment before the full assessment. This, for example, can be the case when the cost of making a false negative prediction regarding the diagnostic outcome is far greater than that of false positives. Overall, when using Weka the best performing algorithms were typical dense neural networks and random forest and the best performing interpretable algorithm was SANN. In the case of JADBio, the best performance was achieved using SVM and the best performing interpretable algorithm was ridge logistic regression.

4. Autism Screening Questionnaire

The analysis using machine learning demonstrated the potential but also the limitations of machine learning applications using current datasets, since either the user adopts a low selection threshold which eliminates the false negative results but also allows many false positives or increases the threshold risking having false negative cases. In order to overcome these limitations a novel autism screening questionnaire is proposed (consisting of two parts, one for clinicians and another for patients) and although related datasets are still in development, an analysis based on machine learning is thus not yet feasible, preliminary statistical results are also presented. The new questionnaire can be used in order to add future autism datasets with more data points per case and subsequently improve the performance of machine learning methods over these datasets. The first tool (first part of the questionnaire) consists of 15 questions, where only binary answers are allowed. The questionnaire was undertaken by 30 patients; 8 of them have been diagnosed with autism.

The data contain binary answers, demographic information (age, gender) and the final score calculated based on the answers. Figure 4 shows the distribution of ages according to the diagnosis.

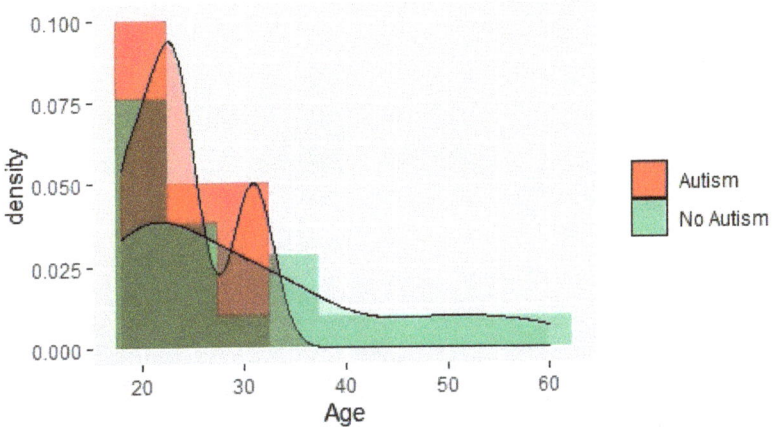

Figure 4. Distribution of ages according to the diagnose.

It can be noticed that ages are strongly skewed towards the younger age. Ages of patients affected by autism lay in the range of 18–31 with the mean being 23.88 years. Ages of patients without autism are strongly skewed to the left and are between 18 and 60 years. The majority of ages are distributed between 20 and 34 years with the mean value of 30.33. The results might be affected by sample size.

Figure 5 demonstrates gender balance for patients affected by autism. It can be concluded that while the collected data shows an equal gender balance for healthy patients, there is a gender imbalanced for patients affected by autism. This result might be affected by sample size.

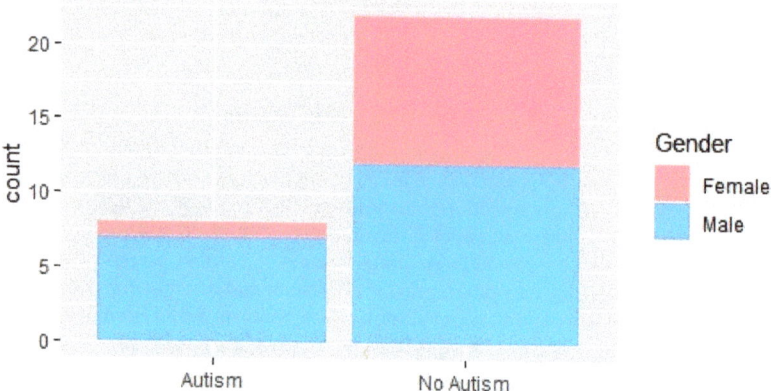

Figure 5. Gender-based frequencies for two diagnoses.

To test the questions for importance the Barnard's exact test was applied. The test gave the indication that questions Q6, Q7, Q10 and Q14 might be important (unadjusted *p*-values are 0.23, 0.13, 0.23, 0.23). However, it can be noticed that *p*-values are higher than 0.05 and additional data are required to prove or disprove the claim. Figures 6 and 7 demonstrate how answers are distributed amongst two categories of patients: healthy and those affected by autism.

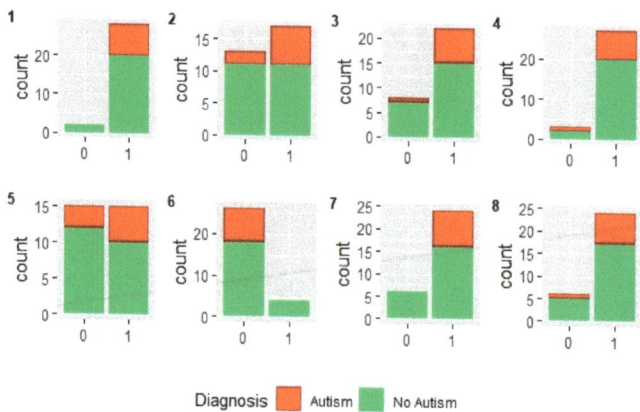

Figure 6. Bar plots demonstrating frequencies of "yes"-"no" answers to questions 1–8; 0 corresponds to "no", 1 corresponds to "yes".

Figure 8 shows that in the Dim1–Dim2 factor space the diagnosis "Autism" is strongly associated with Q5-yes and Q2-yes. The diagnosis "No Autism" does not have any strong associations: Q15-no and Q5-no are the closest points. Q7-no, Q3-no and Q8-no are close to each other. Questions Q4-yes, Q10-yes, Q14-yes, Q1-yes and Q11-yes are strongly associated with male gender while Q6-no and Q15-no are closer to female. It should be noted that the contribution of these questions into variability of data is rather low.

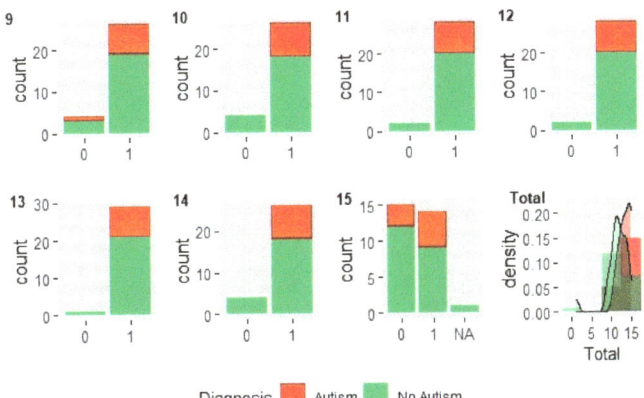

Figure 7. Bar plots demonstrating frequencies of "yes"-"no" answers to questions 9–15; 0 corresponds to "no", 1 corresponds to "yes". The bottom-right plot shows a grouped histogram for total score.

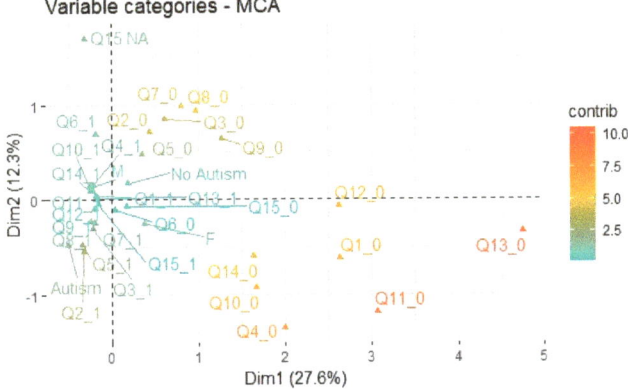

Figure 8. MCA shows the most contributing variables in factor plane Dim1–Dim2.

It can be noticed that Q13-no and Q11-no have a rather strong contribution to variability along Dim1 and Dim2. However, they are far from diagnosis autism/no autism and do not have an association with them.

In factor plane Dim2–Dim3 (see Figure 9) we can see the association of autism and Q14-no as well as no autism and Q11-yes, Q14-yes and Q11-yes. On the other hand, Q6-yes has little association with diagnosis autism/no autism.

In factor plane Dim3–Dim4 (see Figure 10), Q6-yes is still far from diagnosis. Q8-no and Q3-yes are close to no autism while Q3-no and Q9-no seem to have some association with autism.

It can be concluded that being diagnosed with or without autism has little contribution to variability in all five dimensions. Therefore, despite the associations of certain answers with certain diagnoses, at this stage we cannot select them as strong contributing factors.

The second proposed tool consists of 20 questions, where only binary answers are allowed. The questionnaire was undertaken by 18 patients; 4 of them have been diagnosed with autism.

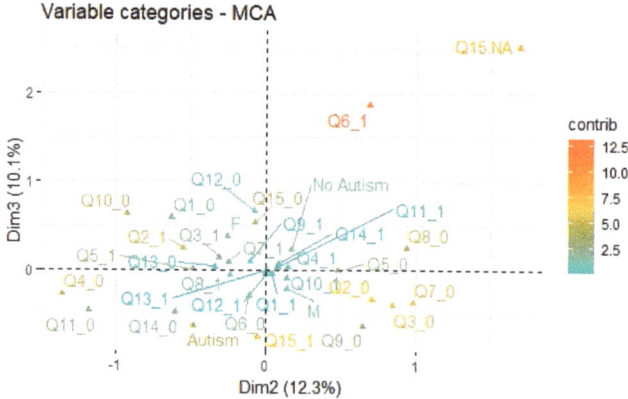

Figure 9. MCA shows the most contributing variables in factor plane Dim2–Dim3.

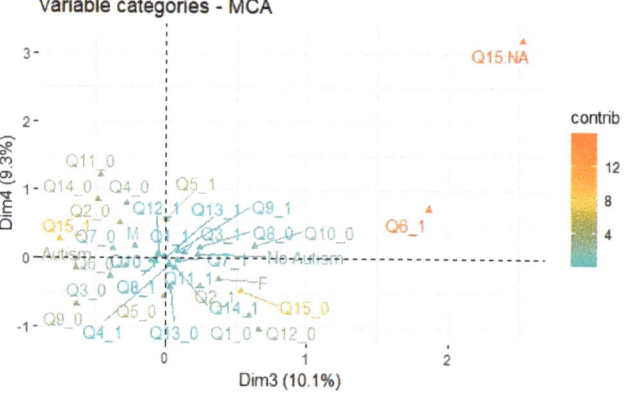

Figure 10. MCA shows the most contributing variables in factor plane Dim3–Dim4.

The data contain binary answers, demographic information (age, gender) and the final score calculated based on the answers. Figure 11 shows distribution of ages according to the diagnosis. It can be noticed that the ages of patients affected by autism are generally older (this can be affected by small sample size). Both samples contain outliers which represent older patients. The mean value of ages of patients affected by autism is 32.25 while the mean value of ages of healthy patients is 27.21. The majority of ages for all patients lay between 20 and 31.

Figure 12 demonstrates gender balance for patients affected by autism. It can be concluded that while the collected data maintains an equal gender balance for healthy patients, there is a gender imbalanced for patients affected by autism. This result might be affected by sample size.

To test the questions for importance the Barnard's exact test was applied. The test gave the indication that questions Q19 and Q15 might be important (unadjusted p-values are 0.0068, 0.1553). Q19 looks particularly promising. However, it can be noticed that additional data are required to prove or disprove the claim.

Figures 13–15 demonstrate how answers are distributed amongst two categories of patients: healthy and those affected by autism.

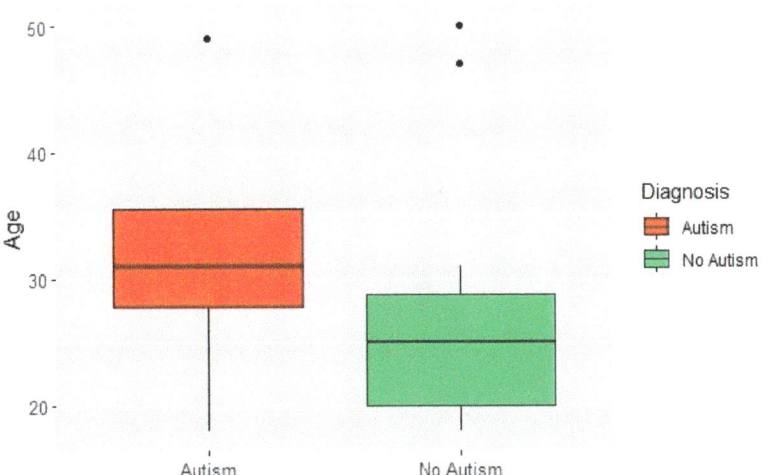

Figure 11. Distribution of ages according to the diagnose.

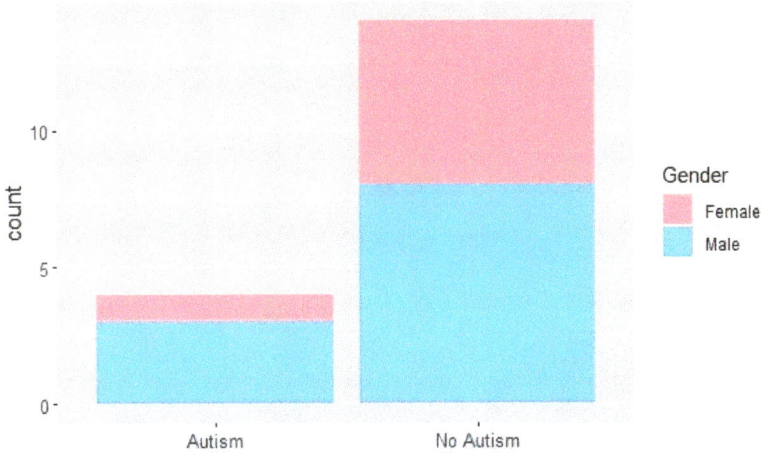

Figure 12. Gender-based frequencies for two diagnoses.

It is interesting to see that all patients answered in the same way to Q18. There seems to be no large difference in ratios autism/no autism in answers to Q6 and Q17 (0.33/0.27). However, it may be worth analyzing answers on the larger sample before making a final decision to discard Q18, Q6 and Q17.

Figures 16 and 17 show that autism mostly contributes to data variability in factor planes Dim3–Dim4 and Dim4–Dim5. It confirms the association of diagnosis "Autism" with Q15-no and Q19-yes as well as Q15-yes and Q19-no and "No Autism". The plots also show associations of "No Autism" with Q3-no and Q16-no.

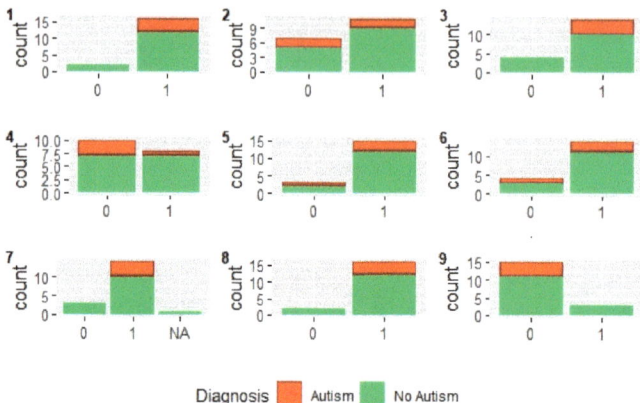

Figure 13. Bar plots demonstrating frequencies of "yes"-"no" answers to questions 1–9; 0 corresponds to "no", 1 corresponds to "yes".

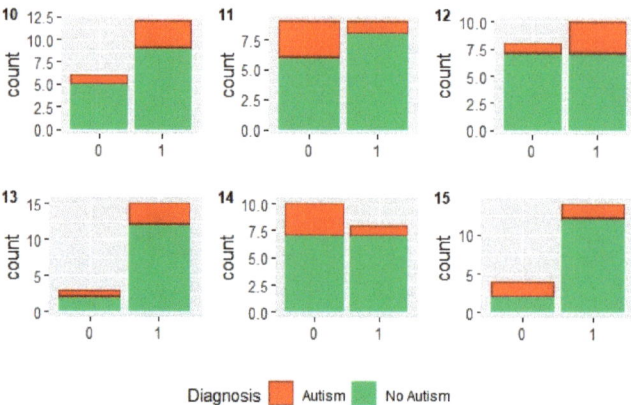

Figure 14. Bar plots demonstrating frequencies of "yes"-"no" answers to questions 10–15; 0 corresponds to "no", 1 corresponds to "yes".

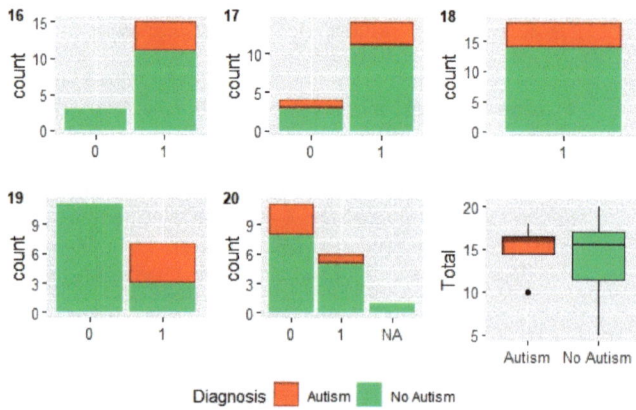

Figure 15. Bar plots demonstrating frequencies of "yes"-"no" answers to questions 16–20; 0 corresponds to "no", 1 corresponds to "yes". The bottom-right plot shows the grouped boxplot for total score.

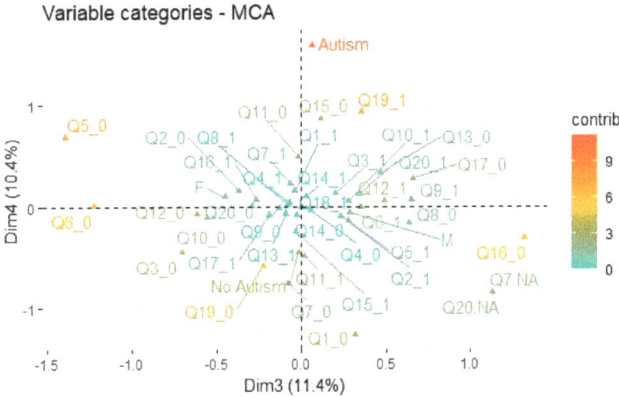

Figure 16. MCA shows the most contributing variables in factor plane Dim3–Dim4.

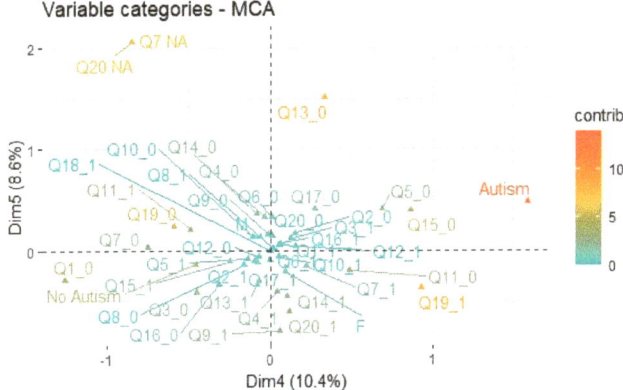

Figure 17. MCA shows the most contributing variables in factor plane Dim4–Dim5.

It is also interesting to note that Q18-yes has zero contribution to variability, which confirms with calculated p-values and grouped bar plot shown above.

Overall, our analysis shows that the novel tool contains information that is statistically relevant for identifying people with autism. This is a promising result, but of course more data is needed for gaining further insights and confidence in the tool's accuracy.

Another interesting question for future exploration is to establish if the new tools will improve prediction accuracy of machine learning methods when applied to dataset containing both the information included in Section 3 and in Section 4.

5. Conclusions and Future Work

This paper presented a data driven analysis over a dataset for autism assessment. Preliminary results showed that various algorithms achieved high performance although the diagnostic outcome classification was not an easy task because of the dataset characteristics (unbalanced, having some features that were not useful and not easily separable i.e., in a linear way). Furthermore, when applying such an analysis in practice, there are other crucial factors besides the total performance, such as the requirement of interpretability and automation of the analysis process, in addition to optimal performance for specific classes and the relative cost of various types of errors when specifying the decision process. In addition, in order to overcome the limitations demonstrated in the performed analysis this work aims to evaluate the validity of an easy to administer new scale, to be used as a self-report screening tool for adult patients referred for an ASD. This study prioritizes the importance of investigation within a clinical environment similar to where it is intended for use. Data was gathered from patients referred to the Adult ADHD and Autism Service, South West Yorkshire Partnership NHS Foundation Trust.

Future work will proceed in various directions. A particular direction will be to consider richer clinical data; there are even ideas to capture either neurological data, facial expressions through video or in combination. Another interesting idea is to expand the AI technologies used by capturing and representing explicitly, through declarative rules, medical knowledge about how clinical data should be interpreted. Such a knowledge model could be used in conjunction with a machine learning model as discussed in this paper, thus deploying a hybrid AI approach.

Author Contributions: Data analysis and writing, S.B.; data gathering and analysis, M.A.; data analysis, I.T.; background and related work analysis, S.J.; novel tools analysis, S.T.; overview and editing G.A.; writing—review and editing, T.K. All authors have read and agreed to the published version of the manuscript.

Funding: This research received no external funding.

Institutional Review Board Statement: Not applicable.

Informed Consent Statement: Informed consent was obtained from all subjects involved in the study.

Data Availability Statement: Not applicable.

Acknowledgments: Authors would like to thank Adult ADHD and Autism Service, South West Yorkshire Partnership NHS Foundation Trust for its support during this work.

Conflicts of Interest: The authors declare no conflict of interest.

References

1. American Psychiatric Association. *Diagnostic and Statistical Manual of Mental Disorder*, 5th ed.; American Psychiatric Press: Washington, WA, USA, 2013.
2. Lord, C.; Cook, E.H.; Leventhal, B.L.; Amaral, D.G. Autism spectrum disorders. *Neuron* **2000**, *28*, 355–363. [CrossRef]
3. Brugha, T.S.; McManus, S.; Bankart, J.; Scott, F.; Purdon, S.; Smith, J.; Bebbington, P.; Jenkins, R.; Meltzer, H. Epidemiology of autism spectrum disorders in adults in the community in England. *Arch. Gen. Psychiatry* **2011**, *68*, 459–465. [CrossRef]
4. Murphy, C.M.; Wilson, C.E.; Robertson, D.M.; Ecker, C.; Daly, E.M.; Hammond, N.; Galanopoulos, A.; Dud, I.; Murphy, D.G.; McAlonan, G.M. Autism spectrum disorder in adults: Diagnosis, management, and health services development. *Neuropsychiatr. Dis. Treat.* **2016**, *12*, 1669–1686. [CrossRef]
5. Harris, J.; Brugha, T.; McManus, S.; Meltzer, H.; Smith, J.; Scott, F.J.; Purdon, S.; Bankart, J. *Autism Spectrum Disorders in Adults Living in Households Throughout England: Report from the Adult Psychiatric Morbidity Survey 2007*; The NHS Information Centre for Health and Social Care: Teddington, UK, 2009.
6. Fombonne, E. Epidemiology of autistic disorder and other pervasive developmental disorders. *J. Clin. Psychiatry* **2005**, *66* (Suppl. S10), 3–8.
7. Kan, C.; Buitelaar, J.K.; Van Der Gaag, R.J. Autism spectrum disorders in adults. *Ned. Tijdschr. Geneeskd.* **2008**, *152*, 1365–1369.
8. Wing, L.; Potter, D. The epidemiology of autistic spectrum disorders: Is the prevalence rising? *Ment. Retard. Dev. Disabil. Res. Rev.* **2002**, *8*, 151–161. [CrossRef]
9. Ritvo, R.A.; Ritvo, E.R.; Guthrie, D.; Ritvo, M.J.; Hufnagel, D.H.; McMahon, W.; Tonge, B.; Mataix-Cols, D.; Jassi, A.; Attwood, T.; et al. The Ritvo Autism Asperger Diagnostic Scale-Revised (RAADS-R): A scale to assist the diagnosis of autism spectrum disorder in adults: An international validation study. *J. Autism Dev. Disord.* **2011**, *41*, 1076–1089. [CrossRef]
10. Barnard, J.; Harvey, V.; Potter, D.; Prior, A. *Ignored or Ineligible? The Reality for Adults with Autism Spectrum Disorders*; National Autistic Society: London, UK, 2001.
11. Le Couteur, A.; Haden, G.; Hammal, D.; McConachie, H. Diagnosing autism spectrum disorders in pre-school children using two standardised assessment instruments: The ADI-R and the ADOS. *J. Autism Dev. Disord.* **2008**, *38*, 362–372. [CrossRef]
12. Molloy, C.A.; Murray, D.S.; Akers, R.; Mitchell, T.; Manning-Courtney, P. Use of the Autism Diagnostic Observation Schedule (ADOS) in a clinical setting. *Autism* **2011**, *15*, 143–162. [CrossRef]
13. National Institute for Health and Care Excellence. *Autism Spectrum Disorder in Adults: Diagnosis and Management (Guideline CG142)*; National Institute for Health and Care Excellence: London, UK, 2016.
14. Barlati, S.; Deste, G.; Gregorelli, M.; Vita, A. Autistic traits in a sample of adult patients with schizophrenia: Prevalence and correlates. *Psychol. Med.* **2019**, *49*, 140–148. [CrossRef]

15. De Crescenzo, F.; Postorino, V.; Siracusano, M.; Riccioni, A.; Armando, M.; Curatolo, P.; Mazzone, L. Autistic symptoms in schizophrenia spectrum disorders: A systematic review and meta-analysis. *Front. Psychiatry* **2019**, *10*, 78. [CrossRef] [PubMed]
16. Bastiaansen, J.A.; Meffert, H.; Hein, S.; Huizinga, P.; Ketelaars, C.; Pijnenborg, M.; Bartels, A.; Minderaa, R.; Keysers, C.; de Bildt, A. Diagnosing autism spectrum disorders in adults: The use of Autism Diagnostic Observation Schedule (ADOS) module 4. *J. Autism Dev. Disord.* **2011**, *41*, 1256–1266. [CrossRef] [PubMed]
17. Berthoz, S.; Hill, E.L. The validity of using self-reports to assess emotion regulation abilities in adults with autism spectrum disorder. *Eur. Psychiatry* **2005**, *20*, 291–298. [CrossRef] [PubMed]
18. Frith, U. *Autism: Explaining the Enigma*, 2nd ed.; Blackwell Publishing: Oxford, UK, 2003.
19. Leyfer, O.T.; Folstein, S.F.; Bacalman, S.; Davis, N.O.; Dinh, E.; Morgan, J.; Tager-Flusberg, H.; Lainhart, J.E. Comorbid psychiatric disorders in children with autism: Interview development and rates of disorders. *J. Autism Dev. Disord.* **2006**, *36*, 849–861. [CrossRef] [PubMed]
20. Gillberg, C. *A Guide to Asperger Syndrome*; Cambridge University Press: Cambridge, UK, 2002.
21. Fusar-Poli, L.; Brondino, N.; Politi, P.; Aguglia, E. Missed diagnoses and misdiagnoses of adults with autism spectrum disorder. *Eur. Arch. Psychiatry Clin. Neurosci.* **2020**, *272*, 187–198. [CrossRef]
22. Gould, J.; Ashton-Smith, J. Missed diagnosis or misdiagnosis? Girls and women on the autism spectrum. *Good Autism Pract.* **2011**, *12*, 34–41.
23. Hull, L.; Petrides, K.V.; Allison, C.; Smith, P.; Baron-Cohen, S.; Lai, M.-C.; Mandy, W. "Putting on my best normal": Social camouflaging in adults with autism spectrum conditions. *J. Autism Dev. Disord.* **2017**, *47*, 2519–2534. [CrossRef]
24. Glascoe, F.P. Screening for developmental and behavioral problems. *Ment. Retard. Dev. Disabil. Res. Rev.* **2005**, *11*, 173–179. [CrossRef]
25. Arun, P.; Chavan, B.S. Development of a screening instrument for autism spectrum disorder: Chandigarh autism screening instrument. *Indian J. Med. Res.* **2018**, *147*, 369–375. [CrossRef]
26. Chakraborty, S.; Bhatia, T.; Sharma, V.; Antony, N.; Das, D.; Sahu, S.; Sharma, S.; Sharma, V.; Brar, J.S.; Iyengar, S.; et al. Protocol for development of the indian autism screening questionnaire: The screening version of the Indian scale for assessment of autism. *Indian J. Psychol. Med.* **2020**, *42* (Suppl. S6), S63–S67. [CrossRef]
27. Thabtah, F. An accessible and efficient autism screening method for behavioural data and predictive analyses. *Health Inform. J.* **2018**, *25*, 1739–1755. [CrossRef] [PubMed]
28. Thabtah, F.; Peebles, D. Early autism screening: A comprehensive review. *Int. J. Environ. Res. Public Health* **2019**, *16*, 3502. [CrossRef] [PubMed]
29. Eaves, L.C.; Wingert, H.D.; Ho, H.H.; Mickelson, E.C.R. Screening for autism spectrum disorders with the social communication questionnaire. *J. Dev. Behav. Pediatrics* **2006**, *27*, S95–S103. [CrossRef] [PubMed]
30. Woodbury-Smith, M.R.; Robinson, J.; Wheelwright, S.; Baron-Cohen, S. Screening adults for asperger syndrome using the AQ: A preliminary study of its diagnostic validity in clinical practice. *J. Autism Dev. Disord.* **2005**, *35*, 331–335. [CrossRef]
31. Sappok, T.; Heinrich, M.; Underwood, L. Screening tools for autism spectrum disorders. *Adv. Autism* **2015**, *1*, 12–29. [CrossRef]
32. Baron-Cohen, S.; Hoekstra, R.A.; Knickmeyer, R.; Wheelwright, S. The autism-spectrum quotient (AQ): Evidence from Asperger syndrome/high-functioning autism, males and females, scientists and mathematicians. *J. Autism Dev. Disord.* **2001**, *31*, 5–17. [CrossRef]
33. Eriksson, J.M.; Andersen, L.M.J.; Bejerot, S. RAADS-14 screen: Validity of a screening tool for autism spectrum disorder in an adult psychiatric population. *Mol. Autism* **2013**, *4*, 49. [CrossRef]
34. Baron-Cohen, S.; Wheelwright, S.; Robinson, J.; Woodbury-Smith, M. The Adult Asperger Assessment (AAA): A diagnostic method. *J. Autism Dev. Disord.* **2005**, *35*, 807–819. [CrossRef]
35. Sizoo, B.B.; Horwitz, E.H.; Teunisse, J.P.; Kan, C.C.; Visser, C.T.W.M.; Forceville, E.J.M.; Van Voorst, A.J.P.; Van Voorst, H.M. Predictive validity of self-report questionnaires in the assessment of autism spectrum disorders in adults. *Autism* **2015**, *19*, 842–849. [CrossRef]
36. Wakabayashi, A.; Baron-Cohen, S.; Wheelwright, S.; Tojo, Y. The Autism-Spectrum Quotient (AQ) in Japan: A cross-cultural comparison. *J. Autism Dev. Disord.* **2006**, *36*, 263–270. [CrossRef]
37. Kenny, H.; Alison, J.S. How useful are the Adult Asperger Assessment and AQ-10 within an adult clinical population of all intellectual abilities? *Adv. Autism* **2016**, *2*, 118–130. [CrossRef]
38. Fusar-Poli, L.; Ciancio, A.; Gabbiadini, A.; Meo, V.; Patania, F.; Rodolico, A.; Saitta, G.; Vozza, L.; Petralia, A.; Signorelli, M.S.; et al. Self-reported autistic traits using the AQ: A comparison between individuals with ASD, psychosis, and non-clinical controls. *Brain Sci.* **2020**, *10*, 291. [CrossRef] [PubMed]
39. Adamou, M.; Jones, S.L.; Wetherhill, S. *AAA Screening in Adults with ASD: A Retrospective Cohort Study*; Emerald Publishing Limited: Bingley, UK, 2021.
40. Ashwood, K.L.; Gillan, N.; Horder, J.; Hayward, H.; Woodhouse, E.; McEwen, F.S.; Findon, J.; Eklund, H.; Spain, D.; Wilson, C.E.; et al. Predicting the diagnosis of autism in adults using the Autism-Spectrum Quotient (AQ) questionnaire. *Psychol. Med.* **2016**, *46*, 2595–2604. [CrossRef] [PubMed]
41. Bishop, S.L.; Seltzer, M.M. Self-reported autism symptoms in adults with autism spectrum disorders. *J. Autism Dev. Disord.* **2012**, *42*, 2354–2363. [CrossRef] [PubMed]

42. Booth, T.; Murray, A.L.; McKenzie, K.; Kuenssberg, R.; O'Donnell, M.; Burnett, H. Brief report: An evaluation of the AQ-10 as a brief screening instrument for ASD in adults. *J. Autism Dev. Disord.* **2013**, *43*, 2997–3000. [CrossRef]
43. Allison, C.; Auyeung, B.; Baron-Cohen, S. Toward brief "red flags" for autism screening: The short autism spectrum quotient and the short quantitative checklist in 1000 cases and 3000 controls. *J. Am. Acad. Child Adolesc. Psychiatry* **2012**, *51*, 202–212. [CrossRef]
44. Kurita, H.; Koyama, T.; Osada, H. Autism-Spectrum Quotient-Japanese version and its short forms for screening normally intelligent persons with pervasive developmental disorders. *Psychiatry Clin. Neurosci.* **2005**, *59*, 490–496. [CrossRef]
45. Lepage, J.-F.; Lortie, M.; Taschereau-Dumouchel, V.; Théoret, H. Validation of French-Canadian versions of the Empathy Quotient and Autism Spectrum Quotient. *Can. J. Behav. Sci.* **2009**, *41*, 272–276. [CrossRef]
46. Ketelaars, C.; Horwitz, E.; Sytema, S.; Bos, J.; Wiersma, D.; Minderaa, R.; Hartman, C.A. Brief report: Adults with mild autism spectrum disorders (ASD): Scores on the autism spectrum quotient (AQ) and comorbid psychopathology. *J. Autism Dev. Disord.* **2008**, *38*, 176–180. [CrossRef]
47. Hirota, T.; So, R.; Kim, Y.S.; Leventhal, B.; Epstein, R.A. A systematic review of screening tools in non-young children and adults for autism spectrum disorder. *Res. Dev. Disabil.* **2018**, *80*, 1–12. [CrossRef]
48. Williams, J.; Brayne, C. Screening for autism spectrum disorders: What is the evidence? *Autism* **2006**, *10*, 11–35. [CrossRef] [PubMed]
49. Posserud, M.-B.; Lundervold, A.J.; Gillberg, C. Validation of the autism spectrum screening questionnaire in a total population sample. *J. Autism Dev. Disord.* **2009**, *39*, 126–134. [CrossRef] [PubMed]
50. Ritvo, R.A.; Ritvo, E.R.; Guthrie, D.; Yuwiler, A.; Ritvo, M.J.; Weisbender, L. A scale to assist the diagnosis of autism and Asperger's disorder in adults (RAADS): A pilot study. *J. Autism Dev. Disord.* **2008**, *38*, 213–223. [CrossRef] [PubMed]
51. Jones, S.L.; Johnson, M.; Alty, B.; Adamou, M. The effectiveness of RAADS-R as a screening tool for adult ASD populations. *Autism Res. Treat.* **2021**, *2021*, 9974791. [CrossRef] [PubMed]
52. Kember, S.M.; Williams, M.N. Autism in Aotearoa: Is the RAADS-14 a valid tool for a New Zealand population? *Eur. J. Psychol. Assess.* **2021**, *37*, 247. [CrossRef]
53. Conner, C.M.; Cramer, R.D.; McGonigle, J.J. Examining the diagnostic validity of autism measures among adults in an outpatient clinic sample. *Autism Adulthood* **2019**, *1*, 60–68. [CrossRef]
54. Picot, M.-C.; Michelon, C.; Bertet, H.; Pernon, E.; Fiard, D.; Coutelle, R.; Abbar, M.; Attal, J.; Amestoy, A.; Duverger, P.; et al. The French version of the revised ritvo autism and Asperger diagnostic scale: A psychometric validation and diagnostic accuracy study. *J. Autism Dev. Disord.* **2021**, *51*, 30–44. [CrossRef]
55. Brugha, T.; Tyrer, F.; Leaver, A.; Lewis, S.; Seaton, S.; Morgan, Z.; Tromans, S.; van Rensburg, K. Testing adults by questionnaire for social and communication disorders, including autism spectrum disorders, in an adult mental health service population. *Int. J. Methods Psychiatr. Res.* **2020**, *29*, e1814. [CrossRef]
56. Horwitz, E.H.; Schoevers, R.A.; Ketelaars, C.E.J.; Kan, C.C.; van Lammeren, A.M.D.; Meesters, Y.; Spek, A.A.; Wouters, S.; Teunisse, J.P.; Cuppen, L.; et al. Clinical assessment of ASD in adults using self- and other-report: Psychometric properties and validity of the Adult Social Behavior Questionnaire (ASBQ). *Res. Autism Spectr. Disord.* **2016**, *24*, 17–28. [CrossRef]
57. Andersen, L.M.J.; Näswall, K.; Manouilenko, I.; Nylander, L.; Edgar, J.; Ritvo, R.A.; Ritvo, E.; Bejerot, S. The Swedish version of the ritvo autism and Asperger diagnostic scale: Revised (RAADS-R). A Validation study of a rating scale for adults. *J. Autism Dev. Disord.* **2011**, *41*, 1635–1645. [CrossRef]
58. Westwood, H.; Eisler, I.; Mandy, W.; Leppanen, J.; Treasure, J.; Tchanturia, K. Using the autism-spectrum quotient to measure autistic traits in anorexia nervosa: A systematic review and meta-analysis. *J. Autism Dev. Disord.* **2016**, *46*, 964–977. [CrossRef] [PubMed]
59. Romero, M.; Aguilar, J.M.; Del-Rey-Mejías, Á.; Mayoral, F.; Rapado, M.; Peciña, M.; Barbancho, M.Á.; Ruiz-Veguilla, M.; Lara, J.P. Psychiatric comorbidities in autism spectrum disorder: A comparative study between DSM-IV-TR and DSM-5 diagnosis. *Int. J. Clin. Health Psychol.* **2016**, *16*, 266–275. [CrossRef] [PubMed]
60. Mannion, A.; Leader, G. Comorbidity in autism spectrum disorder: A literature review. *Res. Autism Spectr. Disord.* **2013**, *7*, 1595–1616. [CrossRef]
61. Lai, M.-C.; Kassee, C.; Besney, R.; Bonato, S.; Hull, L.; Mandy, W.; Szatmari, P.; Ameis, S.H. Prevalence of co-occurring mental health diagnoses in the autism population: A systematic review and meta-analysis. *Lancet Psychiatry* **2019**, *6*, 819–829. [CrossRef]
62. Lugnegård, T.; Hallerbäck, M.U.; Gillberg, C. Asperger syndrome and schizophrenia: Overlap of self-reported autistic traits using the Autism-spectrum Quotient (AQ). *Nord. J. Psychiatry* **2015**, *69*, 268–274. [CrossRef]
63. Tebartz Van Elst, L.; Pick, M.; Biscaldi, M.; Fangmeier, T.; Riedel, A. High-functioning autism spectrum disorder as a basic disorder in adult psychiatry and psychotherapy: Psychopathological presentation, clinical relevance and therapeutic concepts. *Eur. Arch. Psychiatry Clin. Neurosci.* **2013**, *263* (Suppl. S2), S189–S196. [CrossRef]
64. Wigham, S.; Rodgers, J.; Berney, T.; Couteur, A.L.; Ingham, B.; Parr, J.R. Psychometric properties of questionnaires and diagnostic measures for autism spectrum disorders in adults: A systematic review. *Autism* **2018**, *23*, 287–305. [CrossRef]
65. Happé, F.G.; Mansour, H.; Barrett, P.; Brown, T.; Abbott, P.; Charlton, R.A. Demographic and cognitive profile of individuals seeking a diagnosis of autism spectrum disorder in adulthood. *J. Autism Dev. Disord.* **2016**, *46*, 3469–3480. [CrossRef]
66. Sewani, H.; Kashef, R. An autoencoder-based deep learning classifier for efficient diagnosis of autism. *Children* **2020**, *7*, 182. [CrossRef]

67. Kashef, R. ECNN: Enhanced convolutional neural network for efficient diagnosis of autism spectrum disorder. *Cogn. Syst. Res.* **2022**, *71*, 41–49. [CrossRef]
68. Kanimozhiselvi, C.S.; Jayaprakash, D. Machine learning based autism grading for clinical decision making. *Int. J. Recet. Technol. Eng.* **2019**, *8*, 7443–7446.
69. Eslami, T.; Almuqhim, F.; Raiker, J.S.; Saeed, F. Machine learning methods for diagnosing autism spectrum disorder and attention-deficit/hyperactivity disorder using functional and structural MRI: A survey. *Front. Neuroinform.* **2021**, *14*, 62. [CrossRef] [PubMed]
70. Hyde, K.K.; Novack, M.N.; LaHaye, N.; Parlett-Pelleriti, C.; Anden, R.; Dixon, D.R.; Linstead, E. Applications of supervised machine learning in autism spectrum disorder research: A review. *Review J. Autism Dev. Disord.* **2019**, *6*, 128–146. [CrossRef]
71. Batsakis, S.; Adamou, M.; Tachmazidis, I.; Antoniou, G.; Kehagias, T. Data-driven decision support for autism diagnosis using machine learning. In Proceedings of the 13th International Conference on Management of Digital EcoSystems, Hammamet, Tunisia, 1–3 November 2021; pp. 30–34.
72. Hall, M.; Frank, E.; Holmes, G.; Pfahringer, B.; Reutemann, P.; Witten, I.H. The WEKA data mining software: An update. *ACM SIGKDD Explor. Newsl.* **2009**, *11*, 10–18. [CrossRef]
73. Batsakis, S.; Tachmazidis, I.; Baryannis, G.; Antoniou, G. Semantic artificial neural networks. In *European Semantic Web Conference*; Springer: Berlin/Heidelberg, Germany, 2020; pp. 39–44.
74. Došilović, F.K.; Brčić, M.; Hlupić, N. Explainable artificial intelligence: A survey. In Proceedings of the 2018 41st International Convention On Information And Communication Technology, Electronics And Microelectronics (MIPRO), Opatija, Croatia, 21–25 May 2018; pp. 210–215.
75. Shavlik, J.W.; Towell, G.G. An approach to combining explanation-based and neural learning algorithms. In *Applications of Learning and Planning Methods*; World Scientific: Singapore, 1991; pp. 71–98.
76. Towell, G.G.; Shavlik, J.W. Knowledge-based artificial neural networks. *Artif. Intell.* **1994**, *70*, 119–165. [CrossRef]
77. Tsamardinos, I.; Charonyktakis, P.; Lakiotaki, K.; Borboudakis, G.; Zenklusen, J.C.; Juhl, H.; Chatzaki, E.; Lagani, V. *Just Add Data: Automated Predictive Modeling and Biosignature Discovery*; Cold Spring Harbor Laboratory: Laurel Hollow, NY, USA, 2020.
78. Tsamardinos, I.; Greasidou, E.; Borboudakis, G. Boot-strapping the out-of-sample predictions for efficient and accurate cross-validation. *Mach. Learn.* **2018**, *107*, 1895–1922. [CrossRef]

 digital

Article

Intelligence-Led Policing and the New Technologies Adopted by the Hellenic Police

Georgios Gkougkoudis [1,*], Dimitrios Pissanidis [2] and Konstantinos Demertzis [3]

[1] Hellenic Police, General Directorate of Attica Region, Leoforos Alexandras 173, 11522 Athens, Greece
[2] Computer Science Department, Independent Studies of Science & Technology College (IST), Sygrou Avenue 68, 11742 Athens, Greece; d.pissanidis@ist.edu.gr
[3] School of Science & Technology, Informatics Studies, Hellenic Open University, Par. Aristotelous 18, 26335 Patra, Greece; kdemertz@fmenr.duth.gr
* Correspondence: g.gkougkoudis@hellenicpolice.gr

Abstract: In the never-ending search by Law Enforcement Agencies (LEAs) for ways to reduce crime more effectively, the prevention of criminal activity is always considered the ideal solution. Since the 1990s, Intelligence-led Policing (ILP) was implemented in some forms by many LEAs around the world for crime prevention. Along with ILP, LEAs nowadays more and more turn to various new surveillance technologies. As a result, there are numerous studies and reports introducing some compelling results from LEAs that have implemented ILP, offering robust data around how the future of policing could be. In this context, this paper explores the most recent literature, identifying where ILP stands today in Greece and to what extent it could be a viable, practical approach to crime prevention. In addition, it is researched to what degree new technologies have been adopted by the European Union and the Hellenic Police in their "battle" against crime. It is concluded that most technologies are at the research stage, and studies are underway in many areas.

Keywords: policing; security; technology; surveillance; cybercrime; data analysis; AI; law enforcement

1. Introduction

Policing has gone through numerous radical changes over the years. Since the introduction of professional policing under political control in liberal democracies, various models of policing have been tested and implemented [1]. The most typical examples are Community Policing, Zero Tolerance Policing, Intelligence-Led Policing (ILP), Problem Solving Policing, Preventative Policing, Cooperative Policing, etc. [2,3]. The responsibilities and requirements of the police profession used to be simple, and the means used by the police officers, in order to perform duties, unsophisticated and "unadorned" [4]. However, since the 1930s, the policing "world" changed along with the rapid transformation of society and the development of criminality [2,4]. A significant contribution was made in this transformation of policing by J. Edgar Hoover, who introduced how science could contribute to criminal investigations, establishing, in 1932, the first Technical Crime Laboratory in the Federal Bureau of Investigations, focusing on the use of scientific analysis to solve crimes [5]. After that point, using technological innovations for collecting and analyzing criminal information and data to deal with crime and manage risk became the dominant model [2].

Security was always a multifarious subject [2,6]. Threat sources and events, crime vulnerabilities, and risks are many and diverse; thus, a lot of discussions have taken place for decades among scholars and practitioners of policing around how the modern police should respond to crime [2,6]. In this context, numerous academics and researchers [2,3,7] have stated that ILP's holistic approach that focuses on taking advantage of technology in order to accurately assess the social harm of criminality, may allow the police to prevent crime beyond borders.

Citation: Gkougkoudis, G.; Pissanidis, D.; Demertzis, K. Intelligence-Led Policing and the New Technologies Adopted by the Hellenic Police. *Digital* **2022**, *2*, 143–163. https://doi.org/10.3390/digital2020009

Academic Editors: Mirjana Ivanović, Richard Chbeir and Yannis Manolopoulos

Received: 27 November 2021
Accepted: 28 March 2022
Published: 29 March 2022

Publisher's Note: MDPI stays neutral with regard to jurisdictional claims in published maps and institutional affiliations.

Copyright: © 2022 by the authors. Licensee MDPI, Basel, Switzerland. This article is an open access article distributed under the terms and conditions of the Creative Commons Attribution (CC BY) license (https://creativecommons.org/licenses/by/4.0/).

One of the first and more significant steps taken towards the datafication of policing was made by the New York City Police Department in early 1994 when it introduced the Compstat system that exploited crime statistics and mapping technologies to identify crime hotspots and emerging threats [2]. The transition from an investigative ethos to a technologically driven strategic business model to address modern policing problems provided police with a real opportunity to increase its effectiveness against crime [2]. This transition was accelerated after the terrorist attacks of 9 November 2001, which revealed to the world how intelligence operations are of life-and-death importance [7]. Since that day, it was realized that homeland security and local crime prevention are not mutually exclusive; thus, the world's attention has been focused on the need for constructive changes in law enforcement intelligence [7]. That was the point where efforts focused on enhancing state and local law enforcement intelligence operations, making it possible for police to play a major role in homeland security [7]. Therefore, everyday police events and incidents were considered now crucial in the production of valuable intelligence when correlated with homeland security information. What better source for gathering information on all kinds of potential threats and vulnerabilities than police officers "on the beat" [7] (p.vii)?

The future policing environment is expected to be challenging, as it will be characterized by transnational organized criminality, global terrorism, and domestic extremism, while society will be increasingly risk concerned and influenced by intrusive media [2]. The need for convergence between criminal intelligence and national security will become imperative [2]. "Law enforcement can no longer afford to respond to contemporary and future problems with the solutions of yesterday" [7] (p.vii).

As ILP is evolving and widely applied, surveillance mechanisms are increasing [2]. In that sense, although LEAs have been implementing ILP and surveillance technologies for almost 30 years now, there is still much controversy around the use of this data-driven approach to crime prevention, as not much empirical evidence exists to either support or discredit it [8–13].

However, LEAs continue to expand their technology to obtain, retain, and search numerous non-criminal data in their effort to identify information on criminal suspects [2]. In this context, the Greek state, along with the European Union (EU), invested a lot of energy and government/EU funds on the technological upgrade of the Hellenic Police (HP) and focused on fully adopting the ILP's philosophy in everyday police work. As a result, the creation of the Aerial Means Division, the use of body-worn cameras by police officers, and innovative technological projects such as "Smart Policing" and "National Passenger Information Unit" signaled the new era that the HP has entered [14–18]. In this sense, this paper, after an extensive review of all the relevant literature, presents a broad-based study of the cutting-edge technology used by LEAs, namely the HP, in their effort to fully implement ILP and adopt its philosophy in their everyday work. However, it should be mentioned that this thorough investigation of sources showed that no significant and extensive research was realized around the subject. This fact indicates how limited the research and investigation around the new technologies that HP has or is about to adopt, has been, and how difficult it turned out to be for us to look into all the details around the theme because of the lack of previous original research data. Nevertheless, this absence of relevant research data proves the value of this research. As a result, a study researching this aspect of ILP's adoption by the HP could be considered important, offering new data in the context of the degree of the technologically driven datafication of policing in Greece.

The study is organized as follows: Section 2 describes the research design and methodology followed by the researchers; Section 3 conceptualizes the ILP doctrine and reviews related work around the new technologies implemented by LEAs in general, that have adopted ILP; Section 4 presents the EU initiatives in the same field; Section 5 presents the main results of our study on the technologies implemented or about to be adopted by the HP in its effort to apply the ILP doctrine; Section 6 gives a detailed description of the main benefits and risks that comprise from the use of such technologies; and finally the last section draws the conclusions and outlines future research directions.

2. Research Design

The general topic/title for this research paper is "Intelligence-led policing (ILP) and the new technologies in the Hellenic Police," and the research question of this study is "To what extent the new police doctrine, ILP, and new technologies are adopted by the HP?". With that in mind, the research aims to acquire knowledge around the ILP doctrine and the degree of its implementation by the HP and identifying any new technologies adopted by the EU and the HP in their effort to reduce crime. In order to achieve these aims, a review of the existing policing literature about ILP was realized in order to comprehend to what extent it is implemented by the HP. Furthermore, a thorough exploration of the existing policing and technology literature was made in order to identify technologies adopted by the EU and the HP and to contribute original data to the ongoing discussions surrounding ILP, and new police adopted technologies in Greece.

The research strategy adopted in this research can be described as a two-step procedure. The first one is collecting indirect (secondary) qualitative data from books, journals, newspaper articles, and the internet, existing data that researchers simply gather and analyze, and the second one is analyzing them using qualitative methods in order to extract valuable conclusions [19]. As a result, the research question will be best examined through conducting desk-based theoretical research [20].

This qualitative methodology was preferred due to the fact that it does not raise major ethical considerations and demand careful sampling in order to guarantee neutrality and credibility [19,21].

However, indirect data may not be custom-built for the research subject, challenging the researcher to adequately and effectively combine them in order to extract the conclusions needed [19]. In secondary data research analysis, the most important is knowing what you are looking for [19]. If the researcher knows what he/she needs, it is easier to identify adequate sources [19].

As a result, it was vital for the researchers, during the collection and analysis stage of the data, to follow some important qualitative techniques that guaranteed the objectivity and credibility of the research conclusions:

- Prolonged engagement—invest sufficient time to understand the context of each source [19];
- Persistent observation—dig further into each source, beyond an initial superficial reading [19];
- Broad representation and triangulation—collect a variety of sources of data to confirm the authenticity of each source and create a collected data sample that will be wide enough to ensure that formed conclusions are remarkable [19].

Right at this time, it should be stated that when conducting secondary research using indirect data, there is an agitation regarding the impartiality of research data collected and their sources [22,23]. As O'Leary [19] states, one's bias could "color" the data interpretations and understandings. It is vital during the analysis process to question a text's origin and the writer's agenda as some sources are by nature subjective (e.g., media coverage expressing political agendas) [19]. As a result, assessing credibility and objectivity during data collection and analysis is essential [19].

In this context, the content analysis method was used by the researchers. More specifically, the researchers moved on, carrying out an in-depth conceptual content analysis of all the data. In order to use conceptual content analysis in analyzing all the findings, we had to break them down into more manageable categories for further analysis [24,25]. As a result, the steps that were followed for the research's secondary data content analysis were as follows:

- Locating data;
- Evaluating relevance of the data;
- Assessing the credibility of the data;
- Categorizing and analyzing the data.

Through this process of content analysis, the researchers analyzed all the gathered material and tried to conceptualize and interpret it attentively, draw conclusions, and spot trends and patterns, as this type of content analysis could only quantify the information [24].

3. ILP and Technology

Globally, the intensive engagement of modern governments in the surveillance of individuals is naturally recognized as an integral part of their overall path to globalization and is closely linked to the broader socio-political conditions and the recent technological developments [26]. Although the events of 9 November 2001 are not genetically related to the already existing surveillance trend, they are nevertheless considered as a major cause of the intensification of the escalation, as most surveillance procedures, in particular the collection, distribution, and information processing, henceforth, was the most dynamic—at the same time, of course, the darkest—approach to managing the terrorist threat [7,26].

The process of legitimizing the collection and processing of information by official Law Enforcement policy bodies has begun to change dramatically, as the formal boundaries between the methods of criminal proceedings and those of the relevant state secret services have ceased to be distinguished and sometimes even to exist [1]. The British LEA, followed by its US counterparts, were the first to formally and systematically adopt a policing model based on the extensive collection of information about individuals, openly embracing very wide and frequently challenged techniques and methods of gathering information, with the aim of improving the effectiveness of counter-terrorism work [10]. At the same time, many other European countries have begun to adopt similar preventive information management practices around individuals, even before their formal involvement in the criminal justice system, only under the vague condition of probable high criminal risk [27].

This trend towards an "information-defined" form of policing, aimed at countering terrorism, soon gained the attention, not only of designers and practitioners but also of theorists and academics who began to contribute systematically to its theoretical foundation and analysis, now calling it ILP [26,28]. It soon gained strong supporters on a practical and academic level, and it was identified as one of the most important innovations of the 21st century in the field of law enforcement [26,28].

At its core, ILP can be conceptualized as a predictive model that uses the inductive method for the export of conclusions [2,7].

3.1. Defining ILP

Attempting to describe this trend presents a small difficulty in its early stages, as there is no, as one would expect, the general and universally accepted definition [2]. ILP is a "definitionally evolving concept" [2] (p. 84), and divergent interpretations of the model around the world are mainly based on the fact that it is relatively new, constantly expanding and changing, applied to jurisdictions of different cultures-necessities and with enormous room for improvement [2,26].

According to many academics [2,3,29], ILP is identified as a tool or an instrument or, as Sheptycki [29] defines it, "the technological effort to manage information about threats and risks in order to strategically manage the policing mission."

However, the recent revisions move ILP away from being a tactic or a tool and identify it as a part of a conceptual policing philosophy [2]. Ratcliffe [2], along with the Organization for Security and Co-operation in Europe (OSCE) [30], follow a more business-oriented terminology, stating that ILP is evolving into a managerial model of evidence-based resource allocation decisions through prioritization.

In most cases, ILP is described as "a strategy, a long-term and targeted approach to crime control that focuses on the identification, analysis and management of existing and growing problems or forms of risk" [3] (p. 2). According to this philosophy, the model moves more towards a problem-solving orientation of problem-oriented policing [2].

All modern definitions of ILP though emphasize the importance of collecting, analyzing and sharing information and data in the "battle" against crime [2,27]. This policing model—inspired by the modern crime management mentality—attempts to be implemented through the systematic collection of information (not only criminological) and the analysis of relevant data in order to help formulate a more general decision-making framework, with the ultimate goal of crime reduction and prevention, both through problem management strategy and effective repression, targeting, in particular, the most dangerous criminals [28].

3.2. LEA and Technology

ILP and the technology that comes with it is transforming LEAs work in the 21st century, introducing new tools to deal with modern crime [26]. From drones and body-worn cameras to facial recognition software and artificial intelligence, new pioneering technologies are equipping LEAs with new capabilities to protect and serve civilians [31,32]. For instance, more and more police departments across the country are deploying drones and unmanned aerial vehicles (UAVs) as "eyes" in the sky to collect crime evidence or even prevent crimes from happening, functioning as a crime deterrence [32,33]. As technology continues to transform nearly every aspect of society, LEAs' leaders now have an arsenal of high-tech systems and tools that are designed to enhance public safety, catch criminals, and save lives [31,34].

After a thorough review of technology and policing literature [16–18,31–45], in order to identify the most important ILP technologies that are equipping LEAs with new capabilities to perform their duties, it can be said that these technologies are divided in 10 main categories, which are described briefly below.

3.2.1. Artificial Intelligence

The ever-growing expansion of the Internet of Things (IoT) signifies that more data are being generated, collected, and analyzed every day—much of which could be proved to be incredibly valuable for LEAs [6]. However, the process of deriving actionable insights from exploiting huge amounts of data can be incredibly time-consuming and costly when performed by police officers [2].

This Big Data challenge is recently confronted by Artificial Intelligence (AI) [8]. Technologies such as ShotSpotter, facial recognition, and biometrics contain AI algorithms [31,46]. AI is also used for crime mapping in order to more effectively pinpoint high-crime areas that should be monitored [34].

AI, in general, is mostly used by LEAs in their effort to deploy a predictive policing model. AI utilizes the so-called "deep learning" algorithms that train computers to analyze big data in order to actually predict when and where crimes are more likely to occur and help LEAs to distribute police staff accordingly to the crime hotspot areas identified [44,45].

3.2.2. Facial Recognition Software

Facial recognition capabilities came along with the development of AI that was achieved thanks to the newly introduced innovative deep learning techniques [47]. Thus, a deep learning-based face recognition system, typically when it detects a face, it starts normalizing the image and extracting facial features in order to compare them against any given face or a pool of faces existed in a database [48]. Such a system was tested for live identification of people of interest at Brussels Airport in 2017 [49].

Though advanced forms of facial recognition could prove to be a valuable tool for crime prevention with its capabilities in identifying potential terrorists and tracking criminals and missing people, such technologies are considered to be among the most controversial emerging police technologies in the 21st century [50].

3.2.3. Biometrics

In addition to fingerprints, which have been used globally for over a century, and DNA profiling, which has been used for the last 40 years by LEAs to identify criminals, now LEAs have access to an ever-expanding array of biometric and behavioral characteristics [31].

Some of the most important are emotion detection, voice recognition, gait analysis, wrist veins, iris recognition, palmprints, and even heartbeats [17,31].

For example, emotion detection technologies are used to identify the mental state and emotions of a target, examining facial expressions and other physiognomic characteristics such as gaze, voice, heart rate, body temperature, body movement, and gestures [47]. Emotion detection applications based on AI technology are already exploited in monitoring mental health, evaluating children's social and emotional skills, assessing job candidates, and detecting potential shoplifters [47].

3.2.4. Robots

In this category, one of the hottest trends is the development and construction of self-driving cars that continue to challenge the automotive industry until today [40]. This new technology was recently used by the automaker FORD to patent a self-driving police car that was equipped with artificial intelligence and was designed to identify traffic law violators by transmitting data to police officers on duty [41]. In this context, according to McGuire [30] (p.29), "the requirement for a police presence behind the wheel of patrol vehicles is itself now under threat... form the technology of driverless vehicles."

Moreover, there were some cases that LEAs, in order to obtain visual and audio access to specific potential crime scenes that were considered too dangerous or hard to reach, used next-generation robotic cameras, which were able to capture more complex movements and offer the level of optical resolution for close up action and consistency of coverage, space-saving and unique angles in comparison with automated cameras [42].

In the same context, a lot of ongoing research is focused on the development of police robot officers [42]. China introduced, in 2016, a security and service robot called "AnBot" that would be used to patrol banks, airports, and schools. According to Chinese Authorities [42], the "AnBot" is still under development, and in the near future, it will be deployed on the field, using facial recognition to identify criminals and was capable of following them until the police arrive [42]. In the same context, in Dubai, the Sanbot, a touchscreen-equipped robot officer that uses IBM's Watson AI system, is already on duty, patrolling tourist attractions [41]. The policing agencies in Dubai introduced this robot patrol officer in 2016, which was able to feed video to a command center, forward reported crimes to police, settle fines, run facial recognition processes, and speak nine languages. According to the United Arab Emirates Police Force, these robot officers will replace 25% of their forces by 2030 [42].

3.2.5. ShotSpotter

ShotSpotter is a new technology implemented in many cities, mainly in the United States, that detects gunfire through sensors, helping police analysts to track down the event and notify operational police officers to arrive at the scene more quickly than ever before [51]. According to Carr's research [51] in Washington and Oakland, where ShotSpotter tools were used, it was identified that only 12% of gunfire incidents resulted in a 911 call to report gunshots. However, a lot of concerns are still being raised around whether ShotSpotter can reliably distinguish the sound of gunfire from other loud, impulsive noises [52].

3.2.6. Thermal Imaging

Thermal imaging is a vastly used tool in border surveillance as it is especially effective in the dark [50]. Thermal image cameras exploit infrared imaging technology to detect heat emitted by objects such as humans and animals [36,37]. This technology is vastly used by HP in its effort to monitor and protect the borders [53]. After the migrant crisis that took place in February 2020 on the Greek-Turkish border, the HP deployed a huge number of thermal cameras, which detect human movement from body heat in a range of up to 12 km [38]. As a result, the HP monitors the movement on the border, inside the Turkish territory, in order to be prepared in case of a mass movement of people [38].

3.2.7. Automatic License (or Number) Plate Recognition (ALPR or ANPR)

The ALPR technology that is vastly used by toll collectors to automatically identify the registration numbers and letters on a car's license plate is now exploited by LEAs in their effort to identify stolen cars, arrest people with active warrants, and locate declared missing people (Amber Alerts)" [44].

This technology helped the police to automate and speed up the process of checking a license plate against LEA databases [39]. ALPR cameras are mounted at police cars and, in some cases, at streetlights, allowing LEAs to capture images of the same license plate could potentially offer the ability to track a vehicle's movements over time, which could prove to be vital in catching criminals [39].

This technology is used by the HP since 2016 in Athens and was recently deployed at the border crossings to locate both stolen vehicles and those used for illegal or criminal activities [38].

3.2.8. CCTV Systems

CCTV systems have become increasingly popular among municipalities and LEAs, as they provide important surveillance and prevention perspectives and serve as a tool for police investigation [54]. These systems are extensively exploited in London; however, the cameras used are configured to not being able to listen to conversations and capture clear pictures of public interactions [54]. They simply monitor people's behavior by covering a public space thus that it can be seen if a crime has been committed, gathering evidence at the same time ready to be used if needed, in a transubstantiation of an evidence-based policing strategy [55].

Of course, the proliferation of smartphones in the modern digital age has also exponentially increased the ability to record events, especially during police and citizen's contact [56]. As a result, video and audio recording have become a widespread integral part of the 21st-century culture [56].

In this context, video technology has been increasingly used as a surveillance mechanism, both by citizens and LEAs [6]. The first police-used video camera was introduced in the early 1990s in the US when various police patrol cars were equipped with in-car cameras that were recording real-time the police officers perform their duties [57].

3.2.9. Enhanced Body-Worn Cameras

Apart from CCTV systems and in-car cameras, body-worn police cameras that record the interactions and contacts of an on-duty police officer have also been used lately by LEAs around the world in order to provide transparency and accountability [58]. Despite the early resistance of the police personnel to the use of these cameras, research [59] showed that as accountability and transparency in the police increased, the sense of security and trust to the police officers by the citizens was augmented. A recent example of transparency was the case of George Floyd in the US, as the video recording from the police vehicle's camera was used in order to convict the police officer that shot and killed him [60,61].

This technology was recently in the center of public debate in Greece, especially after the announcements made by the Minister of Civil Protection that riot police would wear cameras to monitor the events during public demonstrations [14]. The use of body-worn cameras by the police has set in motion an ongoing debate around the importance and the impact of this technology in concepts such as privacy and data protection [14].

Nowadays, videos of police officers performing their duties in a number of high-profile incidents flood the internet and social media in an instance, drawing intense public and media scrutiny [14]. However, these videos, in most cases, do not display the whole picture of an incident as it does not depict all of the events; thus, body-worn cameras allow police supervisors and the public to gain an objective view of on-duty police work [62]. This technology, in some cases, was designed to integrate with police car systems in order to provide synchronized video of an event from multiple angles [58]. In addition, a smart holster has been developed that can activate the body-worn camera when the police officer draws his or her firearm [14]. Moreover, there are some technological reports indicating that body-worn cameras could, in the near future, be capable of issuing an alert when an officer falls down or is hurt [58]. The facial recognition capabilities of body-worn cameras are still in the development process [31].

3.2.10. Drones

Police forces are deploying more and more drones in their everyday tasks [42]. From traffic monitoring to border control surveillance, drones have proved to be a great tool in the police's efforts against crime [42]. LEAs in certain US states have already passed legislation that allows the use of non-lethal force by robots and drones. Therefore, the US border patrol has been actively considering weaponizing its drones to immobilize potential suspects in using non-lethal force against targets of interest [42].

In that sense, the Unmanned Aircraft Service of the HP was founded in 2017 and has the responsibility of monitoring all Greek territory and transiting information to the ground police forces regarding the prevention and suppression of crime, the treatment of illegal immigration in border areas, the control of order and traffic, the support firefighters in dealing with fires, natural disasters, floods, earthquakes or serious accidents and incidents [33,35]. The Service has nine UAVs at its disposal that were recently used to monitor the traffic during quarantine hours due to COVID-19 [16,38].

In general, drones are mostly used by police to gain aerial vantage points for collecting evidence from crime scenes, crowd monitoring, and search and rescue efforts [35]. Some drones are equipped even with cameras with thermal imaging, 3D mapping, and enhanced zoom capabilities [33,35].

4. EU Initiatives

Before examining the case of HP, it is imperative to investigate the EU's involvement in adopting new police technologies as EU's decisions and actions are interconnected significantly with HP's future [63].

The EU has, for the last five years, focused its energy and resources on improving border control and mitigating security risks related to cross-border terrorism and transnational crime [47]. EU member states proved to be rather flexible in adopting new technologies that offer accurate identification of individuals in order to control mobility and reduce crime [47].

The most commonly used technology is the automated fingerprint identification technology that is currently used in three European information systems; the Schengen Information System (SIS); the European dactyloscopy database (Eurodac); and the Visa Information System (VIS) [47]. It is also about to be used in the Entry/Exit System and the European Criminal Record Information System for third-Country nationals (ECRIS-TCN) [47].

Along with fingerprint identification, DNA profiling is a new SIS feature that is expected to be fully implemented by the end of 2021 [47].

Apart from these technologies, and according to a recent study for the European Commission (EC) [64], significant opportunities were identified, all involving the use of AI such as chat bots and virtual assistants, data management and analytics tools, and risk assessment applications [64].

In this context, although not yet used, automated FRT is configured in almost all EU information systems that would allow LEAs in the near future to process facial images for identification purposes [47]. The most common example of how FRT is used in the EU is the Automated Border Control (ABC) that is deployed at the EU airports [47]. More specifically an ABC system is "an automated system which authenticates the electronic machine-readable travel document or token, establishes that the passenger is the rightful holder of the document or token, queries border control records, then determines eligibility of border crossing according to the pre-defined rules" [65]. According to FRONTEX [65], these EU ABC systems support a number of biometrics, including facial and iris recognition.

Currently, they are used only for comparing a traveler's face against the facial image of his/her travel document, thus they are about to be enhanced as soon as the biometric passports are adopted worldwide [65].

Moreover, one of the most controversial applications of AI, emotion detection technologies, although not deployed in the EU, is explored and tested in a number of EU-funded projects and initiatives for developing border control mechanisms [47].

Apart from identification processes, AI algorithms are also used by the EU for profiling persons of interest based on specific data-based risk profiles [47]. This algorithmic intelligence-driven profiling technology that assesses individual risks of security, is carried out by Member States in the framework of the Passenger Name Record (PNR) data exchange and is being developed in the context of the VIS and the European Travel Information Authorization System (ETIAS) [47].

Finally, a recent study for the EC researched the development of an AI forecasting and early warning tool for migration trends and security threats [66]. The European Asylum Support Office (EASO) has already used such a tool in order to predict the future number of asylum applications [47]. In the same context, the European Border Surveillance System (EUROSUR) that became operational in 2014 and is based on such AI forecasting technology, is now considered a well-established intelligence and risk analysis driven framework for information exchange between EU Member States and the European Border and Coast Guard Agency (Frontex) [47].

5. ILP and Technology in Greece

Technology is considered to be, along with the ILP model and information management, a mechanism for improving the efficiency and effectiveness of LEAs in relation to crime detection [67].

The ILP model, taking advantage of technology, is now a key pillar of the HP's modern anti-crime policy [2]. This approach takes place in the context of the predictive model of policing, based on processed information (intelligence); thus that the operations of the police officers could be mainly predictive—preventive and secondarily repressive [11].

The HP in its effort to implement the ILP model, allocated a lot of resources and funding mechanisms (approximately 391.465.834,73 € of EU funding) available in acquiring cutting-edge police technology that could help police officers to be more effective [68]. Furthermore, HP is experimenting with FRT and other biometric processing technologies while at the same time consolidating the use of drones for policing and border control [18].

5.1. The Role of DIDAP

One of the main representatives responsible for this effort to adopt and implement ILP by the HP is the Directorate for Management and Analysis of Intelligence (DIDAP), which was established in 2014 (Presidential Decree 178/2014). DIDAP is HP's central point of information collection, where data are evaluated, classified, and analyzed in order to identify threats and signs of high crime—crime hotspots, consolidating the predictive-led policing as a best practice [7].

In this context, DIDAP recently implemented the project for the establishment and operation of an Operational Intelligence Center through the procurement of specialized software for interconnection of databases and analysis of information related to organized crime and terrorism [27,69].

Furthermore, as of May 2018, the EU countries registered all passengers on flights to and from the EU, storing all the data in huge databases and forwarded it to the authorities of other countries [15]. In this setting, DIDAP was responsible for the implementation of another important project, aiming at the establishment of the National Passenger Information Unit (PIU) for the Development of the PNR System [15]. The PNR project was initialized after the European Council obliged all air carriers to share all passenger data (biographic information and travel route information) with the Member States [47]. The primary objective of this system is to enforce border control and prevent irregular migration to Europe as it enables LEAs to detect unknown persons of interest before they arrive at the borders [47].

5.2. Drones and the COVID-19 Pandemic

During 2019, the HP could only use drones to monitor forests and observe traffic in motorways, was allowed to deploy drones in policing and border control activities (Presidential Decree 98/2019) [33,70]. More specifically, the Presidential Decree 98/2019 gives HP the right to use drones for any kind of policing and border control activities without a previous judicial authorization [70]. As drones are now deployed in policing and border control operations, images, and video of people's activity will be obtained [70].

In this context, HP moved on a bit further, exploiting drones during the COVID-19 pandemic [16]. According to the Hellenic Deputy Minister of Citizen Protection, Mr. Eleftherios Oikonomou, the HP used drones during the Easter holidays to ensure compliance with the movement restriction measures related to COVID-19 [33]. Many news media also reported the deployment of drones in urban areas, such as Athens and Thessaloniki, to monitor population movement [16].

Furthermore, HP has recently moved forward in procuring more UAVs and drones to augment its operational needs [33,35]. In June 2020, HP announced the acquisition of two drones through a public procurement contract of 136.000 euro, in the context of a European project called "HEFESTOS," while a few months later, the Western Greece Region concluded a contract with the HP in order to acquire drones for policing activities within the framework of the European project "INTERREG 2014–2020" [16,33,35].

5.3. Body-Worn Cameras and CCTV

The debate around the use of on-duty video recording by police officers has recently entered the Greek public discussion, after the announcements made by the Minister of Civil Protection in December 2019, about the pilot use of body-worn cameras by officers serving at the Public Order Restoration Unit and lately at the Immediate Response Unit [14,58,62]. In the same context, HP announced the realization of a project called "Smart Policing" that included the purchase and use of body-worn cameras by police officers that could identify people using Facial Recognition Technology (FRT) [17,18].

The image and sound recorded by the mobile cameras give LEAs and the public the opportunity to understand firsthand what the modern police officer is called to face during his shift [55].

Body-worn cameras can be both repressive and preventive [58]. Their primary role is of a repressive nature as the recording of video and audio carried by the police makes it easy to recall any interaction, observation or other behavior that could be used to extract useful evidence in identifying crime at an intelligence and judiciary level [58,62]. As a result, this repressive role mentioned could lead to the prevention of crime, as cameras are expected to act as police agents, capturing any misconduct on the part of both citizens and police officers [14]. As Farrar [43] (p.9) mentions "human beings can change their behavior when they know they are being observed and their movements are being recorded and are more likely to adopt more socially acceptable behavior, compliance with the rule of law and a greater sense of cooperation with the police".

In this framework, Couderta et al. [14] stated that such cameras are expected to increase the transparency of police action by documenting events that may involve police officers. This video recording documentation will serve as a reliable source of evidence of any interactions between police and citizens, exposing bad and good behavior [14]. Thus, it will prevent the misuse of violence and discrimination by the police or the violent behavior of citizens against the police [14]. Consequently, it is expected that policing will be improved, and public trust and confidence in the operation of the police will be restored to some degree, providing more public legitimacy [58].

However, many reservations exist around the use of such technology by the police, as there are concerns about privacy taking into account the issue of handling such personal data recorded by those portable police cameras [71]. Furthermore, there are a lot of concerns raised by police unions about the changes this technology will bring in police working conditions [62]. More specifically, there were some discussions around the mental health issues and the stress of police officers that will derive from wearing such devices that will monitor their actions on a daily basis [62].

5.4. Smart Policing—Facial Recognition

The milestone of the effort of the HP to adopt ILP is considered to be the "Smart Policing" project for the implementation of which, during 2019, the HP offered 4 million euro to a global telecommunication systems vendor, funded by the Internal Security Fund (ISF) of the EC. This project will provide police officers with 1000 mobile devices equipped with integrated software enabling facial recognition and automated fingerprint identification that will help them increase their effectiveness during security checks [72]. More specifically, these mobile devices will be the size of a smartphone, and police officers will be able to use them during police stops and patrols, taking face photographs of suspects and collecting their fingerprints that will immediately be compared with data already stored in central databases for identification purposes [31].

The devices will be able to store at least 1,500,000 photos [72]. The new system will provide links to 20 national databases such as those of the Ministries of Justice, Transport, Interior and Foreign Affairs, as well as to European and global databases, such as those of Europol and Interpol [72].

According to the basic network architecture of the system, during the implementation of the project, a private access network will be created and supported by the Contractor that will be inserted between the thousands of mobile devices and the HP's network [46,73]. However, this will signify that a private corporation will have access to all the activity of these devices.

The HP's answer to these concerns was that these smart policing devices would offer a more coherent way to identify individuals, especially foreign nationals overstaying in Greece, in comparison to the current course of action that obliges police officers to bring any individual who does not carry identification documents to the nearest police station [73–75]. The HP elaborated that the processing of biometric data, such as the data collected by these devices, follows all National and European legislation and is in accordance with the HDPA directives [31].

5.5. Research Programs

As many will argue, research projects lie at the heart of innovation and make a critical contribution to the development of Europe's societies and cultures. In this context, apart from the already implemented projects and procurements of specialized technological equipment, the HP has agreed to take part in important European research programs that gather the global interest around the future of the modern police. These research projects that focus on the field of smart policing and border management are funded by the EC under the Horizon 2020 scheme "Secure societies—Protecting freedom and security of Europe and its citizens" [76].

More specifically, the research projects that the HP has been implementing until today are mostly focused on enhancing surveillance capabilities exploiting the IoT technology and improving the information and data stream management (big data analytics).

5.5.1. PREVISION

PREVISION (Prediction and Visual Intelligence for Security Information) is a project that focuses on the development of technological tools in the field of information and data stream management that will help LEAs to deal with (cyber)crime and terrorism [77–79].

The project is coordinated by the Institute of Communication and Computer Systems, a non-profit Academic Research Body established in 1989 by the Greek Ministry of Education.

The project's consortium consists of IT companies, organizations, and LEAs from all around Europe [77–79].

The project will deliver applications that will be able to integrate, fuse, and process heterogeneous data streams collected from the web-darkweb [80], video, road traffic, financial institutions, telecommunications, social network, and information security systems [77–79]. These applications aim at providing LEAs the capability to apply predictive analytics and detect anomalies [11,69].

5.5.2. DARLINE Deep AR Law Enforcement Ecosystem

DARLINE's objective is to investigate how augmented reality (AR) technology can be exploited by LEAs in order to help first responders in making more informed and rapid decisions in challenging incidents [81]. More specifically, the project aims at developing innovative AR tools that will exploit AR smart glass technology and powerful computer vision algorithms with 5G network architectures, allowing agile processing of real-time data and improving situational awareness when responding to criminal and terrorist incidents [81]. According to the project's deliverables, DARLENE will develop:

- AR glasses that will provide real-time information analysis and intelligence provision through capabilities such as facial recognition [31];
- Personalized Heads-Up Display (HUD) that will monitor the users' physiological state and improve situational awareness [75];
- Devices that will enable police officers to see through concrete walls of buildings, the locations of people [32];
- A 5G radio network for the DARLENE AR-based law enforcement ecosystem [32].

This project is coordinated by the Center for Research and Technology-Hellas, a Greek research center [81]. The project's consortium consists of IT companies and organizations from all around Europe and LEAs from Spain, Portugal, Germany, Cyprus, Lithuania, and Greece [81].

5.5.3. ROXANNE

ROXANNE will provide an analytics platform that will enhance investigation capabilities, improving identification of persons of interest by developing an integrated interface, fusing speech, text, and video processing technologies with criminal intelligence analysis [82]. The project will use speech processing exploiting multiple technologies such as speaker identification, multilingual automatic speech recognition, video and geographical meta-data processing, and network analysis [83].

The project is coordinated by the Idiap Research Institute, a non-profit foundation, Idiap was founded by the City of Martigny, the Canton du Valais, EPFL, the University of Geneva, and Swisscom [83]. The project's consortium consists of INTERPOL, IT companies, organizations, universities, and LEAs from all around Europe [83].

5.5.4. AIDA

AIDA, exploiting AI and Deep Learning (DL) techniques to big data analytics, will develop a descriptive and predictive data analytics platform along with its tools in order to detect, analyze, and prevent organized crime and terrorism [17]. With AIDA's platform, LEAs will be capable of dealing with huge amount of heterogeneous data (structured or unstructured) and data sets (text, images, videos, communication and traffic data, financial transactions, etc.), fusing them to produce raw intelligence through applications of big data processing, Machine Learning (ML), AI, predictive and visual analytics [31,79].

The project is coordinated by the private company Engineering Ingegneria Informatica SpA, and the project's consortium consists of EUROPOL, other IT companies, organizations, universities, and LEAs from all around Europe [31,79].

5.5.5. SHIELD

7SHIELD aims at providing a holistic framework to LEAs to allow the effective confrontation of complex cyber and physical threats by enabling the deployment of innovative technological solutions, taking advantage of IoT technology for cyber and physical protection such as e-fences, passive radars, and laser technologies, multimedia AI technologies from CCTV cameras and UAVs [31,84].

This framework will try to integrate all these technologies aiming at correlating all the data produced in an integral hub that will allow the holistic processing, analysis, and visualization and provide better security and cyber threat detection-protection [16,85]. For this purpose, pilot schemes will take place in Spain, Athens, and Finland in order to produce valuable intel to be used in the development process of the framework.

7SHIELD consortium is composed of 22 partners from 12 different countries. It includes Private companies, Centers of Excellence, Research and Technology Centers, Regulation Authorities, Meteorological Institutes, Law Enforcements, and Research Foundations [31,84].

5.5.6. CREST

The CREST project will deliver a platform that will use targeted monitoring, tracking, and analytics solutions, exploiting IoT technology to develop an autonomous system for better surveillance that will allow LEAs to improve operational and investigation capabilities, produce reliable crime and terrorism predictions and preventions [86,87]. CREST Project Consortium showcases an overall representation of 23 partners from 16 countries. The eight LEAs participating in the CREST project originated from eight countries. CREST consortium also comprises seven Research and Academic Institutions, seven Industry Partners, and one Civil Organization [86,87].

5.5.7. TRESSPASS (Robust Risk Based Screening and Alert System for Passengers and Luggage)

TRESSPASS aims at modernizing the way the security checks at border crossing points are carried out by transforming the old-fashioned "Rule based" security check protocol to a new "Risk based" one [88–90].

More specifically, a system will be developed that will enable efficient and reliable well-targeted passenger checks through the exploitation of biometric and sensing technologies (passport/id readers, CCTV systems, body, and cargo scanners) [89] and pre-existing systems and databases such as VIS, SIS, and PNR [88].

The project is coordinated by the National Center for Scientific Research "Demokritos" in Greece, and the project's consortium consists of other IT companies, organizations, universities, and LEAs from all around Europe [88].

5.5.8. BORDERUAS

BORDERUAS aims to facilitate effective border surveillance and prevent cross-border criminal activities by taking advantage of cutting-edge UAV technology available [35]. The project will provide the technology of combining a "lighter-than-air" UAV with sophisticated surveillance technology [33,35]. The project is coordinated by Vicomtech, an applied research technology center specialized in Artificial Intelligence, Visual Computing and Interaction, and the project's consortium consists of other IT companies, organizations, universities, and LEAs from all around Europe [35].

5.5.9. FOLDOUT

FOLDOUT focuses on the development of a system that will combine various sensors and technologies in order to penetrate and monitor border regions with dense foliage in extreme climates [38]. Foliage monitoring is an important unsolved part of border surveillance, especially in the heavily forested areas on the Greek-Turkish border in Evros [35,38].

According to the project's specifications, the system will collect events analyzing them with ML tools in order to continuously increase its detection and tracking capability [38].

The project is coordinated by the Austrian Institute of Technology, and the project's consortium brings together IT companies, organizations, universities, and LEAs from all around Europe. The HP in this project is represented by the Center of Security Studies of Greece (KEMEA), which is a scientific, consulting and research organization overseen by the Minister of Citizen Protection [38].

5.5.10. EWISA (Early Warning for Increased Situational Awareness)

This project aims at increasing intelligence in video surveillance, through the development of smart video surveillance mechanism that will exploit multiple technologies such as motion detection, face recognition, picture enhancement, object counting, pattern and anomaly recognition [47,84]. EWISA will provide better assessment and management of illegal migration flows at the Greek land borders as it will increase the operational situation awareness and enhance the reaction capacity of the land border security service of the HP [47,91].

The project is coordinated by the Center of Security Studies of Greece (KEMEA) along with the HP, and the project's consortium consists of the LEA of Spain and the Border Control Agencies of Romania and Finland [47,84].

6. Discussion

Many reports [2,3,16,29,31,47,63,64,84,92] indicate that the careful adoption of ILP and new technologies, such as Artificial Intelligence (AI), enhanced biometrics and surveillance tools, by LEAs in the context of policing, security, and border control, could offer numerous benefits that are vital for the future of modern policing.

The greatest pitfall in researching such technologies lies in the fact that there is little evidence on the scope of their application to strongly confirm both the expected benefits and risks arising from the use of police technology in the EU and Greece [8,10,11,13,16,31,84]. This is mainly due to the fact that there is no universal application of such technologies by any large-scale LEA.

As a result, from the scientific literature reviewed, there is little evidence to strongly confirm most of the expected benefits and risks arising from the use of police technology in the EU and Greece. For instance, little is known about the attitude of European citizens towards police officers who are equipped with cameras. Does technology increase citizens' trust in the police, as well as the legitimacy and transparency with which the police operate?

Therefore, there is an imperative need for further research of the subject. In this setting, the fact that all new technologies used for policing, security, and border control in Greece and the EU are mostly at a research level indicates that the EU is trying to find the silver lining between the risks and benefits of the implementation of such technologies. Thus, demonizing radical technological solutions is not the answer. LEAs should research and test such technologies and regulate their mode of implementation, in order to mitigate all the risks posed by their use [47,48,63,66,93,94]. That is why state and global efforts to control this technological upheaval is realized through the discussions initiated for regulatory initiatives [11,63,94].

6.1. Benefits

According to academics [47,58,64,84,95–99], the benefits offered by a careful adoption of new technologies in the context of policing, security, and border control, such as increased transparency, capacity to identify criminals, detect fraud and abuses, and access to relevant intel for guiding decisions, that are significant for the future of modern LEAs.

In a data-driven world, criminal activity is more and more interconnected with technology and the internet. In this context, the role of Big Data, at this point, should be underlined as through the adaptation of such technologies, a huge amount of data are generated that can be utilized to provide complete information to LEAs, leading to the successful dismantlement of criminal groups. In addition, this approach may lead police officers to rely less on stereotypes about race and class [100]. In that sense, the use of big data by LEAs may reduce mass surveillance of minority neighborhoods and at the same time promote transparency through the exploitation of big data in order to "police the police" [89] (p.997) as digital trails are susceptible to oversight [100]. As a result, the accumulation of Big Data by LEAs could be used to make previous police practices that were based on individual-level bias disappear, providing an opportunity to increase transparency and accountability [100].

6.2. Risks

These powerful new technologies may also pose significant challenges related to their questionable reliability and accuracy that lead to multiple fundamental rights risks such as bias and discrimination, data protection and privacy, and unlawful profiling [47].

To an extent, the benefits of these technologies described above need to be carefully balanced against the significant ethical risks posed by such technologies to fundamental human rights [47,95]. Therefore, Dumbrava [36] (p. II) argues that developing and adopting powerful AI technologies without facing "pitfalls such as technological determinism and the myth of technological neutrality" would further increase the risk posed to fundamental rights, transparency, and accountability.

This unconditional adaptation of new policing technologies, according to surveillance scholars [97,98,101–104], led to the increase in surveillance that is now considered one of the major institutional dimensions of modern societies. According to Lyon [104], in these modern "surveillance societies" [103], which give room for the emergence of mass surveillance, some individuals, groups, and institutions are surveilled more than others, while different populations are monitored for different reasons and purposes.

In this context, the use of FRT, biometric identification technologies, and drones by the HP, according to the civil society, is in conflict with the fundamental human rights of privacy and data protection, while it encroaches on the freedom of expression and assembly [105]. This argument is reinforced by the fact that through the project "Smart Policing" that the HP is implementing, exploiting AI technologies, a private access network will be created and supported by the Contractor that will be inserted between the thousands of mobile devices and the HP's network [84]. This raises questions around whether a private corporation will have access to all the data collected from the operation of the "Smart Policing" system.

In many respects, the risk of increased state-sponsored societal control outweighs any alleged benefits that these technologies promise. To sum up, according to many technology- and society-related studies, technologies are now researched also from a social, political, and cultural context [74]. In that sense, if the current development of FRT is investigated only as science-driven progress, a one-sided perception is created, leaving outside important subjects such as the "securitization" of identity and the global surveillance culture built the last two decades [74]. In this context, the adoption of such technologies is often considered as a series of purely technical procedures and improvements [47]. Such an approach constructs a false sense of objectivity to technologies that separate technological advances from the broader legal, social, and ethical implications they may pose [47]. This false sense is also depicted in the fact that in order to deal with data complexity, a series of cognitive simplifications had to be made during information processing [2,7,10]. These simplifications though could "infect" the procedure and, to an extent, the decision with biases.

As a result, it should be mentioned that no technology adopted for policing is as neutral, impartial, and accurate as it claims to be. This, however, should not limit the implementation of such a model, as ILP methods such as statistical investigations, forensic laboratories, and information systems incorporate the basic assumptions about science and technology (neutrality, validity, and progress), building the image of efficiency and neutrality.

7. Conclusions

The primary aim of this paper was to provide insights on the degree of ILP's implementation by the HP while identifying the innovative police technologies used in the EU and Greece against crime. To accomplish these aims, an extensive and thorough review of the existing literature was conducted to establish a good knowledge base around the theme. This exploration of the academic discourse on the subject divulged some gaps in knowledge; presented the absence of comparable and comprehensive data; and highlighted that although police technology is something that concerns researchers, the research around its implementation and use in the EU and Greece is not vast.

The discussions around these new technologies are best depicted as a continuous "battle" between skeptics, who see technologies such as AI as tools of "destruction," and proponents of progress that see them as tools of "salvation" [47]. Both sides seem to agree though that new technologies are powerful tools that will have a significant impact on modern society [47]. The risk that lurks, however, is in assuming that, given their disruptive power, these technologies will inevitably have such consequences, regardless of what policies and restrictions we may pose to control them. In this context, a recent eu-LISA report [106] underlined that the adaptation of new technologies, such as AI, in policing, security and border control, is not a question of "if", but "when" and "to what extent".

Kuskonmaz and Guild [93] expressed interesting parallelism, lumping together the current haste to implement new digital technologies and the way humanity has addressed previous technological challenges. More specifically, they analogized the car technology to AI, underlining the fact that although cars can run really fast, it has not stopped policy makers from imposing driving speed limits for reasons of public safety [93]. Another great example of such a successful regulation posed on technological progress was realized on the non-proliferation of nuclear weapons through international agreements [47]. In that sense, it can be noted that "just because some technologies are possible, it does not mean that they should be accepted" [93].

As a result, state, and global response to the uncontrollable technological upheaval are taking form through the discussions initiated for regulatory initiatives [47,48,63,66,93,94]. In this regulatory effort, the EU mobilized funding mechanisms in order to move forward the implementation of numerous research projects, as the ones mentioned above, that would test the application of new AI and surveillance technologies in policing and border control. Through these research projects, it is aimed to locate any existing flaws and identify the risks posed by the use of such technologies by the EU LEAs.

In this context, in January 2021 the EC accepted a European Citizens' Initiative put forward by the "Reclaim Your Face" coalition, which calls for a ban on biometric mass surveillance [107]. Furthermore, in April 2021, the EC introduced a proposal for an AI act, which would classify all AI systems used in the fields of migration, asylum, and border control management as high-risk [47,107]. These "high-risk" systems will need to meet certain criteria concerning the quality of data collected, cybersecurity, human oversight, transparency, and technical documentation and record keeping accuracy [47].

As far as the HP is concerned, through the numerous EU research projects that are implemented in Greece regarding the use of new AI and surveillance technologies by the police, the Greek LEA benefits from turning into a technological hotbed of Europe.

Regarding the HP's projects that are already in the implementation phase and not at a research-level, such as the "Smart Policing", the body-worn cameras and the "PNR System," the HP has reassured multiple times that all the technologies adopted, comply with EU and INTERPOL legal and ethical frameworks and have been reviewed by internal experts and external ethics and stakeholder boards. In addition, it should be noted that the operation of DIDAP, the key police service for the ILP implementation, is supervised by a senior Prosecutor and the external control of HDPA, whose responsibility is to guarantee legality and enhance transparency.

After researching the use of these technologies by the HP, it was realized that the only technological solution used that needs further discussion is "Smart Policing". Although the "Smart Policing" system offers a more efficient way to identify individuals, especially third country nationals overstaying in Greece, in comparison to the current procedure that obliges police officers to bring any individual who do not carry identification documents to the nearest police station, it creates an unanswered question around whether the private concessionaire of the project would have access to the data collected as the crypto channel created will operate at the company's network.

Regarding the body-worn cameras, it was never stated by HP that it would implement FRT. The cameras are just used to monitor the police officers doing their job with transparency and, if needed, to collect evidence for a crime committed either by the police or some suspected criminal [14]. Furthermore, the PNR system collects data that are already available to the HP legally through border security checks and airlines databases [15].

As far as the drones are concerned, until today, they were only used for border surveillance and monitoring riots, while recently, they were used for surveilling suspected criminals during police operations in order to collect evidence and capture them committing a crime [16]. The only drone use that was considered to be outside the criminal spectrum was during the COVID-19 pandemic [108] when the HP operated drones to monitor traffic during movement restrictions [16,61]. However, it was not used to identify cars and car holders and did not collect personal data, as the aim of the operation was to evaluate the risk of COVID-19 transmission, depending on the level of mobility of citizens [16,33].

Overall, it can be said that emergent technologies are reshaping policing. This raises serious questions on the limits of the automation of policing and whether automation will ultimately lead to an 'end' of professional police forces [42]. The proliferation of this "technological policing net" [42] is a phenomenon that raised concerns primarily in terms of its surveillance or privacy implications. However, this is only one aspect of the discussion. Increasingly concerning are the damaging effects of intensifying technologization upon the police and the public. Further discussion should be made on the impacts of replacing police forces as "visible societal guardians" [42] with more invisible forms of automated policing. This could be considered to be more corrosive for the public good than any privacy violation [42].

In that sense, the exploitation of new technologies in a data-driven [109,110] policing concept, although important for the goal of preventing crime, is only one part of the solution [10]. ILP, wherever implemented, was considered only as one segment of an overall policing strategy that included staff education [10]. In this context, people, software, and equipment need to be aligned as "the human factor is the primary driver of success" [10]. Always in the end police officers are the ones that analyze, interpret data, decide how to use it, and ensure their success [10].

Concluding, it is worth mentioning that the examination of all the related literature showed that there is still not enough evidence for the universal application of such technologies by any large-scale LEA. All new technologies used for policing, security, and border control in Greece and the EU are mostly at a research-level. Therefore, those agencies that want to proceed with the adoption of such technologies should carefully consider the ethical issues that arise and recognize that most of the claims (advantages and disadvantages) made will have to be re-tested in an implementation environment of each society, at a trial stage. In that sense, the Greek and European Panopticon is still far away.

Author Contributions: Conceptualization: G.G. and D.P.; methodology: G.G., D.P. and K.D.; validation: G.G., D.P. and K.D.; formal analysis: G.G., D.P. and K.D.; investigation: G.G. and D.P.; writing—original draft preparation: G.G.; writing—review and editing: G.G., D.P. and K.D.; supervision: D.P.; project administration: K.D. All authors have read and agreed to the published version of the manuscript.

Funding: This research received no external funding.

Institutional Review Board Statement: Not applicable.

Informed Consent Statement: Not applicable.

Data Availability Statement: Not applicable.

Conflicts of Interest: The authors declare no conflict of interest.

References

1. Burcher, M.; Whelan, C. Intelligence-Led Policing in Practice: Reflections From Intelligence Analysts. *Police Q.* **2019**, *22*, 139–160. [CrossRef]
2. Ratcliffe, J. *Intelligence-Led Policing*; Willan Publishing: Cullompton, UK, 2008.
3. Maguire, M. Policing by risks and targets: Some dimensions and implications of intelligence-led crime control. *Polic. Soc. Int. J.* **2000**, *9*, 316. [CrossRef]
4. Flanagin, A. The impact of contemporary communication and information technologies on police organizations. In *Law Enforcement, Communication and Community*; John Benjamins Publishing: Amsterdam, The Netherlands, 2002; pp. 85–106. ISBN 1588112551/9781588112552.
5. Hoover, J.E. Science, Crime Detection and the Federal Bureau of Investigation. *Stud. Lawyer J.* **1961**, *6*, 14–23.
6. Newburn, T.; Hayman, S. *Policing, Surveillance and Social Control*; Routledge: New York, NY, USA, 2012.
7. Peterson, M. *Intelligence-Led Policing: The New Intelligence Architecture*; Bureau of Justice Assistance: Washington, DC, USA, 2005.
8. Dignum, V. Ethics in artificial intelligence: Introduction to the special issue. *Ethics Inf. Technol.* **2018**, *20*, 1–3. [CrossRef]
9. Islam, Y.; Zahidul, A. Data Mining and Privacy of Social Network Sites' Users: Implications of the Data Mining Problem. *Sci. Eng. Ethics* **2015**, *21*, 941–966. [CrossRef]
10. LeCates, R. Intelligence-led Policing: Changing the Face of Crime Precention. In *Police Chief Magazine*; 2018; Available online: https://www.policechiefmagazine.org/changing-the-face-crime-prevention/ (accessed on 27 November 2021).
11. Seele, P. Predictive Sustainability Control: A review assessing the potential to transfer big data driven 'predictive policing' to corporate sustainability management. *J. Clean. Prod.* **2017**, *153*, 673–686. [CrossRef]
12. Spiegel, J. The Ethics of Virtual Reality Technology: Social Hazards and Public Policy Recommendations. *Sci. Eng. Ethics* **2018**, *24*, 1537–1550. [CrossRef]
13. Wessel, M.; Helmer, N. A Crisis of Ethics in Technology Innovation. *MIT Sloan Manag. Rev.* **2020**, *61*, 71–76.
14. Couderta, F.; Butin, D.; Le Métayer, D. Body-worn cameras for police accountability: Opportunities and risks. *Comput. Law Secur. Rev.* **2015**, *31*, 749–762. [CrossRef]
15. Bîrzu, B. Prevention, Detection, Investigation and Prosecution of Terrorist Offenses and Other Serious Crimes by Using Passenger Name Record (PNR) Data. Critical Opinions. Delege Ferenda Proposals. *Perspect. Bus. Law J.* **2016**, *5*, 195–206.
16. Wen, L.; Du, D.; Zhu, P.; Hu, Q.; Wang, Q.; Bo, L.; Lyu, S. Detection, Tracking, and Counting Meets Drones in Crowds: A Benchmark. In Proceedings of the IEEE/CVF Conference on Computer Vision and Pattern Recognition, Nashville, TN, USA, 20–25 June 2021; pp. 7812–7821.
17. Taskiran, M.; Kahraman, N.; Erdem, C.E. Face recognition: Past, present and future (a review). *Digit. Signal Process.* **2020**, *106*, 102809. [CrossRef]
18. Rezende, I.N. Facial recognition in police hands: Assessing the 'Clearview case' from a European perspective. *New J. Eur. Crim. Law* **2020**, *11*, 375–389. [CrossRef]
19. O'Leary, Z. *The Essential Guide to Doing Your Research Project*; Sage Publications: London, UK, 2010.
20. Vartanian, T.P. *Secondary Data Analysis*; Oxford University Press: Oxford, UK, 2011.
21. Robson, C.; McCartan, K. *Real World Research*, 3rd ed.; Wiley: Chichester, UK, 2011.
22. Reiner, R. *The Politics of the Police*; Oxford University Press: Oxford, UK, 2000.
23. Hostli, O.R. Content Analysis. In *The Handbook of Social Psychology*; Lindzey, G., Aronson, E., Eds.; Amerind Publishing Co.: New Delhi, India, 1968; pp. 596–692.
24. Elo, S.; Kääriäinen, M.; Kanste, O.; Utriainen, K.; Pölkki, T.; Kyngäs, H. Qualitative Content Analysis: A Focus on Trustworthiness. *Sage Open* **2014**, *4*, 2158244014522633. [CrossRef]
25. Hsief, H.-F.; Shannon, S.E. Three Approaches to Qualitative Content Analysis. *Qual. Health Res.* **2005**, *15*, 1277–1288.
26. Manning, P. Information Technologies and the Police. *Crime Justice* **1992**, *15*, 349–398. [CrossRef]
27. Carter, D. *Law Enforcement Intelligence: A Guide for State, Local, and Tribal Law Enforcement Agencies*; Michigan State University: East Lansing, MI, USA, 2009.
28. Innes, M.; Graef, R. 'The Anvil' in the Information Age: Police, Politics and Media. In *Policing: Politics, Culture and Control*; Bloomsbury Publishing: London, UK, 2012; pp. 155–172. ISBN 184731967X/9781847319678.
29. Sheptycki, J. Transnational Policing. *Can. Rev. Polic. Res.* **2005**, *1*, 1–7.
30. OSCE. *Project Report: Intelligence-Led Policing (ILP) 2017–2020*; OSCE: Vienna, Austria, 2021.
31. Nunn, S. Police technology in cities: Changes and challenges. *Technol. Soc.* **2001**, *23*, 11–27. [CrossRef]
32. Custers, B. Technology in policing: Experiences, obstacles and police needs. *Comput. Law Secur. Rev.* **2012**, *28*, 62–68. [CrossRef]
33. Wen, L.; Du, D.; Zhu, P.; Hu, Q.; Wang, Q.; Bo, L.; Lyu, S. Drone-based Joint Density Map Estimation, Localization and Tracking with Space-Time Multi-Scale Attention Network. *arXiv* **2019**, arXiv:1912.01811.
34. Schultz, P. Future is Here: Technology in Police Departments. *Police Chief* **2008**, *75*, 20–22,24,25.

35. Hayrapetyan, N.; Hakobyan, R.; Poghosyan, A.; Gabrielyan, V. Border Surveillance Using UAVs with Thermal Camera. In *Meeting Security Challenges Through Data Analytics and Decision Support*; Shahbazian, E., Rogova, G., Eds.; IOS Press: Amsterdam, The Netherlands, 2016; pp. 219–226. ISBN 1614997152/9781614997153.
36. Akula, A.; Ghosh, R.; Sardana, H.K. Thermal Imaging And Its Application In Defence Systems. In *The AIP Conference Proceedings 1391*; Predeep, P., Thakur, M., Ravi Varma, M.K., Eds.; American Institute of Physics: Kerala, India, 2011; pp. 333–335.
37. Dumpert, D.; Dirksen, S. Networked thermal imaging and intelligent video technology for border security applications. In Proceedings of the SPIE 6203, Optics and Photonics in Global Homeland Security II, Orlando (Kissimmee), FL, USA, 17–21 April 2006; Volume 6203.
38. Dijstelbloem, H. *Borders as Infrastructure: The Technopolitics of Border Control*; MIT Press: Cambridge, UK, 2021; ISBN 0262366371/9780262366373.
39. Kirby, S.; Turner, G. Think Crime, Think Car, Think ANPR: The Use of ANPR in Major Crime Investigations. *J. Homicide Major Incid. Investig.* **2007**, *3*, 35–42.
40. Joh, E. Policing Police Robots. *UCLA Law Rev. Discl.* **2016**, *64*, 516.
41. Szocik, K.; Abylkasymova, R. Ethical Issues in Police Robots. The Case of Crowd Control Robots in a Pandemic. *J. Appl. Secur. Res.* **2021**, 1–16. [CrossRef]
42. McGuire, M.R. The laughing policebot: Automation and the end of policing. *Polic. Soc.* **2021**, *31*, 20–36. [CrossRef]
43. Tanner, S.; Meyer, M. Police work and new 'security devices': A tale from the beat. *Secur. Dialogue* **2015**, *46*, 384–400. [CrossRef]
44. Tombul, F.; Cakar, B. Police use of technology to fight against crime. *Eur. Sci. J.* **2015**, *11*, 286–296.
45. Willis, J. Police Technology. In *The Handbook of Social Control*; Deflem, M., Ed.; Wiley Blackwell: Hoboken, NJ, USA, 2018.
46. Haskins, C.; Mac, R.; McDonald, L. Clearview AI Wants to Sell Its Facial Recognition Software to Authoritarian Regimes around the World. Available online: https://www.buzzfeednews.com/article/carolinehaskins1/clearview-ai-facial-recognition-authoritarian-regimes-22 (accessed on 15 June 2021).
47. Dumbrava, C. *Artificial intelligence at EU Borders*; European Parliamentary Research Service: Brussels, Belgium, 2021.
48. Galbally Herrero, J.; Ferrara, P.; Haraksim, R.; Psyllos, A.; Beslay, L. *Study on Face Identification Technology for Its Implementation in the Schengen Information System*; Publications Office of the European Union: Luxembourg, 2019.
49. Peeters, B. *Facial Recognition at Brussels Airport: Face down in the Mud*; CiTiP Blog: Leuven, Belgium, 2020.
50. Nunn, S. Police Information Technology: Assessing the Effects of Computerization on Urban Police Functions. *Public Adm. Rev.* **2001**, *61*, 221–234. [CrossRef]
51. Carr, J.; Doleac, J.L. The Geography, Incidence, and Underreporting of Gun Violence: New Evidence Using Shotspotter Data. *SSRN Electron. J.* **2016**, *17*. [CrossRef]
52. Doucette, M.; Green, C.; Dineen, J.N.; Shapiro, D.; Raissian, K. Impact of ShotSpotter Technology on Firearm Homicides and Arrests Among Large Metropolitan Counties: A Longitudinal Analysis, 1999–2016. *J. Urban Health* **2021**, *98*, 609–621. [CrossRef]
53. Lambert, N.; Clochard, O. Mobile and Fatal: The EU Borders. In *Borderities and the Politics of Contemporary Mobile Borders*; Palgrave Macmillan: London, UK, 2015; pp. 119–137.
54. Goold, B.J. *CCTV and Policing: Public Area Surveillance and Police Practices in Britain*; Oxford University Press: Oxford, UK, 2004.
55. Papadimitrakopoulos, G. Evidence-based policing (EBP) as a strategy for accomplishing police goals more effectively, the challenges EBP faces, and the prospects for it being adopted widely in Greece. In *Europe in Crisis: Crime, Criminal Justice, and the Way Forward*; Ant. N. Sakkoulas Publishers L.P.: Athens, Greece, 2017; pp. 881–899.
56. Erpenbach, M. Whole World is Watching: Camera Phones Put Law Enforcement Under Surveillance. *Law Enforc. Technol.* **2008**, *35*, 40–44.
57. Williams, C. Police Surveillance and the Emergence of CCTV in the 1960s. *Crime Prev. Community Saf.* **2003**, *5*, 27–37. [CrossRef]
58. Farrar, T. *Self-Awareness to Being Watched and Socially-Desirable Behavior: A Field Experiment on the Effect of Body-Worn Cameras on Police Use-of-Force*; National Policing Institute: Arlington, VA, USA, 2013.
59. Pilant, L. Spotlight on In-Car Video Systems. *Police Chief* **1995**, *62*, 30–31.
60. Europol. *How COVID-19-Related Crime Infected Europe during 2020*; Europol: Den Haag, The Netherlands, 2020.
61. Knight, A.; Oriala, T. COVID-19, George Floyd and Human Security. *Afr. Secur.* **2020**, *13*, 111–115. [CrossRef]
62. Sousa, W.; Sakiyama, M.; Miethe, T. Inconsistencies in Public Opinion of Body-Worn Cameras on Police: Transparency, Trust, and Improved Police–Citizen Relationships. *Polic. A J. Policy Pract.* **2018**, *12*, 100–108. [CrossRef]
63. Renda, A.; Arroyo, J.; Fanni, R.; Laurer, M.; Sipiczki, A.; Yeung, T.; Maridis, G.; Fernandes, M.; Endrodi, G.; Milio, S.; et al. *Study to Support an Impact Assessment of Regulatory Requirements for Artificial Intelligence in Europe*; European Commission: Brussels, Belgium, 2021.
64. Deloitte. *Opportunities and Challenges for the Use of Artificial Intelligence in Border Control, Migration and Security*; European Commission: Brussels, Belgium, 2020.
65. Frontex. *Best Practice Operational Guidelines for Automated Border Control (ABC) Systems*; Frontex: Warsaw, Poland, 2015.
66. Ecorys. *Feasibility Study on a Forecasting and Early Warning Tool for Migration Based on Artificial Intelligence Technology*; European Commission: Brussels, Belgium, 2020.
67. Braga, A.; Papachristos, A.; Hureau, D.M. The Effects of Hot Spots Policing on Crime: An Updated Systematic Review and Meta-Analysis. *Justice Q.* **2014**, *31*, 633–663. [CrossRef]
68. Papadopoulos, V.; Marketakis, P.; Alexopoulos, P. *National Programme (ISF)*; Ministry of Interior: Athens, Greece, 2021.

69. Lozada, B. The Emerging Technology of Predictive Analytics: Implications for Homeland Security. *Inf. Secur. J. A Glob. Perspect.* **2014**, *23*, 118–122. [CrossRef]
70. FRA. *Coronavirus Pandemic in the EU—Fundamental Rights Implications*; Publications Office of the European Union: Luxembourg, 2020.
71. Goold, B.J. Public Area Surveillance and Police Work: The Impact of CCTV on Police Behaviour and Autonomy. *J. Surveill. Soc.* **2003**, *1*, 191–203. [CrossRef]
72. Smart Policing. Available online: https://innovation.gov.gr/en/innovationscaten/smart-policing/ (accessed on 4 November 2021).
73. FRA. *Facial Recognition Technology: Fundamental Rights Considerations in the Context of Law Enforcement*; Publications Office of the European Union: Luxembourg, 2019.
74. Gates, K. *Our Biometric Future: Facial Recognition Technology and the Culture of Surveillance*; New York University Press: New York, NY, USA, 2011.
75. Barrett, L.F.; Adolphs, R.; Marsella, S.; Martinez, A.M.; Pollak, S.D. Emotional Expressions Reconsidered: Challenges to Inferring Emotion From Human Facial Movements. *Psychol. Sci. Public Interes.* **2019**, *20*, 1–68. [CrossRef] [PubMed]
76. European Commission. *Horizon Europe Strategic Plan (2021–2024)*; European Commission: Brussels, Belgium, 2021.
77. Pawlicka, A.; Choraś, M.; Kozik, R.; Pawlicki, M. First broad and systematic horizon scanning campaign and study to detect societal and ethical dilemmas and emerging issues spanning over cybersecurity solutions. *Pers. Ubiquitous Comput.* **2021**. [CrossRef]
78. Pawlicki, M.; Choraś, M.; Kozik, R.; Hołubowicz, W. Missing and Incomplete Data Handling in Cybersecurity Applications. In Proceedings of the Asian Conference on Intelligent Information and Database Systems, Phuket, Thailand, 7–10 April 2021; Nguyen, N.T., Chittayasothorn, S., Niyato, D., Trawiński, B., Eds.; Springer: Cham, Switzerland, 2021; pp. 413–426.
79. Gerostathopoulos, I.; Fernández, D.M.; Zarras, A. Can Today's Machine Learning Pass Image-Based Turing Tests? In Proceedings of the International Conference on Information Security, Paris, France, 11–12 December 2019; Lin, Z., Papamanthou, C., Polychronakis, M., Eds.; Springer: Cham, Switzerland, 2019; pp. 129–148.
80. Demertzis, K.; Tsiknas, K. Darknet Traffic Big-Data Analysis and Network Management for Real-Time Automating of the Malicious Intent Detection Process by a Weight Agnostic Neural Networks Framework. *Electronics* **2021**, *10*, 781. [CrossRef]
81. Iosu, A. Improving Situational Awareness with DARLENE Augmented Reality Tools to Combat Crime and Terrorism. Available online: https://www.darleneproject.eu/improving-situational-awareness-with-darlene-augmented-reality-tools-to-combat-crime-and-terrorism/ (accessed on 8 November 2021).
82. Duszynska-Trojanowska, A. The Intelligence Cycle and the ROXANNE Platform. Available online: https://www.roxanne-euproject.org/news/blog/the-intelligence-cycle-and-the-roxanne-platform (accessed on 8 November 2021).
83. Shivam, G. Social Network Analysis for Criminology in ROXANNE. Available online: https://www.roxanne-euproject.org/news/blog/social-network-analysis-for-criminology-in-roxanne (accessed on 8 November 2021).
84. Gonzales Fuster, G. *Artificial Intelligence and Law Enforcement—Impact on Fundamental Rights*; European Parliament: Brussels, Belgium, 2020.
85. Andreadis, S.; Antzoulatos, G.; Mavropoulos, T.; Giannakeris, P.; Tzionis, G.; Pantelidis, N.; Ioannidis, K.; Karakostas, A.; Gialampoukidis, I.; Vrochidis, S.; et al. A social media analytics platform visualising the spread of COVID-19 in Italy via exploitation of automatically geotagged tweets. *Online Soc. Netw. Media* **2021**, *23*, 100134. [CrossRef]
86. Gkountakos, K.; Touska, D.; Ioannidis, K.; Tsikrika, T.; Vrochidis, S.; Kompatsiaris, I. Spatio-temporal activity detection and recognition in untrimmed surveillance videos. In Proceedings of the ACM International Conference on Multimedia Retrieval, Taipei, Taiwan, 21–24 August 2021.
87. Altobelli, C.; Johnson, E.; Forgó, N.; Napieralski, A. To Scrape or Not to Scrape? The Lawfulness of Social Media Crawling under the GDPR. In *Deep Diving into Data Protection*; Herveg, J., Ed.; Larcier: Namur, Belgium, 2021.
88. Thanos, K.G.; Kyriazanos, D.; Thomopoulos, S. TRESSPASS risk and behaviour data fusion and analysis for border crossing points security. In Proceedings of the Mediterranean Security Event (MSE) 2019, Fodele Crete, Greece, 29–31 October 2019; Springer: Berlin/Heidelberg, Germany, 2020; pp. 29–31.
89. Vora, S.; Shahriari, M.; Thomopoulos, S.; Fischer, L.; Hoch, T. A scoring algorithm for abnormal traveller behaviour in border crossing areas. In Proceedings of the Counterterrorism, Crime Fighting, Forensics, and Surveillance Technologies IV, Online, 21–25 September 2020; Volume 11542.
90. Thanos, K.G.; Kyriazanos, D.; Thomopoulos, S. Fairness-by-design dempster-shafer reasoning system. In Proceedings of the Signal Processing, Sensor/Information Fusion, and Target Recognition XXX, Online, 12–16 April 2021; Volume 11756.
91. Israel, T. *Facial Recognition at a Crossroads: Transformation at Our Borders & Beyond*; CIPPIC: Ottawa, Canada, 2020.
92. Batabyal, A.A.; Kourtit, K.; Nijkamp, P. Technological Forecasting & Social Change A political-economy analysis of the provision of urban anti-crime technologies in a model with three cities. *Technol. Forecast. Soc. Chang.* **2020**, *160*, 120211. [CrossRef]
93. Kuskonmaz, E.M.; Guild, E. *COVID-19: A New Struggle over Privacy, Data Protection and Human Rights?* European Law Blog: Trier, Germany, 2020.
94. Flynn, M.J. *Study on Technical Requirements for Data Spaces in Law Enforcement*; European Commission: Brussels, Belgium, 2020.
95. Dintino, J.; Martens, F. *Police Intelligence Systems in Crime Control: Maintaining a Delicate Balance in a Liberal Democracy*; Charles C. Thomas: Springfield, IL, USA, 1983.

96. Drozdowski, P.; Rathgeb, C.; Dantcheva, A.; Damer, N.; Busch, C. Demographic Bias in Biometrics: A Survey on an Emerging Challenge. *IEEE Trans. Technol. Soc.* **2020**, *1*, 89–103. [CrossRef]
97. Marx, G. *Windows into the Soul: Surveillance and Society in an Age of High Technology*; University of Chicago Press: Chicago, IL, USA, 2016.
98. Marx, G. *Undercover: Police Surveillance in America*; University of California Press: Berkeley, CA, USA, 1988.
99. Rule, J. *Private Lives and Public Surveillance: Social Control in the Computer Age*; Schocken Books: New York, NY, USA, 1974.
100. Brayne, S. Big Data Surveillance The Case of Policing. *Am. Sociol. Rev.* **2017**, *82*, 977–1008. [CrossRef]
101. Ball, K.; Webster, F. *The Intensification of Surveillance: Crime, Terrorism & Warfare in the Information Age*; Pluto Press: London, UK, 2003.
102. Giddens, A. *The Consequences of Modernity*; Stanford University Press: Stanford, CA, USA, 1990.
103. Lyon, D. *The Electronic Eye: The Rise of Surveillance Society*; University of Minesota Press: Minneapolis, MN, USA, 1994.
104. Lyon, D. *Surveillance as Social Sorting: Privacy, Risk, and Digital Discrimination*; Routledge: New York, NY, USA, 2003.
105. Rogers, C.; Scally, E.J. Police use of technology: Insights from the literature. *Int. J. Emerg. Serv.* **2018**, *7*, 100–110. [CrossRef]
106. Eu-LISA. *Artificial Intelligencein the Operational Management of Large-Scale IT Systems*; Eu-LISA: Tallinn, Estonia, 2020.
107. Europa.eu Civil Society Initiative for a Ban on Biometric Mass Surveillance Practices. Available online: https://europa.eu/citizens-initiative/initiatives/details/2021/000001_en (accessed on 14 July 2021).
108. Demertzis, K.; Taketzis, D.; Tsiotas, D.; Magafas, L.; Iliadis, L.; Kikiras, P. Pandemic Analytics by Advanced Machine Learning for Improved Decision Making of COVID-19 Crisis. *Processes* **2021**, *9*, 1267. [CrossRef]
109. Demertzis, K.; Iliadis, L.; Pimenidis, E. Geo-AI to aid disaster response by memory-augmented deep reservoir computing. *Integr. Comput. Aided Eng.* **2021**, *28*, 383–398. [CrossRef]
110. Demertzis, K.; Iliadis, L.; Anezakis, V.-D. An innovative soft computing system for smart energy grids cybersecurity. *Adv. Build. Energy Res.* **2018**, *12*, 3–24. [CrossRef]

Article

A Regulatory Readiness Assessment Framework for Blockchain Adoption in Healthcare

Olanrewaju Sanda, Michalis Pavlidis and Nikolaos Polatidis *

School of Architecture, Technology and Engineering, Moulsecoomb Campus, University of Brighton, Brighton BN2 4GJ, UK; o.sanda@brighton.ac.uk (O.S.); m.pavlidis@brighton.ac.uk (M.P.)
* Correspondence: n.polatidis@brighton.ac.uk

Abstract: Blockchain is now utilized by a diverse spectrum of applications and is proclaimed as a technological innovation that transforms the way that data are stored. This technology has the potential to transform the healthcare sector, especially the prevalent issues of patient's data-privacy and fragmented healthcare data. However, there is no evidence-based effort to develop a readiness assessment framework for blockchain that combines all the different social and economic factors and involves all stakeholders. Based on a systematic literature review, the proposed framework is applied to Portugal's healthcare sector and its applicability is outlined. The findings in this paper show the unique importance of regulators and the government in achieving a globally acceptable regulatory framework for the adoption of blockchain technology in healthcare and other sectors. The business entities and solution providers are ready to leverage the opportunities of blockchain, but the absence of a widely acceptable regulatory framework that protect stakeholders' interests is slowing down the adoption of blockchain. There are several misconceptions regarding blockchain laws and regulations, which has slowed stakeholder readiness. This paper will be useful as a guideline and knowledge base to reinforce blockchain adoption.

Keywords: blockchain; healthcare; regulatory readiness assessment framework

Citation: Sanda, O.; Pavlidis, M.; Polatidis, N. A Regulatory Readiness Assessment Framework for Blockchain Adoption in Healthcare. *Digital* **2022**, *2*, 65–87. https://doi.org/10.3390/digital2010005

Academic Editors: Mirjana Ivanović, Richard Chbeir and Yannis Manolopoulos

Received: 7 December 2021
Accepted: 9 March 2022
Published: 11 March 2022

Publisher's Note: MDPI stays neutral with regard to jurisdictional claims in published maps and institutional affiliations.

Copyright: © 2022 by the authors. Licensee MDPI, Basel, Switzerland. This article is an open access article distributed under the terms and conditions of the Creative Commons Attribution (CC BY) license (https://creativecommons.org/licenses/by/4.0/).

1. Introduction

Blockchain has been around for over a decade but has faced regulatory barriers that have slowed its adoption in key sectors. Some of these sectors handle sensitive data and information, such as the healthcare and finance sector [1,2]. Blockchain is, simply put, a distributed database or consensus existing on multiple computers at the same time [3,4]. The longest existing blockchain started in 1995 at the New York Times Newspaper, where the time-stamping service surety was publishing a hash-value in the ad-section of the newspaper every week [5]. There is a widespread misconception that "Bitcoin is Blockchain", which is false. Bitcoin was introduced to the world in 2008 by Satoshi Nakamoto. It is a new form of digital currency called cryptocurrency that facilitates transactions without a central authority [3,6]. The controversy and misconception surrounding Bitcoin is what has led to the issues with regulation and compliance in blockchain technology today [3,7,8].

Despite the advantages of blockchain, the technology is in contrast with existing data-protection laws, which has led to sanctions, lawsuits, and fines in many cases [9]. History has shown that disruptive technologies and the law will eventually find common ground, but this has not yet proved true for blockchain. The year of 2021 marks a milestone for cryptocurrency, as the first Bitcoin ETF was approved in the U.S. in October 2021 [10]. This means that Bitcoin will be traded as a regular investment stock with less volatility [10,11]. This also marks a huge milestone in blockchain regulation, as financial regulators are gradually understanding the opportunities that blockchain technology can provide.

Blockchain technology has seen a rise in adoption in sectors such as supply chain management and manufacturing because of the data and authenticity issues facing these sectors. There is a call for a legal and regulatory framework to take account of blockchain in sectors that manage the personal information of stakeholders [3,12]. The healthcare sector is overwhelmed with data and multi-level stakeholders. If blockchain is applied to healthcare, it can provide patients and healthcare providers with easy and safe access to medical history. Access to patient data will be provided securely and privately, with the functionality to track authorized access. At present, patient data are fragmented among multiple providers and the web of healthcare systems. Blockchain can offer the patient control of their data in real-time and guarantee data integrity.

Activities, collaborations, and research are ongoing in this area and will eventually see that blockchain is regulated. Cryptocurrency, which is the most popular application of blockchain technology, has not gained much popularity among regulators and big financial houses to date, due to a lack of central control measures, which has left stakeholders exposed. According to Reference [13], hackers have made away with over 2.5 billion USD of cryptocurrency in the last five years. The news of Japan's Coincheck hack of over five hundred ($500) million dollars and Tokyo MtGox Exchange, which lost over 850,000 bitcoins, among others, have made national news headlines [13]. These incidents have given birth to a new wave of regulatory laws that distributed ledger applications have to follow to remain compliant and avoid fines or total shutdown [3,13]. Our review of the regulatory readiness assessment framework for blockchain will guide business entities, solution providers, customers, regulators, and the government on how to develop blockchain-based applications that protect the assets, privacy, and rights of all stakeholders.

In their paper, Gozman et al. [14] proposed a proof-of-concept blockchain system for the regulatory reporting of mortgages in the UK. The benefits of the framework were greater transparency in compliance reporting, a reduction in cost through digitization and a better customer experience. In this paper, we will develop our review based on the lessons learnt from, and discussions on, this prototype. In the future, blockchain may be a solution to data integrity and information-sharing challenges for digital applications. Many business providers and business entities have declared that they are considering leveraging blockchain into their business process. They are aware of blockchain's capabilities but also deterred by regulatory issues in the new technology.

Based on this, we argue that the state-of-art of blockchain regulatory issues have received limited focus. There are some reviews that focus on their application to regulatory reporting; others focus on data enforcement laws on decentralized systems. This has shown a gap for a systematic literature review assessing the regulatory readiness of blockchain adoption and implementation, which was the motivation for this research. Our solution will contribute to the understanding of regulatory issues in blockchain and provides a snapshot of current data laws across some countries. It should be noted that this review cannot be considered all-inclusive as blockchain is growing very fast.

Despite the limited studies on blockchain regulatory frameworks, this paper attempts to answer the following research questions:

RQ1: What are the major regulatory issues of blockchain applications and solutions from a business and technical standpoint?

RQ2: What are the impacts of data laws on blockchain adoption and innovation?

RQ3: How can we examine the regulatory readiness for blockchain in healthcare?

Contributions

There is a growing knowledge repository for the development and adoption of blockchain that will help all stakeholders make more informed decisions [13,15]. The intended benefits of this paper are to reduce the cost of regulatory obligations, accelerate innovation within the blockchain ecosystem and promote collaboration among regulators, business entities, end-users, and solution providers. As a comprehensive study on regulatory readiness for blockchain, this paper makes the following contributions:

- Introduces the regulatory readiness framework research area, presenting a proper foundation, emphasizing definitions, and highlighting terminologies for both industry

and academic affairs. We demonstrate the impact of data laws on blockchain and their enforcement.
- Propose a regulatory readiness assessment framework for blockchain; a framework defining the criteria to assess regulatory readiness and reduce regulatory burdens when adopting blockchain.
- The study is provided in a timely fashion and offers a guiding lamp to strengthen blockchain adoption.
- The proposed framework fills a considerable void in the literature, especially in healthcare, where there is still lack of trust among stakeholders.
- This paper addresses the lack of clarity in blockchain regulatory laws; these issues have become deterrents for stakeholders.
- The proposed framework is adaptable to several sectors and will be of value to policymakers as a tool for assessing readiness for blockchain adoption.

The rest of the paper is as follows: we provide a brief outline of blockchains' architecture and summarize some applications of blockchain in Section 2, followed by the relationship between stakeholders and the proposed framework, in Section 3. We present the application of the framework in Section 4, followed by materials and methods in Section 5. In Section 6, we review the impact of regulatory laws on blockchain adoption. Sections 7 and 8 contain a discussion, the conclusions and future work.

2. Background

In the following paragraphs, we provide a brief overview of the basic architecture and concepts of blockchain. We also offer a summary of some blockchain applications with a focus on regulatory concerns and government impact on blockchain adoption.

Blockchain architecture can be grouped into two categories: private (Permissioned) and public (Permissionless) blockchain [16,17]. Permissionless or public blockchain permits all participants to create a consensus; that is, there is no need for permission to be added as a node on the network [11,16,18]. In this blockchain layout, all participants can read and carry out transactions over the network. A private or permissioned blockchain is when access to participate is granted to only a few on the network [3]. One of the major differences between the public and private is that public blockchains require proof of work or mining, which is used to authenticate transactions [19,20] Another major difference is that, on a private blockchain, all the participants are known, while on a public blockchain, the participants are unknown [16]. A private key is used to sign transactions, while a public key is used to access the transaction. The hash value is encrypted using the private key, and this transaction can be confirmed between two participants on a blockchain network using the public key [16].

The distributed architecture of blockchain means that each block is a reference point to the previous block, which is a hash value from the preceding block, called the Parent Block (as depicted in Figure 1). The block header (Block X) and the block body are composed of the hash value that refers to the previous block. The size of each transaction and size of each block are two very important aspects for maximizing the transactions in a block.

This blockchain layout promotes Confidentiality, Authenticity, and Integrity (CIA) of data and eliminates the risk of both internal and external attacks [19,21]. At present, the major technical drawbacks for blockchain applications are its speed, power usage and scalability [3].

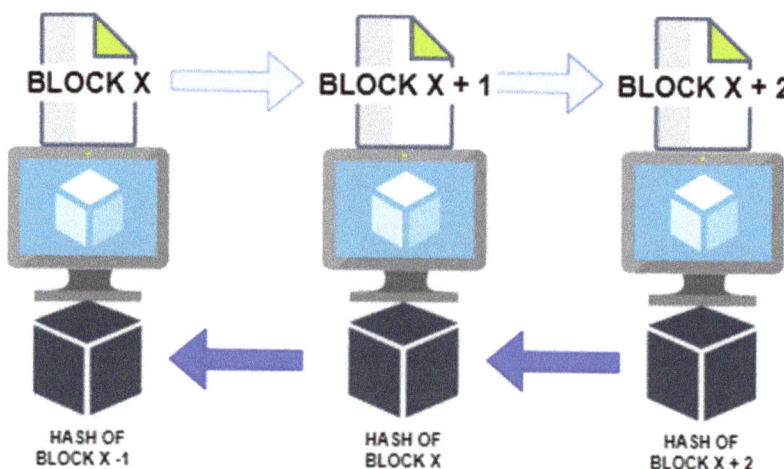

Figure 1. Example of Blockchain Architecture.

Blockchain has shown immense potential to transform the authentication and validation of data assets, but recent studies have emphasized a need for a framework that promotes regulatory compliance [22]. The EU is currently working on a sandbox that brings together regulators, investors, tech experts and companies to test innovative solutions in a controlled environment [22,23]. These solutions will embody the intentional regulations and laws that will be implemented in the pre-coding or pre-design stage of the blockchain application to eliminate bias or undermine traditional regulatory laws [22]. For instance, a blockchain application that is used to provide access to Life Insurance based on the community collectively verifying a person's credit score before the insurance can be approved has a different impact from another that grants approval according to medical and financial history. The first one promotes bias in the community, while the latter encourages socialism [22]. These types of social impacts and issues must be mitigated to create fairness in the use of the technology.

Gozman and Aste, in Reference [14], explored the potential of adopting blockchain technology into regulatory compliance reporting to reduce the burden, cost, and duplication of regulators. They proposed a conceptual blockchain system for the regulatory reporting of UK mortgages. The benefits of this project were a drastic reduction in the cost of regulatory reporting, transparency among all participants, automation of the reporting process and a better end-user experience. Unfortunately, the project did not scale to full implementation, but this created a knowledge pool for financial regulators and businesses to improve on regulatory reporting.

In their article, the Global Systems for Mobile Communications Association (GSMA) [24], propose investment in emerging and disruptive technologies, such as Blockchain, Internet of Things (IOT) and Artificial Intelligence (AI), that have proven to shape the future of companies, allowing them to reach a wider audience and create new integral channels of opportunity. Their report has focused on blockchain as a solution allowing mobile operators, the government, and key stakeholders to work hand-in hand to deliver a better experience in terms of financial services, health, digital identity, and agriculture. The project was a huge success, helping those in rural areas where there is a pressing need for proof of identity. This project faced major drawbacks regarding government regulations. For this project to be a total success, it required some form of government and regulatory approval. This proved to be a challenge because there is no widely accepted regulatory framework that ensures fairness and non-discrimination in the adoption of blockchain. This gave merit to the idea that there is a pressing need for an approved regulatory framework for blockchain that will cut across many sectors.

Esposito, in Reference [16], explored the potential use of blockchain to safeguard medical data hosted in the cloud. The motivation for the research was the increase in data accumulated within the healthcare sector [25]. Their findings showed a growing need for healthcare data to be shared among medical practitioners, for healthcare data to be accessed in real-time by authorized parties, and for these data to be leveraged for a better diagnosis. The current system is a stand-alone Electronic Medical Record (EMR) and lacks interoperability. With new medical smart devices being created, there needs to be a way to accumulate and share these data securely. Their research proposed a blockchain EMR ecosystem, where patient data are stored in a distributed manner, and the patient has control and ownership of their data [16]. This proposed solution was not without its challenges, especially with the data protection laws, such as GDPR, state laws, federal laws, and HIPAA, that exist in the EU and US. Blockchain has not been certified fit to store medical data due to the lack of a regulatory framework within the blockchain ecosystem.

Heston, in Reference [26], conducted a case study in blockchain healthcare innovation to observe how blockchain application can reduce the cost and complexity of managing healthcare records and insurance. The case study focused on the Estonian Government and how they partnered with a private blockchain company called "Guardtime" to create a secure blockchain healthcare record system for its citizens [27]. This innovative approach sprung from a growing population that are unable to pay for their medical bills and an increase in the need for medical care. Heston, in Reference [26], describes how the Estonia government leveraged blockchain to provide a more secure way to share medical data among all necessary participants. The rationale for adopting blockchain technology into the medical sector was the ability to reduce healthcare costs by properly coordinating insurance claims. This new blockchain healthcare initiative was a success, largely because it was supported by Estonia's Health Information System Act of 2007 and the Government Regulation Act of Health Information Exchange in 2008. This has promoted the growth of blockchain in other areas, such as education, tax, and elections, in Estonia. This has put Estonia at the forefront of blockchain adoption in almost every sector of the country. The only challenge faced in the e-health blockchain application was scalability. From these studies, we can extract that the success and failure of a country implementing blockchain into its services not only depends on the layout of the blockchain, but on the data and privacy laws that exist in the country and how the government backs new technologies [26,28]. Therefore, the regulatory readiness assessment for blockchain developed in this research must be in accordance with the data and privacy laws that exist today.

A futuristic approach to the challenges faced by regulators in the EU and US was discussed in their review [29,30]. This research described how public sector services could be revolutionized by a distributed ledger technology. Blockchain regulation has attracted the attention of EU state members, the US Presidency, big financial houses, and big software companies since its exponential growth [30]. The key challenge faced by blockchain adoption stems from the illegal use-cases within the bitcoin community. Some very popular cases involve the money laundering scandal by Liberty Reserve in the US, and the use of bitcoin on shadowy sites and the darknet for malicious purposes. His research proposed a regulatory environment governed by both legal and technical codes to ensure the compliance of blockchain assets. While the EU regulators have adopted a hands-off regulatory approach, the US are focused on regulation after full scalability of the technology; this is not to say that there are no regulations in place [30]. Table 1 provides a summary of the limitations of the studies discussed in the background section. This offers an outline of the research efforts to overcome regulatory barriers in recent years.

Table 1. Summary table of research on blockchain technology.

Citation Number	Authors Name	Year of Publish	Topic	Limitations
[23]	Correia et al.	2021	Evolution of Blockchain Market	Lack of evidence-based studies of regulatory issues associated with blockchain.
[13]	Ekblaw et al.	2016	A Case Study for Blockchain in Healthcare: "MedRec" prototype for electronic health records and medical research data MedRec: Using Blockchain for Medical Data Access and Permission Management.	Security and scalability of the solution are not discussed.
[16]	Esposito et al.	2018	Blockchain: A Panacea for Healthcare Cloud-Based Data Security and Privacy?	The study did not address HIPAA and GDPR laws that guide the use of information technology in healthcare.
[14]	Gozman and Aste	2020	A case study of using blockchain technology in regulatory technology.	The solution was not scaled to production to test its applicability.
[28]	Guardtime	2016	Estonia e-health authority partners with Guardtime to accelerate transparency and auditability in healthcare.	The adaptability and scalability of the solution was not addressed.
[24]	GSMA	2017	Blockchain for Development: Emerging opportunities for Mobile, Identity and Aid.	Regulatory drawbacks have not been considered in detail.
[26]	Heston	2017	A case study in blockchain healthcare innovation.	Lack of applicability to other scenarios.
[22]	Lapointe and Fishbane	2019	The Blockchain Ethical Design Framework. Innovations: Technology, Governance, Globalization.	The research did not go into detail to address the current data laws and how these govern the adoption of blockchain technology.
[29]	Park and Park	2020	Regulation by selective enforcement.	Selective enforcement is difficult to apply in a broader context.
[30]	Yeoh	2017	Regulatory issues in Blockchain Technology.	Their solution requires an approved regulatory framework and standard before implementation can be carried out.

3. The Proposed Readiness Assessment Framework for Blockchain Regulation

In this section of the paper, we propose a readiness assessment framework for blockchain with the key stakeholders and the relationship between each entity. We then introduce some parameters to assess design framework readiness. The key components of this framework have been selected based on the systematic literature review of the blockchain structure and its applications, the key regulatory issues of blockchain, and the stakeholders that will benefit from a regulatory readiness assessment framework for blockchain. The approach to developing this framework is divided into three sections: First, are the facilitating conditions to support blockchain regulation, which involve the creation of regulatory sandboxes, multi-disciplinary research, data protection laws and anonymity. Then, we identify the key stakeholders, which are the regulators and government, business entities, solutions providers, and blockchain end-users [20,27]. In addition, our framework will be based on the dimensions of motivational readiness, structural readiness, engagement readiness and technological readiness, as shown in (Figure 2). Most research done on blockchain, and regulation focuses more on the legal and judicial side of the spectrum; we propose a regulatory readiness assessment framework to test stakeholder readiness for blockchain adoption from a regulatory standpoint. The key stakeholders and their relationships are discussed in the subsections that follow.

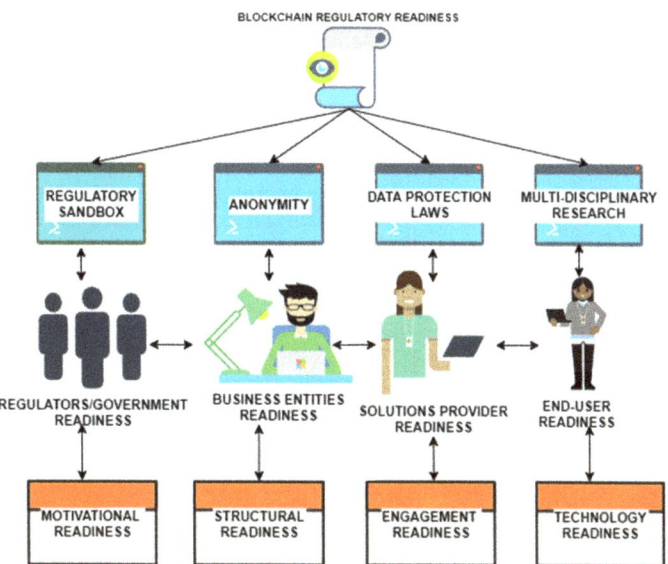

Figure 2. Proposed Regulatory Readiness Assessment Framework.

3.1. Key Stakeholders

3.1.1. Regulators

Regulators can be regarded as the most important blockchain stakeholder because of their direct influence over the blockchain ecosystem. Regulators can determine how easy it will be for other stakeholders to implement blockchain solutions [18]. Regulators are at the forefront of creating legislation and rules-of-engagement for those adopting blockchain solutions.

3.1.2. Business Entities

This refers to the components and processes that make up an organisation. In supply chain management for drug manufacturing, pharmacies, healthcare service providers, research centers and insurance providers will be the business entities that make up the organisation. These will vary according to the blockchain solution that is being adopted and how each business entity will collaborate. Business entities such as healthcare services providers can develop their own blockchain solution or be part of a wider solution.

3.1.3. Solutions Providers

These are the companies that provide the infrastructure need to create blockchain applications and solutions. The number of blockchain solutions providers is gradually increasing, creating healthy competition among these stakeholders. Blockchain solution providers such as IBM and Amazon have continued to show innovation in this space. For example, during the pandemic, IBM launched a blockchain initiative called IBM Rapid Supplier Connect to match frontline workers with essential medical equipment, which was a success.

3.1.4. Blockchain End-Users

These are the direct customers of the blockchain solution. Blockchain has always been a customer-centric solution as opposed to focusing on the organisation. It was created to give the users control over their data and how their data are used. For example, a permissioned or private blockchain solution to manage patient records will give the users control over how their data are shared and stored. The question of who has access and issues of unauthorized access will be reduced.

3.2. Relationship between Stakeholders to Develop a Regulatory Readiness Assessment Framework for Blockchain

3.2.1. Regulators and Business Entities

The adoption of a regulatory readiness assessment framework for blockchain will require extensive collaborative effort between the public sector (regulators) and private sector (business entities). For example, the "RegTech" blockchain prototype was designed to reduce the burden of regulatory compliance and reporting that is placed on organisations. The initiative proposed a decentralized approach for reporting mortgage sales in the UK. This was achieved by a collaborative effort between the Financial Conduct Authority (FCA), which is the public sector, and the banks, which are the private business entities for the success of this project.

3.2.2. Regulators and Solutions Provider

Creating a healthy ecosystem of collaboration and communication between the regulators and the solution providers will improve the implementation of larger projects as well as the scalability of the solution. The Estonian government and regulators have proved the validity of this model through their partnership with 'Guardtime', a blockchain solutions provider [26,28]. This collaborative approach has made Estonia one of the top countries in terms of blockchain adaptability into both public and private services, such as healthcare, finance, and government services.

3.2.3. Regulators and Blockchain End-User

It is important for the government/regulators to work together with blockchain users when creating and regulating blockchain services. This means that regulation will be approached not just from the perspective of solution providers and business entities but from the feedback of end-users. For example, the Estonian government works directly with citizens on the blockchain healthcare system, thereby creating trust and making regulatory compliance easier.

3.2.4. Business Entities and Solutions Providers

A close working relationship between business entities and solutions providers, both large and small, to ensure regulatory compliance and the interoperability of blockchain solutions is key to creating a working framework.

3.2.5. Business Entities and End-Users

There is a need for a direct relationship between business entities and end-users to incentivize users to adopt blockchain technology. Some business entities offer tokens and coins each time a user downloads their blockchain application. This creates trust and better customer relationships. This will also show that the business entities are liable and responsible for their customers' experience.

3.2.6. Solutions Providers and End-Users

This stakeholder relationship is important to protect customers and end-users; it is a key component for the success of blockchain regulation. For instance, in the financial sector, blockchain solutions providers have developed the Know-Your-Customer (KYC) concept to protect users and promote fairness in using the technology. This can be replicated for other sectors and applied in a broader context.

3.3. Regulatory Design Framework Readiness

3.3.1. Motivational Readiness

This refers to the dissatisfaction with the existing or legacy system and the motivation to create a better service for all stakeholders. Motivational readiness is characterised by problem definition, requirement gathering and mapping this to the features offered by blockchain to make it a preferred solution. This creates the catalyst for change in an organization, for example, a change in healthcare records management due to the duplication and tampering of data. Some examples of the requirements for motivational readiness for blockchain adoption include a need for shared data storage, need for a tamper-proof log of all transactions, automation of business processes, visibility of transactions among all stakeholders, removal of a central authority, and creation of data integrity and trust among stakeholders.

3.3.2. Structural Readiness

Implementing a regulatory readiness assessment framework for blockchain will require expertise, time, money, and resources from organisations. This refers to the workforce and non-technical resources in blockchain adoption. Organisations that are structurally strong in blockchain adoption will be one step closer to implementing a readiness assessment framework into their practices.

3.3.3. Engagement Readiness

This will include, but is not limited to, the ecosystem value proposition, the potential participants, the blockchain ecosystem model, how the ecosystem will be governed, the existing infrastructure and the development costs of the readiness assessment framework. These requirements will be mapped to other components of the framework to promote collaboration.

3.3.4. Technology Readiness

This refers to the technological infrastructure that is currently in place and the required information and communication resources for blockchain adoption. Embracing and complying with blockchain regulation and adopting a regulatory readiness assessment framework will require access to certain levels of technology. Some examples of technological readiness include cloud storage, computers, smart phone, and mobile connectivity.

4. Application of Framework in Case Study

In this section of the paper, we introduce the application of the proposed framework and demonstrate its applicability using Portugal's healthcare sector (Appendix A). The Portuguese healthcare sector has grown significantly and was ranked as the 13th best in Europe [31]. The Portuguese government is pushing for patient rights and secure access to information. They are considering blockchain as an innovative solution to address this problem.

4.1. Regulatory/Government Readiness

The Portuguese government/regulators are the most important stakeholders when creating an acceptable regulatory framework for blockchain. Since the global COVID-19 pandemic, the Portuguese government has been slow in their adoption of blockchain into sector specific services, unlike other EU countries, such as Malta and the UK [23,32].

There have been some improvement since the publication of the digital transition action plan, in April 2020, in preparation for the regulations on and legislation of digital technologies [33]. Since then, there has been significant blockchain research in the energy, smart contracts, health, and Non-Fungible Tokens (NFT) sectors [34]. Most of the research into adopting blockchain into healthcare in Portugal is still at the inception stage. This will prove to be a complexity in getting the stakeholders in our case study to accept a blockchain solution, and the lack of regulatory framework in this sector is one of the major deterrents.

This validates the need for a blockchain regulatory readiness in the areas of technology and structural readiness, but points to a lack of motivational and engagement readiness in the Portuguese healthcare sector. Our regulatory readiness assessment framework can assist the government in creating a widely acceptable regulatory framework for blockchain technology by identifying the readiness of key stakeholders and mapping them to the key facilitating conditions that can promote blockchain regulatory and knowledge. This can be designed into a template to promote blockchain innovation and bridge the gap with legislation.

4.2. Business Entity Readiness

From our findings, we outlined a slow growth into blockchain research among many small and large companies in Portugal. This highlights the fact that most are familiar with the term "Bitcoin" but unfamiliar with the term "Blockchain" [35]. The foreign interest in the Portuguese blockchain market has grown since the release of the government's publication regarding the creation of Technology-Free Zones [23]. This created anticipation that, when the TFZ legislative framework is created, it will create a more stable platform for blockchain solutions. Some of the most successful use-case areas of blockchain in Portugal are in Ethereum, charity and gaming. There are considerable limitations from a structural and technological perspective. Therefore, the readiness for a regulatory framework for blockchain solution within business entities is very high, but motivational and engagement readiness is very low.

4.3. Solutions Providers Readiness

Information from the relevant literature on the current state of blockchain technology in Portugal show that many blockchain consulting firms have already been established with a firm foundation. From our findings, we can point to a readiness for solution providers in our four dimensions. Technology, motivation, structure, and engagement readiness are relatively high. This can create a solid foundation for a nationwide, accepted regulatory framework and practice when creating blockchain solutions. Our regulatory readiness assessment framework can assist solution providers in gauging readiness to achieve regulatory compliance when implementing blockchain solutions. Solution providers are focusing more on blockchain in the financial sector because Portugal is tax-free for cryptocurrency [35]. The successful implementation of blockchain into healthcare in Portugal has yet to be achieved, but this may change after the COVID-19 pandemic due to the pressure on the healthcare sector to share and manage a high volume of information.

4.4. End-User Readiness

There is high motivation for a new way of managing healthcare records among patients (end-users) in Portugal; this shows a decent motivation to extend blockchain to the healthcare sector [31,36]. This will have to be achieved in compliance with EU data laws, which is where our regulatory readiness framework can be applied. From our findings in recent studies, there is a growing concern regarding patient autonomy over their data in Portugal. As with the issue of the data breach in our case study, there is news of several other hacks into medical record and breaches into solution providers [11,21]. We highlight strong evidence of engagement, motivation, structural and technology readiness for a healthcare record blockchain solution.

The stakeholder readiness and their corresponding regulatory facilitating conditions were explored by applying our regulatory readiness framework to the case study in Portugal. This showed readiness for a widely acceptable blockchain regulatory framework to boost innovation in the blockchain space in Portugal [31,33,34]. The motivational and engagement readiness for regulators and business entities is *low*, while that of the solution providers and end-users is *high*. On the other hand, the structural and technological readiness for all key stakeholders is *high*.

The key facilitating conditions for regulators to achieve regulatory readiness will include *regulatory sandbox* and *data protection laws*, while the business entities and solution providers will be facilitated by regulatory sandbox, anonymity, and data protection laws. Finally, the key facilitating conditions for end-users will be anonymity and data protection laws.

4.5. Applying Key Regulatory Facilitating Conditions to Stakeholder Readiness

4.5.1. Regulatory Sandbox

A regulatory sandbox will allow innovators and researchers to test out new technology and business models without the rules and consequences of the real world. Most of the discussion concerning blockchain is centered around bitcoin, and we clarified, earlier in our research, that Bitcoin is not Blockchain. There is still no clear regulatory framework for blockchain in Portugal, especially for the healthcare sector. Therefore, we propose a regulatory sandbox among regulators/government, business entities and solutions providers. A regulatory sandbox will allow for the testing of new innovative blockchain solutions within a controlled environment. This will contribute to the knowledge sharing of data laws and provide evidence on blockchain regulatory issues and how key stakeholders can harmonize legislation and blockchain solutions.

4.5.2. Anonymity

For blockchain solutions, especially in healthcare and finance, there is a need to balance the anonymity of blockchain assets with anti-money-laundering laws, KYC and GDPR laws. Defining this clearly from the design to the implementation stage will have huge impact on a globally accepted regulatory framework. This is one of the major facilitating conditions that will harmonize legislation and blockchain technology in Portugal and can be applied in a broader context in other countries. Anonymity is considered a key facilitating condition for business entities, solutions providers, and end-users. There are technologies in place, such as zero knowledge (zk-SNARks) and ring signature, that can be used to hide the identity of the transaction sender on the network. Encryption can also be used to protect the user's privacy.

4.5.3. Data Protection Laws

For Portugal, this falls under the category of enhanced privacy and trust in data. There is a big push for a more effective data-management platform, especially in the country's healthcare sector [23]. The government is discussing initiatives to secure patients' rights regarding how their data are shared and accessed among healthcare practitioners. Understanding the current data protections laws, such as the GDPR "right to be forgotten" and implementing these across the blockchain ecosystem will reinforce the confidence of stakeholders. This key regulatory facilitating condition will be important to regulators, end-users, business entities and solution providers.

4.5.4. Multi-Disciplinary Research

This is one of the most important components of the framework. This promotes engagement readiness among all stakeholders, irrespective of academic background and discipline. It is the catalyst to achieving an industry/sector-wide regulatory framework for blockchain and its assets. The process of multi-disciplinary research will require a collaborative approach among several countries, sectors, disciplines, and businesses that indirectly or directly influence blockchain regulation. This is quite different from the regulatory sandbox and promotes stakeholder engagement at a high level by exploring new opportunities and ideas. Each person or entity will provide a unique and diverse set of skills and knowledge that will add to the knowledge pool of blockchain and how to achieve effective regulation that will not harm innovation efforts. For example, multidisciplinary research into blockchain regulation will involve the legal sector, business sector, the social-science sector, computer science, healthcare, economics and technical and non-technical blockchain experts.

5. Materials and Methods

The search for relevant papers for the Systematic Literature Review was carried out using the Scopus Database. This is a concise database that encompasses a wide array of journal articles, so the enquiry was limited to this search engine. The goal was to retrieve the literature directly relating to blockchain regulations and blockchain in healthcare records' management. The keyword used for the initial search was "Blockchain", with the inclusion criteria for "business & management studies", "Computer Science" and "Healthcare". Conference papers, conference reviews, book chapters and unpublished works were excluded. After removing duplicates and categorizing the literature based on these inclusion criteria, our initial search provided 25,680 articles on blockchain. Following further title-, abstract- and keyword-screening for studies that focus on regulatory concerns of blockchain in healthcare, blockchain regulation and regulatory impacts on blockchain, we shortlisted our list of articles to 135. Highly technical studies, such as blockchain analytics and algorithms, were excluded from the search. After further consideration and review, we selected 23 articles for the review. Figure 3 shows a flowchart of the literature search and selection criteria.

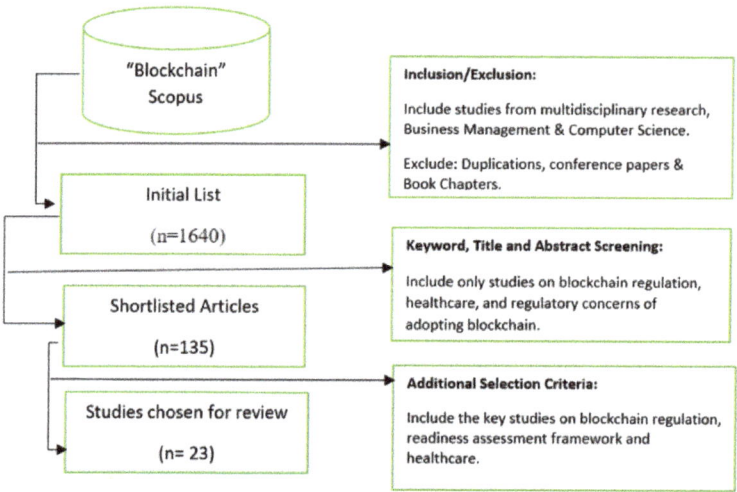

Figure 3. Systematic Review of Blockchain Regulation and Adoption.

Our review of the chosen literature revealed gaps in blockchain regulation research and its adoption within the healthcare space and other sectors. We present a summary table of the chosen studies (as shown in Table 2). Attempts to gain primary data on blockchain regulatory frameworks were limited but it a growing area. Most research studies showed a lack of understanding of key facilitating conditions for blockchain regulation. Despite these gaps and after a careful synthesis of studies, we were able to:

- Gain more knowledge and understand the various applications of blockchain.
- Understand the implications of regulations and data laws on blockchain.
- Understand the roles of the key stakeholders associated with blockchain regulation in the healthcare sector.
- Understand their concerns regarding regulation, privacy, and security.

This systematic literature review provides the conceptual and theoretical foundation for our proposed regulatory readiness assessment framework. While we accept that there is no single framework that is sufficient to assess the regulatory readiness of a sector or country to adopt blockchain, we combined all effort and knowledge to ensure the reproducibility of the proposed framework [37]. We addressed the limitations of blockchain from a technical, economic, and social perspective, then carefully applied this to our proposed framework. We successfully identified the key stakeholders that can promote or limit blockchain regulation, which is very important to ensure that blockchain can gain the popularity required for proper regulation.

Table 2. Summary of the important literature for blockchain regulation and adoption in healthcare and other sectors.

Study/Summary	Methodology	Key Stakeholders
Belchior et al. (2021) [6] Summary: A framework for blockchain interoperability among blockchain entities. Benefits: Reducing attacks through interoperability; improving data standards and privacy; insight into blockchain interoperability use-cases. Challenges: Fast-paced development of blockchain, security, trust and privacy issues related to GDPR.	Systematic Literature Review	Business Entities Regulators Service Providers
Berdik et al. (2021) [18] Summary: Reports on the issues and adoption of blockchain applications in information systems. Benefits: Promotes blockchain adoption and interoperability among components; open source blockchain tools. Challenges The layout and architecture of blockchain is crucial to its widespread adoption.	Secondary Sources (Survey)	End-Users Solutions Providers
Casino et al. (2019) [38] Summary: The use of blockchain in supply chains, healthcare, IOT and data management. Benefits: It contributes to the knowledge base and understanding of applying blockchains to real-world problems. Challenges: Lack of review of current state-of-the-art devices due to limited information and research.	Literature Review	Blockchain Researchers Regulators Business Entities
Charles et al. (2019) [7] Summary: Explores the use of blockchain-based application for clinical research, managing patient and laboratory data. Benefits: Contributes to the knowledge and understanding of the regulatory constraints of adopting blockchain into the healthcare sector. Challenges: Adhering to regulatory requirements, privacy regulations and guideline on how to achieve compliance when managing healthcare records.	Secondary Sources	Patients Regulators/Government Healthcare Providers Solutions Providers
Dameri (2009) [9] Summary: How to improve IT governance and compliance of digital applications. Compliance requirements when implementing IT governance into digital applications. Benefits: Development of a compliance-automated system. Challenges: Transparency, costs, data protection laws.	Secondary Sources	Solutions Providers Regulators/Government
Dorri et al. (2017) [19] Summary: An investigation into the use of blockchain in a smart-home setting. Benefits: Proposed a blockchain smart-home framework that is secure, and secure access control for IOT devices. Challenges: Confidentiality, high costs and security issues.	Experiment	Solutions Provider Blockchain Developers
Ekblaw et al. (2016) [13] Summary: Proposed the use of blockchain to manage medical records. Benefits: The development of a working prototype to analyse the potential of blockchain in healthcare, improved interoperability of systems among healthcare providers and quality data for medical researchers. Challenges: 51% attack on the private blockchain, high volume of medical data.	Case Study (Experiment)	Patients Healthcare Providers Regulators Public Health Authorities.
Esposito (2018) [16] Summary: Proposed a blockchain solution to protect healthcare data hosted within the cloud. Benefits: Recommends off-chain storage to combat GDPR "Right to be forgotten' law. Challenges: GDPR Laws, scalability, and storage of data.	Secondary Sources	Patients Healthcare Providers Regulators Solutions Providers

Table 2. Cont.

Study/Summary	Methodology	Key Stakeholders
Filippi and Hassan (2016) [39] Summary: An overview into the legal challenges of blockchain applications. Benefits: Proposed automated legal governance using blockchain, improved transparency in carrying out regulatory obligations. Challenges: Issues with GDPR's right to be forgotten and immutability of blockchain transactions.	Secondary sources	Regulators Law Makers Business Entities
Gozman et al. (2020) [14] Summary: Automating the process of regulatory reporting using blockchain technology. Benefits: Reduce duplication, efficient regulatory reporting system, and creating a better understanding of blockchain for regulators by making them use the technology in regulatory reporting. Challenges: Educating regulators and other stakeholders, confidentiality issues.	Secondary Sources	Regulators/Government Financial Houses Business Entities
Gupta and Sadoghi (2019) [40] Summary: Proposed the use of blockchain in processing transactions. Benefits: Improves trust and data integrity, tamper-proof solution, reduce fraud and accountability of data. Challenges: High costs of maintenance and regulatory issues.	Secondary Sources	Business Entities Solutions Providers
Heston (2017) [26] Summary: The application of blockchain in healthcare innovation using Estonia as a case study. Benefits: Promotes better understanding of regulators, governments, and healthcare providers on the use of blockchain in the healthcare sector and how to leverage the opportunities provided by blockchain to improve healthcare data integrity. Puts the patient's welfare at the forefront of innovation. Challenges: 51% attack can occur; size of medical data can cause storage problems and end-user is responsible for data.	Case Study	Patients Regulators/Government Healthcare Providers Business Entities
Kwok and Koh (2018) [4] Summary: Explores the use of blockchain to boost tourism among small economies. Benefits: Increased commercial opportunities for small countries and improved stakeholder knowledge on blockchain. Challenges: Educating stakeholders on blockchain and regulatory gaps.	Secondary Sources	End-users Business Entities Regulators/Government
Lim et al. (2021) [36] Summary: How blockchain technology can be used to improve supply chain activities. Benefits: Improve stakeholder knowledge of using blockchain in supply chain tracking and management. Challenges: Transparency, high costs and lack of expertise.	Literature Review	Solutions Providers Business Entities
Lin et al. (2017) [12] Summary: The security issues and challenges of blockchain, and how these have shaped regulation laws and the adoption of blockchain as a solution. Benefits: Easy access to data, integration of multiple tasks and less maintenance. Challenges: Privacy issues.	Secondary Sources	Regulators Solutions Providers
Kwok (2018) [41] Summary: This research focused on the adoption of blockchain technology into Tourism and the implications for tourism development in the Caribbean economy. Benefits: Boosting of tourism revenue and the launching of the first digital legal tender in the Caribbean. Challenges: Lack of IT infrastructure and government support for new technologies.	Survey	End-users Government Business Entities

Table 2. *Cont.*

Study/Summary	Methodology	Key Stakeholders
Nguyen et al. (2021) [32] Summary: An extensive survey into the application of blockchain and AI into combating the COVID-19 virus. An integration of blockchain and AI to revolutionize the healthcare sector. Benefits: Early detection of outbreaks, ordering of medical data, support drug manufacturing and virus tracing. Challenges: Lack of a regulatory framework for blockchain, data privacy concerns, implementation issues and interoperability of medical record systems.	Survey	Patients Government Healthcare Providers
Prashanth (2018) [21] Summary: A survey into the challenges and opportunities of using blockchain as a solution to privacy concerns. Benefits: Improves trust in and credibility of data and has no third parties. Challenges: Fear of strict regulations.	Secondary Sources	Solutions Providers Business Entities
Sarmah (2018) [2] Summary: A study into understanding the use of blockchain and how to it can be applied to several industries and sectors, as well as their challenges and advantages. Benefits: Promotes a better understanding of how to leverage blockchain as a solution for organisations. Challenges: A lack of regulatory framework is slowing down the pace of adoption and a lack of understanding of blockchain architecture by the key stakeholders.	Secondary Sources	Solutions Providers Regulators
Siyal (2019) [42] Summary: An overview into blockchain application in the healthcare sector, focusing on Electronic Health Records, clinical research, medical fraud detection, neuroscience, and biomedical research. Benefits: New research opportunities for biomedical research. Challenges: Storage and scalability, requires regulatory standards, social acceptance, and interoperability of healthcare systems.	Secondary Sources	Healthcare providers Biomedical researchers R&D Specialist Patients Solutions Providers
Yeoh (2017) [30] Summary: This research examines the key regulatory challenges of blockchain adoption in the EU and US. It discusses the hands-off approach initiated by both countries, and how this has accelerated the growth of blockchain, in detail. Benefits: Support for the right innovation for blockchain that will continue to add value to the technology and make it more accessible. It also promotes a better understanding between cryptocurrency and blockchain. Challenges: Lack of adequate knowledge and blockchain expertise from regulators.	Primary Sources Secondary sources	Regulators Governments Solutions Providers
Kant (2021) [43] Summary: Blockchain as a solution to organisations' needs and a source of competitive advantage. Benefits: Contributes to the body of knowledge of blockchain adoption. Challenges: Social and legal issues.	Secondary Sources	Blockchain Researchers Solutions Providers
Pal (2021) [44] Summary: Explores the possibility of applying blockchain to business management and business activities to create a safer transaction process. Benefits: Safer business transactions, reduces error in transactions, helps prevent fraud. Challenges: Regulatory and social challenges.	Systematic Literature Review	Business Entities Solution Providers Blockchain Researchers

Table 2. *Cont.*

Study/Summary	Methodology	Key Stakeholders
Rajeb (2020) [45] Summary: Explores the application of blockchain to food supply chains (FSC) to combat the issue of food traceability, improve health and safety standards of food, provide verifiable information on food nutrients. Benefits: Improve supply chain transparency, effective traceability, automate data collection and minimize logistic errors. Challenges: Limited scalability, technological immaturity, lack of industry standard, lack of a blockchain regulatory framework and privacy concerns.	Systematic Literature Review Bibliometric Analysis.	Food Manufacturers Food Regulators Business Entities End-Users
Sung (2021) [46] Summary: This study focuses on the adoption of blockchain in an identity management system, with a focus on the Korean Government. Benefits: Blockchain provides better control of data, integrity and data reliability and reduces the cost of delivery to public services. This system is a user-centric personal data management without a central authority. This will allow for quicker data access by leveraging the decentralized nature of blockchain. Challenges: Educating public sector on blockchain, privacy concerns, regulatory concerns.	Design Case Literature Review	End-users Government Regulators Public Sector

Some of the studies, such as Casino et al., Charles et al., Dameri, Dorri et al., Gupta and Sadoghi, Kwok and Koh, Lim et al., Sarmah, Siyal, Kant, Pal and Sung, proposed different methods for blockchain adoption and highlighted some related and non-related regulatory issues pertaining to blockchain. The primary components of the framework were chosen from framework- and regulatory-related studies on blockchain (Belchior et al., Berdik et al., Ekblaw et al., Esposito., Filippi and Hassan, Gozman et al., Heston, Lin et al., Nguyen et al., Prashanth, Yeoh and Rajeb). Most of these reviews and studies were limited in scope but offered a good theoretical foundation for the proposed framework. Most reviews focused on one aspect of organisations and stakeholders, while ours considers different levels of stakeholder readiness. Defining the stakeholders responsible for adopting new technology is very important to the framework, especially for a multi-stakeholder sector such as healthcare.

6. Impact of Regulatory Laws on Blockchain Adoption

Blockchain-enabled applications are currently fighting the battle of compliance and how to navigate the parameters of data privacy laws such as GDPR, Health Insurance Portability and Accountability Act (HIPAA), SEC, California Consumer Privacy Act (CCPA), tax laws, state laws, anti-money-laundering laws, and anti-corruption laws [8,35,47]. Policymakers and business entities will have to collaborate on the laws and rules of engagement that surround blockchain for innovation to continue at a fast pace [9,38]. This proposes the question of whether the existing laws will be modified to suit blockchain or whether there will be entirely new set of rules for blockchain assets [40].

Blockchain is built on transparency, trust, and immutability; therefore, many sectors are adopting it into their business process. This unique characteristic is also the reason it is facing resistance from regulators [4,5]. Blockchain has been envisioned to become a new tool of democracy, giving control over personal data back to the users, as well as the power to monetize their data [7,38,40]. The lack of compliance, governance, and adequate regulations in blockchain technology is slowing down its adoption and innovation in several sectors and industries [8,35]. This is one of the major challenges faced by emerging technologies such as Artificial Intelligence (AI), Internet of Things (IOT), 3D Printing and Virtual Reality (VR) [48].

Blockchain is a catalyst for change and will eventually blend with regulation and legislation [3,28]. The impact of data laws and regulations on blockchain applications is no longer passive. The EU, according to GDPR laws, has rules and regulations regarding how data are managed and transmitted; these are enforced across all traditional digital assets. For instance, the GDPR Regulation (2016/679) of the European parliament and Council protects the processing of personal information and the free movement of such data [49]. This creates an issue in the world of blockchain technology due to its special characteristics, such as the anonymity/pseudonymity, immutability, and distributed nature of this innovative technology [7,15,41]. The decentralized structure of blockchain violates the first rule of the GDPR, which is the "Right to be Forgotten"; this is the right for an individual to request that their personal data are removed or erased, which is impossible on a blockchain ledger [49].

According to Siegel [50], the HIPAA laws consist of two major categories: the HIPAA Privacy Rule and the HIPAA Security Rule. The HIPPA Privacy rule is a collection of national standards for the protection of certain patient information, while the HIPAA Security Rule is a collection of security standards for patient information that is transferred or exchanged in the US [50]. The current HIPAA laws are in direct contention with blockchain because encryption or cryptography is in direct violation of HIPPA privacy and security rules. This is a challenge when proposing solutions using blockchain to the authentication and verification of medical data in the US. Companies such as Timcoin are currently working on blockchain uses in the healthcare industry that can navigate the HIPAA rules [33,50].

There are also laws such as state laws, tax laws and anti-corruption laws that vary from country to country. Blockchain companies must consider these laws according to where data will be stored and transmitted, who will have access to data, and the purpose of the blockchain [35].

6.1. Key Issues between Blockchain and Current Data Protection Laws

At present, digital applications operate using a central or single database that serves as a single source of truth [16,35]. This master database can easily be shared with regulators and authorities for enforcement and investigations. Blockchain, on the other hand, operates as a distribution of nodes and acts as a consensus version of the truth [47]. This has made regulation complex because it is difficult to ascertain ownership of the network in a decentralized network. Blockchain is characterized by anonymity and pseudonymity, making it difficult for enforcement agencies and police to enforce laws [39,50,51]. Blockchain is an immutable ledger, which means that transactions cannot be deleted once they are entered [41,52]. This creates another dilemma with regulatory laws and regulators due to data privacy laws. These are some of the major gaps that exist between enterprise blockchain and regulation.

There are some major key legal hurdles that blockchain companies must overcome to comply with data laws and regulations. Some of these hurdles are due to the technical features of blockchain, while others are based on territory. They are as follows.

6.1.1. Recognizing Blockchain-Based Signatures

On a blockchain ledger, it is easy to know who owns the stored data and prove that data have not been manipulated by users. According to the regulators, this is insufficient, as they are not legally binding. For blockchain-based signatures to be legally binding, regulators will need to know who made the transactions, the time stamp, who validated the transactions, the data associated with the transaction, and was it carried out under a trusted Internet Service Provider (ISP) [31,51]. To mitigate these legal hurdles, regulators will be required to broaden their knowledge of blockchain timestamping methods and how this can fit into the current regulations [35].

6.1.2. Location of Nodes

Permissionless or public blockchains such as Bitcoin are not hosted in one precise location, but a combination of nodes that are spread out across the globe [41]. This can make it difficult for regulators, especially in the finance sector, where there are anti-money-laundering laws and know-your-customer (KYC) laws. This will require a cross-jurisdiction effort on the part of regulators to comply with data laws. There is also the drawback of being unable to control risks and monopolies that exist in the blockchain ecosystem. EU regulators focus on the location of a dispute to determine the appropriate laws that will govern damage recovery [31]. The place where the harmful event or hacking occurs usually determines which court will have jurisdiction. The decentralized structure of blockchain will make it difficult to determine in which place or country the damage occurred and will make it hard for the law to take its course.

6.1.3. Anonymity

When a law is broken, law enforcement does their job by enforcing sanctions and penalties. For this to happen, the law will have a clear idea of who the lawbreakers are and where they reside. For blockchain, this is quite impossible or very difficult to ascertain. For permissioned or consortium blockchains, this will not be a problem because all participants are identified, but for a permissionless blockchain, where the actors are unknown, this can be quite difficult and will require forensic analysis of the blockchain network [32]. To mitigate this issue in Bitcoin, for instance, the regulators will need to police the gateway between cryptocurrency and fiat currency [34,35]. Regulators will be able to monitor the access points that are key to the running of the blockchain application. By policing these access points, lawbreakers can be unmasked and traced.

6.1.4. Liability Constraints

Who is liable? The question of who will be liable and responsible for data breaches or violating data laws can be confusing in blockchain. This lack of liability can create an obstacle for regulators to establish with compensation rights for defrauded users [34,53]. The issue of who is most liable among blockchain developers, users, and business entities is still under debate, so the government has decided to find a different way of enforcing liability in blockchains [32,34].

6.1.5. Data Protection Laws

The EU has enforced GDPR rules since 2018, whose sole purpose is to consider all developments in the online world for the last 25 years [49,51]. The GDPR laws were designed before the popularity of blockchain grew to its present levels. This has created tension between blockchain technology and EU data regulators. There are three major areas of contention between blockchain and GDPR laws, which are as follows:

- The identification of data controllers and processors is law under GDPR.
- Anonymity of personal data.
- The GDPR right to be forgotten.

The third contention, which is the "Right to be Forgotten", can be mitigated if the blockchain is designed with this data law in mind [50]. The use of an off-chain storage and processing data management platform can mitigate this issue.

6.2. Some Key Guidelines to Aid Regulators and Policy Makers on Their Journey to Regulate Blockchain Technology

- A simple dictionary of blockchain terminologies written by regulators, which defines blockchain EU Laws and data laws to ensure shared definitions among countries.
- Communication of these terminologies so that they reach a wider audience.
- Creation of a balance between blockchain terminologies and laws that will not deter innovation.
- A sandbox to improve understanding between regulators and the blockchain ecosystem.
- Use of case testing to obtain a clearer picture of the gap between blockchain and GDPR.
- Monitoring and reiteration in smaller use cases to test resistance to blockchain assets.

- A based regulatory tool is a good way of improving the understanding between regulators and blockchain. In their work Gozman and Aste [14] proposed a solution that involved the application of blockchain to regulatory reporting. This will help bridge the gap and harmonize the current situation between the data-protection regulators and blockchain solutions as they utilize this technology first-hand.

7. Discussion

The authenticity of a framework is ascertained when its explanations are concise, categories are properly formed, interpretations and terminology are easy to understand, and transferability and dependability are established [47]. We present a summary of the regulatory readiness assessment framework for the Portuguese healthcare sector, as shown in Table 3. We provide a snapshot of the findings based on the key regulatory facilitating conditions, which is key to the framework. We categorize facilitating conditions from '*high*' to '*low*' based on key stakeholder readiness. We capture how the key regulatory facilitating conditions influence stakeholders and highlight their readiness for a regulatory framework for blockchain technology. These findings are based on our Portuguese healthcare case study.

Table 3. Summary of the regulatory readiness assessment framework for Portugal's Healthcare Sector (case study) in terms of key regulatory facilitating conditions.

Key Regulatory Facilitating Conditions	Regulators/Government	Business Entities	Solutions Providers	End Users
Regulatory Sandbox	Low — There are plans to launch a Trade-Free Zone in Portugal, but there is no ongoing collaborative approach between regulators and blockchain providers. There is a need for a regulatory sandbox to improve the understanding of regulators in Portugal that Bitcoin is not Blockchain.	Low — There is little to no collaborative effort among business entities to improve blockchain adoption and minimize regulatory concerns.	High — There are collaborative research plans among the bigger technology companies to reduce regulation concerns by following regulatory practices when providing their blockchain solution.	High — High stakeholder motivation for blockchain adoption and innovation, especially due to Portugal's tax-free law on cryptocurrency, but fear of harsh regulation causes concern.
Anonymity	Low — Regulators and government understanding of blockchain anonymity is based on the darknet uses of Bitcoin. Regulators must have a technical understanding that blockchain anonymity is not a threat but an opportunity if leveraged correctly. There are always ways to reduce anonymity within a technology, but only through an understanding of its technology and terminology.	High — Business entities are individually taking advantage of blockchain in Portugal, especially cryptocurrency, which is the most popular use-case at present.	High — Solution providers such as Amazon and IBM are trying to figure out ways to blend anonymity when developing blockchain platforms with regulatory requirements.	Low — There are concerns regarding how issues will be resolved and the high risk of losing their investments if everyone is anonymous.
Data Protection Laws	High — The EU is considering blockchain regulation despite most laws still being at the planning phase.	Low — Concerns relating to GDPR data laws and fines.	Low — Concerns relating to GDPR laws, Portuguese data laws and anti-money-laundering laws.	Low — Concerns relating to laws of the regulatory framework and how these will impact their data.
Multi-Disciplinary Research	High — There is motivation for research on blockchain regulation to cut across all sectors, even though most research is still in the planning phase. There is also a good IT infrastructure in Portugal.	Low — There is no known multi-disciplinary research on blockchain regulation among business entities in Portugal.	Low — There is limited multi-disciplinary research among small and large solution providers.	High — End-users show motivation to be part of multi-disciplinary research that forms a knowledge pool for the creation of a regulatory framework.

One of the key results is that all stakeholders need to understand the technology and terminologies, which will require extensive collaboration. Most blockchain initiatives have faced challenges in gathering all stakeholders together to discuss a roadmap for a widely acceptable regulatory framework. The key concern of most business entities and end-users relates to data protection laws. Addressing these concerns by creating a regulatory sandbox to test blockchain solutions in a controlled environment will boost blockchain's adoption into the healthcare sector and other industries.

There is strong evidence of blockchain adoption and innovation in Portugal. This willingness to adopt blockchain as a solution provides the correct ecosystem for a widely approved framework that supports innovation. The fault tolerance of the proposed solution is synonymous with distributed systems. By design, the proposed readiness assessment framework will maintain its functionalities if one or more of the components fail due to their unexpected behaviors. The issue of scalability will heavily depend on the number of stakeholders that are involved in the process and the transactions of the blockchain application. There is a need for a regulatory readiness framework that will address the concerns of all stakeholders without comprising the innovative potential of blockchain technology.

8. Conclusions and Future Work

The blockchain phenomenon has now moved from an exaggeration to a reality. This innovative technology is gradually disrupting the digital ecosystem and has the power to transform not only the financial industry, but almost every industry and sector in the world. There is ongoing research and collaborative efforts toward regulating this technology but no evidence of any research into the regulatory readiness assessment for blockchain technology. In this study, we proposed a conceptual regulatory readiness assessment framework for blockchain. This was then applied to the Portuguese healthcare case study to test its usefulness. We identified the key stakeholders that are needed to achieve a regulatory framework, the technology, motivational, engagement and structural readiness, and the key regulatory facilitating conditions for blockchain. This gave a good insight to the application of blockchain to manage healthcare records, with Portugal as a focus point for our case study. Our findings showed positivity regarding the adoption of blockchain, especially in the healthcare sector, where patients want full control over their data, there are issues of fragmented data, and healthcare providers require data integrity. The downside in our findings points to a lack of harmony between regulators and blockchain stakeholders due to the lack of a dependable regulatory framework. Applying a regulatory readiness framework to blockchain will speed up its adoption, guarantee knowledge dissemination, reduce loss of data, avoid fines, and improve regulatory reporting. Blockchain development and regulatory compliance will be approached simultaneously at every level of the framework, with the key stakeholders as variables.

Blockchain can enhance data integrity in many sectors especially healthcare but there must be trust between the technology providers, regulators/government, business entities and end-users. Much is still unknown about blockchain regulation at this stage and, as it grows from strength to strength, regulation will become mandatory. This will have to be done on a use-case-by-use-case basis, rather than using one-size-fits all approach. Although our framework was based on a wide view of blockchain in terms of its regulation, adoption, and innovation, it does not cover every aspect of blockchain regulation.

For future research, we propose research into a web application tool for blockchain adoption and a regulatory readiness assessment. This will be conducted using a collaborative approach with a wider number of researchers, with a focus on its application in the healthcare sector. The healthcare sector is slow to accept digital transformation and has limited information when it comes to blockchain application. Despite these limitations, we believe that our regulatory readiness assessment framework will improve regulatory knowledge for the use of blockchain in healthcare and other sectors.

Author Contributions: Conceptualization, O.S., M.P. and N.P.; methodology, O.S.; validation, M.P. and N.P.; writing—original draft preparation, O.S.; writing—review and editing, M.P. and N.P.; supervision, M.P. and N.P. All authors have read and agreed to the published version of the manuscript.

Funding: This research received no external funding.

Institutional Review Board Statement: Not applicable.

Informed Consent Statement: Not applicable.

Data Availability Statement: Not applicable.

Conflicts of Interest: The authors declare no conflict of interest.

Appendix A. Case Study Brief

We selected a hospital in Portugal that was fined for GDPR infringement and violating data regulatory laws for our case study. After evaluating several pieces of secondary data (research journals and articles) on regulation in the EU, we chose Portugal because of its recent effort towards blockchain adoption and nation-wide regulation. A case study approach seems appropriate because of the limited information regarding blockchain adoption and regulatory research in the healthcare sector. We have looked through extensive news coverage and information on this case study to obtain a comprehensive understanding, and most of the data were compiled from secondary data sources. We focused on secondary data that showed the anticipated challenges regarding blockchain in Portugal, the current state of regulation, and stakeholder readiness for blockchain technology. We used secondary data corresponding to our themes, which were the key facilitating conditions for blockchain, identification of relevant stake holders and stakeholder readiness, when selecting our case study.

From our findings, we identified several news headlines about the 400,000 EUR fine slammed on the hospital for violating data laws, which was the first of its kind [34]. The Portuguese-based hospital was accused of violating three EU data laws, as follows: indiscriminate access to patient's data, lack of secure processing, and violation of confidentiality and integrity. The hospital blamed this breach on the outdated information technology system provided by the public sector [34]. This could have been avoided if the hospital had adopted a more secure way of managing and accessing healthcare records, in accordance with data laws. This provided the opportunity to suggest a more innovative system that manages data assets efficiently, such as blockchain technology. The hospital focuses on general medical diagnosis, treatment, and tests. We then applied our regulatory readiness assessment framework to a proposed, blockchain-based, healthcare-record-management system for the hospital to improve the confidentiality, integrity, and authenticity of medical records, restrict unauthorized access and give patients full control over their data within the hospital.

The hospital has over 50 staff members, both external and internal, and their patient size has recently increased from 100 patients to 150 patients in the past year. The previous electronic health record system used in the hospital can no longer serve this growing customer database. In the past, there have been losses and comprises of patient information, and fragmented sharing of data. There is also a lack of integrity regarding medical data and patients cannot access their data conveniently.

We propose the implementation of a permissioned blockchain architecture to manage patient data and replace or enhance the current HER system. If set up correctly, patients will have full control over their records, and can revoke access to information. Patients would also be able review doctor's visits, online medical diagnoses, secure data exchange and the interoperability of systems with other health care providers, and secure data collection for ministry and government surveys.

References

1. Nakamoto, S. Bitcoin: A Peer-to-Peer Electronic Cash System. 2008. Available online: https://www.researchgate.net/publication/228640975_Bitcoin_A_Peer-to-Peer_Electronic_Cash_System (accessed on 7 December 2021).
2. Sarmah, S.S. Understanding Blockchain Technology. *Comput. Sci. Eng.* **2018**, *8*, 23–29. [CrossRef]
3. Crosby, M.; Kalyanaraman, V. Blockchain Technology: Beyond Bitc'in. *Appl. Innov. Rev.* **2016**, *2*, 6–19.
4. Lim, M. 81 of Top 100 Companies Use Blockchain Technology. 2021. Available online: https://forkast.news/81-of-top-100-companies-use-blockchain-technology-blockdata/ (accessed on 13 November 2021).

5. Genov, E. The Longest Running Blockchain Has Existed on NYT Pages Since 1995. 2018. Available online: https://toshitimes.com/the-longest-running-blockchain-has-existed-on-nyt-pages-since-1995/ (accessed on 7 December 2021).
6. Belchior, R.; Vasconcelos, A.; Guerreiro, S.; Correia, M. A Survey on Blockchain Interoperability: Past, Present, and Future Trends. *ACM Comput. Surv.* **2022**, *54*, 1–44. [CrossRef]
7. Charles, W.; Marler, N.; Long, L.; Manion, S. Blockchain Compliance by Design: Regulatory Considerations for Blockchain in Clinical Research. *Blockchain Distrib. Res.* **2019**, *2*, 18. [CrossRef]
8. Tasca, P.; Widmann, S. The Challenges Faced by Blockchain Technology. *J. Digit. Bank.* **2017**, *2*, 132–147.
9. Dameri, R.P. Improving the Benefits of IT Compliance Using Enterprise Management Information Systems. *Electron. J. Inf. Syst. Eval.* **2009**, *12*, 27–38. Available online: http://search.ebscohost.com/login.aspxdirect=true&db=bth&AN=37568214&lang=fr&site=ehost-live (accessed on 2 October 2021).
10. Haar, R. New Bitcoin ETF Grows at Record Speed. 2021. Available online: https://time.com/nextadvisor/investing/cryptocurrency/bitcoin-etf-approved/ (accessed on 10 October 2021).
11. Dore, K. What the First Bitcoin Futures Exchange-Traded Fund Means for the Cryptocurrency Industry. 2021. Available online: https://www.cnbc.com/2021/10/24/what-first-bitcoin-futures-etf-means-for-cryptocurrency-industry.html (accessed on 13 November 2021).
12. Lin, I.C.; Liao, T.C. A survey of blockchain security issues and challenges. *Int. J. Netw. Secur.* **2017**, *19*, 653–659. [CrossRef]
13. Ekblaw, A.; Azaria, A.; Halamka, J.D.; Lippman, A.; Original, I.; Vieira, T. A Case Study for Blockchain in Healthcare: "MedRec" prototype for electronic health records and medical research data MedRec: Using Blockchain for Medical Data Access and Permission Management. In Proceedings of the 2016 2nd International Conference on Open and Big Data (OBD), Vienna, Austria, 22–24 August 2016; pp. 1–13. [CrossRef]
14. Gozman, D.; Liebenau, J.; Aste, T. A case study of using blockchain technology in regulatory technology. *MIS Q. Exec.* **2020**, *19*, 19–37. [CrossRef]
15. Hermstrüwer, Y. *The Limits of Blockchain Democracy: A Transatlantic Perspective on Blockchain Voting Systems*; TTLF Working Papers No. 49; Stanford-Vienna Transatlantic Technology Law Forum: Stanford, CA, USA, 2020.
16. Esposito, C.; De Santis, A.; Tortora, G.; Chang, H.; Choo, K.K.R. Blockchain: A Panacea for Healthcare Cloud-Based Data Security and Privacy? *IEEE Cloud Comput.* **2018**, *5*, 31–37. [CrossRef]
17. Ismail, L.; Materwala, H. A review of blockchain architecture and consensus protocols: Use cases, challenges, and solutions. *Symmetry* **2019**, *11*, 1198. [CrossRef]
18. Berdik, D.; Otoum, S.; Schmidt, N.; Porter, D.; Jararweh, Y. A Survey on Blockchain for Information Systems Management and Security. *Inf. Process. Manag.* **2021**, *58*, 102397. [CrossRef]
19. Dorri, A.; Kanhere, S.S.; Jurdak, R.; Gauravaram, P. Blockchain for IoT security and privacy: The case study of a smart home. In Proceedings of the 2017 IEEE International Conference on Pervasive Computing and Communications Workshops, PerCom Workshops, Kona, HI, USA, 13–17 March 2017; pp. 618–623. [CrossRef]
20. Oham, C.; Michelin, R.A.; Jurdak, R.; Kanhere, S.S.; Jha, S. B-FERL: Blockchain based framework for securing smart vehicles. *Inf. Process. Manag.* **2021**, *58*, 102426. [CrossRef]
21. Prashanth, J.A.; Han, M.; Wang, Y. A survey on security and privacy issues of blockchain technology. *Math. Found. Comput.* **2018**, *1*, 121–147. [CrossRef]
22. Lapointe, C.; Fishbane, L. The Blockchain Ethical Design Framework. *Innov. Technol. Gov. Glob.* **2019**, *12*, 50–71. [CrossRef]
23. Correia, T.; Correia, H.; Gamito, C.; Kindylidi, I. Evolution of Blockchain Market. 2021. Available online: https://practiceguides.chambers.com/practice-guides/blockchain-2021/portugal (accessed on 12 November 2021).
24. GSMA. Blockchain for Development: Emerging Opportunities for Mobile, Identity and Aid. 2017. Available online: https://www.gsma.com/mobilefordevelopment/wp-content/uploads/2017/12/Blockchain-for-Development.pdf (accessed on 15 October 2021).
25. Prisco, G. The blockchain for Healthcare: Gem Launches Gem Health Care Network with Philips Blockchain Lab. Available online: https://bitcoinmagazine.com/articles/the-blockchain-for-heathcare-gem-launches-gem-health-network-with-philips-blockchain-lab-1461674938 (accessed on 27 November 2021).
26. Heston, T. A case study in blockchain healthcare innovation. *Int. J. Curr. Res.* **2017**, *9*, 60587–60588.
27. Batubara, F.R.; Ubacht, J.; Janssen, M. Challenges of blockchain technology adoption for e-government. In Proceedings of the 19th Annual International Conference on Digital Government Research Governance in the Data Age—Dgo '18, Delft, The Netherlands, 30 May–1 June 2018; pp. 1–9. Available online: http://dl.acm.org/citation.cfm?doid=3209281.3209317 (accessed on 13 November 2021).
28. Guardtime. Estonia e-Health Authority Partners with Guardtime to Accelerate Transparency and Auditability in Healthcare. 2016. Available online: https://guardtime.com/blog/estonian-ehealth-partners-guardtime-blockchain-based-transparency (accessed on 27 August 2021).
29. Park, J.; Parkm, H. Regulation by Selective Enforcement: The SEC and Initial Coin Offerings. 2020. Available online: https://openscholarship.wustl.edu/law_journal_law_policy/vol61/iss1/11/ (accessed on 13 November 2021).
30. Yeoh, P. Regulatory Issues in Blockchain Technology. *J. Financ. Regul. Compliance* **2017**, *25*, 196–208. [CrossRef]
31. Marques, F.; Albuquerque, M.; Verissimo, D. Blocckchain & Cryptocurrency Laws and Regulation 2022. Available online: https://www.globallegalinsights.com/practice-areas/blockchain-laws-and-regulations/23Portugal (accessed on 17 November 2021).

32. Nguyen, D.C.; Ding, M.; Pathirana, P.N.; Seneviratne, A. Blockchain and AI-Based Solutions to Combat Coronavirus (COVID-19)-Like Epidemics: A Survey. *IEEE Access* **2021**, *9*, 95730–95753. [CrossRef]
33. Monteiro, A. First GDPR Fine in Portugal Issued against Hospital for Three Violations. 2019. Available online: https://iapp.org/news/a/first-gdpr-fine-in-portugal-issued-against-hospital-for-three-violations/ (accessed on 10 October 2021).
34. Mettler, M. Blockchain technology in healthcare: The revolution starts here. In Proceedings of the 2016 IEEE 18th International Conference on E-Health Networking, Applications and Services, Healthcom, Munich, Germany, 14–16 September 2016; pp. 18–20. [CrossRef]
35. Dewey, J. Global Legal Insight—Blockchain & Cryptocurrency Regulations. 2021. Available online: https://www.mlgts.pt/xms/files/site_2018/publicacoes/2020/GLI_Blockchain__Cryptocurrency_Regulation_2021_Portugal.pdf (accessed on 2 October 2021).
36. Lim, M.K.; Li, Y.; Wang, C.; Tseng, M.L. A literature review of blockchain technology applications in supply chains: A comprehensive analysis of themes, methodologies, and industries. *Comput. Ind. Eng.* **2021**, *154*, 107133. [CrossRef]
37. Peffers, K.; Tuunaanen, T.; Rothenberger, M.; Chatterjee, S. A design science research methodology for information systems. *J. Manag. Inf. Syst.* **2008**, *24*, 45–77. [CrossRef]
38. Casino, F.; Dasaklis, T.K.; Patsakis, C. A systematic literature review of blockchain-based applications: Current status, classification, and open issues. *Telemat. Inform.* **2019**, *36*, 55–81. [CrossRef]
39. Filippi, P.D.; Hassan, S. Blockchain Technology as a Regulatory Technology. First Monday. *arXiv* **2016**, arXiv:1801.02507.
40. Gupta, S.; Sadoghi, M. Blockchain Transaction Processing. *Encycl. Big Data Technol.* **2019**, *2019*, 366–376. [CrossRef]
41. Kwok, A.; Koh, S. Is blockchain technology a watershed for tourism development. *Curr. Issues Tour.* **2018**, *22*, 2447–2452. [CrossRef]
42. Siyal, A.A.; Junejo, A.Z.; Zawish, M.; Ahmed, K.; Khalil, A.; Soursou, G. Applications of blockchain technology in medicine and healthcare: Challenges and future perspectives. *Cryptography* **2019**, *3*, 3. [CrossRef]
43. Kant, N. Blockchain: A strategic resource to attain and sustain competitive advantage. *Int. J. Innov. Sci.* **2021**, *13*, 520–538. [CrossRef]
44. Pal, A.; Tiwari, C.K.; Haldar, N. Blockchain for business management: Applications, challenges, and potentials. *J. High Technol. Manag. Res.* **2021**, *32*, 100414. [CrossRef]
45. Rejeb, A.; Keogh, J.G.; Zailani, S.; Treiblmaier, H.; Rejeb, K. Blockchain Technology in the Food Industry: A Review of Potentials, Challenges and Future Research Directions. *Logistics* **2020**, *4*, 27. [CrossRef]
46. Sung, C.S.; Park, J.Y. Understanding of blockchain-based identity management system adoption in the public sector. *J. Enterp. Inf. Manag.* **2021**, *34*, 1481–1505. [CrossRef]
47. Donovan, A. Blockchain: Developing Regulatory Approaches for the Use of Technology in Legal Services. 2019. Available online: https://www.legalservicesboard.org.uk/wp-content/uploads/2019/10/Blockchain-Developing-Regulatory-Approaches-for-the-Use-of-Technology-in-Legal-Services.pdf (accessed on 3 October 2021).
48. Kshetri, N. Strengthen the Internet of. Securing IT, August. 2017; pp. 68–72. Available online: https://pdfs.semanticscholar.org/e870/9e2906361ade9064cc605b9c7637bec474a0.pdf (accessed on 10 December 2021).
49. European Parliament. Blockchain and the General Data Protection Regulation'. European Parliamentary Research Service. 2019. Available online: https://www.europarl.europa.eu/RegData/etudes/STUD/2019/634445/EPRS_STU(2019)634445_EN.pdf (accessed on 5 December 2020).
50. Siegel, S. Is Blockchain HIPAA Complaint? 2018. Available online: https://masur.com/lawtalk/is-blockchain-hipaa-compliant/#:~{}:text=HIPAA%20prohibits%20the%20use%20of,industry%20non%2Dcompliant%20with%20HIPA (accessed on 2 November 2021).
51. Sayegh, E. When Crypto Meets Compliance: Is Blockchain Ready for Enterprise? 2018. Available online: https://www.forbes.com/sites/emilsayegh/2020/07/07/when-crypto-meets-compliance-is-blockchain-ready-for-the-enterprise/#713d7fab4aad (accessed on 11 September 2021).
52. Wang, J.; Wu, P.; Wang, X.; Shou, W. The outlook of blockchain technology for construction engineering management. *Front. Eng. Manag.* **2017**, *4*, 67. [CrossRef]
53. Upadhyay, A.; Mukhuty, S.; Kumar, V.; Kazancoglu, Y. Blockchain technology and the circular economy: Implications for sustainability and social responsibility. *J. Clean. Prod.* **2021**, *293*, 126130. [CrossRef]

 *digital*

Communication

Use of Internet Technology among Older Adults in Residential Aged Care Facilities: Protocol for a Systematic Review and Meta-Analysis

Sandesh Pantha *, Sumina Shrestha and Janette Collier

Australian Institute for Primary Care & Ageing, La Trobe University, Bundoora, VIC 3086, Australia; s.shrestha@latrobe.edu.au (S.S.); janette.collier@latrobe.edu.au (J.C.)
* Correspondence: s.pantha@latrobe.edu.au

Citation: Pantha, S.; Shrestha, S.; Collier, J. Use of Internet Technology among Older Adults in Residential Aged Care Facilities: Protocol for a Systematic Review and Meta-Analysis. *Digital* **2022**, *2*, 46–52. https://doi.org/10.3390/digital2010003

Academic Editors: Mirjana Ivanović, Richard Chbeir and Yannis Manolopoulos

Received: 1 December 2021
Accepted: 22 February 2022
Published: 25 February 2022

Publisher's Note: MDPI stays neutral with regard to jurisdictional claims in published maps and institutional affiliations.

Copyright: © 2022 by the authors. Licensee MDPI, Basel, Switzerland. This article is an open access article distributed under the terms and conditions of the Creative Commons Attribution (CC BY) license (https:// creativecommons.org/licenses/by/ 4.0/).

Abstract: Internet usage may help promote the physical and mental health of older adults living in Residential Aged Care Facilities (RACF). There is little evidence of how these older citizens use internet services. This systematic review aims to explore the trends and factors contributing to internet use among aged care residents. A systematic search will be conducted on nine online databases—MEDLINE, EMBASE, PsycInfo, CINAHL, AgeLine, ProQuest, Web of Science, Scopus, and the Cochrane Library. Two reviewers will independently conduct title and abstract screening, full-text reading, critical appraisal, and data extraction. Any discrepancies will be resolved by consensus. Methodological risk of bias will be assessed using the Effective Public Health Practice Project measure and Joanna Briggs Institute checklist. We will report a narrative synthesis of the evidence. Information on factors contributing to internet use and their strength of association will be reported. If feasible, we will undertake a meta-analysis and meta-synthesis. Our review will provide information on the factors predicting internet use among older adults in residential aged care facilities. The evidence from this review will help to formulate further research objectives and, potentially, to design an intervention to trial internet access for these groups. (Protocol Registration: PROSPERO-CRD 42020161227).

Keywords: internet usage; older adults; elderly; digitalisation; residential aged care; nursing home; computer; smartphone

1. Introduction

Older adults (people aged 65 years and above) choose to use the internet for many reasons. Understanding these reasons is essential when planning internet services targeted at this group. Few studies have explored the reasons for internet usage among older adults living in the United States [1], Germany [2], Australia, and New Zealand [3–5]. For example, Szabo et al. (2019) [3] analysed data from three waves of New Zealand's health, work, and retirement study (NZHWR) involving 1165 older adults aged 60–77. Social connectivity, online banking, and acquiring health information constituted the top three reasons for internet usage among older people. In a survey of 1040 Australian adults, it was reported that around two-thirds of older Australians aged ≥ 65 years used the internet for medical consultation [5]. Some evidence suggests that older adults participate in online health promotion activities such as cancer screening [6]. These studies reflect internet usage among older adults but are not specific to those living in Residential Aged Care Facilities (RACFs).

A few studies report lower internet use among the residents in aged care facilities compared with community-dwelling older adults of similar age [7,8]. For example, Seifert et al. (2017) [7] reported a survey of 1212 residents from 24 aged care facilities in Switzerland. The authors note that only one in six (15%) aged care residents used internet services. It was further reported that community-dwelling older adults were two times more likely to browse the internet compared with residents in RACFs [7]. In another study, it was reported that only three per cent of residents aged 85 and above spent time on the internet, a figure eight times lower than that for community-dwelling older adults of similar age [8]. Residents of RACFs are older, frail, and have poor physical and mental health [9,10], and this could potentially explain the lower penetration of the internet into this population. Two pilot studies investigated internet usage in RACFs [11,12]. In one of the pilot crossover randomised controlled trials, nine older adults with dementia were scheduled to talk with their family members using Skype or telephone. The residents were less aggressive and had lower levels of agitation when using video calls [12]. Loh et al. (2005) evaluated reasons for the low uptake of internet technology in two RACFs in Australia [13]. Low internet utilisation was attributed to the limited access to computers. It was further reported that neither facility had a broadband internet connection. However, the study was conducted in 2005 when internet services had low penetration in the community. Since then, there have been changes in internet service provision. Many RACFs have incorporated digital technologies into their service; however, providing internet facilities does not mean residents are using internet services [9]. Besides, many governments provide online services to older residents. For example, the Australian Government is encouraging people to utilise internet media for health-related services. Australia has implemented a national digital health system, 'My Health Record' [14] and a national internet portal for aged care assistance, 'My Aged Care' [15]. With poor or no access to the internet, older adults in RACFs are prevented from accessing these services.

These studies provide a reflection on the perceived benefits of internet usage among RACF residents. While internet technology plays an important role in an older person's life in residential aged care by promoting social connectedness and physical and mental wellbeing, very little is known about its access and use among these residents. To date, no systematic reviews have synthesised evidence on internet use among residents of RACFs. Our systematic review and meta-analysis will investigate the factors influencing internet usage among the residents. We will further explore the strength of association of factors predicting internet use and the models used to determine this relationship.

2. Materials and Methods

The manuscript adheres to the preferred reporting guidelines for systematic review protocols. A complete checklist reporting guidelines is provided with this manuscript (Supplementary material File S1: PRISMA-P Checklist).

2.1. Eligibility Criteria

We will include studies based on the following criteria:
- Population: Older adults (aged 65 years or over) living in residential aged care facilities
- Exposure: Internet usage (describes internet usage or explores factors associated with internet usage)
- Study design: experimental, quasi-experimental, before and after design, observational, and qualitative
- Language: English
- Publication time: Published after 1990
- We will exclude case studies, literature reviews, commentaries, editorials, and letters to the editor as these do not involve primary data.

2.2. Information Source

We will scientifically explore the following online data sources: MEDLINE, EMBASE, PsycInfo, CINAHL, AgeLine, Web of Science, Scopus, the library of the Cochrane Collaboration, and four ProQuest databases: 1. public health, health, and medical; 2. healthcare administration; 3. nursing and allied health; and 4. dissertations and theses. These databases were included based on the existing systematic review literature [16,17], aiming to identify as many studies as possible. MEDLINE, PUBMED, and Cochrane Library are the three major databases used for systematic reviews [18]. There is some evidence to suggest that bias can be reduced when an extensive database search is carried out [18]. There will be no language restriction in the search strategy, but studies in languages other than English will be excluded.

We will undertake the citation search (of the included studies) to identify any additional studies relevant to our review.

We will not search grey literature as there is evidence that a search strategy used for grey literature may not be replicable [19].

2.3. Search Strategy

We identified three search concepts to address our research question—older adults, residential aged care, and internet-based technology. The Peer Review of Electronic Search Strategies (PRESS) guidelines [20] were followed to develop the search strategy. We incorporated the technical inputs from an information scientist during the development of the search strategy. A second information scientist peer-reviewed our search strategy. The MEDLINE search is presented along with this manuscript (Supplementary Material File S2: MEDLINE Search).

2.4. Screening and Selection of Studies

The output from each database will be imported to Endnote 9.2 and combined. The final list of citations will be exported to Covidence [21,22]. Duplicates will be identified and removed using Covidence.

We will undertake a two-step screening process for selecting the study: 1. title and abstract screening, and 2. full-text screening. Two reviewers will independently conduct screening at each stage against set criteria for inclusion and exclusion. A third member of the review team will resolve the disagreements, and the final decision will be made by consensus within the review team.

Two reviewers will undertake a thorough assessment of citations of the included studies to locate any potentially relevant studies. Such studies will be selected based on consensus among the reviewers.

A PRISMA flowchart will be presented to describe the flow of articles at each stage of the review [23].

2.5. Risk of Bias Assessment

Quantitative studies will be assessed using the Effective Public Health Practice Project (EPHPP) tool. This measure has eight sections, each scored as "strong", "moderate", or "weak". Depending on the number of weak ratings, studies will be graded as strong, moderate, or weak [24].

Similarly, Joanna Briggs Institute (JBI) critical appraisal checklist will be used to evaluate the methodological robustness of qualitative studies [25]. The JBI tool coherently evaluates the intrinsic methodological quality of a qualitative study. It has ten questions to evaluate the congruity between the research methodology with five components—proposed theoretical framework, research questions, data collection methods, data analysis process, and the interpretation of results [25,26]. Each question is answered either 'yes', 'no', 'unclear', or 'not applicable'.

We will use a table to narrate the findings from the risk of bias.

We will check the manuscript for ethics approval. We will not include any studies that have been retracted post publication..

2.6. Data Extraction

We will design and pilot test the data extraction tool. The tool will be amended if necessary. This task will be undertaken independently by the two reviewers. Any discrepancies during extraction will be resolved by verifying the data in the article. If the article(s) is/are not clear, we will email the author for clarification.

If multiple manuscripts are reported from a data set, we will report the first published study with the outcome of interest as the primary source. Information from the multiple sources will be collated, compared for consistency before data synthesis, and reported in the review. There is a possibility that some cohort studies may include analysis at different points in time. In such cases, we will include both manuscripts and make a note of it.

We will obtain the following data:

1. Citation
2. Country
3. Period of data collection
4. Study design (randomised control trial, quasi-experimental, before and after study, cohort, case control, survey, qualitative, other)
5. Sampling strategy
6. Participant characteristics (total participants, frequency distribution based on gender, mean and standard deviation of age)
7. Internet usage (frequency of internet usage, the purpose of internet usage, the device used for the internet, the mean and standard deviation of time spent on the internet);
8. Factors predicting with internet use (we will extract information on factors related to internet use (associated or no association), the model used to determine the association (bivariate or multivariate), strength (coefficient and 95% confidence interval), effect size (power) of the tested model (adjusted or non-adjusted), and report whether those models were standardised or non-standardised)
9. From qualitative studies, we will also collect information about the study's philosophical or theoretical basis, methodological approach, and specific details about participants. We will also report the study population's context and culture, phenomena of interest, quotes from participants, and statements, assumptions, and interpretations from the researchers.

2.7. Data Synthesis

We will follow the convergent segregated approach for systematic reviews with quantitative and qualitative methods [27]. Quantitative and qualitative findings will be synthesised separately at first, then linked together to generate a conclusion. We will report a narrative synthesis for outcomes lacking adequate data.

2.7.1. Meta-Analysis

If sufficient information is available, we will undertake a meta-analysis to pool findings from included studies [28] using the Review Manager (RevMan, Version 5.3, Revman International Inc., New York, NY, USA) software package. We anticipate a substantial variety in the study design and outcome variables. Information on the prevalence and factors predicting internet use will be extracted and pooled across different outcomes and study designs, followed by a subgroup analysis. We will extract the following information for the meta-analysis: participant characteristics (age, standard deviation), gender, the prevalence of internet usage (percentage and standard deviation), factors contributing to internet usage (risk ratio, 95% confidence interval). The analysis will be conducted at the study level, not individual participants.

The model for meta-analysis will be determined using the test of heterogenicity (I^2 test). We will use a fixed-effects model if the observed heterogeneity is low (i.e., $I^2 < 25\%$) and a random-effects model if heterogeneity is moderate to high (i.e., $I^2 \geq 25\%$) [29]. For each factor that is tested, a summary statistic of each included study will be reported using a Risk Ratio (RR) and 95% confidence interval. Where individual studies report an Odds Ratio (OR) as a measure of association, we will convert it to Risk Ratio using the procedures in RevMan Version 5.3. A forest plot of the pooled estimates as a risk ratio (95% confidence intervals) will be presented for each outcome. A sensitivity analysis will be carried out to understand the methodological robustness of a study. If the study involves ten or more studies, we will perform a funnel plot analysis to detect any publication bias among the included studies [30,31].

If the information provided in the manuscript is not complete, we will email the corresponding author for the missing values. We will document such communication in our report. If the information could not be obtained even after a follow-up email (sent 14 days after the initial email), we will exclude incomplete studies from the final analysis.

Sensitivity Analysis

Sensitivity analysis allows us to check if the results from a meta-analysis were affected by the inclusion of certain studies based on predefined criteria. We will undertake a sensitivity analysis to determine if the outcome is influenced by omitting one or more studies from the analysis. For example, we will conduct a sensitivity analysis to examine the effect of bias by removing studies with a high risk of bias.

Subgroup Analysis

Subgroup analysis will help us to understand the mean effect and variation in different study populations and different study designs. For example, we will consider a subgroup analysis to determine if there are studies with a control group and without a control group. Gender influence on internet use will also be explored through subgroup analysis. A further subgroup analysis will be based on the year of publication to check if there were any differences before and after 2010 when the technological advances became more prominent. For example, Facebook and other social media applications became popular after 2010. We will calculate the mean effect and variance for each group and compare subgroups. There is some evidence to suggest that subgroup analysis needs to be undertaken with caution and may produce misleading inferences [31]. We will consider a subgroup analysis if there are at least five studies [28] in each subgroup.

Meta-Biases

We will conduct a funnel plot analysis to identify publication bias among the studies included in the review. However, it has been suggested that the sensitivity of a funnel plot analysis to detect publication bias is limited if the meta-analysis is conducted with less than ten studies [30,31].

2.7.2. Meta-Aggregation

We will conduct a meta-aggregation to synthesise qualitative data [27]. Contextual information will be compiled and categorised into groups based on similarity. These statements will be referred to as findings from the review synthesised from the qualitative data of studies included in the review. If sufficient studies are not available to conduct textual pooling, findings will be presented in narrative form.

3. Discussion

Our systematic review will generate evidence on internet usage among older adults living in RACFs. It will further explore the barriers and enablers that contribute to older residents' use of internet technology. Outcomes from this review will facilitate improving services to the consumers of residential aged care facilities.

Residential aged care facilities offer standard services such as meals and personal care. Internet access is not a component of these essential services. We believe this review's impact and further intervention work would be to add internet provision as a standard service offered by a facility.

Supplementary Materials: The following supporting information can be downloaded at: https://www.mdpi.com/article/10.3390/digital2010003/s1, Supplementary Material File S1: PRISMA-P statement and Supplementary Material File S2: MEDLINE Search strategy.

Author Contributions: Conceptualization and consultation with the information scientist from La Trobe University, S.P. and J.C.; abstract and full-text screening, S.P. and S.S.; writing—original draft preparation S.P.; additional inputs for the protocol, S.S. and J.C. All authors have read and agreed to the published version of the manuscript.

Funding: The research received no external funding. The authors were funded through existing projects.

Institutional Review Board Statement: Not applicable.

Informed Consent Statement: Not applicable.

Data Availability Statement: Not applicable.

Acknowledgments: We would like to acknowledge Ange Johns-Hayden and Hannah Buttery for their technical inputs during the development of the search strategy.

Conflicts of Interest: The authors declare that they have no conflict of interest. This protocol was presented as a poster at the 54th Annual conference (virtual) of the Australian Association of Gerontology (9–11 November 2021).

Protocol Registration and Amendments: We prospectively registered our review protocol with the International Prospective Register of Systematic Reviews (PROSPERO) (Registration number: CRD 42020161227). Any changes in the registered protocol will be documented and reported in the manuscript.

References

1. Choi, N.G.; DiNitto, D.M. Internet Use among Older Adults: Association with Health Needs, Psychological Capital and Social Capital. *J. Med. Internet Res.* **2013**, *15*, e97. [CrossRef]
2. Schehl, B.; Leukel, J.; Sugumaran, V. Understanding differentiated internet use in older adults: A study of informational, social, and instrumental online activities. *Comput. Hum. Behav.* **2019**, *97*, 222–230. [CrossRef]
3. Szabo, A.; Allen, J.; Stephens, C.; Alpass, F. Longitudinal analysis of the relationship between purposes of internet use and well-being among older adults. *Gerontologist* **2019**, *59*, 58–68. [CrossRef] [PubMed]
4. Russell, C.; Campbell, A.; Hughes, I. Research: Ageing, social capital and the Internet: Findings from an exploratory study of Australian 'silver surfers'. *Australas. J. Ageing* **2008**, *27*, 78–82. [CrossRef] [PubMed]
5. Research Australia. *Health and Medical Research Public Opinion Poll 2016*; Research Australia: Darlinghurst, NSW, Australia, 2016.
6. Hunsaker, A.; Hargittai, E. A review of Internet use among older adults. *New Media Soc.* **2018**, *20*, 3937–3954. [CrossRef]
7. Seifert, A.; Doh, M.; Wahl, H.-W. They also do it: Internet use by older adults living in residential care facilities. *Educ. Gerontol.* **2017**, *43*, 451–461. [CrossRef]
8. Schlomann, A.; Seifert, A.; Zank, S.; Woopen, C.; Rietz, C. Use of Information and Communication Technology (ICT) devices among the oldest-old: Loneliness, anomie, and autonomy. *Innov. Aging* **2020**, *4*, igz050. [CrossRef]
9. Deloitte. *Australia's Aged Care Sector: Economic Contribution and Future Directions*; Deloitte Access Economics: Sydney, NSW, Australia, 2016.
10. Holloway, E.E.; Constantinou, M.; Xie, J.; Fenwick, E.K.; Finkelstein, E.A.; Man, R.E.K.; Coote, M.; Jackson, J.; Rees, G.; Lamoureux, E.L. Improving eye care in residential aged care facilities using the Residential Ocular Care (ROC) model: Study protocol for a multicentered, prospective, customized, and cluster randomized controlled trial in Australia. *Trials* **2018**, *19*, 650. [CrossRef]
11. Ballantyne, A.; Trenwith, L.; Zubrinich, S.; Corlis, M. 'I feel less lonely': What older people say about participating in a social networking website. *Qual. Ageing Older Adults* **2010**, *11*, 25. [CrossRef]
12. Van der Ploeg, E.S.; Eppingstall, B.; O'Connor, D.W. Internet video chat (Skype) family conversations as a treatment of agitation in nursing home residents with dementia. *Int. Psychogeriatr.* **2016**, *28*, 697–698. [CrossRef]
13. Loh, P.K.; Flicker, L.; Horner, B. Attitudes toward information and communication technology (ICT) in residential aged care in Western Australia. *J. Am. Med. Dir. Assoc.* **2009**, *10*, 408–413. [CrossRef] [PubMed]
14. Australian Institute of Health Welfare. *Australia's Health 2018*; AIHW: Canberra, Australia, 2018.
15. Smith, C. *Navigating the Maze: An Overview of Australia's Current Aged Care System*; Royal Commission into Aged Care Quality and Safety, Commonwealth of Australia: Canberra, Australia, 2019.
16. Bandari, R.; Khankeh, H.R.; Shahboulaghi, F.M.; Ebadi, A.; Keshtkar, A.A.; Montazeri, A. Defining loneliness in older adults: Protocol for a systematic review. *Syst. Rev.* **2019**, *8*, 26. [CrossRef] [PubMed]
17. Rosa, M.V.; Perracini, M.R.; Ricci, N.A. Usefulness, assessment and normative data of the Functional Reach Test in older adults: A systematic review and meta-analysis. *Arch. Gerontol. Geriatr.* **2019**, *81*, 149–170. [CrossRef]
18. Betrán, A.P.; Say, L.; Gülmezoglu, A.M.; Allen, T.; Hampson, L. Effectiveness of different databases in identifying studies for systematic reviews: Experience from the WHO systematic review of maternal morbidity and mortality. *BMC Med. Res. Methodol.* **2005**, *5*, 6. [CrossRef]

19. Adams, R.J.; Smart, P.; Huff, A.S. Shades of grey: Guidelines for working with the grey literature in systematic reviews for management and organizational studies. *Int. J. Manag. Rev.* **2017**, *19*, 432–454. [CrossRef]
20. McGowan, J.; Sampson, M.; Salzwedel, D.M.; Cogo, E.; Foerster, V.; Lefebvre, C. PRESS Peer Review of Electronic Search Strategies: 2015 Guideline Statement. *J. Clin. Epidemiol.* **2016**, *75*, 40–46. [CrossRef]
21. Kellermeyer, L.; Harnke, B.; Knight, S. Covidence and Rayyan. *J. Med. Libr. Assoc.* **2018**, *106*, 580–583. [CrossRef]
22. Babineau, J. Product review: Covidence (systematic review software). *J. Can. Health Libr. Assoc.* **2014**, *35*, 68–71. [CrossRef]
23. Liberati, A.; Altman, D.G.; Tetzlaff, J.; Mulrow, C.; Gøtzsche, P.C.; Ioannidis, J.P.; Clarke, M.; Devereaux, P.J.; Kleijnen, J.; Moher, D. The PRISMA statement for reporting systematic reviews and meta-analyses of studies that evaluate health care interventions: Explanation and elaboration. *J. Clin. Epidemiol.* **2009**, *62*, e1–e34. [CrossRef]
24. Thomas, B.H.; Ciliska, D.; Dobbins, M.; Micucci, S. A Process for Systematically Reviewing the Literature: Providing the Research Evidence for Public Health Nursing Interventions. *Worldviews Evid.-Based Nurs.* **2004**, *1*, 176–184. [CrossRef]
25. Hannes, K.; Lockwood, C.; Pearson, A. A Comparative Analysis of Three Online Appraisal Instruments' Ability to Assess Validity in Qualitative Research. *Qual. Health* **2010**, *20*, 1736–1743. [CrossRef] [PubMed]
26. Aromataris, E.; Munn, Z. Assessment of Methodological Quality. Available online: https://reviewersmanual.joannabriggs.org/ (accessed on 25 November 2020).
27. Aromataris, E.; Munn, Z. MMSR Questions That Take a Convergent Segregated Approach to Synthesis and Integration. Available online: https://reviewersmanual.joannabriggs.org/ (accessed on 25 November 2020).
28. Borenstein, M.; Hedges, L.V.; Higgins, J.P.T.; Rothstein, H.R. *Introduction to Meta-Analysis*, 1st ed.; John Wiley and Sons: Hoboken, NJ, USA, 2009; p. 419.
29. Rao, G.; Lopez-Jimenez, F.; Boyd, J.; D'Amico, F.; Durant, N.H.; Hlatky, M.A.; Howard, G.; Kirley, K.; Masi, C.; Powell-Wiley, T.M. Methodological standards for meta-analyses and qualitative systematic reviews of cardiac prevention and treatment studies: A scientific statement from the American Heart Association. *Circulation* **2017**, *136*, e172–e194. [CrossRef] [PubMed]
30. Egger, M.; Smith, G.D.; Schneider, M.; Minder, C. Bias in meta-analysis detected by a simple, graphical test. *BMJ* **1997**, *315*, 629–634. [CrossRef] [PubMed]
31. Higgins, J.P.; Thomas, J.; Chandler, J.; Cumpston, M.; Li, T.; Page, M.J.; Welch, V.A. *Cochrane Handbook for Systematic Reviews of Interventions*; John Wiley & Sons: Chichester, UK, 2019.

Review

Unlocking the Power of Digital Commons: Data Cooperatives as a Pathway for Data Sovereign, Innovative and Equitable Digital Communities

Michael Max Bühler [1,*], Igor Calzada [2,3,4], Isabel Cane [5], Thorsten Jelinek [6], Astha Kapoor [7], Morshed Mannan [8], Sameer Mehta [9], Vijay Mookerje [10], Konrad Nübel [11], Alex Pentland [12], Trebor Scholz [13], Divya Siddarth [14], Julian Tait [15], Bapu Vaitla [16] and Jianguo Zhu [17]

1 Faculty of Civil Engineering, Konstanz University of Applied Sciences (HTWG), 78462 Konstanz, Germany
2 School of Social Sciences, WISERD, Cardiff University, Cardiff CF10 3AT, UK; calzadai@cardiff.ac.uk
3 Ikerbasque, Basque Foundation for Science, 48009 Bilbao, Spain
4 Faculty of Social Sciences and Communication, University of the Basque Country, 48940 Leioa, Spain
5 Public Governance Directorate, Organization for Economic Co-Operation and Development (OECD), 75016 Paris, France; isabel.cane@oecd.org
6 Center for Digital Governance, Hertie School of Governance, 10117 Berlin, Germany; t.jelinek@hertieschool.org
7 Aapti Institute, Bengaluru 560042, Karnataka, India; astha@aapti.in
8 Robert Schuman Centre, European University Institute, Piazza S. Domenico, 50014 Firenze, Italy; morshed.mannan@eui.eu
9 Rotterdam School of Management (RSM), Erasmus University Rotterdam, 3062 PA Rotterdam, The Netherlands; mehta@rsm.nl
10 Naveen Jindal School of Management, University of Texas at Dallas, Richardson, TX 75080, USA; vijaym@utdallas.edu
11 Construction Process Management, Technical University Munich, 80333 Munich, Germany; konrad.nuebel@tum.de
12 Connection Science, MIT Media Lab, Cambridge, MA 02139, USA; sandy@media.mit.edu
13 Platform Cooperativism Consortium, The New School, New York, NY 10003, USA; scholzt@newschool.edu
14 Collective Intelligence Project, Stanford, CA 94305, USA; divya@cip.org
15 Open Data Manchester, Manchester M60 0AS, UK; julian@opendatamanchester.org.uk
16 Data2X, Washington, DC 20006, USA; bvaitla@data2x.org
17 Centre for Future Energy Networks, University of Sydney, Sydney, NSW 2006, Australia; jianguo.zhu@sydney.edu.au
* Correspondence: mbuehler@htwg-konstanz.de; Tel.: +49-151-143-144-99

Abstract: Network effects, economies of scale, and lock-in-effects increasingly lead to a concentration of digital resources and capabilities, hindering the free and equitable development of digital entrepreneurship, new skills, and jobs, especially in small communities and their small and medium-sized enterprises ("SMEs"). To ensure the affordability and accessibility of technologies, promote digital entrepreneurship and community well-being, and protect digital rights, we propose data cooperatives as a vehicle for secure, trusted, and sovereign data exchange. In post-pandemic times, community/SME-led cooperatives can play a vital role by ensuring that supply chains to support digital commons are uninterrupted, resilient, and decentralized. Digital commons and data sovereignty provide communities with affordable and easy access to information and the ability to collectively negotiate data-related decisions. Moreover, cooperative commons (a) provide access to the infrastructure that underpins the modern economy, (b) preserve property rights, and (c) ensure that privatization and monopolization do not further erode self-determination, especially in a world increasingly mediated by AI. Thus, governance plays a significant role in accelerating communities'/SMEs' digital transformation and addressing their challenges. Cooperatives thrive on digital governance and standards such as open trusted application programming interfaces ("APIs") that increase the efficiency, technological capabilities, and capacities of participants and, most importantly, integrate, enable, and accelerate the digital transformation of SMEs in the overall process. This review article analyses an array of transformative use cases that underline the potential of cooperative data governance. These case studies exemplify how data and platform cooperatives, through their innovative value creation mechanisms, can elevate digital commons and value chains to a new dimension of collaboration, thereby addressing pressing societal issues. Guided by our research aim, we propose a policy framework that supports the practical implementation of digital federation platforms and data cooperatives. This policy blueprint intends to facilitate sustainable development in both the Global South and North, fostering equitable and inclusive data governance strategies.

Keywords: data; cooperatives; open data; data stewardship; data governance; digital commons; data sovereignty; open digital federation platform

1. Introduction

Understanding the urgent need to democratize the digital landscape requires a clear acknowledgment of the problems we are facing today. As the digital world continues to evolve, we witness an alarming concentration of power within a small number of "cloud empires" [1]. This dominance not only undermines market competition but also poses significant threats to data privacy, autonomy, and equitable access to digital resources. These cloud empires exercise overwhelming control over markets and consumer data, creating an environment that often lacks transparency and accountability. They also dictate the terms of data usage, commodification, and sharing, often side-lining individual and community rights over their own data. These trends are fundamentally problematic as they exacerbate digital inequality and stifle the potential for innovation and participatory digital engagement.

Responding to this state of affairs, our research argues for the transformative potential of data cooperatives as a viable solution. Data cooperatives, rooted in principles of democratic governance, collective ownership, and equitable data practices, offer a promising alternative. They empower individuals and communities by enabling them to assert control over their data, thus challenging the dominance of cloud empires. Through the detailed case studies and policy recommendations presented in our paper, we seek to not only contribute to the ongoing discussions around digital commons but also to provide actionable strategies for achieving a more equitable, inclusive, and democratic digital world.

Our research aim is to integrate the digital commons [2] discourse with the practical execution of data cooperatives [3,4] and digital federation platforms. Through a comprehensive analysis of various case studies, we strive to develop a robust policy framework designed to facilitate the adoption and effective operation of these digital structures. We contend that such structures offer a potential solution to the prevailing issue of digital resources and capabilities being disproportionately concentrated in the hands of a few entities. Our objective, therefore, is to articulate a roadmap towards more equitable and inclusive digital data governance, underpinned by cooperative principles and communal benefits.

1.1. Challenges That Must Be Overcome

The primary challenges addressed by this review article are the concentration of digital resources and capabilities in the hands of a few dominant players, the subsequent erosion of digital entrepreneurship and job opportunities, and the negative impacts on small communities and SMEs. These issues hinder the achievement of Sustainable Development Goals (SDGs) 8, 9, and 11, which emphasize inclusive and sustainable economic growth, innovation, and resilient communities. Key challenges that can be addressed by data and platform cooperatives are summarized in Table 1 and Figure 1.

Table 1. Key challenges to be addressed by data and platform cooperatives.

Key Challenge	Description
Market Concentration	The network effects, economies of scale, and lock-in effects experienced by large technology companies have led to an increasing concentration of digital resources and capabilities. This creates a barrier for new entrants, particularly SMEs and small communities, stifling competition, and innovation.
Digital Exclusion	Due to the monopolistic nature of the digital landscape, small communities and SMEs often lack affordable and accessible digital infrastructure and resources, leading to digital exclusion and perpetuating inequality.
Insufficient Data Governance	Many small communities and SMEs lack robust data governance structures and open standards, making it difficult for them to harness the full potential of data-driven insights and decision-making.
Underdeveloped Skills and Capacity	The existing concentration of resources and capabilities in the digital landscape contributes to a skills gap in small communities and SMEs, limiting their ability to participate in the digital economy and adapt to technological advancements.
Eroding Self-Determination and Data Sovereignty	The increasing influence of AI-driven decision-making and the dominance of a few major players in the digital landscape undermine the self-determination of small communities and SMEs, restricting their ability to shape their digital futures through data sovereignty [5].

This review article aims to address these challenges by proposing the establishment of open digital federation platforms and data cooperatives, which can foster a more equitable and inclusive digital ecosystem, empower small communities and SMEs, and support the achievement of SDGs 8, 9, and 11. Data and platform cooperatives represent a novel approach to digital governance, emphasizing democratic decision-making, equitable benefit distribution, and user rights protection. However, several challenges must be addressed to ensure the viability and success of these models. These challenges span legal and regulatory frameworks, funding acquisition and financial sustainability, scalability and growth, technological infrastructure development, and effective governance implementation.

Additionally, cooperatives must tackle issues related to awareness and adoption among users, interoperability and data portability, data privacy and security, competitive pressures from established businesses, and advocacy for supportive regulatory and policy frameworks. A comprehensive examination of these challenges can provide valuable insights into the factors influencing the development and adoption of data and platform cooperatives, paving the way for future research and practical applications in the digita landscape.

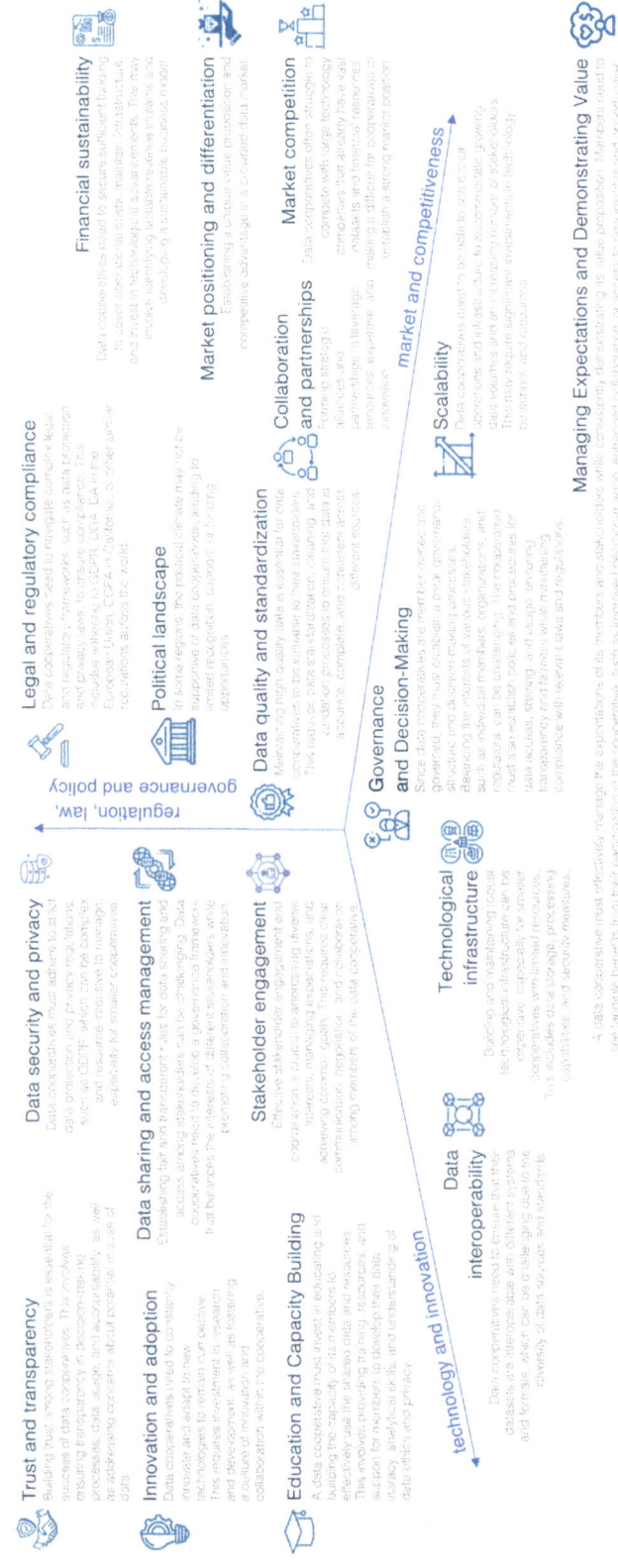

Figure 1. Challenges that might arise for data and platform cooperatives in the areas of regulation, law, governance, and policy; technology and innovation as well as market and competitiveness (own depiction).

1.2. Definitions of Key Concepts

Data sovereignty [5,6], open digital federation platforms, data cooperatives, and platform cooperatives are interrelated concepts central to our research. Our study's central argument lies in their intersection and the cooperative and democratic principles they embody. Data sovereignty pertains to the legal assertion that digital information conforms to the laws and governance structures of the jurisdiction where it is collected, processed, or stored [7,8]. This principle requires that organizations and individuals exercise control, management, and protection of their data in accordance with the relevant legal and regulatory framework [9]. In the context of data privacy, cross-border data transfer, and cloud computing, data sovereignty has become a critical factor that underscores the need to adhere to local privacy, security, and compliance requirements when handling and transferring data across international borders [7,8,10–14]. Data sovereignty extends beyond formal institutional structures and involves various modes of governance, including informal mechanisms that prioritize specific cultural contexts and rights. An essential dimension of this broader understanding of data sovereignty is Indigenous Data Sovereignty, a concept that goes beyond the traditional jurisdictional laws and governance structures. The CARE Principles for Indigenous Data Governance, as articulated by Carroll et al., 2020 [15], are an enlightening example of such an informal yet vital governance model. The principles emphasize the right of Indigenous peoples to govern the collection, ownership, and application of data about their communities. The acronym "CARE" stands for Collective Benefit, Authority to Control, Responsibility, and Ethics. Collective Benefit means that data activities should align with Indigenous values and deliver discernible benefits to the Indigenous communities from which the data originates. Authority to Control reaffirms the Indigenous peoples' right to control information about their people, traditions, and territories. Responsibility refers to the duty to consult with and include Indigenous communities in data processes and uses. Ethics necessitates respect for Indigenous peoples' values and rights in all data practices. In acknowledging these principles, we recognize the pluralistic nature of data sovereignty, emphasizing that it must always be rooted in the local context and respect local rights and traditions. Such an understanding of data sovereignty illuminates our exploration of data cooperatives and emphasizes the importance of cultural sensitivity, inclusivity, and ethical responsibility in data governance practices. Open digital federation platforms, or federated platforms, represent collaborative online ecosystems that encourage data sharing, interoperability, and cooperation among various stakeholders through a federated structure. In such a setting, the term "federation" denotes a group of entities united under a central system or governance structure, maintaining autonomy and control over their resources. The platform's openness promotes transparency, innovation, and collaboration, thus fostering a more inclusive and interconnected digital environment. A data cooperative (Figure 2) is also known as a data co-op (whereas data trusts are a different data stewardship model to a data cooperative. The trust model is based on a board of trustees who have a fiduciary duty towards data subjects and are not necessarily controlled directly be them, whereas data cooperatives have stronger democratic governance and data decisions are made either by the cooperative members themselves or officers that are employed by the members to act on their behalf [16]). Refs. [3,4,17–21], is a member-owned and governed organization that facilitates the design, collection, processing, pooling, management, analysis, and/or sharing of data among its members in a collective, democratic, and transparent manner. This collaborative structure allows members to retain control over their data while benefiting from the collective resources, knowledge, and expertise within the cooperative. As noted by the European Union's Data Governance Act, data cooperatives can also be used by individuals and micro-entrepreneurs through data donation/altruism to negotiate and informedly choose terms and conditions for data processing prior to consent and allow for mechanisms to exchange views on data processing purposes and conditions that would best represent their interests. As such, data cooperatives aim to promote data sovereignty and overcome the data divide. In the context of data cooperatives, "democratic" governance emphasizes the representational power of the cooperative, empowering traditionally underrepresented or misrepresented individuals in the digital space by providing them with a self-determined voice and equitable participation in decision-making processes [22], equitable data access, and data-driven innovation by fostering an environment of trust and cooperation. By enabling the sharing and repurposing of data, data cooperatives can generate significant economic, social, and environmental benefits for their members and the wider community [3,17–20,23–28]. A platform cooperative, or platform co-op, also referred to as a co-operative platform in some instances, is a type of digital platform that is owned and governed by its members, who are often the platform's users, workers, or other stakeholders [29]. It is an alternative to the traditional model of digital platforms, which are typically owned and controlled by private corporations seeking to maximize profits for shareholders. Platform cooperatives emphasize democratic governance, fair distribution of profits, and the well-being of their members. They often operate based on cooperative principles, which include voluntary and open membership, democratic member control, member economic participation, autonomy, and independence, education and training, cooperation among cooperatives, and concern for the community based on the International Co-operative Alliance's seven principles of the cooperative identity. These platforms can be found in various sectors, such as ride-sharing, e-commerce, social networking, online marketplaces, and even agriculture [30,31]. By shifting the ownership and control to the users and workers themselves, platform cooperatives aim to create more equitable, sustainable, and socially responsible alternatives to traditional digital platforms [32–37]. Platform co-operatives include sub-category data co-operatives, not vice versa [32–38]. Digital commons, a shared virtual realm where digital knowledge, information, and assets are managed collectively by a community, serve as a foundation for our research. This concept encompasses open-source software, research data, creative works, educational materials, and various digital content. With principles of collaboration, openness, and participatory governance, digital commons offer users the freedom to access, create, modify, and disseminate resources within a defined set of guidelines or rules. Digital commons present an alternative to traditional models of intellectual property by fostering open access, collaborative innovation, and knowledge sharing. In doing so, they alleviate barriers to information, encourage community ownership, and contribute to knowledge democratization, fostering more inclusive, sustainable digital ecosystems.

Our study builds upon the concept of digital commons, harnessing its ethos to propose the implementation of data cooperatives and digital federation platforms. We argue that these structures have the potential to address the issues of concentrated digital resources and capabilities while bolstering the democratic ethos of the digital commons. To this end, the essential role of digital commons in our research question is highlighted. We aim to enhance the reader's understanding of the unique contributions of our study to the existing literature by contextualizing our arguments within the broader digital commons framework [39–45].

Digital rights encompass the human rights and legal protections that individuals and organizations possess in the context of digital technology, the internet, and the online environment. These rights extend traditional human rights, such as privacy, freedom of expression, and access to information, to the digital realm. Key aspects of digital rights include the right to protect personal information, share and access information and opinions online, seek and receive information through digital channels, protect one's creations and innovations, and use digital technology without fear of surveillance, cyberattacks, or harassment. Digital rights advocacy aims to promote and defend these rights against challenges such as government surveillance, corporate data collection, and online censorship, ensuring a more open, inclusive, and democratic digital environment for all [7,23,46–52]. Barcelona, NYC, and Amsterdam established the Cities Coalition for Digital Rights advocated by the UN, and now encompasses more than 50 global cities in the protection of citizens' digital rights [47–49].

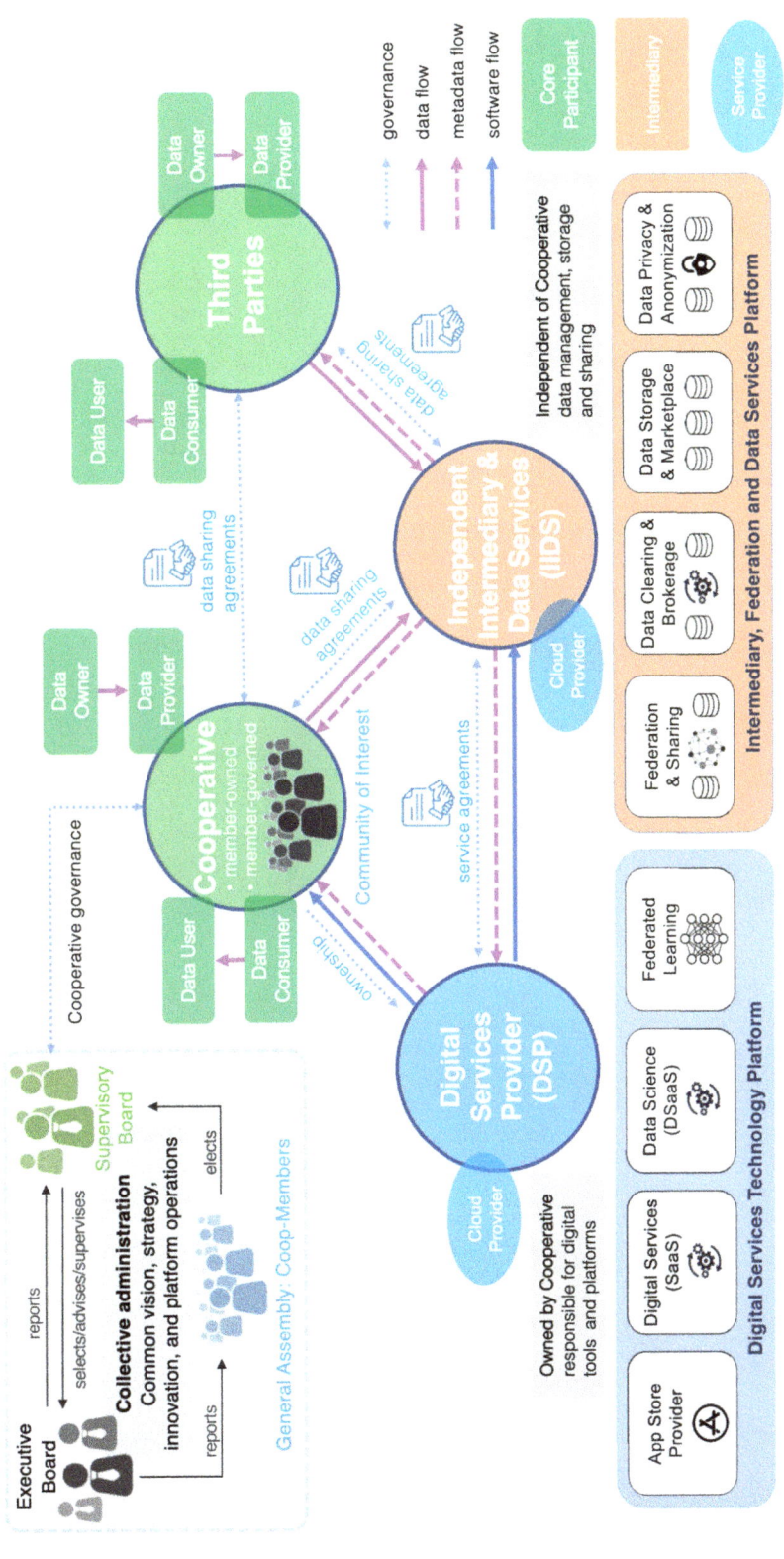

Figure 2. Example of the organizational structure of a data cooperative (own depiction).

2. Methods

Our research adopted a systematic and criterion-based approach to explore the concepts of digital commons, data cooperatives, and digital federation platforms. The primary sources of our data were academic literature, case studies, policy documents, and regulatory frameworks. To gather these, we followed a detailed methodological process outlined below.

We commenced our research with a comprehensive literature search, primarily using databases such as Google Scholar, Scopus, Web of Science, and the IEEE Xplore Digital Library. Our search encompassed a broad range of keywords and combinations thereof, including "digital commons", "data cooperatives", "digital federation platforms", "platform cooperatives", "data governance", and "data sovereignty", among others. The search was not confined to a particular time frame to capture the rich history and development of these concepts. However, we prioritized recent literature to maintain the relevance and applicability of our research. The titles, abstracts, and keywords of the searched articles were screened based on their relevance to our research topic. Full-text articles that met the initial screening criteria were then downloaded for detailed review.

For the selection of case studies, we followed a criterion-based approach. We sought case studies that provide substantial insight into the implementation and impact of data cooperatives, digital federation platforms, and platform cooperatives. We looked for examples that depict their governance structures, operational mechanisms, challenges, and achievements. The case studies were obtained from a variety of sources, including academic articles, reports from research institutions, grey literature, and online databases dedicated to platform cooperatives and digital commons. The selected case studies were then used to inform the analysis and provide real-world evidence for the discussions and arguments presented in the research.

In terms of analysis, we employed a thematic approach. Once the relevant literature and case studies were identified, we extracted and synthesized information related to the key themes of our research. We mapped the relationships between the key concepts of digital commons, data cooperatives, and digital federation platforms, and highlighted how they can contribute to more equitable and sustainable digital ecosystems. We also performed a critical analysis of the successes, challenges, and limitations associated with these concepts, thereby addressing the need for a balanced evaluation. Moreover, we explored how the structures and principles of digital commons, data cooperatives, and digital federation platforms can be harnessed to develop a policy framework that addresses the challenges of data concentration and digital inclusivity. Our analytical methods were systematically structured to develop our policy recommendations. It involved a rigorous process of synthesizing evidence from diverse sources, assessing various policy approaches, and shaping our recommendations accordingly. The step-by-step process we employed is outlined as follows:

The initial phase of our analysis involved synthesizing the collected evidence. After carefully reviewing the selected literature and case studies, we extracted and compiled relevant data regarding digital commons, data cooperatives, and digital federation platforms. This compilation was comprehensive, covering diverse dimensions, such as their structure, operation, impact, and challenges faced in implementation. Our evidence synthesis did not just rely on empirical data but also involved a critical interpretation of the findings in relation to the overall research context.

The synthesized evidence allowed us to identify various policy approaches, which were then thoroughly assessed. The assessment considered the feasibility, sustainability, effectiveness, and inclusivity of these approaches. This evaluation was not conducted in isolation; it was linked to the potential challenges of concentrated digital resources and capabilities. We conducted an in-depth analysis of the pros and cons of each policy approach, taking into account the complexities of the digital ecosystem and the diverse stakeholders involved.

The final phase of our analysis involved shaping our policy recommendations. The aim here was to develop policy suggestions that not only address the current challenges but also anticipate future developments in the digital ecosystem. The recommendations were drawn from our comprehensive understanding of the strengths and limitations of different policy approaches and their alignment with the principles of digital commons, data cooperatives, and digital federation platforms. Our recommendations underwent a rigorous refinement process, which involved revisiting the synthesized evidence, reassessing the policy approaches, and realigning the recommendations to ensure their relevancy and appropriateness. In conclusion, our analytical methods involved a systematic and iterative process of synthesizing evidence, assessing policy approaches, and shaping recommendations. This approach facilitated the development of robust, evidence-based, and forward-thinking policy recommendations that can guide the future of digital commons, data cooperatives, and digital federation platforms.

We acknowledge the inherent limitations of our approach. The literature and case study selection may be influenced by the availability and accessibility of resources, and there may be relevant studies or examples not included in our review. Additionally, the complex and evolving nature of the concepts studied means that our analysis is context and time-sensitive. Despite these limitations, we strived to provide a comprehensive, balanced, and up-to-date overview of our research topic, guided by the principles of rigor and reflexivity.

3. Economic, Social, and Environmental Impact of Our Proposal

The implementation of our recommendations, including the establishment of digital federation platforms and data cooperatives, has the potential to generate significant economic and social benefits for small communities and SMEs [3]. Data's non-depletable nature and reusability in the 21st century knowledge economy make it a valuable form of capital [5]. Beneficial spill-overs arise when data are shared and repurposed for unforeseen growth opportunities or societal benefits [6]. Data cooperatives can enhance trust, create an environment for informed consent increasing data sharing, and consequently foster data-driven innovation [2]. Data access and sharing can create "super-additive" insights, leading to increasing returns to scope [53]. Under certain conditions, data may be considered an infrastructural resource. Data access and sharing have been shown to generate positive social and economic benefits for data providers, so-called direct impact, suppliers and users, so-called indirect impact, and the wider economy, called induced impact. However, quantifying these benefits is challenging [54]. Most recent studies [55] suggest that data access and sharing can increase the value of data for holders, create 10 to 20 times more value for users, i.e., indirect impact, and 20 to 50 times more value for the wider economy, i.e., induced impact. In some cases, data access and sharing may reduce data holders' producer surplus [56]. Overall, data access and sharing can generate benefits worth 0.1% to 1.5% of GDP for public-sector data and 1% to 2.5% of GDP (up to 4% in some studies) when including private sector data [57]. Data, akin to R&D for 21st century innovation systems, shares properties such as being an intangible asset, enabling knowledge creation with societal spill-overs, and facing investment incentive challenges [58]. Organizations may capture private benefits but not always recognize broader societal benefits [5]. Significant potential for value generation in an economy by cooperative data sharing and subsequent data value generation can be expected in those sectors which already have the activities with the largest share of total value added (value added by activity shows the value added created by the various industries (such as agriculture, industry, utilities, and other service activities). The indicator presents value added for an activity, as a percentage of total value added. All OECD countries compile their data according to the 2008 System of National Accounts (SNA). i.e., services (46–80%), industry (14–32%), etc. (Figure 3, [59]). However, it should be highlighted that sectors with low productivity and low digital maturity, i.e., construction, forestry, etc., might actually have the highest value growth potential. Data cooperatives play a crucial role in leveraging the collective strength of their members, resulting in various positive outcomes. While the correlation between the value generation of data cooperatives and the value added by producing goods and services might be apparent, it is essential to note that one does not necessarily cause the other directly. The interplay is complex and influenced by a host of factors. For instance, the value generated by data cooperatives is multi-dimensional, encompassing not just economic but also social, democratic, and individual empowerment facets. It influences the decision-making, operational efficiency, and strategic planning that contribute to the production of goods and services. On the other hand, the value added by these sectors, such as services or industry, can enhance the resources and capabilities of data cooperatives, fueling their growth and strengthening their value proposition.

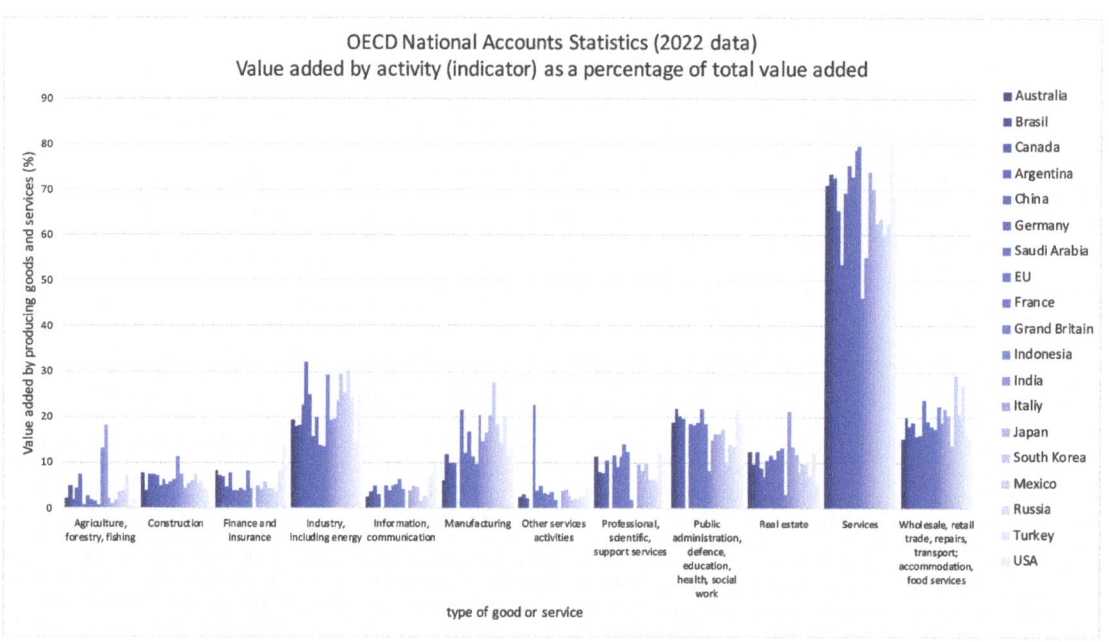

Figure 3. Value added by activity for all G20 economies [59]. Value added reflects the value generated by producing goods and services and is measured as the value of output minus the value of intermediate consumption. Value added also represents the income available for the contributions of labor and capital to the production process (own depiction).

Moreover, sectors with low productivity and digital maturity, such as construction and forestry, may hold untapped potential. Given the right digital tools, data-sharing infrastructure, and cooperative framework, these sectors could witness significant value growth. Therefore, the relationship between data cooperatives and value-added sectors is not linear causality but a complex, intertwined process influenced by multiple variables, both internal and external. In essence, it is a dynamic, symbiotic relationship where growth and value generation in one can potentially foster progress in the other.

By pooling cooperative resources (Figure 4A), these organizations promote improved resource allocation and job creation, which contributes to economic growth and supports community development. As members work together, sharing knowledge, skills, and resources, social cohesion within the community is also strengthened, fostering a sense of unity and collaboration. Data cooperatives can lead to improved resource efficiency and can lead to the collection of better data through the direct relationship that members have with the data governance mechanisms of the cooperative and shared aspirations by optimizing the use of available assets and reducing waste, ultimately promoting more sustainable practices. Furthermore, they can help establish fair and equitable compensation systems, ensuring that members receive appropriate rewards for their contributions. In summary, data cooperatives harness the power of shared resources to drive economic, social, and environmental benefits, making them an essential component of modern data-driven ecosystems. The virtuous cycle of data cooperatives (Figure 4) encompasses four interconnected dimensions: (A) collaborative resource pooling, (B) cooperative innovation, (C) cooperative data market expansion, and (D) cooperative ROI. This cycle starts with pooling resources, which fosters innovation and expands market opportunities. As cooperative investments yield sustainable and inclusive returns, the cycle circles back to optimizing resources, reinforcing the positive economic, social, and environmental impacts. This interconnected cycle promotes a sustainable and inclusive future for data cooperative members and their communities.

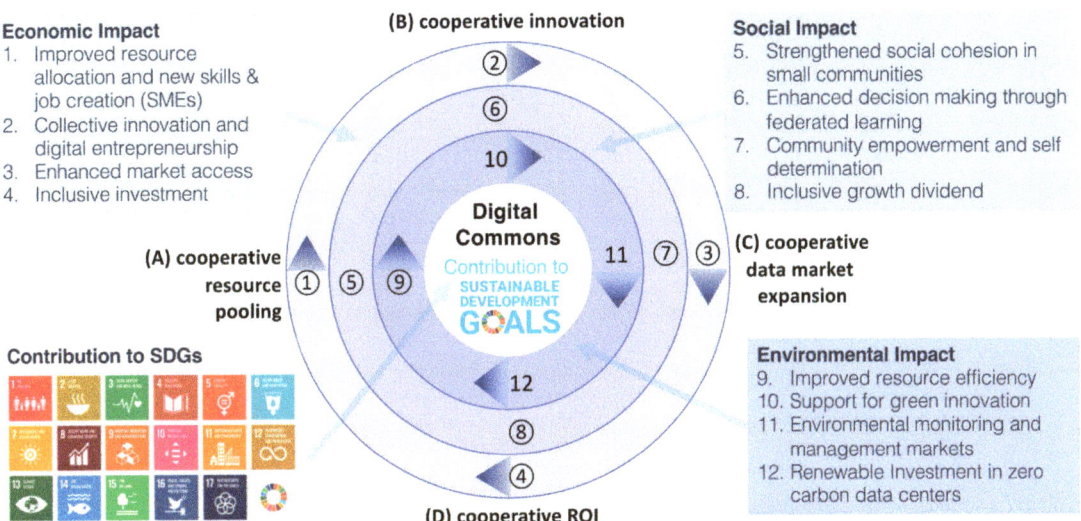

Figure 4. Virtuous cycle of economic, social, and environmental impact of data cooperatives (own depiction).

Cooperative innovation (Figure 4B) emphasizes the power of collaborative efforts within data cooperatives to drive ground-breaking ideas and solutions. By leveraging shared knowledge and resources, members can make better-informed decisions and explore novel approaches to challenges. This collective spirit not only fuels technological advancements and process improvements but also nurtures environmentally conscious practices and sustainable development. Through synergistic collaboration, data cooperatives enable their members to tackle complex global issues while fostering a culture of creativity and sustainability.

Cooperative data market expansion (Figure 4C) highlights how data cooperatives facilitate greater market access and empower their members including individuals and SMEs. By pooling resources and sharing knowledge, cooperatives enable small businesses and communities to tap into new opportunities, extending their reach beyond geographical constraints. Additionally, data cooperatives play a vital role in promoting self-determination and fostering growth in environmental monitoring and management markets. This market expansion helps drive sustainable development, ensuring the prosperity of both members and the environment.

Cooperative ROI (return on investment, see Figure 4D) emphasizes the shared value creation and inclusive growth resulting from cooperative investment in data cooperatives. By prioritizing sustainable investments, such as renewable energy in zero-carbon data centers, cooperatives minimize their environmental impact while maximizing the benefits for their members. This approach ensures that the economic gains from the cooperative are distributed equitably and reinvested in the cooperative itself, promoting a sustainable and inclusive growth model.

By highlighting the economic, social, and environmental impact of our proposal, we emphasize the importance and potential benefits of digital federation platforms and data cooperatives in fostering inclusive and sustainable growth for small communities and SMEs. These impacts serve as a compelling rationale for supranational organizations to act and support the implementation of our recommendations.

4. A Path to Transformation—10 Case Studies

This section demonstrates the practical application of our recommendations by showcasing transformative use cases and case studies from Asia and Africa, with limited examples from Europe and America (Table 2). It highlights the barriers and shortcomings that demand policy action proposed in Sections 5 and 6.

Table 2. Exemplary transformative case studies.

Case Study	Description
Case Study 1: Mobile Money in Africa (Kenya's M-Pesa)	M-Pesa, a mobile money platform launched in Kenya, revolutionized financial inclusion by providing affordable, accessible, and secure digital financial services to millions of unbanked individuals [60–62]. This example illustrates the transformative potential of a digital platform that effectively empowers small communities and businesses. However, the challenge remains to extend the benefits of such platforms to other sectors, including education, healthcare, and supply chain management, by establishing data cooperatives and adopting open standards [63,64].
Case Study 2: Digital Agriculture in Asia (India's eKutir)	eKutir [65,66], a social enterprise in India, leverages digital technologies to empower smallholder farmers through data-driven agricultural advice, access to finance, and market linkages. By pooling data and resources from various stakeholders, eKutir demonstrates the potential of a data cooperative to drive sustainable development in rural communities. Yet, scalability and replicability of this model require supportive policies and a robust digital governance framework [67,68]
Case Study 3: Collaborative Land Management in Africa (Ghana's Farmerline)	Farmerline [69], a Ghanaian agriculture technology company, provides smallholder farmers with timely and accurate agricultural information through mobile technology. By pooling data from various sources, Farmerline exemplifies the potential of data cooperatives to drive sustainable development and food security in rural areas. To scale and replicate this model, supportive policies and a strong digital governance framework are essential, along with financial support from international partners [69,70].
Case Study 4: Decentralized Renewable Energy in Asia (Bangladesh's SOLshare)	SOLshare [71], a peer-to-peer energy trading platform in Bangladesh, enables rural communities to access affordable, clean energy by connecting solar home systems in a decentralized network. The platform exemplifies the transformative potential of data cooperatives in promoting sustainable development. Nevertheless, the broader adoption of such models requires the development of open standards, APIs, and legal frameworks that support data sharing and collaboration [72,73].
Case Study 5: Fintech for Financial Inclusion in South America (Brazil's Nubank)	Nubank [74], a Brazilian digital bank, has successfully expanded access to financial services for millions of underserved individuals in the region. By leveraging digital technologies and data-driven solutions, Nubank illustrates the potential of innovative platforms to empower small communities and businesses. Further development of data cooperatives in this sector can facilitate better credit access and risk assessment for SMEs, requiring supportive policies and collaboration between stakeholders [75].
Case Study 6: Telemedicine in Asia (Indonesia's Halodoc)	Halodoc [76], an Indonesian telemedicine platform, connects patients in remote areas with healthcare professionals through digital consultations, improving access to quality healthcare services. This initiative demonstrates the value of digital platforms in addressing critical challenges faced by rural communities. The expansion of such platforms, combined with the establishment of data cooperatives, can empower local communities and healthcare providers to make more informed decisions. However, this requires the development of robust data governance structures and open standards [77,78].

Table 2. *Cont.*

Case Study	Description
Case Study 7: Community Networks in Africa (South Africa's Zenzeleni)	Zenzeleni [79,80], a community-owned telecommunications network in South Africa, provides affordable internet access to rural communities by leveraging cooperative ownership and management [81]. The initiative highlights the importance of local ownership and collaboration in bridging the digital divide. However, regulatory barriers and limited resources impede the expansion of such initiatives, calling for policy interventions and financial support from G20 countries [82,83].
Case Study 8: Construction Industry in Bavaria, Germany (Germany's GemeinWerk)	GemeinWerk [3] proposed the first construction data cooperative in Munich, Germany. The case study of this Bavarian Construction Data Cooperative, which was launched by the Bavarian Construction Industry Association and GemeinWerk Ventures and will be operated by cooperative members, aims to provide small and medium-sized enterprises in the construction industry with access to shared services and construction data via a digital collaborative platform and data cooperative. This platform improves collaboration and organization within the construction value chain. The project primarily targets governance innovations to intensify industry collaboration, enable trust-based data sharing among stakeholders, and create a pre-competitive space of trust that drives productivity and innovation among SMEs through ecosystem collaboration.
Case Study 9: Smart City Initiatives in Europe (Barcelona, Spain and Salus Coop, Spain)	Barcelona's smart city initiatives [84–86] leverage digital technologies and data-driven solutions to improve urban services and enhance the quality of life for its residents. By utilizing data from various sources, such as sensors and citizen feedback, the city has implemented projects related to transportation, waste management, and energy efficiency. This case study demonstrates the potential of data cooperatives and digital federation platforms to facilitate collaboration among stakeholders in urban environments, i.e., Salus Coop [10,20,38,49]. However, the expansion of such initiatives requires the development of open standards, robust data governance structures, and the active involvement of citizens in decision-making processes as the case of Barcelona has shown reverting the technocratic approach to smart city paradigm [87–90].
Case Study 10: Ride-hailing platform initiative. (Driver's Seat, USA)	Driver's Seat Cooperative [91] is a driver owned cooperative that operates in a number of cities in the US. It enables gig-economy workers working in the ride-hailing sector to collect, pool and analyze data collected on a smartphone whilst undertaking work for ride-hailing platforms such as Uber and Lyft. The pooled data allows insights to be fed back to members so that they can optimize their incomes. The cooperative also sells data and insights to city agencies to enable better policy decisions with the profits from sales being redistributed back to members.

4.1. Insights and Lessons from Case Studies: Unraveling the Potential of Data Cooperatives

Our diverse selection of case studies encapsulates the essence of data cooperatives from various angles. They provide tangible examples that elucidate the transformative potential of data cooperatives and showcase how they can overcome the hurdles of the digital age, further substantiating our general arguments. Let us delve into the details of some notable instances.

The M-Pesa platform in Kenya exemplifies the potency of digital platforms in enhancing financial inclusion (Case Study 1). While M-Pesa itself is not a data cooperative, the way it has leveraged data to empower communities demonstrates the value of data cooperatives. By extending such platforms to sectors such as education and healthcare through data cooperatives, we can further disseminate benefits at a broader level.

Similarly, the Farmerline initiative in Ghana (Case Study 3) presents an effective model of data cooperation that amalgamates data from various sources. It demonstrates how data cooperatives can enhance sustainable development and food security in rural regions. However, scaling and replication of this model require supportive policies and a robust digital governance structure, underlining the necessity of political will and agency in the growth of data cooperatives.

A striking example of the transformative potential of data cooperatives can be found in SOLshare (Case Study 4). This decentralized energy trading platform has brought affordable, clean energy to rural communities in Bangladesh. It emphasizes that with the right framework supporting data sharing and collaboration, data cooperatives can significantly contribute to sustainable development.

Zenzeleni (Case Study 7), a community-owned telecommunications network in South Africa, serves as an excellent example of how local ownership and collaboration can help bridge the digital divide. It also highlights the challenges such initiatives face, such as regulatory hurdles and limited resources, illustrating the critical need for policy interventions and financial support.

The Bavarian Construction Data Cooperative, GemeinWerk (Case Study 8), presents a unique model of a sector-specific data cooperative. Facilitating trust-based data sharing among stakeholders creates a pre-competitive space of trust that drives productivity and innovation among SMEs.

Lastly, Barcelona's smart city initiatives (Case Study 9) demonstrate the potential of data cooperatives in urban environments. The city has successfully leveraged data from various sources to improve urban services and enhance residents' quality of life. However, the expansion of such initiatives requires robust data governance structures, open standards, and active citizen participation, emphasizing the importance of multi-stakeholder engagement in data cooperatives.

In conclusion, these case studies validate our argument for the significance of data cooperatives in overcoming the challenges of the digital age. They illustrate that while potential hurdles exist, with the right blend of policy support, technological framework, and stakeholder collaboration, data cooperatives can become a critical player in democratizing data governance and fostering an inclusive digital common.

4.2. Barriers and Shortcomings of Data Cooperatives and Digital Federation Platforms

1. Regulatory Barriers: Existing regulations in many countries may not adequately support or even hinder the establishment and operation of data cooperatives and digital federation platforms, limiting their potential impact.
2. Limited Resources: Small communities and SMEs often face resource constraints that restrict their ability to develop and implement digital governance structures, open standards, and cooperative models.
3. Digital Divide: Unequal access to digital infrastructure, skills, and resources exacerbates existing inequalities, making it more challenging for marginalized communities to participate in and benefit from digital transformation efforts.
4. Data Privacy and Security: Ensuring data privacy and security is critical for the success of digital federation platforms and data cooperatives, requiring the development of robust governance frameworks and technical solutions.

These case studies highlight the transformative potential of data cooperatives and digital federation platforms in addressing the challenges faced by small communities and SMEs. However, overcoming the barriers and shortcomings highlighted above necessitates policy action, as proposed in the following sections. Additional case studies from the Global South, including South America, highlight the transformative potential of data cooperatives and digital federation platforms in various sectors. Overcoming the barriers and addressing the shortcomings highlighted in the previous section requires policy action and support from both national governments and international organizations. The case studies from Europe and the United States display the potential of data cooperatives and digital federation platforms to drive transformative change across various sectors and contexts. To fully realize the benefits of such models, it is crucial to address the identified barriers and shortcomings through policy action, capacity building, and the development of supportive legal and regulatory frameworks.

5. Data Cooperatives and Their Governance

5.1. Navigating the Data Governance Spectrum

In the intricate matrix of data governance, numerous solutions have emerged, including multistakeholderism, top-down regulation, technical decentralization, digital rights constitutionalism, and the notion of middleware companies and mediators of individual data. While these solutions present their merits, their ability to foster data sovereignty and promote an equitable digital world remains questionable. Here, we argue that data cooperatives offer a more comprehensive and effective approach, outperforming these alternatives in several crucial ways.

1. Multistakeholderism and top-down regulation: While these approaches aim to create a balanced digital ecosystem by integrating various stakeholders or enforcing strict regulations, they often fall short in promoting true data sovereignty. Multistakeholderism risks marginalizing less influential parties in decision-making processes, and top-down regulations can inadvertently stifle innovation and competition. In contrast, data cooperatives ensure that each member has an equal voice, fostering a more democratic governance structure that empowers individuals and communities.
2. Technical decentralization: While this approach champions technological solutions for data privacy, it lacks a holistic perspective. Technology alone cannot address the complex social, economic, and political issues associated with data governance. Data cooperatives, however, adopt an integrative approach that couples technological advancements with robust governance mechanisms to address these complex dimensions.
3. Digital constitutionalism: Although codifying digital rights into law is a significant step towards safeguarding data sovereignty, these rights remain theoretical unless individuals and communities are empowered to exercise them effectively. Data cooperatives provide the necessary framework for individuals to collectively assert and protect their digital rights, making these constitutional provisions a lived reality.

The proposals by Fukuyama [92] and Lanier [93], suggesting middleware companies and mediators of individual data, do share intellectual proximity to our data cooperative proposition. These approaches, much like data cooperatives, seek to foster a middle layer of governance, offering a balanced approach to data management. However, data cooperatives surpass these concepts in their emphasis on collective ownership, democratic decision-making, and an inherently cooperative ethos.

While middleware companies serve as third-party entities managing the interaction between end-users and internet companies, they still operate within a commercial logic that may not prioritize user interests. Similarly, while mediators of individual data can provide negotiation power for individuals, they do not inherently ensure an equitable distribution of benefits derived from data. On the other hand, data cooperatives operate on principles of democracy, openness, equality, and solidarity, ensuring that their members' rights and interests are paramount.

We echo Lanier and Weyl's [93] robust defense of mid-level solutions and extend it to champion data cooperatives specifically. They offer a promising avenue for just data governance, striking a balance between individual and state-level management, and providing a more participatory, equitable, and democratic model of data governance.

While we have addressed the distinguishing elements of data cooperatives, it is essential to recognize that no solution can operate in a vacuum. All these mentioned models and approaches have their unique strengths, and the ideal data governance framework will likely include components from each of them. Yet even in this amalgamated model, we posit that data cooperatives stand as an essential element due to their unique principles and potential. To reiterate, data cooperatives are fundamentally anchored in democratic governance, ensuring equitable involvement of all members. This cooperative ethos goes beyond the mere management of data; it is a conscious effort to reshape the power dynamics in the digital realm. It provides individuals and communities with the agency to determine how their data are used and how the benefits from this usage are distributed. It is this decentralization of power that is lacking in many of the other approaches discussed.

However, the integration of data cooperatives within the broader ecosystem requires strategic collaboration with other models. For instance, the legal structures provided by data trusts could be valuable in fortifying the legal standing of data cooperatives. Similarly, the technological advancements heralded by the idea of technical decentralization could enhance the secure and efficient operation of cooperatives. The principles of digital constitutionalism can complement the protective mechanisms within cooperatives, promoting a rights-respecting digital environment. In this vein, we need to carefully consider the insights from works such as Fukuyama's and Lanier and Weyl's [92,93]. The concept of middleware companies, for example, presents an interesting interface between the user and the internet companies. These entities can potentially be orchestrated within the cooperative framework, functioning as service providers that uphold the cooperative's principles. Similarly, the mediators of individual data could serve a role within cooperatives, representing collective interests in negotiation with external entities.

Ultimately, the argument for data cooperatives is not just about the efficient management of data or the safeguarding of privacy. It is about fostering a democratic digital culture where power is distributed, voices are heard, and benefits are shared. It is a vision of the digital world that is inclusive, equitable, and just, where data sovereignty is a reality, not just a catchphrase. Therefore, while we acknowledge the value of the varied approaches toward data governance, we firmly believe that data cooperatives should take center stage in these discussions, given their transformative potential.

5.2. Evaluation of Current Policies in the Context of Data Cooperatives

Current policy measures, particularly within the European Union, have already begun to address several aspects related to data governance. The EU's Data Governance Act and forthcoming Data Act are crucial developments in establishing a framework for data sharing and handling, yet their alignment with the policy recommendations for the advancement of data cooperatives deserves further scrutiny.

The EU Data Governance Act, currently in effect, establishes a mechanism to facilitate data sharing among businesses, citizens, and government bodies while respecting data sovereignty. The Act provides for the establishment of data intermediaries, which will operate under stringent neutrality requirements, thereby offering a stepping stone towards our recommended structure of data cooperatives. However, the Act lacks explicit support for cooperative models and does not offer specific mechanisms to foster trust and engagement from data subjects, elements we deem critical for successful data cooperatives.

Furthermore, the Data Governance Act promotes sector-specific data spaces, which can be likened to our proposal for sector-specific data cooperatives. Yet, the Act does not sufficiently articulate ways to ensure that these data spaces cater to the interests of all stakeholders, particularly individuals and smaller businesses, which is a cornerstone of our recommendations.

The proposed Data Act, aimed at ensuring fair and open access to data generated by businesses and public bodies, is another promising policy development. While the Act embodies the principles of fair and equitable data sharing, the exact mechanisms to ensure these principles remain somewhat nebulous. Our policy recommendations advocate for clear, implementable strategies that not only ensure equitable access but also foster active participation of data subjects in data governance, elements not yet thoroughly addressed in the proposed Data Act.

In conclusion, while the current and proposed policy measures by the EU form a significant stride toward fair and equitable data governance, there are gaps that need to be addressed. These primarily pertain to explicit support for data cooperative models, fostering trust and engagement from data subjects, and implementing clear strategies to ensure equitable access and participation. Further policy development should aim to address these gaps, considering data cooperatives as a viable and effective model for democratic and inclusive data governance.

6. Recommendations for Implementation

To ensure the equitable development of digital entrepreneurship and promote community well-being, we present the following recommendations (Figure 5 and Table 3). These recommendations are supported by strong arguments and evidence from the case studies discussed earlier.

By implementing these recommendations, governments and civil society around the world can create an enabling environment for the growth of digital federation platforms and data cooperatives, fostering a more inclusive and equitable digital ecosystem that supports the sustainable development of small communities and SMEs.

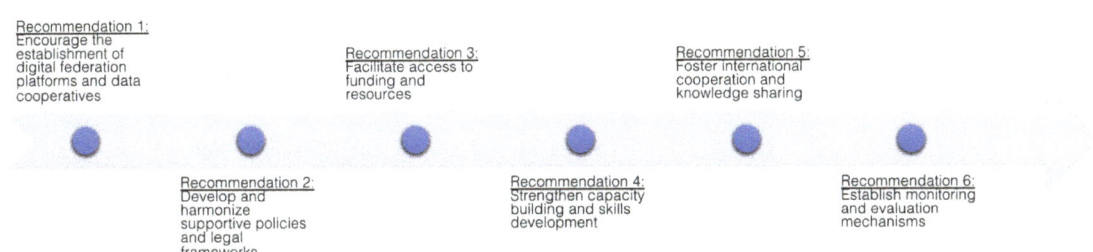

Figure 5. Proposed chronical order of recommendation implementation (own depiction).

Table 3. Recommendations to interested governments and civil society.

Recommendation	Description
Recommendation 1: Encourage the establishment of digital federation platforms and data cooperatives	❖ Promote the creation of digital federation platforms and data cooperatives to empower small communities and SMEs by providing access to resources, information, and decision-making power. ❖ Facilitate knowledge sharing and provide technical assistance to support the development and implementation of these platforms and cooperatives. ❖ Initiate and support creative programs such as "Digital Innovation Hubs" that bring together SMEs, communities, and technology experts to collaboratively develop and implement digital solutions tailored to local needs, fostering a culture of innovation and entrepreneurship in the digital space.
Recommendation 2: Develop and harmonize supportive policies and legal frameworks	❖ Develop and align policies and legal frameworks that foster digital inclusion, open standards, and data governance. ❖ Encourage member countries to remove regulatory barriers that hinder the establishment and operation of data cooperatives and digital federation platforms. ❖ Create a "Digital Policy Innovation Lab"—a collaborative, multi-stakeholder platform that brings together policymakers, technologists, SMEs, and community representatives to co-design, pilot, and refine innovative regulatory frameworks and policy solutions that promote digital entrepreneurship and ensure a fair and inclusive digital ecosystem.
Recommendation 2: Develop and harmonize supportive policies and legal frameworks	❖ Develop and align policies and legal frameworks that foster digital inclusion, open standards, and data governance. ❖ Remove regulatory barriers that hinder the establishment and operation of data cooperatives and digital federation platforms. ❖ Create a "Digital Policy Innovation Lab"—a collaborative, multi-stakeholder platform that brings together policymakers, technologists, SMEs, and community representatives to co-design, pilot, and refine innovative regulatory frameworks and policy solutions that promote digital entrepreneurship and ensure a fair and inclusive digital ecosystem.

Table 3. Cont.

Recommendation	Description
Recommendation 3: Facilitate access to funding and resources	❖ Establish funding mechanisms, such as grants, low-interest loans, or other financial instruments, to support the development and implementation of digital federation platforms and data cooperatives, particularly in resource-constrained regions. ❖ Explore partnerships with multilateral organizations, regional development banks, and private sector stakeholders to mobilize resources and support capacity building initiatives. ❖ Launch a "Digital Entrepreneurship Challenge," a global competition that encourages SMEs and communities to develop innovative digital solutions using data cooperatives and digital federation platforms. Winners would receive financial support, mentorship, and access to resources, fostering a culture of innovation and collaboration in the digital space.
Recommendation 4: Strengthen capacity building and skills development	❖ Support the development and delivery of capacity building and skills development programs for small communities and SMEs, enabling them to effectively participate in the digital economy. ❖ Collaboration with international organizations, educational institutions, and the private sector should be leveraged to create and implement relevant training programs. ❖ To inject creativity into capacity building and skills development, promote the establishment of "Digital Skill-Share Networks", which are peer-to-peer learning platforms where SMEs, communities, and experts can exchange knowledge and skills in digital technologies and data governance. These networks would foster a collaborative learning environment, encouraging participants to share experiences, insights, and best practices in a dynamic and engaging manner.
Recommendation 5: Foster international cooperation and knowledge sharing	❖ Promote international cooperation and knowledge sharing among member countries to identify and disseminate best practices related to digital federation platforms and data cooperatives. ❖ Collaboration with multilateral organizations, regional development banks, and other stakeholders should be encouraged to facilitate the exchange of experiences and insights. ❖ Organize an annual "Global Digital Commons Summit" that brings together representatives from member countries, SMEs, communities, multilateral organizations, and the private sector. This summit would serve as a platform for showcasing innovative projects, exchanging best practices, and forming new partnerships related to digital federation platforms and data cooperatives, thus strengthening the global digital ecosystem.
Recommendation 6: Establish monitoring and evaluation mechanisms	❖ Develop mechanisms to monitor and evaluate the impact of digital federation platforms and data cooperatives on small communities and SMEs. ❖ Use this information to identify areas for improvement and ensure that these initiatives effectively contribute to the achievement of SDGs 8, 9, and 11. ❖ Launch a "Digital Impact Dashboard"—an interactive, publicly accessible platform that visualizes the progress and impact of digital federation platforms and data cooperatives on small communities and SMEs. This dashboard would not only increase transparency and accountability but also facilitate the identification of success stories and areas for improvement, encouraging continuous learning and adaptation within the digital ecosystem.

7. Governments' Role and Beyond

Governments around the world play a crucial role in addressing the policy challenges identified in this review article. Supranational organizations' (such as the OECD, G20, G7, EU, ASIAN etc.) collective influence, resources, and commitment to fostering inclusive and sustainable growth make them well-positioned to create viable opportunities for small communities and SMEs in the digital landscape. Those supranational organizations can contribute to the establishment and support of open digital federation platforms and data cooperatives in several ways (Table 4):

Table 4. Summary table of proposed roles of supranational organizations in supporting data and platform cooperatives.

Recommendation	Description
Policy Harmonization	Encourage member countries to develop and align policies that promote digital inclusion, support the establishment of data cooperatives, and foster a more equitable digital economy. This can include measures such as incentives for SMEs to participate in cooperatives and the adoption of open standards and APIs.
Financial Support	Facilitate access to funding for the development and implementation of digital federation platforms and data cooperatives, particularly in regions where resources are scarce. This can include grants, low-interest loans, or other financial instruments that help kickstart these initiatives.
Capacity Building	Support capacity building and skills development programs for small communities and SMEs, empowering them to participate in the digital economy and make effective use of digital resources. This may involve collaborating with international organizations, educational institutions, NGOs, and the private sector to develop and deliver relevant training programs. This could include using the existing knowledge in established and flagship co-operative groups (i.e., Mondragon [94]) to leverage through this organizational model further implementations in the current digital economy and society.
Knowledge Sharing	Promote knowledge sharing and the exchange of best practices among member countries regarding the implementation of digital federation platforms and data cooperatives. This can help identify effective models and strategies that can be adapted and scaled across different contexts.
International Cooperation	Foster international cooperation and partnerships to support the development of digital federation platforms and data cooperatives, including collaboration with multilateral organizations, regional development banks, and other stakeholders.
Monitoring and Evaluation	Establish mechanisms for monitoring and evaluating the impact of digital federation platforms and data cooperatives on small communities and SMEs. This can help to identify areas for improvement and ensure that these initiatives are effectively contributing to the achievement of SDGs 8, 9, and 11.

By actively engaging in these efforts, supranational organizations can create an environment that encourages the growth of digital federation platforms and data cooperatives, supporting a more inclusive and equitable digital ecosystem for small communities and SMEs. In doing so, supranational organizations can make significant strides in addressing the policy challenges identified in this brief, promoting sustainable development, and advancing the global digital economy [95,96].

8. Addressing Key Considerations in Data Cooperative Implementation

In our quest to explore the transformative potential of data cooperatives for digital commons, we aim to bridge the gap between theory and practice by delving into the intricate aspects of their implementation. This paper navigates through the complex landscape of data cooperatives by providing a comprehensive understanding of their associated nuances. Consequently, this section unravels four critical dimensions, which surfaced from our in-depth exploration of relevant case studies and literature: potential risks and limitations, interconnected data governance, the Global North–South divide, and the dynamics of political agency. It is essential to approach our investigation of data cooperatives through an integrative lens, thereby weaving together the threads of risks, limitations, geopolitical contexts, and political agency. This approach facilitates a more holistic and pragmatic comprehension of the data cooperative environment, thereby contributing to the understanding and successful realization of digital commons.

8.1. Risks and Limitations of Data Cooperatives

While data cooperatives present a promising avenue toward the democratization of the digital sphere, our comprehensive analysis underscores that this potential is not devoid of its challenges. Primary among these are concerns related to data privacy, operational scalability, and regulatory compliance.

The delicate balance of individual privacy within the data cooperative model necessitates the deployment of robust safeguards. In an environment characterized by extensive data sharing, the implementation of rigorous data anonymization protocols and stringent cybersecurity measures are imperative to uphold the sanctity of privacy.

Furthermore, as cooperatives scale, the complexity of maintaining effective, participatory decision-making processes magnifies. Balancing the growth in data volume with active participatory governance becomes an increasingly nuanced task, demanding careful strategizing and adept management.

Lastly, the multifaceted nature of regulatory landscapes poses additional challenges. With the rules governing data usage varying widely across jurisdictions, creating a unified operational framework is a daunting endeavor. The need for a sophisticated regulatory approach that accommodates these variations is thus highlighted.

While we have underscored the transformative potential of data cooperatives, our responsibility is to also illuminate their inherent pitfalls, challenges, and constraints. This balanced perspective offers a holistic view of the data cooperative landscape, enabling us to explore solutions while being mindful of the potential hurdles.

8.2. Interconnected Data Governance

Data governance encompasses a vast array of policies, regulations, and practices, rendering it a complex, interconnected concept rather than an isolated one. The potency of data cooperatives, therefore, can be amplified significantly when harmoniously integrated with other data governance paradigms, including data trusts and personal data stores.

For instance, data trusts could serve as legal scaffolds, facilitating collective decision-making pertaining to data, and thereby strengthening the cooperative model's structure. Concurrently, personal data stores have the potential to enhance individual autonomy by offering individuals greater control over their data.

When these governance models are strategically amalgamated with the data cooperative paradigm, the result could be a substantial boost to equitable data practices and an increased agency for individuals in the digital arena. Hence, our exploration of data cooperatives must consider the larger context, recognizing the valuable role played by other forms of data governance and their potential to synergistically enhance the effectiveness of data cooperatives, thereby further advancing the cause of digital inclusivity.

8.3. The Global North–South Divide

The distinct divide between the Global North and South delineates unique implications for data cooperatives, presenting both distinct challenges and opportunities. Disparities in technological advancements and resource availability have etched an uneven digital terrain, typically characterizing the Global North with superior technological capabilities compared to the Global South.

Though this scenario poses certain hurdles, it also unveils opportunities for fostering digital solidarity. Data cooperatives in the Global North could function as a lighthouse, sharing resources, insights, and technology with their counterparts in the Global South, thus cultivating a more balanced digital ecosystem.

However, these initiatives must be judiciously crafted to respect local contexts and uphold the principles of data sovereignty to ensure genuine efficacy. The dichotomy between the Global North and South influences the growth trajectory of data cooperatives in intricate ways.

The inherent uneven development, a by-product of diverse technological resources and availability, has created a digital divide between these two regions. Our proposed policy framework and the establishment of digital federated platforms are meticulously designed to provide blueprints relevant to both contexts. Yet, the disparities in resource availability, digital infrastructure, and data governance policies call for a finely calibrated, context-sensitive application.

By emphasizing the promotion of local capacity-building, stimulating South–South collaborations, and endorsing context-sensitive policies, we could potentially navigate toward a more balanced and inclusive digital landscape.

8.4. The Role of Political Agency

The realization and expansion of data cooperatives hinge significantly on political agency and willpower, spanning the roles of local, national, and supranational entities in cultivating a conducive environment. For instance, local authorities can weave data cooperatives into their smart city initiatives, while national governments can lay the groundwork for supportive legislation and funding. Supranational entities, such as the European Union, are primed to harmonize regulations across borders, thereby streamlining the functioning of cross-border cooperatives. It is paramount, however, to calibrate these efforts to ensure they do not compromise the democratically driven ethos integral to cooperatives.

In addressing these pivotal aspects, we aspire to furnish a balanced, comprehensive perspective on the data cooperative model. Our intent is to deliver a nuanced understanding capable of guiding effective policymaking and fostering an equitable, inclusive digital commons.

Political agencies' role in nurturing data cooperatives is multi-layered, extending beyond the top-down influence of supranational organizations. Indeed, local, community-driven data access, usage, and governance serve as the vital lifeline for initiating and sustaining data cooperatives. Nonetheless, transformative change often hinges on facilitative policies, regulatory backing, and financial incentives, most effectively offered at the national and supranational levels.

In acknowledging these dynamics, it is essential to appreciate the hybrid nature of governance arrangements across various geographical scales. Power and politics within data governance regimes are distributed, mirroring the involvement of a spectrum of actors ranging from community members to global institutions. Consequently, data cooperatives should be perceived as components of a broader socio-political ecosystem, requiring active participation from stakeholders across all tiers.

To encapsulate, this thorough understanding of the complexities surrounding data cooperatives provides a more robust foundation for executing our policy recommendations. It arms us with the acuity to foresee challenges, to strategically align with complementary data governance models, to adapt to geographical disparities, and to engage optimally with political agencies. The ultimate aim is democratizing digital resources and capabilities.

9. Conclusions

The digital age, characterized by rapid technological advancements and data-driven economies, poses unique challenges and opportunities for small communities and small and medium enterprises (SMEs). Data cooperatives and digital federation platforms have emerged as viable solutions to tackle these challenges, enabling the democratization of digital resources and providing avenues for collective decision-making and shared value creation. Through the detailed exploration presented in this paper, we underscored the transformative potential of data cooperatives and digital federation platforms. We delved into their nuances, highlighting key considerations such as risks and limitations, interconnected data governance, the Global North–South divide, and the dynamics of political agency.

Our study reaffirms that data cooperatives are not a panacea and come with their inherent challenges, such as privacy concerns, operational scalability, and regulatory compliance. Nevertheless, they offer promising prospects for fostering a more inclusive and equitable digital ecosystem, especially when intertwined with other data governance models such as data trusts and personal data stores. The geopolitical context, characterized by the North–South divide, influences the trajectory of data cooperatives. Although it introduces disparities in technological advancements and resource availability, it also presents opportunities for fostering digital solidarity. A key strategy toward a balanced digital ecosystem is the promotion of local capacity-building, fostering South–South collaborations, and endorsing context-sensitive policies.

The role of political agency is vital in shaping an environment conducive to the growth of data cooperatives. From local to supranational entities, supportive legislation, and funding, as well as harmonization of regulations, can facilitate the expansion of these cooperatives. Yet, it is crucial to ensure these efforts do not compromise the democratically driven ethos integral to cooperatives. The recommendations we propose for governments and civil society provide a strategic blueprint to harness the potential of data cooperatives and digital federation platforms effectively. From encouraging the establishment of these platforms to harmonizing supportive policies, providing access to resources, strengthening capacity building, fostering international cooperation, and establishing evaluation mechanisms—these steps would drive a more inclusive and equitable digital ecosystem.

The establishment and successful implementation of data cooperatives and digital federation platforms represent an essential step towards a digital commons that serve the needs of all stakeholders. By providing a platform for collective decision-making and shared value creation, they offer a promising route toward digital equity and inclusivity. The insights gleaned from this study lay a robust foundation for executing policy recommendations and advancing toward a democratized digital landscape.

Author Contributions: Conceptualization, M.M.B. and A.P.; methodology, I.C. (Igor Calzada) and T.S.; validation, K.N., T.S., J.T. and D.S.; formal analysis, M.M.B., K.N., T.J., S.M. and V.M.; investigation, I.C. (Isabel Cane), D.S., J.T., S.M. and J.Z.; resources, M.M.B.; data curation, I.C. (Isabel Cane), B.V. and J.Z.; writing—original draft preparation, M.M.B., I.C. (Igor Calzada), M.M., B.V. and A.P.; writing—review and editing, A.K., T.S., M.M., M.M.B., I.C. (Igor Calzada) and M.M.; visualization, M.M.B.; supervision, A.P. and J.T.; project administration, M.M.B.; funding acquisition, M.M.B. All authors have read and agreed to the published version of the manuscript.

Funding: The article processing charges (APC) were fully funded by the Baden-Württemberg Ministry of Science, Research and Culture (Ministerium für Wissenschaft, Forschung und Kunst Baden-Württemberg) and the University of Applied Sciences Konstanz (HTWG Hochschule Konstanz Technik, Wirtschaft und Gestaltung). Furthermore, an overall discount of 10% on the APC was granted within the framework of the Open Access Program, in which one of the authors of the TU Munich participates.

Conflicts of Interest: The authors declare no conflict of interest.

References

1. Lehdonvirta, V. *Cloud Empires: How Digital Platforms Are Overtaking the State and How We Can Regain Control*; MIT Press: Cambridge, MA, USA, 2022.
2. Bresciani, S.; Ciampi, F.; Meli, F.; Ferraris, A. Using big data for co-innovation processes: Mapping the field of data-driven innovation, proposing theoretical developments and providing a research agenda. *Int. J. Inf. Manag.* **2021**, *60*, 102347. [CrossRef]
3. Bühler, M.M.; Nübel, K.; Jelinek, T.; Riechert, D.; Bauer, T.; Schmid, T.; Schneider, M. Data cooperatives as a catalyst for collaboration, data sharing and the digital transformation of the construction sector. *Buildings* **2023**, *13*, 442. [CrossRef]
4. Tait, J. Open Data Cooperation—Building a Data Cooperative. Available online: https://www.opendatamanchester.org.uk/947/ (accessed on 4 April 2023).

5. Organisation for Economic Co-operation and Development (OECD). *Data-Driven Innovation: Big Data for Growth and Well-Being*; OECD Publishing: Paris, France, 2015.
6. Corrado, C.; Hulten, C.; Sichel, D. Intangible capital and US economic growth. *Rev. Income Wealth* **2009**, *55*, 661–685. [CrossRef]
7. Hummel, P.; Braun, M.; Tretter, M.; Dabrock, P. Data sovereignty: A review. *Big Data Soc.* **2021**, *8*, 2053951720982012. [CrossRef]
8. Jarke, M.; Otto, B.; Ram, S. Data sovereignty and data space ecosystems. *Bus. Inf. Syst. Eng.* **2019**, *61*, 549–550. [CrossRef]
9. Institute, A.L. *Exploring Legal Mechanisms for Data Stewardship*; Ada Lovelace Institute and UK AI Council: London, UK, 2021.
10. Calzada, I. Data co-operatives through data sovereignty. *Smart Cities* **2021**, *4*, 1158–1172. [CrossRef]
11. Cuno, S.; Bruns, L.; Tcholtchev, N.; Lämmel, P.; Schieferdecker, I. Data governance and sovereignty in urban data spaces based on standardized ICT reference architectures. *Data* **2019**, *4*, 16. [CrossRef]
12. Floridi, L. The Fight for Digital Sovereignty: What It Is, and Why It Matters, Especially for the EU. *Philos. Technol.* **2020**, *33*, 369–378. [CrossRef]
13. Jelinek, T. Technology Silos of Today or the End of Global Innovation. In *The Digital Sovereignty Trap*; Springer: Berlin/Heidelberg, Germany, 2023; pp. 19–33.
14. Walter, M.; Kukutai, T.; Carroll, S.R.; Rodriguez-Lonebear, D. *Indigenous Data Sovereignty and Policy*; Taylor & Francis: London, UK, 2021.
15. Carroll, S.R.; Garba, I.; Figueroa-Rodríguez, O.L.; Holbrook, J.; Lovett, R.; Materechera, S.; Parsons, M.; Raseroka, K.; Rodriguez-Lonebear, D.; Rowe, R. The CARE principles for indigenous data governance. *Data Sci. J.* **2020**, *19*, 43. [CrossRef]
16. Bunting, M.; Lansdell, S. Designing Decision Making Processes for Data Trusts: Lessons from Three Pilots. 2019. Available online: https://theodi.org/wp-content/uploads/2019/04/General-decision-making-report-Apr-19.pdf (accessed on 26 June 2023).
17. Baars, H.; Tank, A.; Weber, P.; Kemper, H.-G.; Lasi, H.; Pedell, B. Cooperative Approaches to Data Sharing and Analysis for Industrial Internet of Things Ecosystems. *Appl. Sci.* **2021**, *11*, 7547. [CrossRef]
18. Ferdinand-Steinbeis-Institut (FSTI). Datengenossenschaft.com (Data Cooperative). Available online: https://www.datengenossenschaft.com/ (accessed on 14 November 2022).
19. Miller, K. Radical Proposal: Data Cooperatives Could Give Us More Power over Our Data. Available online: https://hai.stanford.edu/news/radical-proposal-data-cooperatives-could-give-us-more-power-over-our-data (accessed on 14 November 2022).
20. Scholz, T.R.; Calzada, I. Data cooperatives for pandemic times. In *Data Cooperatives for Pandemic Times*; Public Seminar: New York, NY, USA, 2021.
21. Tait, J. The Case for Data Cooperatives. Available online: https://thedataeconomylab.com/2021/09/06/the-case-for-data-cooperatives/ (accessed on 26 June 2023).
22. Sgarro, V. *Understanding Democratic Decision-Making in Cooperatives*; Platform Cooperatives: New York, NY, USA, 2023.
23. Calzada, I. Postpandemic technopolitical democracy: Algorithmic nations, data sovereignty, digital rights, and data cooperatives. In *Made-to-Measure Future(s) for Democracy? Views from the Basque Atalaia*; Springer International Publishing: Cham, The Netherlands, 2022; pp. 97–117.
24. Hardjono, T.; Pentland, A. Empowering artists, songwriters & musicians in a data cooperative through blockchains and smart contracts. *arXiv* **2019**, arXiv:1911.10433.
25. Hardjono, T.; Pentland, A. Data cooperatives: Towards a foundation for decentralized personal data management. *arXiv* **2019**, arXiv:1905.08819.
26. Marjanovic, O.; Zhu, J.; Krivokapic-Skoko, B.; Lewis, C. Will the real data coop stand up!: Data cooperatives in the coop sector–current challenges and future opportunities. In Proceedings of the 14th ICA CCR Asia-Pacific Research Conference, Newcastle, Australia, 12–14 December 2019.
27. Salau, A.; Dantu, R.; Morozov, K.; Upadhyay, K.; Badruddoja, S. Towards a Threat Model and Security Analysis for Data Cooperatives. In Proceedings of the 19th International Conference on Security and Cryptography-SECRYPT, Lisbon, Portugal, 11–13 July 2022; pp. 707–713.
28. Shah, P.R.; Juenke, E.G.; Fraga, B.L. Here Comes Everybody: Using a Data Cooperative to Understand the New Dynamics of Representation. *PS Political Sci. Politics* **2022**, *55*, 300–302. [CrossRef]
29. Mannan, M.; Schneider, N. Exit to community: Strategies for multi-stakeholder ownership in the platform economy. *Geo. L. Tech. Rev.* **2021**, *5*, 1.
30. Mannan, M. Theorizing the emergence of platform cooperativism: Drawing lessons from role-set theory. *Ondernem. Tijdschr.* **2022**, *2*, 64–71.
31. Mannan, M.; Pek, S. *Solidarity in the Sharing Economy: The Role of Platform Cooperatives at the Base of the Pyramid*; Springer: Berlin/Heidelberg, Germany, 2021.
32. Bunders, D.J.; Arets, M.; Frenken, K.; De Moor, T. The feasibility of platform cooperatives in the gig economy. *J. Co-Oper. Organ. Manag.* **2022**, *10*, 100167. [CrossRef]
33. Kuncoro, E.A. Platform Cooperative as a Business Model: An Innovation toward a Fair Sharing Economy in Indonesia. Available online: https://binus.ac.id/wp-content/uploads/2022/09/Orasi-Ilmiah_Engkos-Achmad-Kuncoro-English-24-September-2022_FA-NEW-3.pdf (accessed on 26 June 2023).
34. Pentzien, J. *The Politics of Platform Cooperativism*; Institute for Digital Cooperative Economy: New York, NY, USA, 2020. Available online: https://ia801701.us.archive.org/10/items/jonas-pentziensingle-web_202012/Jonas%20Pentzien_single_web.pdf (accessed on 26 June 2023).

35. Platform Cooperativism Consortium, Platform Co-op Directory. "The Platform Co-Op Directory Is a Place Where You Can Search for and Connect with Co-Operatives and Other Members of the Co-Operative Community". 2021. Available online: https://directory.platform.coop/#1/31.1/-84.8 (accessed on 26 June 2023).
36. Scholz, T. Platform cooperativism. In *Challenging the Corporate Sharing Economy*; Rosa Luxemburg Foundation: New York, NY, USA, 2016.
37. Scholz, T. A Portfolio of Platform Cooperativism, in Progress. *Ökol. Wirtsch. Fachz.* **2018**, *33*, 16–19. Available online: https://www.oekologisches-wirtschaften.de/index.php/oew/article/view/1646 (accessed on 26 June 2023).
38. Calzada, I. Platform and data co-operatives amidst European pandemic citizenship. *Sustainability* **2020**, *12*, 8309. [CrossRef]
39. Chan, A.; Bradley, H.; Rajkumar, N. Reclaiming the Digital Commons: A Public Data Trust for Training Data. *arXiv* **2023**, arXiv:2303.09001.
40. Dulong de Rosnay, M.; Stalder, F. Digital commons. *Internet Policy Rev.* **2020**, *9*, 1–22. [CrossRef]
41. Huang, S.; Siddarth, D. Generative AI and the Digital Commons. *arXiv* **2023**, arXiv:2303.11074.
42. Ostrom, E. *Governing the Commons: The Evolution of Institutions for Collective Action*; Cambridge University Press: Cambridge, UK, 1990.
43. Sharma, C. Tragedy of the Digital Commons. *N. Carol. Law Rev. Forthcom.* **2022**, *101*, 4. [CrossRef]
44. Siddarth, D.E.G.W. The Case for the Digital Commons. 2021. World Economic Forum. Available online: https://www.weforum.org/agenda/2021/06/the-case-for-the-digital-commons/ (accessed on 26 June 2023).
45. Walljasper, J. Elinor Ostrom's 8 Principles for Managing a Commons. on the Commons 2011. Available online: https://www.onthecommons.org/magazine/elinor-ostroms-8-principles-managing-commmons/index.html (accessed on 26 June 2023).
46. Bechtold, S. *Vom Urheber-Zum Informationsrecht: Implikationen des Digital Rights Management*; Beck München: Munich, Germany, 2002.
47. Calzada, I. The right to have digital rights in smart cities. *Sustainability* **2021**, *13*, 11438. [CrossRef]
48. Calzada, I.; Almirall, E. Data ecosystems for protecting European citizens' digital rights. *Transform. Gov. People Process Policy* **2020**, *14*, 133–147. [CrossRef]
49. Calzada, I.; Pérez-Batlle, M.; Batlle-Montserrat, J. People-centered smart cities: An exploratory action research on the cities' coalition for digital rights. *J. Urban Aff.* **2021**, 1–26. [CrossRef]
50. Monti, A. *The Digital Rights Delusion: Humans, Machines and the Technology of Information*; Taylor & Francis: London, UK, 2023.
51. Pangrazio, L.; Sefton-Green, J. Digital rights, digital citizenship and digital literacy: What's the difference? *NAER J. New Approaches Educ. Res.* **2021**, *10*, 15–27. [CrossRef]
52. Polona, C. Digital Rights and Principles. 2023. EPRS: European Parliamentary Research Service. Belgium. Available online: https://policycommons.net/artifacts/3370762/digital-rights-and-principles/4169587/ (accessed on 26 June 2023).
53. Lim, Y. Tech Wars: Return of the Conglomerate-Throwback or Dawn of a New Series for Competition in the Digital Era. *J. Korean L.* **2020**, *19*, 47. [CrossRef]
54. Organisation for Economic Co-operation and Development (OECD). *Mapping Approaches to Data and Data Flows*; OECD: Paris, France, 2020.
55. Reimsbach-Kounatze, C. Enhancing access to and sharing of data: Striking the balance between openness and control over data. In *Data Access, Consumer Interests and Public Welfare*; Nomos: Baden-Baden, Germany, 2021; pp. 25–68. [CrossRef]
56. Organisation for Economic Co-operation and Development (OECD). *OECD Digital Economy Outlook 2020*; OECD: Paris, France, 2020.
57. Organisation for Economic Co-operation and Development (OECD). *Enhancing Access to and Sharing of Data*; OECD: Paris, France, 2019.
58. Organisation for Economic Co-operation and Development (OECD). Responding to societal challenges with data: Access, sharing, stewardship and control. In *OECD Digital Economy Papers*; OECD Publishing: Paris, France, 2022; Volume 342. [CrossRef]
59. Organisation for Economic Co-operation and Development (OECD). Value added by activity (indicator). *Natl. Acc. A Glance* **2023**. [CrossRef]
60. Jack, W.; Suri, T. *Mobile Money: The Economics of M-PESA*; National Bureau of Economic Research: Cambridge, MA, USA, 2011. [CrossRef]
61. Kingiri, A.N.; Fu, X. Understanding the diffusion and adoption of digital finance innovation in emerging economies: M-Pesa money mobile transfer service in Kenya. *Innov. Dev.* **2019**, *10*, 67–87. [CrossRef]
62. Mbiti, I.; Weil, D.N. Mobile banking: The impact of M-Pesa in Kenya. In *African Successes*; Volume III: Modernization and Development; University of Chicago Press: Chicago, IL, USA, 2015; pp. 247–293.
63. Omwansa, T. Omwansa, T. M-PESA: Progress and Prospects. Innovations. 2009, pp. 107–123. Available online: https://d1wqtxts1xzle7.cloudfront.net/87040674/innov-gsma-omwansa-libre.pdf?1654464218=&response-content-disposition=inline%3B+filename%3DM_PESA_Progress_and_prospects.pdf&Expires=1688009710&Signature=BezXWNQdUqfT4EoqqikY8R-vb6WqKtQ7xHYBZnf7lke0c7c5LLVY46jH9pMNcZJsHvwl1tU~v1DGQ7CFOTTuUUhkYOPW-vOM1m-9sW4aAqw4tMqucMx~~39v7i5Iu4wDPPgfThHrKmfkmue0r8qNZJaIRVoYXwwgKLm3TuBUtVu2iGloa68dlkq4x0uw1e5zQZKEhlcFV-IiOHLXZLxKexNnyn-RBMkwUuBPZNu-eG7WwxS6cMQZ3Yz~XKxLShOARvaQp7W4cQnnsM-0xmll5k0Ig-thOEA1oVq~EuIBxYuflC-IxtnJP8rGJStEF6CEDwicxW2EIb1HVg5Rtp-WHg__&Key-Pair-Id=APKAJLOHF5GGSLRBV4ZA (accessed on 26 June 2023).
64. Van Hove, L.; Dubus, A. M-PESA and financial inclusion in Kenya: Of paying comes saving? *Sustainability* **2019**, *11*, 568. [CrossRef]

65. Dubé, L.; McRae, C.; Wu, Y.-H.; Ghosh, S.; Allen, S.; Ross, D.; Ray, S.; Joshi, P.K.; McDermott, J.; Jha, S. Impact of the eKutir ICT-enabled social enterprise and its distributed micro-entrepreneur strategy on fruit and vegetable consumption: A quasi-experimental study in rural and urban communities in Odisha, India. *Food Policy* **2020**, *90*, 101787. [CrossRef]
66. McRae, C.; Annosi, M.; Dubé, L. Tracing Digital Transformation Pathways from Subsistence Farming to Equitable and Sustainable Modern Society: Revisiting the eKutir ICT Platform-Enabled Ecosystem as an Interstitial Space. In Proceedings of the ICIS 2022 Proceedings, Copenhagen, Denmark, 9–14 December 2022.
67. Moore, S.; Annosi, M.C.; Gilissen, T.; Mandelbaum, J.; Dube, L. The social impact of ICT-enabled interventions among rural Indian farmers as seen through eKutir's VeggieLite intervention. In *How Is Digitalization Affecting Agri-Food?* Routledge: London, UK, 2020; pp. 93–98.
68. Sengupta, T.; Narayanamurthy, G.; Hota, P.K.; Sarker, T.; Dey, S. Conditional acceptance of digitized business model innovation at the BoP: A stakeholder analysis of eKutir in India. *Technol. Forecast. Soc. Chang.* **2021**, *170*, 120857. [CrossRef]
69. Senyo, W. Farmerline: A for-profit agtech company with a social Mission. In *Digital Technologies for Agricultural and Rural Development in the Global South*; CAB International: Wallingford, UK, 2018; pp. 123–126.
70. Delinthe, L.; Zwart, S.J. Digital Services for Agriculture. In Accelerating Impacts of CGIAR Climate Research for Africa (AICCRA). 2022. Available online: https://hdl.handle.net/10568/126217 (accessed on 26 June 2023).
71. Agnihotri, A.; Bhattacharya, S. SOLshare: Revolutionary Peer-to-Peer Solar Energy Trading in a Developing Market. In *SAGE Business Cases*; SAGE Business Cases Originals; SAGE Publications: Thousand Oaks, CA, USA, 2022.
72. Flanagan, K. For the common good. *Renew Technol. A Sustain. Future* **2020**, 76–79. Available online: https://www.jstor.org/stable/48587590 (accessed on 26 June 2023).
73. Groh, S.; Zürpel, C.; Waris, E.; Werth, A. Analytics on pricing signals in peer-to-peer solar microgrids in Bangladesh. *Econ. Energy Environ. Policy* **2022**, *11*, 2022. [CrossRef]
74. Sirota, F.; Fratini, G. A Case about Nubank: The Story of an Innovative Fintech in Brazil. Master's Thesis, Politecnico di Milano, Milan, Italy, 2019.
75. da Rosa, S.C.; Schreiber, D.; Schmidt, S.; Junior, N.K. MANAGEMENT PRACTICES THAT COMBINE VALUE COCREATION AND USER EXPERIENCE An Analysis of the Nubank Startup in the Brazilian Market. *Rev. De Gestão Finanças E Contab.* **2017**, *7*, 22–43.
76. Kushendriawan, M.A.; Santoso, H.B.; Putra, P.O.H.; Schrepp, M. Evaluating User Experience of a Mobile Health Application 'Halodoc'using User Experience Questionnaire and Usability Testing. *J. Sist. Inf.* **2021**, *17*, 58–71.
77. Mangkunegara, C.N.; Azzahro, F.; Handayani, P.W. Analysis of factors affecting user's intention in using mobile health application: A case study of Halodoc. In Proceedings of the 2018 International Conference on Advanced Computer Science and Information Systems (ICACSIS), Yogyakarta, Indonesia, 27–28 October 2018; pp. 87–92.
78. Tarmidi, D. The influence of product innovation and price on customer satisfaction in halodoc health application services during COVID-19. *Turk. J. Comput. Math. Educ.* **2021**, *12*, 1716–1722.
79. Bidwell, N.; De Tena, S.L. Alternative Perspectives on Relationality, People and Technology during a Pandemic: Zenzeleni Networks in South Africa. In *COVID-19 From the Margins*; Institute of Network Cultures: Amsterdam, The Netherlands, 2021.
80. Hussen, T.S.; Bidwell, N.J.; Rey-Moreno, C.; Tucker, W.D. Gender and participation: Critical reflection on Zenzeleni networks in Mankosi, South Africa. In Proceedings of the First African Conference on Human Computer Interaction, Nairobi, Kenya, 21–25 November 2016; pp. 12–23.
81. Academy of Science of South Africa (ASSAf) and Department of Science and Innovation (DSI). Building Profitable and Sustainable Community Owned Connectivity Networks. 2020. Available online: https://doi.org/10.17159/assaf.2019/0065 (accessed on 26 June 2023).
82. Pather, S. Op-ed1: Towards an enabling environment for a digital ecosystem: A foundation for entrepreneurial activity. *J. Entrep. Innov.* **2021**. [CrossRef]
83. Rey-Moreno, C.; Pather, S. Advancing rural connectivity in south africa through policy and regulation: A case for community networks. In Proceedings of the 2020 IST-Africa Conference (IST-Africa), Virtual, 18–22 May 2020; pp. 1–10.
84. Bakıcı, T.; Almirall, E.; Wareham, J. A smart city initiative: The case of Barcelona. *J. Knowl. Econ.* **2013**, *4*, 135–148. [CrossRef]
85. Bibri, S.E.; Krogstie, J. The emerging data–driven Smart City and its innovative applied solutions for sustainability: The cases of London and Barcelona. *Energy Inform.* **2020**, *3*, 1–42. [CrossRef]
86. Capdevila, I.; Zarlenga, M.I. Smart city or smart citizens? The Barcelona case. *J. Strategy Manag.* **2015**, *8*, 266–282. [CrossRef]
87. Gascó-Hernandez, M. Building a smart city: Lessons from Barcelona. *Commun. ACM* **2018**, *61*, 50–57. [CrossRef]
88. Smith, A.; Martín, P.P. Going beyond the smart city? Implementing technopolitical platforms for urban democracy in Madrid and Barcelona. In *Sustainable Smart City Transitions*; Routledge: London, UK, 2022; pp. 280–299.
89. Calzada, I.; Cobo, C. Unplugging: Deconstructing the smart city. *J. Urban Technol.* **2015**, *22*, 23–43. [CrossRef]
90. Calzada, I. (Smart) citizens from data providers to decision-makers? The case study of Barcelona. *Sustainability* **2018**, *10*, 3252.
91. Driver's Seat. Driver's Seat—Know More. Earn More. Use Your Data to Maximize Rideshare And Delivery Earnings and Take Control of Your Work. Available online: https://driversseat.co/ (accessed on 3 April 2023).
92. Fukuyama, F.; Richman, B.; Goel, A. How to save democracy from technology: Ending big tech's information monopoly. *Foreign Aff.* **2021**, *100*, 98.
93. Lanier, J.; Weyl, E.G. A blueprint for a better digital society. *Harv. Bus. Rev.* **2018**, *26*, 2–18.

94. Calzada, I. 16. knowledge building and organizational behavior: The Mondragón case from a social innovation perspective. In *The International Handbook on Social Innovation: Collective Action, Social Learning and Transdisciplinary Research*; Edward Elgar Publishing: Northampton, MA, USA, 2013; p. 219.
95. Massimo, C.; Marina, M.; Jiri, H.; Igor, C.; Steven, L.; Marisa, P.; Jaap, B. *Digitranscope: The Governance of Digitally-Transformed Society*; Publications Office of the European Union: Luxembourg, 2021.
96. Bignami, F.; Calzada, I.; Hanakata, N.; Tomasello, F. Data-driven citizenship regimes in contemporary urban scenarios: An introduction. *Citizsh. Stud.* **2023**, *27*, 145–159. [CrossRef]

Disclaimer/Publisher's Note: The statements, opinions and data contained in all publications are solely those of the individual author(s) and contributor(s) and not of MDPI and/or the editor(s). MDPI and/or the editor(s) disclaim responsibility for any injury to people or property resulting from any ideas, methods, instructions or products referred to in the content.

Opinion

Mouse Tracking as a Method for Examining the Perception and Cognition of Digital Maps

Vassilios Krassanakis * and Loukas-Moysis Misthos

Department of Surveying and Geoinformatics Engineering, School of Engineering, University of West Attica, Egaleo Park Campus, Ag. Spyridonos Str., 12243 Egaleo, Greece
* Correspondence: krasvas@uniwa.gr

Abstract: This article aims to present the authors' perspective regarding the challenges and opportunities of mouse-tracking methodology while performing experimental research, particularly related to the map-reading process. We briefly describe existing metrics, visualization techniques and software tools utilized for the qualitative and quantitative analysis of experimental mouse-movement data towards the examination of both perceptual and cognitive issues. Moreover, we concisely report indicative examples of mouse-tracking studies in the field of cartography. The article concludes with summarizing mouse-tracking strengths/potential and limitations, compared to eye tracking. In a nutshell, mouse tracking is a straightforward method, particularly suitable for tracking real-life behaviors in interactive maps, providing the valuable opportunity for remote experimentation; even though it is not suitable for tracking the actual free-viewing behavior, it can be concurrently utilized with other state-of-the-art experimental methods.

Keywords: mouse tracking; mouse-movement analysis; map perception and cognition; cartographic design evaluation; cartography

Citation: Krassanakis, V.; Misthos, L.-M. Mouse Tracking as a Method for Examining the Perception and Cognition of Digital Maps. *Digital* **2023**, *3*, 127–136. https://doi.org/10.3390/digital3020009

Academic Editors: Mirjana Ivanović, Richard Chbeir and Yannis Manolopoulos

Received: 26 April 2023
Revised: 26 May 2023
Accepted: 29 May 2023
Published: 30 May 2023

Copyright: © 2023 by the authors. Licensee MDPI, Basel, Switzerland. This article is an open access article distributed under the terms and conditions of the Creative Commons Attribution (CC BY) license (https://creativecommons.org/licenses/by/4.0/).

1. Introduction

A map constitutes a medium designed to communicate generalized spatial information as well as existing relationships among geographic entities [1]. Cartographic products aim to transfer spatial information from mapmakers (cartographers) to the map readers/users taking also into account the third (i.e., time) dimension. Depending on the nature of the used medium, maps could be either analog or digital. Nowadays, the majority of the maps are distributed as digital products using the World Wide Web; they can be either static, animated, or interactive. In any case, the maps' design is directly connected to the implementation of visual [2], dynamic [3] and/or sound [4] variables which are utilized towards the representation of qualitative and/or quantitative differences that characterize geographical entities and/or phenomena. Compared to other types of spatial representations (e.g., satellite images, orthophotos, etc.), both the effectiveness and the efficiency of the map-reading process are directly influenced by the selections made during the cartographic design process. The effectiveness and the efficiency are connected to the accuracy and the corresponding completion time required for the execution of map-reading tasks, accordingly [5].

The examination of map perception and cognition is mainly based on the performance of experimental research studies in which cartographic products act as visual stimuli and certain research hypotheses are tested under map-reading conditions [6]. More specifically, in cartographic research it is important to rate and/or rank the performance of the design tools (i.e., visual, dynamic and sound variables) utilized towards the visualization of spatiotemporal phenomena, as well as to analyze and model the strategies followed by map readers during the execution of basic or more complex map tasks. Over the last decades, several experimental methods, including questionnaire analysis (e.g., [7]), think-aloud protocols (e.g., [8]), reaction-time measures (e.g., [9]), eye tracking (e.g., [10]), mouse tracking (e.g., [11]), electroencephalography (EEG) (e.g., [12]), and functional Magnetic Resonance Imaging (fMRI) [13], as well as combinations among them (e.g., [14]), have been employed for the examination of perceptual and cognitive aspects related to the map-reading process. These approaches constitute well-established behavior research methods implemented in several fields related to cartography, such as psychology and neuroscience. In addition, the research outcomes produced by the performance of scientific experimentation have a direct influence on the process of cartographic design, especially for the production of modern multimedia and interactive maps distributed either as standalone applications or through the internet.

The aim of this work is to briefly present the methodology of mouse-tracking and mouse-movement analysis, as well as to highlight both the opportunities and the limitations it provides towards the examination of perceptual and cognitive issues related to the map-reading process. The higher-level goal of this article is to provide the future perspectives and potential directions in cartographic research, based on authors' viewpoints.

In Section 2, mouse tracking is presented as an experimental method providing specific metrics and visualization techniques used for the analysis of the collected experimental data. Moreover, existing software solutions are reported in the same section. Section 3 summarizes recent cartographic studies which are based on the implementation of mouse-tracking techniques. Section 4 provides an outline of the strengths and future potential on the discussed research field, while the associated limitations are presented in Section 5. Section 6 showcases some concluding remarks of this perspective work.

2. The Mouse-Tracking Methodology

Mouse-tracking methodology constitutes one of the simplest methods used towards capturing user response during the execution of typical computer tasks (i.e., a task that is performed on a graphical user interface (GUI) presented on a digital display (e.g., mouse clicking/logging on specific linear elements)). Hence, this methodology could be utilized for the examination of both perceptual and cognitive processes related to the executed tasks [15]. Indeed, over the last decades, several applications have appeared in different domains (see, e.g., the examples presented by [15]).

2.1. Basic Description of the Method

The methodology of mouse tracking involves the process of recording and analyzing computerized mouse-movement trajectories [16]. In practice, the implementation of mouse-tracking techniques enables the collection of spatiotemporal mouse-movement data, also including mouse pointer events (i.e., single- and double-clicking). Hence, each mouse-movement data record mainly includes both horizontal and vertical coordinates of the mouse cursor position expressed in a display monitor coordinate system (usually referred to as pixel system), as well as the corresponding timestamp (usually expressed in msec). In other words, each record is mainly characterized by two spatial (x,y) and one temporal (t) value. Since the recording frequency of mouse-movement data is mainly influenced by the capabilities of the utilized system, such data can be characterized by high density. Therefore, the nature of mouse-movement data can be considered similar to other types of movement data, such as GPS trajectories and eye-tracking data. As a result, quantitative and qualitative approaches that are implemented in the aforementioned types of data could be adapted to mouse-movement data analysis and visualization (see, e.g., the studies provided by [15,17]).

The trajectories of the captured movements could reveal critical patterns regarding the strategies followed by the users. Moreover, the computation of specific metrics leads to the standardization of the analysis process, especially for the case of scientific experimentation. Besides, the computed indices are usually supported by simple or more sophisticated visualization techniques (see Section 2.2 for further details). Visualization techniques are able to qualitatively express existing patterns of the users' searching behavior.

In order to highlight the potential provided by the method during a 'real-world' scenario, a simple example in the field of cartographic research is presented in Figure 1. In this example, experimental participants are asked to detect a specific (point) symbol on a cartographic background. Using mouse-tracking and analysis software, participants' behavior could be modelled considering either specific metrics or different types of visualizations. Figure 1 involves different aspects of mouse trajectory produced by the MatMouse toolbox [15].

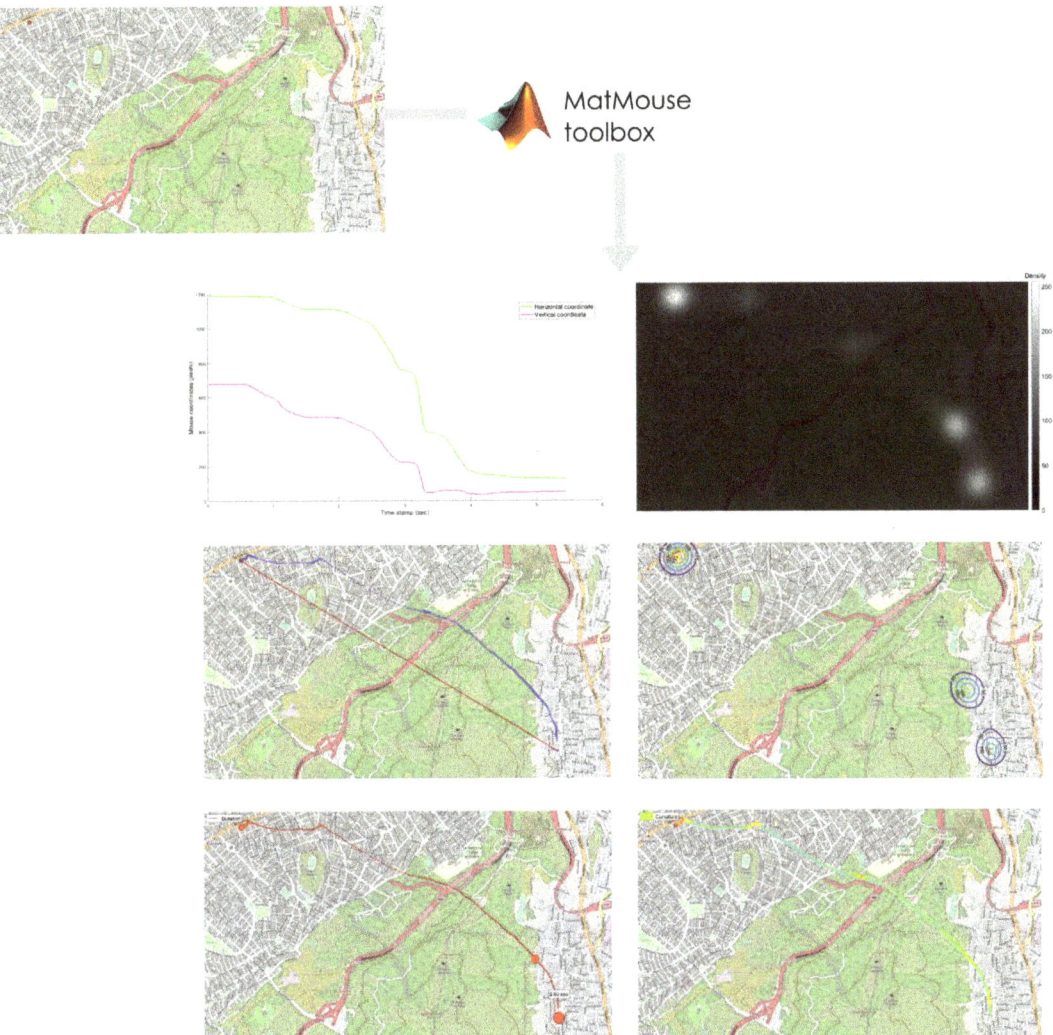

Figure 1. Different ways to visualize and/or quantify the same raw (experimental) data of mouse trajectory produced by the MatMouse toolbox [15] during a task-based map-reading procedure.

2.2. Metrics and Visualization Methods

Both the quantitative and the qualitative analyses of mouse-tracking experimental data are based on the computation of specific metrics which mainly aim to describe the individual (each participant's) mouse-movement trajectories, as well as on the development of specific visualization methods that are used for highlighting either individual or aggregated (i.e., several/all participants') searching strategies. The mouse-movement metrics, visualization techniques and software tools reported in the following sections (Sections 2.2.1, 2.2.2 and 2.3) are indicative, whereas their reporting aims to reveal several opportunities that are offered towards addressing research questions connected to different aspects of visual perception and cognition.

2.2.1. Mouse-Movement Metrics

Mouse-movement trajectories indicate the searching strategies during the execution of a task (or a series of tasks) on a visual stimulus presented on a digital display. The principal aim behind the computation of specific metrics is to describe such strategies in a quantitative way, also providing the capability for statistical comparisons. Mouse-movement metrics include the computation of specific values that characterize the mouse trajectories' deviations either temporally or geometrically [18]. More specifically, mouse-movement strategies could be described based on the relative reaction times, changes in direction, as well as on the corresponding trajectory velocity and acceleration [16]. The geometry-based description of mouse-movement trajectories includes quantitative measures that are able to reveal the existing differences compared to the optimal trajectory that corresponds to a straight line [15]. The most typical metrics in this category are the Maximum Absolute Deviation (MAD), the Area Under Curve (AUC), the Maximum Deviation (MD), and the Convex Hull (CH) area [15,19–21].

More precisely, such metrics provide fine-grained quantification of the *conflict* or *uncertainty* among *response options* [16]. For instance, MD quantifies the response between two elements of potential choice (e.g., icons in a website) by calculating the furthest point on the actual (mouse) trajectory from the optimal/ideal (straight) trajectory, while AUC calculates the area between the actual and the optimal straight trajectory [20]. Trajectories that approach the straight trajectory tend to reflect less conflict between the two options [22]. In cartographic research, the application of such metrics can significantly support the quantification of the amount of conflict for decisions regarding the elements existing in interactive cartographic products (e.g., map symbols) and/or GUIs (e.g., interactive tools). Aside from these mouse-tracking metrics, there are other, less standardized ones that quantify the *temporal development* of mouse trajectories (e.g., acceleration and velocity [23], or entropy analyses [24]) in order to assess the way a decision *evolves* [20,22].

2.2.2. Visualization Techniques

Visualization techniques could be used for supporting the analysis of experimental data in qualitative means. Although representing mouse trajectories as simple lines seems to be the more intuitive method for representing individual behaviors, several techniques have been reported in mouse-tracking studies over the last years. More specifically, considering the similarity between mouse- and eye-movement data in terms of their spatiotemporal nature, the corresponding techniques for data collection and analysis could share the approaches followed towards the visualization of both individual and aggregated experimental data. Hence, aside from the simple representation in horizontal plane as reported above, mouse-tracking data referring to an individual behavior during the execution of a task or a series of tasks on a visual scene could be also illustrated in both horizontal and vertical coordinates over time [15] and/or using Space–Time Cubes (STC) [25]. Furthermore, duration diagrams that depict the stationary situations (as happened with fixation events in eye-movement analysis) during searching, as well as curvature diagrams that highlight the corresponding curvature changes, could be utilized [15]. Additionally, mouse-movement data could be visualized using grayscale statistical heatmaps and isolines [15], as well as contiguous irregular cartograms [26]. These three techniques are also suitable for the visualization of aggregated behavior (i.e., cumulative outcome produced by different users' searching strategies). Among them, grayscale statistical heatmaps could also serve as statistical products expressing the possibility (per each pixel of an image) of having mouse activity during search on a visual stimulus [11].

2.3. Software Tools

The practical implementation of mouse-tracking studies requires the utilization of software tools that are capable of supporting the process of experimental design, data analysis and visualization. Table 1 includes a collection of software tools described in scientific articles and delivered to the scientific community since 2006.

Table 1. Mouse-tracking software tools described in scientific articles.

Tool	Programming Language	Tracking Mode	Data Analysis	Interface	Year	Reference
MouseTrack	PHP/JavaScript	Yes	Yes (basic visualizations)	Use through web page	2006	[27]
OGAMA	C#.NET	Yes	Yes	GUI	2008	[28]
MouseTracker	N/A	Yes	Yes	GUI	2010	[22]
Mousetrap	R	Yes	Yes	Extension of OpenSesame	2017	[29]
Qualtrics mouse-tracking	JavaScript/CSS/R	Yes	Yes	Command line-based	2019	[30]
MatMouse	MATLAB	Yes	Yes	Command line-based	2020	[15]

3. Mouse-Tracking Techniques in Cartographic Research

Since in our days the majority of cartographic products are digital and usually interactive, mouse-tracking techniques have been incorporated in cartographic research in order to examine how people interact with such modern products. Moreover, existing studies highlight that the mouse-tracking method is used as an alternative or as a supplementary approach to eye-tracking techniques [8,11,31,32]. Indeed, an experimental study presented by [25] has shown that there is a connection between eye and mouse movements during the execution of map-related tasks.

Previous studies highlight that mouse-tracking and -logging techniques have been utilized for the examination of usability issues in the map-reading process [33], for the interpretation of the existing patterns and the identification of differences between novice and expert users [34]. Mouse events, in conjunction with other inputs that may reveal user behavior (e.g., eye movements), have been employed for the examination of specific GUIs or cartographic interfaces (see, e.g., the work presented by [35]), which are also characterized by interactivity [36].

Mouse movements could also serve as one of the inputs in order to develop specific indices towards the evaluation of the effectiveness of interactive cartographic products (see, e.g., the recent work presented by [37]). Furthermore, mouse tracking has also been used for the examination of preattentive attributes of vision in cartographic symbols [11].

In a nutshell, the aforementioned studies confirm that the method is well accepted by the cartographic community. As it is obvious, the total number of empirical studies which utilize mouse tracking as the main experimental method is not that high, especially after comparing it with the existing applications of eye tracking in cartography and spatial research [38–41]. However, considering the main strengths and future potential discussed in the following section, mouse tracking could serve as one of the most powerful methods in cartographic research.

4. Strengths and Future Potential

In order to identify the future potential of mouse-tracking techniques in cartographic research and, more specifically, in the examination of both perceptual and cognitive issues related to map reading, it is important to highlight the main advantages of the discussed method compared to others.

Mouse tracking constitutes a simple method providing quantitative data during the performance of an experimental study. Hence, the analysis of the collected data can be based on the computation of specific metrics, as well as on the implementation of specific visualization methods (as discussed in Section 2.2). The description of participants' behavior with quantitative indices allows the performance of statistical comparisons of the produced results. Therefore, the method appears to be quite suitable for the performance of cartographic experimentation since it aims to examine map-reading procedures under different conditions, including different cartographic designs, environmental conditions, as well as participants with different characteristics (e.g., age or level of expertise). In this way, the mouse-tracking method could substantially contribute towards meeting the clear need of understanding how map users behave when exploring modern interactive cartographic products [42].

The methodology could also be executed remotely through the internet (see, e.g., the technical framework recently provided by [32], as well as the experimental study described in [8]). Although this approach could have some limitations (e.g., different experimental conditions per participant, influence by network connection quality and/or connected device specifications [32]), it is considered much simpler than eye tracking in terms of implementation. This can be confirmed taking into consideration two additional (except for its suitability for remote testing) facts: it does not require any calibration process, and it can provide high-frequency spatiotemporal data using typical computers. Consequently, the method permits the ease of experimental data collection by a high overall number of participants. This advantage is quite important, especially when the examined research hypotheses are connected to several factors (see also the recent study provided by [43] where this issue is analyzed and discussed in the framework of the performance of map-user studies).

Since mouse tracking is mainly based on mouse events and trajectories, the method is suitable for the examination of task-based processes. Especially when dealing with more complex map GUIs in which the main map display is combined with multiple accompanying data displays [35], or in cases where interaction with the map GUI plays an inextricable role for map reading (through specific 'digital activities' such as zooming, panning, etc.) [36], mouse tracking appears to provide a unique advantage in recording and further quantifying the users' mouse trajectories, as if these trajectories were executed in real-life conditions. Mouse tracking extends the data that are collected by the traditional experimental approach of recording the reaction times—an approach widely implemented in psychological research [44]—by providing spatiotemporal information related to participants' searching strategies. Examining the behavior of map users under different types of tasks could reveal critical outcomes regarding several aspects related to the map-reading process. Typical examples in cartographic research involve the examination of identification, memorability and recognition issues [45], as well as the examination of visual complexity influence [46–49].

The collection of large-scale experimental data could also result in the distribution of the corresponding datasets to the scientific community. This is a common practice in research studies related to visual attention, including cartography and geographic information science (see, e.g., the eye-tracking datasets distributed by previous research studies [45,46,50]). In a recent study [40], the twofold advantages of this approach are explained: freely distributed datasets are considered as objective ground truths for the analysis and the modeling of searching behavior; at the same time, open science is promoted by providing the collected data to the scientific community for further research.

Finally, as also can be shown by the research studies reported in Section 3, mouse tracking could be easily combined with other experimental methods (i.e., questionnaire analysis, eye tracking, EEG, and fMRI), permitting the multimodal description of participants' reactions. Moreover, the development of the existing tools in common programming language and/or frameworks could support the integrated manipulation of all stages in cartographic experimentation, including designing, analysis and visualization.

5. Limitations

Although mouse tracking has the potential to serve as a robust technique in cartographic experimentation, it has some limitations. These exact limitations can be particularly identified when mouse tracking is compared with eye tracking. Several studies report the correlation between eye and mouse movements (e.g., [25,51–57]). However, mouse movements cannot replace the detection of the so-called 'point of regard'. Hence, even though task-based and interactive procedures can be adequately or even properly supported, mouse tracking is not that suitable in the examination of free-viewing procedures. Even in the cases in which the visual stimulus corresponds to an interactive map which requires mouse cursor panning for navigation, mouse trajectory is not necessarily connected to the salient locations of the visual stimulus. Therefore, mouse tracking cannot be utilized for generating ground truth towards modeling the unconscious reaction of map users.

Mouse tracking constitutes a computer-based method. Therefore, it can be used only for examining digital (cartographic) products or analog products that have been digitized and presented on a digital monitor. In other words, compared to other experimental methods, we are not able to implement this method in a real-world scenario which involves the execution of a typical map task using a traditional paper map, or a map printed in any other type of a physical analog medium.

The method is not quite suitable for capturing the reaction of map users during the utilization of touch-screen displays (e.g., smartphones and tablets). However, although the trajectory of map-user response is not recorded, response events referring to clicks, pan and zoom in/out could be used for higher-level analyses.

Summarizing both strengths/future potential and limitations presented in Sections 4 and 5, a comparison table is provided (Table 2). More specifically, Table 2 summarizes the strengths/potential, as well as the limitations of mouse tracking—mainly compared to eye tracking—with a special focus on experimental procedures in cartographic research.

Table 2. Mouse-tracking strengths/potential and limitations (compared to eye tracking).

Strengths/Potential	Limitations
• Simple method, providing quantitative experimental data	• Not suitable for tracking the 'point of regard' (gaze position)
• Suitable for the experimental examination of task-based exploration processes	• Not suitable for the experimental examination of free-viewing exploration processes
• Uniquely suitable for understanding the map-user behavior when exploring modern interactive cartographic products and GUIs	• Not suitable for conducting experimental studies on traditional (i.e., printed) maps
• Particularly proper for the conduction of experimental studies remotely (i.e., via the internet)	• Not quite suitable for capturing the reaction of map users during the utilization of touch-screen displays (e.g., smartphones)
• Suitable for the experimental examination of map-reading procedures under different conditions and of different participant groups	
• Particularly proper for being combined with other experimental methods (i.e., questionnaire, eye tracking, EEG, and fMRI)	

6. Concluding Remarks

Capturing and analyzing mouse movements and events constitutes a valuable method towards the examination of both perceptual and cognitive issues related to digital map-reading processes. Despite the existing limitations, the method is simple and straightforward, it appears particularly suitable for tracking real-life behaviors in interactive maps, also providing the valuable opportunity for remote experimentation. At the same time, considering the relatively common spatiotemporal nature between mouse- and eye-movement raw data, similar metrics and visualization techniques can be used in order to examine the response of map users during the execution of task-based procedures on digital cartographic products. This particularity also permits the direct comparison between mouse and eye movements, while the simplicity of the method grants its concurrent utilization with other state-of-the-art experimental methods.

Author Contributions: Conceptualization, V.K. and L.-M.M.; investigation, V.K.; writing—original draft preparation, V.K.; writing—review and editing, V.K. and L.-M.M. All authors have read and agreed to the published version of the manuscript.

Funding: This research received no external funding.

Data Availability Statement: Not applicable.

Conflicts of Interest: The authors declare no conflict of interest.

References

1. Lapaine, M.; Midtbø, T.; Gartner, G.; Bandrova, T.; Wang, T.; Shen, J. Definition of the Map. *Adv. Cartogr. GIScience ICA* **2021**, *3*, 9. [CrossRef]
2. Bertin, J. *Semiology of Graphics*; University of Wisconsin Press: Madison, WI, USA, 1983; ISBN 0299090604.
3. DiBiase, D.; MacEachren, A.M.; Krygier, J.B.; Reeves, C. Animation and the Role of Map Design in Scientific Visualization. *Cartogr. Geogr. Inf. Syst.* **1992**, *19*, 201–214. [CrossRef]
4. Krygier, J.B. Chapter 8—Sound and Geographic Visualization. In *Visualization in Modern Cartography*; MacEachren, A.M., Taylor, D.R.F.-M.C.S., Eds.; Academic Press: Cambridge, MA, USA, 1994; Volume 2, pp. 149–166. ISBN 1363-0814.
5. Çöltekin, A.; Heil, B.; Garlandini, S.; Fabrikant, S.I. Evaluating the Effectiveness of Interactive Map Interface Designs: A Case Study Integrating Usability Metrics with Eye-Movement Analysis. *Cartogr. Geogr. Inf. Sci.* **2009**, *36*, 5–17. [CrossRef]
6. Ciołkosz-Styk, A. The visual search method in map perception research. *Geoinf. Issues* **2012**, *4*, 33–42.
7. Beitlova, M.; Popelka, S.; Voženílek, V.; Fačevicová, K.; Janečková, B.A.; Matlach, V. The Importance of School World Atlases According to Czech Geography Teachers. *ISPRS Int. J. Geo-Inf.* **2021**, *10*, 504. [CrossRef]
8. Knura, M.; Schiewe, J. Map Evaluation under COVID-19 restrictions: A new visual approach based on think aloud interviews. *Proc. ICA* **2021**, *4*, 60. [CrossRef]
9. Michaelidou, E.; Filippakopoulou, V.; Nakos, B.; Petropoulou, A. Designing point map symbols: The effect of preattentive attributes of shape. In Proceedings of the 22th International Cartographic Association Conference, La Coruña, Spain, 9–16 July 2005.
10. Cybulski, P.; Krassanakis, V. The effect of map label language on the visual search of cartographic point symbols. *Cartogr. Geogr. Inf. Sci.* **2022**, *49*, 189–204. [CrossRef]
11. Pappa, A.; Krassanakis, V. Examining the preattentive effect on cartographic backgrounds utilizing remote mouse tracking. *Abstr. ICA* **2022**, *5*, 111. [CrossRef]
12. Keskin, M.; Ooms, K.; Dogru, A.O.; De Maeyer, P. EEG & Eye Tracking User Experiments for Spatial Memory Task on Maps. *ISPRS Int. J. Geo-Inf.* **2019**, *8*, 546. [CrossRef]
13. Lobben, A.; Lawrence, M.; Olson, J.M. fMRI and Human Subjects Research in Cartography. *Cartogr. Int. J. Geogr. Inf. Geovis.* **2009**, *44*, 159–169. [CrossRef]
14. Burian, J.; Popelka, S.; Beitlova, M. Evaluation of the Cartographical Quality of Urban Plans by Eye-Tracking. *ISPRS Int. J. Geo-Inf.* **2018**, *7*, 192. [CrossRef]
15. Krassanakis, V.; Kesidis, A.L. MatMouse: A Mouse Movements Tracking and Analysis Toolbox for Visual Search Experiments. *Multimodal Technol. Interact.* **2020**, *4*, 83. [CrossRef]
16. Kieslich, P.J.; Schoemann, M.; Grage, T.; Hepp, J.; Scherbaum, S. Design factors in mouse-tracking: What makes a difference? *Behav. Res. Methods* **2020**, *52*, 317–341. [CrossRef] [PubMed]
17. Karagiorgou, S.; Krassanakis, V.; Vescoukis, V.; Nakos, B. Experimenting with polylines on the visualization of eye tracking data from observations of cartographic lines. In Proceedings of the CEUR Workshop Proceedings, Vienna, Austria, 23–24 September 2014; Volume 1241.

18. Di Palma, M.; Carioti, D.; Arcangeli, E.; Rosazza, C.; Ambrogini, P.; Cuppini, R.; Minelli, A.; Berlingeri, M. The biased hand. Mouse-tracking metrics to examine the conflict processing in a race-implicit association test. *PLoS ONE* **2022**, *17*, e0271748. [CrossRef] [PubMed]
19. Yamauchi, T.; Leontyev, A.; Razavi, M. Mouse Tracking Measures Reveal Cognitive Conflicts Better than Response Time and Accuracy Measures. In Proceedings of the CogSci, Montreal, QC, Canada, 24-27 July 2019; pp. 3150–3156.
20. Stillman, P.E.; Shen, X.; Ferguson, M.J. How Mouse-tracking Can Advance Social Cognitive Theory. *Trends Cogn. Sci.* **2018**, *22*, 531–543. [CrossRef]
21. Tian, G.; Wu, W. A Review of Mouse-Tracking Applications in Economic Studies. *J. Econ. Behav. Stud.* **2020**, *11*, 1–9. [CrossRef]
22. Freeman, J.B.; Ambady, N. MouseTracker: Software for studying real-time mental processing using a computer mouse-tracking method. *Behav. Res. Methods* **2010**, *42*, 226–241. [CrossRef]
23. Wojnowicz, M.T.; Ferguson, M.J.; Dale, R.; Spivey, M.J. The Self-Organization of Explicit Attitudes. *Psychol. Sci.* **2009**, *20*, 1428–1435. [CrossRef]
24. Calcagnì, A.; Lombardi, L.; Sulpizio, S. Analyzing spatial data from mouse tracker methodology: An entropic approach. *Behav. Res. Methods* **2017**, *49*, 2012–2030. [CrossRef]
25. Demšar, U.; Çöltekin, A. Quantifying gaze and mouse interactions on spatial visual interfaces with a new movement analytics methodology. *PLoS ONE* **2017**, *12*, e0181818. [CrossRef]
26. Krassanakis, V. Aggregated Gaze Data Visualization Using Contiguous Irregular Cartograms. *Digital* **2021**, *1*, 130–144. [CrossRef]
27. Arroyo, E.; Selker, T.; Wei, W. Usability Tool for Analysis of Web Designs Using Mouse Tracks. In Proceedings of the CHI '06 Extended Abstracts on Human Factors in Computing Systems, Montreal, QC, Canada, 22–27 April 2006; Association for Computing Machinery: New York, NY, USA, 2006; pp. 484–489.
28. Voßkühler, A.; Nordmeier, V.; Kuchinke, L.; Jacobs, A.M. OGAMA (Open Gaze and Mouse Analyzer): Open-source software designed to analyze eye and mouse movements in slideshow study designs. *Behav. Res. Methods* **2008**, *40*, 1150–1162. [CrossRef] [PubMed]
29. Kieslich, P.J.; Henninger, F. Mousetrap: An integrated, open-source mouse-tracking package. *Behav. Res. Methods* **2017**, *49*, 1652–1667. [CrossRef] [PubMed]
30. Mathur, M.B.; Reichling, D.B. Open-source software for mouse-tracking in Qualtrics to measure category competition. *Behav. Res. Methods* **2019**, *51*, 1987–1997. [CrossRef]
31. Knura, M.; Schiewe, J. Analysis of User Behaviour While Interpreting Spatial Patterns in Point Data Sets. *KN J. Cartogr. Geogr. Inf.* **2022**, *72*, 229–242. [CrossRef]
32. Krassanakis, V.; Kesidis, A.L.; Pappa, A.; Misthos, L.-M. Performing cartographic visual search experiments online: Opportunities and challenges. In Proceedings of the Workshop on Adaptable Research Methods for Empirical Research with Map Users, Virtual Workshop, 6 May 2021.
33. Manson, S.M.; Kne, L.; Dyke, K.R.; Shannon, J.; Eria, S. Using Eye-tracking and Mouse Metrics to Test Usability of Web Mapping Navigation. *Cartogr. Geogr. Inf. Sci.* **2012**, *39*, 48–60. [CrossRef]
34. McArdle, G.; Tahir, A.; Bertolotto, M. Interpreting map usage patterns using geovisual analytics and spatio-temporal clustering. *Int. J. Digit. Earth* **2015**, *8*, 599–622. [CrossRef]
35. Golebiowska, I.; Opach, T.; Rød, J.K. Breaking the Eyes: How Do Users Get Started with a Coordinated and Multiple View Geovisualization Tool? *Cartogr. J.* **2020**, *57*, 235–248. [CrossRef]
36. Ooms, K.; Coltekin, A.; De Maeyer, P.; Dupont, L.; Fabrikant, S.; Incoul, A.; Kuhn, M.; Slabbinck, H.; Vansteenkiste, P.; Van der Haegen, L. Combining user logging with eye tracking for interactive and dynamic applications. *Behav. Res. Methods* **2015**, *47*, 977–993. [CrossRef]
37. Horbiński, T.; Cybulski, P.; Medyńska-Gulij, B. Web Map Effectiveness in the Responsive Context of the Graphical User Interface. *ISPRS Int. J. Geo-Inf.* **2021**, *10*, 134. [CrossRef]
38. Steinke, T.R. Eye Movement Studies in Cartography and Related Fields. *Cartogr. Int. J. Geogr. Inf. Geovis.* **1987**, *24*, 40–73. [CrossRef]
39. Krassanakis, V.; Cybulski, P. A review on eye movement analysis in map reading process: The status of the last decade. *Geod. Cartogr.* **2019**, *68*, 191–209. [CrossRef]
40. Krassanakis, V.; Cybulski, P. Eye Tracking Research in Cartography: Looking into the Future. *ISPRS Int. J. Geo-Inf.* **2021**, *10*, 411. [CrossRef]
41. Kiefer, P.; Giannopoulos, I.; Raubal, M.; Duchowski, A. Eye tracking for spatial research: Cognition, computation, challenges. *Spat. Cogn. Comput.* **2017**, *17*, 1–19. [CrossRef]
42. Roth, R.E.; Çöltekin, A.; Delazari, L.; Filho, H.F.; Griffin, A.; Hall, A.; Korpi, J.; Lokka, I.; Mendonça, A.; Ooms, K.; et al. User studies in cartography: Opportunities for empirical research on interactive maps and visualizations. *Int. J. Cartogr.* **2017**, *3*, 61–89. [CrossRef]
43. Martins, V.B.; Amorim, F.R.; Schmidt, M.A.R.; Delazari, L.S. Study about the appropriate number of participants in map user studies. *Int. J. Cartogr.* **2023**, *9*, 1–14. [CrossRef]
44. Draheim, C.; Mashburn, C.A.; Martin, J.D.; Engle, R.W. Reaction time in differential and developmental research: A review and commentary on the problems and alternatives. *Psychol. Bull.* **2019**, *145*, 508–535. [CrossRef]

45. Keskin, M.; Krassanakis, V.; Çöltekin, A. Visual Attention and Recognition Differences Based on Expertise in a Map Reading and Memorability Study. *ISPRS Int. J. Geo-Inf.* **2023**, *12*, 21. [CrossRef]
46. Tzelepis, N.; Kaliakouda, A.; Krassanakis, V.; Misthos, L.-M.; Nakos, B. Evaluating the perceived visual complexity of multidirectional hill-shading. *Geod. Cartogr.* **2020**, *69*, 161–172. [CrossRef]
47. Cybulski, P. Spatial distance and cartographic background complexity in graduated point symbol map-reading task. *Cartogr. Geogr. Inf. Sci.* **2020**, *47*, 244–260. [CrossRef]
48. Keil, J.; Edler, D.; Kuchinke, L.; Dickmann, F. Effects of visual map complexity on the attentional processing of landmarks. *PLoS ONE* **2020**, *15*, e0229575. [CrossRef] [PubMed]
49. Liao, H.; Wang, X.; Dong, W.; Meng, L. Measuring the influence of map label density on perceived complexity: A user study using eye tracking. *Cartogr. Geogr. Inf. Sci.* **2019**, *46*, 210–227. [CrossRef]
50. He, B.; Dong, W.; Liao, H.; Ying, Q.; Shi, B.; Liu, J.; Wang, Y. A geospatial image based eye movement dataset for cartography and GIS. *Cartogr. Geogr. Inf. Sci.* **2023**, *50*, 96–111. [CrossRef]
51. Chen, M.C.; Anderson, J.R.; Sohn, M.H. What can a mouse cursor tell us more? In Proceedings of the CHI '01 Extended Abstracts on Human Factors in Computing Systems (CHI '01), Seattle, WA, USA, 31 March–5 April 2001; p. 281.
52. Guo, Q.; Agichtein, E. Towards predicting web searcher gaze position from mouse movements. In Proceedings of the 28th of the International Conference Extended Abstracts on Human Factors in Computing Systems (CHI EA '10), Atlanta, GA, USA, 10–15 April 2010; p. 3601.
53. Milisavljevic, A.; Hamard, K.; Petermann, C.; Gosselin, B.; Doré-Mazars, K.; Mancas, M. Eye and Mouse Coordination During Task: From Behaviour to Prediction. In Proceedings of the International Conference on Human Computer Interaction Theory and Applications, Funchal, Portugal, 27–29 January 2018; SCITEPRESS—Science and Technology Publications: Funchal, Portugal, 2018; pp. 86–93.
54. Cooke, L. Is the Mouse a "Poor Man's Eye Tracker"? In Proceedings of the Annual Conference-Society for Technical Communication, Las Vegas, NV, USA, 7–10 May 2006; Volume 53, p. 252.
55. Egner, S.; Reimann, S.; Höger, R.; Zangemeister, W.H. Attention and information acquisition: Comparison of mouse-click with eye-movement attention tracking. *J. Eye Mov. Res.* **2018**, *11*. [CrossRef]
56. Liebling, D.J.; Dumais, S.T. Gaze and Mouse Coordination in Everyday Work. In Proceedings of the 2014 ACM International Joint Conference on Pervasive and Ubiquitous Computing: Adjunct Publication, Seattle, WA, USA, 13–17 September 2014; pp. 1141–1150.
57. Rose, J.; Liu, Y.; Awad, A. Biometric Authentication Using Mouse and Eye Movement Data. In Proceedings of the 2017 IEEE Security and Privacy Workshops (SPW), San Jose, CA, USA, 25 May 2017; pp. 47–55.

Disclaimer/Publisher's Note: The statements, opinions and data contained in all publications are solely those of the individual author(s) and contributor(s) and not of MDPI and/or the editor(s). MDPI and/or the editor(s) disclaim responsibility for any injury to people or property resulting from any ideas, methods, instructions or products referred to in the content.

Article

Quality Control Methods Using Quality Characteristics in Development and Operations †

Daiju Kato [1],* and Hiroshi Ishikawa [2]

1. Nihon Knowledge Co., Ltd., Tokyo 111-0042, Japan
2. Graduate School of System Design, Tokyo Metropolitan University, Tokyo 191-0065, Japan; ishikawa-hiroshi@tmu.ac.jp
* Correspondence: d-kato@know-net.co.jp; Tel.: +81-80-4052-2372
† This paper is the conference extension of Proceedings of the 14th International Conference on Management of Digital EcoSystems, Venice, Italy, 19–21 October 2022.

Abstract: Since the Software Quality Model was defined as an international standard, many quality assurance teams have used this quality model in a waterfall model for software development and quality control. As more software is delivered as a cloud service, various methodologies have been created with an awareness of the link between development productivity and operations, enabling faster development. However, most development methods are development-oriented with awareness of development progress, and there has been little consideration of methods that achieve quality orientation for continuous quality improvement and monitoring. Therefore, we developed a method to visualize the progress of software quality during development by defining quality goals in the project charter using the quality model defined in international standards, classifying each test by quality characteristics, and clarifying the quality ensured by each test. This was achieved by classifying each test by quality characteristics and clarifying the quality ensured by each test. To use quality characteristics as KPIs, it is necessary to manage test results for each test type and compare them with past build results. This paper explains how to visualize the quality to be assured and the benefits of using quality characteristics as KPIs and proposes a method to achieve rapid and high-quality product development.

Keywords: DevOps; quality control; quality characteristics; SQuaRE; quality analysis

1. Introduction

In many software development environments, work is often divided between development (Dev) teams, which are responsible for developing features, and operations (Ops) teams, which are responsible for running the service. The Dev team's primary mission is to add new features to the software, while the Ops team's mission is to maintain the current environment and keep the service stable and continuous. The Dev and Ops teams have very different missions, and this can lead to team disagreements. However, faster software development is required to keep up with the rapidly changing business environment. To this end, teams should avoid becoming exhausted due to internal conflicts, and DevOps [1] is attracting attention as a way of thinking that "resolves common conflicts between teams and promotes smooth development through collaboration".

DevOps has a seven-step lifecycle: Plan, Code, Build, Test, Deploy, Operate, and Monitor.

- Plan: Defines the task management and development requirements for the entire project;
- Code: Programmers create code according to development requirements;
- Build: The application that will actually run is built from the source code;
- Test: Test the built application for bugs and other defects;
- Deploy: Deploy the application into production;

- Operation: Perform maintenance and management tasks to ensure continuous service;
- Monitor: Review information obtained from operations, user assessments, requests, etc.

These steps are performed sequentially and continuously to practice DevOps. The main benefits of implementing DevOps are achieving smooth development, increasing productivity, and speeding up releases.

The essence of DevOps, as mentioned above, is to resolve conflicts between Dev and Ops teams. By eliminating the internal drag-and-tug that has been common in the past, the goal is to achieve smooth development and operations.

To implement DevOps, it is necessary to implement a variety of supporting tools at each step of the lifecycle. Typical tools include version control systems that track file changes under project management and CI/CD tools such as Jenkins [2] that automate tasks previously performed manually. Effective use of these tools leads to increased productivity. This increased productivity means that more human resources can be allocated to improving quality and developing new services, which in turn increases the value of the service.

Automating testing and delivery with tools brings benefits in the form of increased productivity and faster work. Acceleration is simply the speed at which the DevOps lifecycle can be executed. In other words, you can increase the number of DevOps lifecycle cycles in a given period of time. More lifecycle cycles mean faster adoption of market requirements and feedback, which in turn means greater responsiveness to changing market needs.

For example, a developer runs unit tests against locally implemented code, and if the unit tests pass, the developer periodically commits changes to the code to a central repository as part of the CI process. The process is then delegated to Jenkins, the CI enabler, to run build, unit test, and build verification tests (BVT). If the BVT passes, the build is automatically deployed. Automated tests such as functional, performance, security, and regression tests are then run to ensure that the added code does not degrade the quality of existing functionality.

In addition to testing for quality, quality control is performed using various metrics and cascading models such as the V-model. Typically, the pass rate, defect rate, and test coverage of each test type (Table 1) are used to monitor project quality. However, these quality indicators are often difficult to use to assess the quality of software under development. Even if the coding rules and test design and implementation rules are clearly defined, it is difficult to objectively judge whether the quality is good or bad unless it is a derivative development project.

Table 1. Famous quality metrics for quality control.

Metrics Types	Metrics
Defect density	Ratio per page of design documents Ratio per line or step of codes Ratio per test cases
Defect removal rates	Removal rate per phases Removal rate per components Removal rate per test cases
Pass rates	Pass rates per test sets Pass rates per test cases Pass rates per function points
Coverages	Documents review coverage Test coverage per line of codes Test coverage per test cases

When considering software quality, the quality model [3] defined in the ISO 25000 series (SQuaRE) [4] can be used to classify the quality required of the software under development in terms of the quality characteristics provided by this quality model, shown in Figure 1, and to judge from test results whether each characteristic has been assured. SQuaRE also defines the metrics for each quality attribute, which can be used to determine whether quality has been assured.

Ito et al. [5] proposed a framework that allows the creation of a strategic test plan to achieve incremental quality building in agile development projects. The framework provides a state in which quality can be explained by releasing the product in a ratable manner and comprehensive quality assurance by incrementally building product quality.

To use quality characteristics effectively, we recommend that project managers classify the quality of software goals by quality characteristics and, if possible, also define the quality to be achieved at each milestone by quality characteristics.

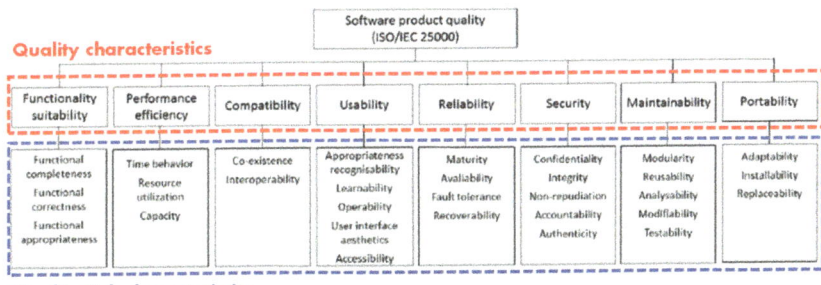

Figure 1. ISO/IEC 25010 quality model for system/software product quality.

Therefore, we have studied how to effectively use quality characteristics and existing quality data in development projects using the V-model. We have studied the international standard, which is also used in countries such as Germany and South Korea. In the JIS (Japanese Industry Standard) standard certification for software [6], we have studied the development process with an awareness of compliance with this standard and have applied it to several projects. With the expansion of the recurring business, several projects are adapting the agile process, so we decided to further expand the development process for the use of quality features and improve it so that it can also be used in projects that use the agile process.

2. Considerations for Using Quality Model in Agile Development Processes

The combination of continuous integration (CI) and continuous deployment (CD) processes as a software engineering practice for rapidly developing and deploying software applications into production is called the CI/CD pipeline. The pipeline is a collection of tools developers, test engineers, and IT operations staff use throughout the continuous software development, delivery, and deployment lifecycle.

The test pyramid, as shown in Figure 2, is a useful technique that allows us to conceptualize how to prioritize the tests in a CI/CD pipeline in terms of their relative number and order of execution. This technique was defined by Mike Cohn [7], with unit tests at the bottom, service tests in the middle, and UI tests at the top. By prioritizing with a test pyramid, you can build a strong foundation of automated unit tests that are quick and easy to execute, then move on to more complex tests that are more complex to write and take longer to execute, and finally, the least complex tests that are fewer in number. The pipeline provides more prioritized feedback.

As in the development process established for the V-model, quality requirements in agile projects are classified and normally described in the project plan. An international standard for quality requirements [8] has already been established, and functional and non-functional requirements can be classified using quality characteristics according to the methodology described in this standard. This method makes it possible to clarify the quality requirements for each actor. The initial quality control is carried out through the various activities of the development process and the rules defined in the project charter.

The project charter is a short, formal document that summarizes the entire project and describes the project objectives, how it will be executed, and who will be involved. It is used throughout the project lifecycle and is an important factor in project planning. These projects can use quality characteristics for key quality management indicators, as shown in Table 2.

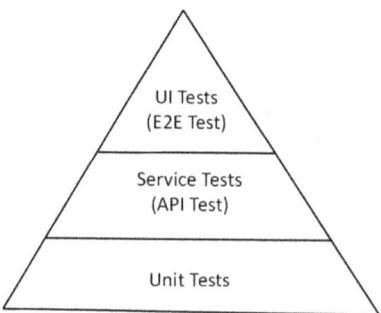

Figure 2. Test pyramid.

By including all the practices related to testing in the Agile process pipeline and the review activities necessary to build quality, such as design reviews, it is possible to organize which quality-enhancing activities are included in each practice.

Build, static analysis, unit testing, front-end and back-end integration testing, and the E2E test pipeline can be used to identify common implementation errors and increase software maturity. It is also possible to measure individual execution times within the CI process to immediately detect degradation due to code additions. For example, if the execution time of a test increases compared to the previous test, it is likely that some performance degradation is occurring, and the impact of the added code should be suspected.

Deploying builds in a continuous delivery (CD) process allows portability properties to be checked during the installation process.

Implementing a general CI/CD process and managing the results will help ensure that quality is continuously improved. In addition, by automating and integrating more testing activities, more quality characteristics can be covered in addition to functional conformance. By defining criteria for testing activities, each quality attribute can be used as a quality KPI on an ongoing basis.

In many development projects, GitHub [9] and Atlassian tools [10] can be used as project management tools, task ticket activities can be visualized as kanban boards, and development and bug-fixing activities can be effective for source code control. Project management tools are effective for managing project progress, but they cannot manage quality progress. Test management tools, on the other hand, can manage test cases and test progress and can play a role in quality management, but it is often difficult to use test results in history management.

Shimizu et.al [11] proposed a test result management tool to analyze and extend the coverage of automated tests and our team enhanced the test result management tool. The tool is written in C# and stores test results in SQL Server; for unit tests with API calls, we decided to implement and integrate a report class that can capture CPU load, memory consumption, I/O load, and network load along with functional tests and output this quality data along with the test results. The purpose of the report class is to provide a performance efficiency assessment. The purpose of the report class is to extend the coverage of unit testing by providing a performance efficiency evaluation.

The report class we built called MSTest [12], an extension of NUnit [13], a unit testing framework, with an extension method to obtain quality data necessary for evaluating performance efficiency and to generate test results in XML format along with functional test results (Figure 3).

Table 2. Famous quality metrics for quality control.

Activities	Quality Characteristics	Quality Sub-Characteristics
\multicolumn{3}{c}{Activities in the Whole Development Process}		
Coding Rules	Security	Confidentiality
		Integrity
	Maintainability	Modularity
		Reusability
		Modifiability
		Testability
Design Review	Functional Suitability	Function completeness
		Function correctness
	Reliability	Maturity
		Availability
		Fault tolerance
		Recoverability
	Maintainability	Testability
Inspection Review	Reliability	Maturity
\multicolumn{3}{c}{Activities in CI process}		
Static Analysis	Reliability	Maturity
	Security	Integrity
	Maintainability	Analysability
Unit test Integration test Regression test	Functional Suitability	Function completeness
		Function correctness
		Function appropriateness
	Reliability	Maturity
E2E test	Functional Suitability	Function completeness
		Function correctness
		Function appropriateness
	Usability	Operability
		User error protection
	Reliability	Maturity
\multicolumn{3}{c}{Trough out the CI process}		
Measurement of processing time	Performance Efficiency	Time behavior
		Resource utilization
	Maintainability	Analysability
\multicolumn{3}{c}{*Activity in CD operations*}		
install test	Portability	Installability

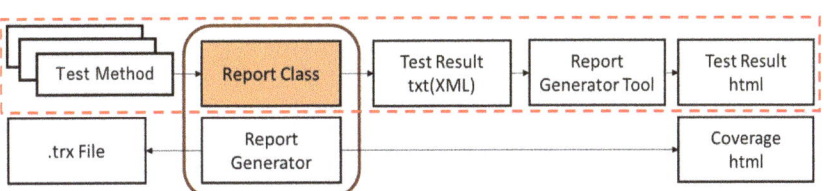

Figure 3. Created report class (upper is process and lower is operation. Square frame is developed area).

The generated XML file can be used with the command line generator tool to generate a test result report in HTML format. The class also reads the .trx file of MSTest results generated by Visual Studio and generates a list of API methods called in HTML format to help understand test coverage.

Although it is possible to open a .trx file in Visual Studio and check the test results, there are problems in analyzing the results as it is difficult to see the cause of the failure. We developed this time to not only generate the results of functional and performance tests by outputting reports that automatically describe the pass/fail list, the logs during the tests, and the performance measurement results but also to convert this result information into HTML files to visualize the test result information, Figure 4.

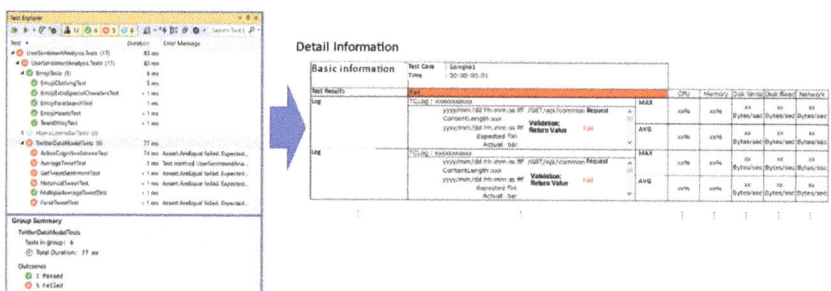

Figure 4. Easy visualization of test results.

Also, for the API tests created in JMeter, we decided to obtain performance data from the API test execution as well as the unit tests and evaluate whether the updated build has any performance degradation.

Both unit and integration tests were able to produce the following benefits while adding performance efficiency assessments.

- Increased development productivity by being able to find features and performance and load degrades in the build pipeline;
- Increased testing efficiency through automation;
- Increased coverage of automated tests to capture more quality data.

As an example of this project, we are using Ranorex [14] as an E2E testing tool to automate scenario testing. The scenarios include use cases that involve more standard operating procedures called golden routes, use cases that check screen transitions when functions are invoked, and use cases that result in errors due to operational errors, so they are considered to include usability evaluations.

In this way, classifying automated tests using quality characteristics not only allows the quality improvement situation to take test coverage into account but also increases development productivity.

3. Enhance of Management of Test Results for Agile Projects

In software package development and service development, DevOps makes it possible to increase development productivity and increase the frequency of product releases. To ensure stable product releases, it is important to maintain the quality of the product and the test results within the project must be well managed. Since the DevOps project has achieved test automation with CI tools, we will also consider using a pipeline for test result management.

Engineers can quickly detect quality degradation if the test management tool can save the test results of unit tests, integration tests, and E2E tests as Jenkins jobs to be developed and easily report comparisons with multiple past versions. The comparison with the previous build is done in the build pipeline, and the comparison with past versions is easily performed in the tool.

When importing the test results, it compares the test results with the specified multiple past versions, compares the pass rate of the functional tests and the performance data, and generates a simple report with the judgment of whether or not the performance is within the registered threshold range. The URL of the generated result will be notified to you via Teams or e-mail. If you want to check the results of past versions in detail, you can use the comparison function of the tool to generate a detailed report.

The image of the job to process the import of test results from Jenkins is shown in Figure 5.

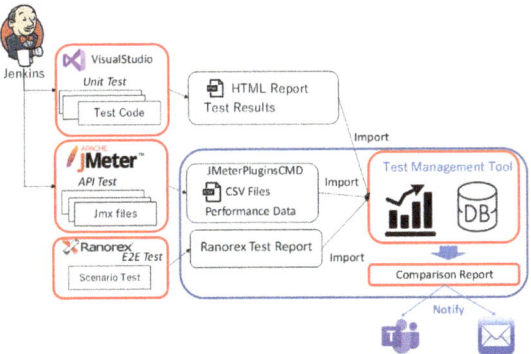

Figure 5. Architecture of test results management (The red part is the process flow and the blue part is the test result management process).

By running it as a Jenkins job, you can automate the process of importing the results of each test performed in the build pipeline and generating a test report.

The ability to manage test results and compare them with past versions makes it easier to ensure maturity and allows for the immediate detection of quality degradation, whether functional or performance.

The quality guaranteed by the expanded coverage of test automation in the CI process, the comparison process in the test result management tool, the distribution in the CD process, and the development rules in the development project are shown in Table 3.

Our projects are able to automate more quality-related tasks, such as static analysis, known as SAST, and dynamic analysis, known as DAST, than typical DevOps, although it requires some time and effort to integrate it into both the CI process and the CD process. Therefore, by preparing multiple test environments, resilience testing is able to perform security-related testing for automated testing.

Also, the use of test result management tools makes it possible to monitor quality progress from test results obtained in the CI process.

Table 3. Quality covered by CI/CD pipeline process.

Quality Characteristics	Quality Sub Characteristics	Evaluation by
Function Suitability	Functional Completeness	• Unit test • Static analysis (SAST) • Integration test • Dynamic analysis (DAST) • Performance test • Regression test • E2E test
	Functional Correctness	
	Functional Appropriateness	
Performance Efficiency	Time Behaviour	
	Resource Utilization	
	Capacity	
Compatibility	Co-existence	-
	Interoperability	

Table 3. Cont.

Quality Characteristics	Quality Sub Characteristics	Evaluation by
Usability	Appropriateness Recognizability	-
	Learnability	-
	Operability	■ Unit test ■ E2E test
	User Error Protection	
	User Interface Aesthetics	
	Accessibility	-
Reliability	Maturity	■ Unit test ■ Static analysis (SAST) ■ Integration test ■ Dynamic analysis (DAST) ■ Performance test ■ Regression test ■ E2E test ■ Test results management
	Availability	
	Fault Tolerance	
	Recoverability	-
Security	Confidentiality	■ Static analysis (SAST) ■ Dynamic analysis (DAST) ■ Regression test
	Integrity	
	Non-repudiation	-
	Authenticity	-
	Accountability	-
Maintainability	Modularity	■ Covered by the development process and project charter
	Reusability	
	Analysability	
	Modifiability	
	Testability	
Portability	Adaptability	-
	Installability	■ CD process
	Replaceability	-

4. Using Quality Characteristics for KPI under Agile Development Projects

We have always used quality characteristics as KPIs for project quality in waterfall software development and have made quality progress visible [15]. In addition, this quality management approach is aware of the international standards [16] used in software certification and the international standards for software testing [17]. Therefore, the use of quality characteristics as KPIs to understand the quality build has also been considered for agile software development projects [18]. In the waterfall model, acceptance testing is planned as a condition for starting testing as the entry criteria for each test level, and acceptance testing is performed by extracting test cases from the test types to be performed at that test level using a stratified method. Since it is impossible to perform acceptance testing in every sprint of the agile process due to time constraints, we decided to investigate the need for acceptance testing and the relationship between the tasks performed in each sprint and quality characteristics through experiments.

We conducted two types of experiments on the impact on quality by conducting software development in an agile process with the following measures to make more effective use of quality characteristics in the agile process.

In the first team, the project manager chose the method of adding quality attributes to the task ticket items so that quality attributes were set when each task was raised, and sub-quality attributes were set for all test cases in the sprint. Second, many rules are defined in the project charter for using quality characteristics for KPIs.

The project manager in the second team adds the definition for the analyzed functional requirements and introduces a process for creating quality requirements at the time of the requirements review, and the following activities are introduced:

- Designing quality requirements created at the time of the business requirements review and quality requirements for the design and development of the software. Ensure traceability of each issue so that the quality requirements created in the business requirements review can be checked for validity in design and evaluation;
- Add quality attribute items to Jira and create a Kanban that quality attributes can reference;
- Before starting a sprint, we created a sprint backlog by selecting tickets to be worked on by the sprint from the product backlog containing the business requirements and mapped the quality characteristics required by the business requirements.

In addition, the following practices are carried out for each sprint;

- Define the quality requirements for each functional requirement and set the criteria by considering the metrics to be used;
- Evaluate the design and implementation checkpoints of the functional elements for each quality attribute;
- Establish evaluation criteria for each quality characteristic and map them to the quality characteristics to be ensured for each test activity;
- Visualize the progress of the established criteria by assessing the conformance of the quality characteristics at each sprint.

Before starting the first sprint, the project prepared a mapping of activities and quality characteristics, as shown in Figure 6.

Also, the project begins with the following quality objectives:

- Projected development scale: 2.6 KL;
- Review density: 20 man-hours/KL;
- Density of test items: 150 items/KL;
- Number of bugs: 10/KL.

Quality characteristics \ Activities	Functional suitability	Performance efficiency	Compatibility	Usability	Reliability	Security	Maintainability	Portability
Each sprint								
Spec analysis	○	○	○	○	○	○	○	○
Design	○	○	○	○	○	○	○	○
Coding	○	○	○	○	○	○	○	○
Static analysis	○					○	○	
Unit test	○			○			○	
Integration test	○			○	○		○	
Security test						○		
Performance test		○						
E2E test	○		○	○				
Only final sprint								
Regression test	○				○			
Release test	○	○	○	○	○		○	○

Figure 6. Mapping quality characteristics to activities.

5. Results of Two Practices

The first project did not establish rules for using quality features in the project and left it up to the developers, which resulted in many tasks being delayed due to the overhead of using quality features. In addition, most tasks were biased toward functional conformance. This result is likely to occur in the waterfall model as well, and without considering the balance of each quality characteristic, the result will be biased toward functional conformance, so efforts are being made to reduce quality characteristics to 70% or less. It was found that simply using quality characteristics would only complicate the work and would not be beneficial.

On the other hand, in the second project, where the use of quality characteristics was specified in the project charter, and the method of using quality characteristics was defined, it became possible to break down the quality status and monitor progress. As a result, smooth project management was realized without disturbing the balance of QCD, and very good results were achieved. In the case of this project, the use of quality characteristics increased the testing density by 144% compared to the case where quality characteristics were not used, resulting in an increase in testing man-hours, but the number of defects detected decreased to 32% of the predicted value. This was a result of the quality characteristics of KPI and the implementation of quality-driven development. In addition, the tasks to be implemented were able to proceed as planned. In other words, using quality characteristics as KPIs makes it possible to proceed with quality-conscious development while being aware of the QCD balance.

Although this experiment was conducted on a small scale of 3.7 KL, similar results can be obtained by determining the quality characteristics to focus on for each sprint and proceeding with development with an awareness of the quality priority order. It was also suggested that the same effect could be achieved by being aware of quality prioritization, such as determining the quality characteristics to focus on in each sprint.

The benefits of using quality characteristics from the experiment are as follows:

- When using quality characteristics in the agile process, it is assumed that if they are applied to a project for which a project plan has already been drawn up, the overhead of using quality characteristics is large and is likely to significantly affect the sprint's activities;
- If the use of quality features is considered from the project planning stage, the following actions can be taken to provide evidence of quality assurance to project management;
- Declaring the use of quality features in the project charter;
- Assigning quality characteristics to different activities;
- The overhead of using quality characteristics should be included in the rough estimate before the project starts.

Finally, an example of a qualitative analysis of a product by quality characteristic in the project is given in Table 4.

Table 4. Example of quality analysis classified by quality characteristics.

Quality Characteristics	Quality Analysis
Function suitability	Functional suitability is ensured because the functional requirements that satisfy the functional requirements are considered in the design document, implemented, and confirmed to work properly through various tests.
Performance efficiency	Compared to the operation before the enhancement, the performance of the functions implemented in the previous version has not deteriorated, and the import of new reports, a new function, is comparable to the import speed of the report functions implemented in the previous version, thus meeting the performance requirements. As load and capacity requirements have not been verified for this project, it can be concluded that ensuring only performance efficiency is not a problem.
Compatibility	There are no problems with interfacing with other systems, such as EXCEL output and ZIP compression, and compatibility is ensured because there are no problems with co-existence with other systems in the same environment and no code-level implementation that would affect others.
Usability	The enhancement does not create new screens but enhances existing screens and identifies no new usability issues, ensuring usability.

Table 4. *Cont.*

Quality Characteristics	Quality Analysis
Reliability	Reliability is ensured because functional requirements are met throughout the process: requirements->specification->design->implementation->testing The quality of the requirements developed during the requirements review is ensured by the associated activities, and any bugs found during the various reviews and tests are fixed.
Security	The same level of security as the previous version has been confirmed by testing. The same level of security as the previous version is guaranteed.
Maintainability	Maintainability is ensured because it is based on coding conventions, various documents are written in the same format as the previous version, and the level of description is written at the same or higher granularity than the previous version.
Portability	The installation procedure is the same as the previous version. Portability is, therefore, guaranteed.

6. Conclusions

Regardless of whether the development process used in a project is the cascade model method or the agile method, quality-oriented development can be achieved by using quality characteristics.

In the case of agile processes, it is possible to confirm that quality is continuously improving by defining the metrics to be achieved in each pipeline in the CI/CD pipeline. From the test engineer's perspective, more time can be spent on test design and automated scripting, leaving more time for exploratory testing. In addition, the results of automated tests become the criteria for initiating manual tests, allowing them to efficiently focus on more complex manual tests. This allows them to efficiently focus on further improving quality.

In an agile process, it is important to design and execute testing activities efficiently in the CI/CD pipeline and to clarify in the sprint plan the quality characteristics that should be prioritized in each sprint. By clarifying the quality characteristics that should be prioritized in each sprint in the sprint plan and by developing a method to use SQuaRE [19] in the agile process, it can be recommended to build quality more efficiently.

In order to use quality characteristics as a KPI in large-scale agile development, it is necessary to prepare a KANBAN for this KPI and check the quality status of each team in a centralized manner. It will be necessary to educate all project members about quality characteristics, specify the purpose and means of using quality KPIs in the project charter, and ensure that project members understand and follow this project charter.

Author Contributions: Conceptualization, methodology, validation, formal analysis, investigation, resources, data curation, writing—review and editing, D.K.; supervision, H.I. All authors have read and agreed to the published version of the manuscript.

Funding: This research received no external funding.

Data Availability Statement: Data are contained within the article.

Conflicts of Interest: Author Daiju Kato was employed by the company Nihon Knowledge Co., Ltd. The remaining authors declare that the research was conducted in the absence of any commercial or financial relationships that could be construed as a potential conflict of interest.

References

1. DevOps, 10+ Deploys Per Day: Dev and Ops Cooperation at Flickr. 2009. Available online: https://www.slideshare.net/jallspaw/10-deploys-per-day-dev-and-ops-cooperation-at-flickr (accessed on 15 January 2022).
2. Jenkins. Available online: https://www.jenkins.io/ (accessed on 1 February 2020).
3. *ISO/IEC 25010*; Systems and Software Engineering—Systems and Software Quality Requirements and Evaluation (SQuaRE)—System and software quality models. ISO: Geneva, Switzerland, 2011.
4. *ISO/IEC 25000*; Systems and Software Engineering—Systems and Software Quality Requirements and Evaluation (SQuaRE)—Guide to SQuaRE. ISO: Geneva, Switzerland, 2014.

5. Ito, J.; Yamaguchi, S.; Okazaki, K.; Yokosuka, S.; Kimoto, K.; Yamanaka, M.; Nagata, A.; Yamaguchi, T.; Hosoya, S. Quality Assurance by Quality Stepwise Refinement in Agile Development. Report on the Results of the Subcommittee Meeting of the Software Quality Control Research Group. 2018, pp. 137–144. Available online: https://www.juse.or.jp/sqip/workshop/report/at-tachs/2018/4_aqa_ronbun.pdf (accessed on 15 January 2022). (In Japanese).
6. *JIS X 25051*; Software Engineering-Systems and Software Quality Requirements and Evaluation (SQuaRE)-Requirements for Quality of Ready to Use Software Product (RUSP) and Instructions for Testing. JISC: Tokyo, Japan, 2016.
7. Cohn, M. The Forgotten Layer of the Test Automation Pyramid. Available online: https://www.mountaingoatsoftware.com/blog/the-forgotten-layer-of-the-test-automation-pyramid/ (accessed on 1 February 2022).
8. *ISO/IEC 25030*; Systems and Software Engineering—Systems and Software Quality Requirements and Evaluation (SQuaRE)—Quality Requirements Framework. ISO: Geneva, Switzerland, 2019.
9. GitHub. Available online: https://github.com/ (accessed on 1 February 2022).
10. Atlassian. Available online: https://www.atlassian.com/ (accessed on 1 February 2020).
11. Kato, D.; Shimizu, A.; Ishikawa, H. Quality classification for testing work in DevOps. In Proceedings of the 14th International Conference on Management of Digital EcoSystems (ACM MEDES 2022), Venice, Italy, 19–21 October 2022.
12. MSTest. Available online: https://github.com/Microsoft/testfx-docs/ (accessed on 1 February 2021).
13. NUnuit. Available online: https://nunit.org/ (accessed on 1 February 2021).
14. Ranorex. Available online: https://ranorex.com/ (accessed on 1 February 2020).
15. Kato, D.; Ishikawa, H. Develop quality characteristics based quality evaluation process for ready to use software projects. Com-put. *Sci. Inf. Technol.* **2016**, *6*, 9–21. [CrossRef]
16. *ISO/IEC 25051*; Software Engineering—Systems and Software Quality Requirements and Evaluation (SQuaRE)—Requirements for Quality of Ready to Use Software Product (RUSP) and Instructions for Testing. ISO: Geneva, Switzerland, 2014.
17. *ISO/IEC/IEEE 29119-3*; Software and Systems Engineering—Software Testing—Part 3: Test Documentation. ISO: Geneva, Switzerland, 2021.
18. Kato, D.; Okuyama, A.; Ishikawa, H. Introduction of test management based on quality characteristics. In Proceedings of the 1st Inter-national Workshop on Experience with SQuaRE Series & Their Future Direction IWESQ 2019), Putrajaya, Malaysia, 2 December 2019.
19. Shang, W. Bridging the divide between software developers and operators using logs. In Proceedings of the 34th International Conference on Software Engineering (ICSE'12), Zurich, Switzerland, 2–9 June 2012.

Disclaimer/Publisher's Note: The statements, opinions and data contained in all publications are solely those of the individual author(s) and contributor(s) and not of MDPI and/or the editor(s). MDPI and/or the editor(s) disclaim responsibility for any injury to people or property resulting from any ideas, methods, instructions or products referred to in the content.

MDPI
St. Alban-Anlage 66
4052 Basel
Switzerland
www.mdpi.com

Digital Editorial Office
E-mail: digital@mdpi.com
www.mdpi.com/journal/digital

Disclaimer/Publisher's Note: The statements, opinions and data contained in all publications are solely those of the individual author(s) and contributor(s) and not of MDPI and/or the editor(s). MDPI and/or the editor(s) disclaim responsibility for any injury to people or property resulting from any ideas, methods, instructions or products referred to in the content.

www.ingramcontent.com/pod-product-compliance
Lightning Source LLC
LaVergne TN
LVHW070409100526
838202LV00014B/1421